BLACK FRANCE

BLACK FRANCE

Colonialism, Immigration,
and Transnationalism

DOMINIC THOMAS

INDIANA UNIVERSITY PRESS
Bloomington & Indianapolis

This book is a publication of
Indiana University Press
601 North Morton Street
Bloomington, IN 47404-3797 USA

http://iupress.indiana.edu

Telephone orders   800-842-6796
Fax orders   812-855-7931
Orders by e-mail   iuporder@indiana.edu

© 2007 by Dominic Thomas

The paper used in this publication meets the minimum requirements of American National Standard for Information Sciences—Permanence of Paper for Printed Library Materials, ANSI Z39.48-1984.

Manufactured in the United States of America

Library of Congress Cataloging-in-Publication Data

Thomas, Dominic Richard David.
Black France : colonialism, immigration, and transnationalism / Dominic Thomas.
p. cm. — (African expressive cultures)
Includes bibliographical references and index.
ISBN 978-0-253-34821-0 (cloth : alk. paper) — ISBN 978-0-253-21881-0 (pbk. : alk. paper)
1. Blacks—France. 2. Blacks—Race identity—France 3. Blacks—France—Social conditions. 4. Africans—France. 5. France—Ethnic relations. 6. Multiculturalism—France.
I. Title.
DC34.5.B55T46 2007
305.896'044—dc22
2006027760

2 3 4 5 12 11 10 09 08 07

FOR DEVEREUX AND ERIN

People think immigrants are naked when they arrive
in a new land at the end of their odyssey, yet migrants
arrive layered with personal stories, and burdened
with what passes for collective memory.

Abdourahman A. Waberi, *Transit* (2003)

Don't immigrants have a history of their own?
Do you cease to have a history when you move
from one point of the globe to another?

J. M. Coetzee, *Slow Man* (2005)

CONTENTS

Preface and Acknowledgments

In 2002, Indiana University Press published my *Nation-Building, Propaganda, and Literature in Francophone Africa.* That work was concerned with questions of nationalism and the importance of adhering to the nation-state as a prerequisite for the assumption of sovereignty and autonomy from colonial rule, and its central focus was an exploration of the relationship between literature and the state in francophone Africa, the contributions of writers to the transition from colonialism to independence, and recent experimentation with democratization. The imperative was to offer a better understanding of the circumstances of African colonization through a more encompassing view of the role literature had played in African history, decolonization, and the complex process of forging modern nation-states. As I analyzed the disorientation that had resulted from colonial and postcolonial rule, the collapse of the nation-state, and the emergence of generations of young, alienated, and disenfranchised individuals, my own research gradually became more engaged with broader contextual frameworks that would allow me to account for these developments. In *Black France,* attention has shifted in order to explore the failure of the nationalist imperative and the resulting impact on African societies and populations of the dissolution and disintegration of state structures. Through a supranational and comparative framework that incorporates writers from Cameroon, Congo, Djibouti, France, Gabon, Guinea, the Ivory Coast, Mali, Senegal, and Togo, *Black France* explores those transnational constituencies that have emerged from colonialism and immigration, and engages with anthropological, sociological, francophone, Diaspora, postcolonial, and transnational/transcolonial studies, offering new ways of thinking about the symbiotic dimension of relations and population flows between France and the francophone world.

I insisted in *Nation-Building, Propaganda, and Literature in Francophone Africa* that a multidisciplinary approach was necessary in order to account for the complex circumstances of decolonization, and, in much the same way, one can only begin to achieve an accurate understanding of transnational cultural productions and global population movements through cultural, economic, historical, political, and sociological contextualizations. Francophone sub-Saharan African literature shares many points of commonality with the Maghrebi context: in both cases, literature has been produced in "Africa in France" by the children of immigrants (in the case of the Maghreb it is known as Beur literature and exemplified by authors such as Azouz Begag, Farida Belghoul, Mehdi Charef, and Soraya Nini, among others), but also by writers who live or publish in France but who do not self-identify as immigrants (such as Tahar Ben Jelloun, Ahmadou Kourouma, Henri Lopes, and Tierno Monenembo). Similarly, these writers intersect with their counterparts who currently reside in or have lived in other regions of Europe, such as Belgium (Bessora), Britain (Chris Abani, Diran Adebayo, Biyi Bandele-Thomas, Bernardine Evaristo, Ben Okri, Helen Oyeyemi, Zadie Smith), Germany (Senouvo Agbota Zinzou, Théo Ananissoh), and Italy (Pap Khouma).

Black France attempts to reframe African, francophone, and postcolonial studies by adopting a transcolonial theoretical model—one that insists upon considering francophone sub-Saharan African literatures across history rather than as sociocultural products symbolically demarcated into colonial and postcolonial categories by political independence around 1960. Colonial-era literatures, rather than being categorized exclusively as the pioneering canon of sub-Saharan African literature, are shown to operate in a reciprocal context that was always already analogous to that of contemporary authors. When it is demonstrated that francophone colonial sub-Saharan African texts operate symbiotically with hexagonal historiography, the constitutive nature of literary production that emerges complicates French and European debates on identity, but also paradoxically questions the cultural and demographic singularity of France and Europe.

Naturally, this book builds on the pioneering studies of Michel Fabre (*From Harlem to Paris: Black American Writers in France, 1840–1980*), Tyler Stovall (*Paris Noir: African Americans in the City of Lights*), Bennetta Jules-Rosette (*Black Paris: The African Writer's Landscape*), and Pascal Blanchard, Eric Deroo, and Gilles Manceron (*Le Paris noir*), and those of Christopher L. Miller (*Nationalists and Nomads: Essays on Francophone African Literature and Culture*), Brent Hayes Edwards (*The Practice of Diaspora*), Paul Gilroy (*The Black Atlantic*), F. Abiola Irele (*The African Imagination: Literature in Africa and the Black Diaspora*), Manthia Diawara (*In Search of Africa*), Mireille Rosello (*Postcolonial Hospitality: The Immigrant as Guest*), and Alec G. Hargreaves (*Voices from the North African Immigrant Community in France: Immigration and Identity in Beur Fiction*). In turn, *Black France* explores the bilateralism and transversal nature of African and French relations. It acknowledges the centrality of Paris but also broadens and decenters the symbolic territory to provincial sites, simultaneously refuting any notion of cultural homogeneity that may be suggested or implied by such a diasporic space. Indeed, the cover to *Black France,* which features the Congolese painter Chéri Samba's striking image of sub-Saharan African immigrants (*Paris est propre* [Paris is Clean]), is specifically intended to capture the image of the Eiffel Tower as a broader iconic symbol for the metropole and Hexagon, and to underscore the ways in which Black Paris and France are often mutable in the imaginations of writers.

Black France reminds us that the myth of Occidental universalism and cultural superiority operated as an intrinsic component of the expansionist project, and that it was initially disseminated through colonial education. Once subjected to scrutiny, it allows us to locate colonialism as a precursor to contemporary intellectual and political debates in France and Europe on globalization and immigration and to underscore how the very transcoloniality of these issues is reflected in new francophone African literature. As William B. Cohen argued in his book *The French Encounter with Africans: White Response to Blacks, 1530–1880,* "Frenchmen's experiences and conceptions of black peoples helped form the image of the African in Western culture."*

This book has been made possible only by the unyielding support of Dee Mortensen, my sponsoring editor at Indiana University Press. At each and every stage Dee provided invaluable feedback and encouragement, and for that I am extremely grateful. Additionally, the tremendous efficiency and professionalism of the editorial and production staff at IUP guided the manuscript through the production process. Alec G. Hargreaves and Bennetta Jules-Rosette were generous enough to place their own projects on hold in order to review the manuscript for IUP; their insightful comments and suggestions have undoubtedly made this a stronger book. In particular, I would like to thank Elisabeth Marsh, my assistant sponsoring editor; and Patrick McNaughton, general editor of the African Expressive Cultures series.

In completing this book, I have benefited enormously from generous critiques, exchanges, and readings by a multiplicity of people—anonymously, in person, at conferences, through correspondence, in edited volumes, and so on. In turn, I have been constantly challenged by the innovative and thought-provoking work of friends for whom I have nothing but complete admiration; they include Emily Apter, Azouz Begag, Mark Behr, John Conteh-Morgan, Gaurav Desai, Anne Donadey, Emmanuel Dongala, Didier Gondola, Alec G. Hargreaves, Francis Higginson, Nicki Hitchcott, F. Abiola Irele, Bennetta Jules-Rosette, Lawrence Kritzman, Michel Laronde, Alain Mabanckou, Daniel Maximin, Achille Mbembe, Jane Moss, Lydie Moudileno, Jean-Marc Moura, H. Adlai Murdoch, David Murphy, Nick Nesbitt, Panivong Norindr, Anjali Prabhu, Mireille Rosello, Abdourahman A. Waberi, Richard Watts, and Winifred Woodhull.

Residency at Cambridge University's Centre for Research in the Arts, Social Sciences, and Humanities (CRASSH) in 2004 allowed me to make considerable progress on the manuscript. I would like to express my appreciation to the other fellows, and particularly to the program director,

---

*William B. Cohen, *The French Encounter with Africans: White Response to Blacks, 1530–1880* (Bloomington: Indiana University Press, 1980), ix.

Ludmilla Jordanova. I also appreciated the warm welcome that was extended to me by Jean Khalfa of Trinity College, and the occasion to converse with Gaurav Desai, who was in residence at Clare Hall.

I am thankful for generous financial support from UCLA's Academic Senate, the Center for African Studies, and the Center for Globalization —Africa. This made it possible for me to conduct multiple research visits to Dakar, London, Marseilles, Paris, Toulon, and Strasbourg.

Exchanges with members of the University of California Multicampus Research Group for Transcolonial and Transnational Studies helped me think through the theoretical framework of my project. Additionally, my involvement with the new Global Studies Program at UCLA has stimulated my work in many ways. I am grateful to the former vice provost and dean of the International Institute, Geoffrey Garrett, for the various opportunities made available to me under its aegis.

Christopher L. Miller continues to serve as an invaluable mentor, providing both encouragement and sound advice, but above all adhering to the kind of rigorous scholarly standard that is the hallmark of all his work, and that I can only aspire to emulate.

I am extremely fortunate to be surrounded by such brilliant minds at UCLA. For various inspirational moments and indispensable support, I would like to thank Andrew Apter, Shu-mei Shih, Ali Behdad, John Mc-Cumber, Efrain Kristal, and Jenny Sharpe. I would also like to thank my undergraduate and graduate students at UCLA, who have been a constant source of inspiration.

Fran Wintroub deserves a special word of thanks for continuing to help me in immeasurable ways.

In writing this book, I was fortunate to have a wonderful departmental chair. Françoise Lionnet encouraged me in innumerable ways, combined administrative demands with an intimidating rate of scholarly productivity, and somehow found the time to provide generous and extremely detailed critiques of most chapters.

My parents, David and Jean Thomas, and my in-laws, J. Patrick and Pamela Cooney, have, as always, provided all kinds of support, for which I am forever grateful.

My son Devereux, whose patience was often tested as he accompanied me on various book and research expeditions, and my wife Erin Joy Cooney, who has been there at every stage of this project, have no idea of the degree to which I love them, and of the extent to which they have helped me. Naturally, this book is dedicated to them.

PERMISSIONS

For permission to reprint various material in this book, I am grateful to the editors and proprietors of *Modern Languages Notes;* the *Journal of*

Romance Studies; Comparative Studies of Africa, Asia, and the Middle East; Culture, Theory, and Critique; Immigrant Narratives in Contemporary France (Susan Ireland and Patrice Proulx, eds.); *Postcolonial Theory and Francophone Literary Studies* (Anne Donadey and H. Adlai Murdoch, eds.); the *Journal of Francophone Studies;* and *Research in African Literatures.* In all instances, my work in this book supersedes earlier versions, has been extensively revised, and has benefited from the incisive comments and critiques of numerous—and mostly anonymous—readers.

Note on Translations

Material included in this book that originally appeared in French has been given in the English of published translations when these were available. Otherwise, translations are my own. In some places the meaning of the original French seemed self-evident or its significance critical.

BLACK FRANCE

ONE

Introduction: Black France in Transcolonial Contexts

But what exactly is a Black? First of all, what's his color?

Jean Genet[1]

I will tear down those Banania smiles from the walls of France.

Léopold Sédar Senghor[2]

Look, a Negro!

Frantz Fanon[3]

Whether one is satisfied or not with the terminological pertinence of globalization or the use of the French term *mondialisation* to designate the nature of human relations at the beginning of the twenty-first century, the fact nevertheless remains that cultural, economic, political, and social discourse is infused with conflicting interpretations of the constitutive or divisive attributes of the local and the global.[4] A broad range of texts, including Benjamin Barber's *Jihad versus McWorld,* Samuel Huntington's *The Clash of Civilizations,* Michael Hardt and Antonio Negri's *Empire* and *Multitude,* and Jean-François Bayart's *Le gouvernement du monde,* have, respectively, privileged categories such as ethnicity or inter-"civilizational" competition, underscored the potential of popular resistance to hegemonic forces by demonstrating how Empire (as distinguished from imperialism) operates as "a *decentered* and *deterritorialized* apparatus," or demonstrated how transnational networks further inscribe the centrality of the nation-state, in order to interpret new configurations and transnational alignments.[5]

Perhaps no other country than France has emerged as such a delicate site for the investigation of these complex formulations, given that all of these issues have contributed to the process of determining what a global Hexagon might look like. A range of factors would seem to corroborate such observations: the questioning of Americanization most powerfully contained in concerns with "the imperialism of Mickey Mouse," "coca-colonization" and the "Starbuckization" of France; the politics of decolonization and post-Empire France; immigration policies and the rise of extreme-right wing agendas; the tenuous relationship between national agendas and broader incorporation in an expanding European Union (such as by abandoning national currency); global security pre- and post-9/11; and the paradoxical "reversed colonization" of the metropole. Immigration and the cultural productions that have emerged from within France's postcolonial communities have generated radically new sociocultural structures, displacing received notions of Frenchness. Lawrence Kritzman once characterized Pierre Nora's seven-volume *Les lieux de mémoire* as "the result of an imaginary process that codifies and condenses a national consciousness of the past,"[6] but one might well ask whether this work accurately reflects the collective memory of those people for whom the Hexagon now represents *home*, a fact that has simultaneously compelled individuals and groups to acknowledge and recognize that memory is now also elsewhere. A study of "Black" France inevitably finds itself at the intersection of these issues, since to explore France from such a perspective is to embark on a journey across the arbitrary lines of demarcation that distinguish the colony from the postcolony and the colonial from the postcolonial period, in order to engage with immigration and identity politics, and to question the origins of the French Republic and challenges to its foundational principles (such as the headscarf and veil affairs). Naturally, this approach will include consideration of the fragile connections between the imperatives of human rights legislation and modern forms of population displacement exemplified by asylum seekers, refugees, and the *sans-papiers* (undocumented subjects or illegals).[7]

If questions of nationalism and the importance of adhering to the nation-state as a prerequisite for the assumption of sovereignty and autonomy from colonial rule provided the concern of my previous book, *Nation-Building, Propaganda, and Literature in Francophone Africa*,[8] then attention in *Black France* has shifted in order to explore the failure of the nationalist imperative and the resulting impact on African societies and populations of the partial dissolution of incorporative state structures in favor of supranational economic, juridical, and political mechanisms. My research has then taken me on what Saskia Sassen has described as a transition from the "emphasis on the sovereignty of the people of a nation and the right to self-determination . . . to the rights of individuals regardless of identity."[9]

In *Nation-Building, Propaganda, and Literature in Francophone Africa*, the central focus was provided by an exploration of the relationship between literature and the state in francophone sub-Saharan Africa, the contributions of writers to the transition from colonialism to independence, and recent experimentation with democratization. The imperative was to provide a better understanding of the circumstances of African colonization through a more encompassing view of the role literature had played in African history, decolonization, and the complex process of forging modern nation-states. By analyzing the disorientation that had resulted from colonial and postcolonial rule, the collapse of the nation-state, and the emergence of generations of young, alienated, and disenfranchised individuals, my own research gradually became more engaged with broader contextual frameworks that would allow me to account for these developments. Through a comparative framework that incorporates writers from Cameroon, Congo, Djibouti, France, Gabon, Guinea, the Ivory Coast, Mali, Senegal, and Togo, *Black France* explores those transnational constituencies that have emerged from colonialism and immigration, and engages with anthropological, sociological, francophone, gender, Diaspora, postcolonial, and transnational and transcolonial studies, offering new ways of thinking about the symbiotic dimension of relations and population flows between France and the francophone world.[10] In fact, as Nancy Green underscores in her book *Repenser les migrations,* a lexicon organized around the notion of fluidity through terms such as *vagues* or *flux* (waves), *courants* (streams), and *marée humaine* (human tide) will help us better understand these "relations of disjuncture,"[11] and these terms have become useful as the central markers of these population movements.[12]

Recent important works, such as Manthia Diawara's *In Search of Africa* (2000), F. Abiola Irele's *The African Imagination: Literature in Africa and the Black Diaspora* (2001), Mireille Rosello's *Postcolonial Hospitality: The Immigrant as Guest* (2001), and Jean-Loup Amselle's *Branchements: Anthropologie de l'universalité des cultures* (2001), have provided useful paradigms and contextual frameworks for exploring the phenomena outlined above.[13] As I distance myself (as Amselle suggests) from traditional anthropological frameworks in order to rethink the relationship between the global and the local, the subsequent recontextualization and emphasis on what are also commonly known as "multisited ethnographies" are tremendously helpful in delineating the objectives of this book. This theoretical apparatus can be put into practice in order to better understand the various ways in which all actors—the colonized and the colonizer, immigrants and receiving countries—are transformed by and in diasporic, multicultural, and transnational spaces through the constitutive dimension of cross-cultural encounters. The challenge comes from identifying and documenting the various ways in which diverse transnational cultural productions intersect and are reformulated within and across national boundaries.

The symbiotic dimension of French-African relations is most convincingly demonstrated in the highly original title of a collection of essays by the Congolese novelist Henri Lopes, namely *Ma grand-mère bantoue et mes ancêtres les Gaulois* (*My Bantu Grandmother and My Ancestors the Gauls*).[14] Indeed, this bilateralism provides one of the central structural markers of *Black France,* as colonial texts are juxtaposed with postcolonial ones within and across chapters (Ousmane Sembene's "La noire de . . . " ["Black Girl"] and *Le docker noir* [*Black Docker*] and Henriette Akofa's *Une esclave moderne* around the problematic of slavery), colonial-era texts are explored as precursors to contemporary immigrant narratives, gender issues are examined in relation to both internal and external African discourses, testimonial narratives are contrasted with works of fiction in which the relationship between fiction and the evidentiary mode is constantly blurred, and the dialogue between African and African American writers (Sembene and Richard Wright), the transnationalism implicit in Calixthe Beyala's *Lettres,* and multiple forms of migration (of students, workers, and *sapeurs,* and clandestine migration) are considered.[15] Most striking has been the remarkable number of works set in both Africa and France characterized for the most part by the bi-directionality of the individual or collective experience, with multiple examples of transcolonialism and transnationalism, in which protagonists move between spaces, depart, descend, return, and leave again. But some questions are more complex. How, for example, can protagonists "return" to a country they never left? As an indication of how this question has changed since the colonial period, one might consider how Bernard Dadié's young protagonist Tanhoe Bertin emphasized that he had received "ONE *round-trip* ticket" (italics mine).[16]

Whereas protagonists of colonial-era texts navigated their way through France primarily for the purpose of education and travel, those in contemporary novels experience detention centers, are faced with legal procedural issues, and are often categorized as illegal, clandestine, or undocumented. If the experience of migration or travel during the colonial era could be characterized as existential, then the trauma of exile itself and the accompanying domestic conditions some protagonists are escaping from in the postcolony are compounded by the deprivation associated with the circumstances of immigration to France. The migration is thus one of people, but also of identities, as the distance between the fictional and evidentiary modes is constantly blurred in works by such authors as Pius Ngandu Nkashama (*Vie et mœurs d'un primitif en Essone quatre-vingt-onze*), Blaise N'Djehoya (*Nègre de Potemkine*), Simon Njami (*African gigolo*), Léandre-Alain Baker (*Ici s'arrête le voyage*), V. Y. Mudimbe (*Entre les eaux*), Denis Oussou-Essui (*La souche calcinée*), Sally N'Dongo (*Exil, connais pas*), Gaston-Paul Effa (*Tout ce bleu*), Monique Ilboudo (*Le mal de peau*), Saïdou Boukoum (*Chaîne*), Sayouba Traoré (*Loin de mon village, c'est la brousse*), Bilguissa Diallo (*Diasporama*), Lauren Ekué (*Icône urbaine*), Léonora Miano (*L'intérieur de la nuit*), Aleth-Felix Tchicaya (*Lumière de femme*), and Gaston-Paul Effa (*Voici le dernier jour du monde*), in the last of which a grown man who left Africa as a teenager prepares to return: "If it is true that I have become a coconut, black on the outside and white on the inside, and that I have grown up like a palm tree forgetting my roots, then I must learn to renounce this natural shame. I was welcomed in France as a foreigner; now, it is as a stranger that I am returning home" (9).[17] These kinds of reformulations and broadenings of the conversation across "multiple spatiotemporal (dis)orders" align themselves with what Romuald Fonkoua has described as "nationals on the inside and the nationals on the exterior."[18] For many writers, exile itself constitutes the entry into writing, the "coming to writing," as one has said before; the Congolese novelist Emmanuel Dongala has underlined how both negritude and the more recent concept of "migritude" emerged from these circumstances.[19] For Jacques Chevrier, "this neologism designates both the thematic of immigration that is at the heart of contemporary African works, but also the expatriate status of most of the writers . . . their inspiration comes from their hybridity and decentered lives, elements that now characterize a kind of French-style 'world literature.'"[20] In this way, "migritude" symbolizes a kind of "third space" that comes from a "questioning of certain prevalent discursive configurations" and "simultaneous disengagement from both the culture of origin and the receiving culture . . . within a new identitarian space" (Chevrier, "Afrique(s)-sur-Seine," 99). In order to unpack these questions, I have found the term "mediation" useful.

The process of mediation is central in numerous ways to the organizing mechanisms that provide the logic behind the book. Mediation is useful (i) in order to read works produced during the colonial era alongside those that emerged after the official end of colonial rule; (ii) in juxtaposing texts written in Africa with those authored in France; (iii) in analyzing the shifting external and internal cartographies and topographies across territorial lines (France in Africa and Africa in France); and finally (iv) in registering the distinctive manner in which aesthetic literary considerations are employed. The figure of mediation in turn engages in a dialogue that rejoins and extends earlier theorizations by considering the African, European, and African American context. The Tunisian writer Albert Memmi, for example, has continued to expand upon the historical mediation of the colonized and the colonizer, a construct that is explicitly recentered in the new coordinates offered in his book *Portrait du décolonisé arabo-musulman et de quelques autres*.[21] His reflections are divided into two parts, and mediation now emerges between the newly decolonized sovereign subject (*le nouveau citoyen*) and the immigrant (*l'immigré*). There are of course precursors to these issues, and the very cyclical nature of debates is central to the broader ways in which mediation functions: the conflict between the "humanist" ideals of the Republic and the exploitative practice of colonization itself was a new manifestation of an earlier problem in which the Société des amis des Noirs (founded in 1788), the decree of human rights after the revolution of 1789, and of course the official abolition of slavery in 1794 were at odds with Napoleon's reinstitution of slavery in 1802, much in the same way as immigration politics in France since the 1980s have been informed by conflicting policies that have to do with both greater social incorporation and exclusionary measures.

In analogous ways, mediation has been central to literature both in Africa and in France, and in particular *between* these two spaces. French historiography has been much informed by and concerned with Africa (*négrophile* literature, Prosper Mérimée, André Gide, Michel Leiris, and so on), and in her book *Rereading Camara Laye,* Adèle King has sought to demonstrate the importance "the support of the French government, specifically the Ministry of France Overseas, gave to Camara's literary career and to those of others who supported French policy on the overseas territories in the period after the Second World War" in disseminating at least an "idea of France."[22] For African writers who had attended colonial schools and whose ancestors had also officially become the "Gauls," literary expression in French would introduce an unavoidable mediation between Africa and France, one that coincided with the material circumstances of French language literacy. For Eileen Julien, this point is crucial, since "the dominance of oral language in Africa is obviously a matter of material conditions" rather than there being "something ontologically oral about Africa" whereby writing emerges as somehow "disjunctive and alien for Africans."[23] As Elisabeth Mudimbe-Boyi has argued, "the writings of missionaries, colonial settlers, and travelers as well as the influence of intertextuality and collective imagination helped perpetuate Europe's stereotyped images of Africa."[24] Whereas new immigrant texts are mediating with earlier francophone texts (the work of Fatou Diome examined in chapter 7 powerfully underscores this intertextuality), their francophone literary predecessors were already mediating with French historiography.[25] Ultimately, these works have allowed for a redrawing of the geographic boundaries of Africa and France in our imagination. As Achille Mbembe lucidly signaled, "what we designate by the term 'Africa' exists only as a series of disconnections, superimpositions, colors, costumes, gestures and appearances, sounds and rhythms, ellipses, hyperboles, parables, misconnections, and imagined, remembered, and forgotten things, bits of spaces, syncopes, intervals, moments of enthusiasm and impetuous vortices—in short, perceptions and phantasms in mutual perpetual pursuit, yet co-extensive with each other."[26]

Black France explores the bilateralism of African and French relations, but simultaneously challenges any notion of cultural homogeneity that may be suggested or implied by such a diasporic space in the Hexagon.[27] While separate identitarian constructs arise from the colonial, immigrant, and transnational experience, some African immigrants may identify only with groups with whom they share national citizenship or linguistic or religious commonalities. Alternatively, individuals or groups may establish connections with other diasporic, immigrant, or refugee structures from sub-Saharan Africa, the Caribbean, Asia, and so forth, and may circulate outside of, or even resist, such community alignments (the Mourides population, for example, in Marseilles, New York, or Los Angeles), preferring instead to navigate autonomously according to the demands and exigencies associated with their dislocated and transplanted status.[28] Emmanuel Todd has, for example, underlined the importance of recognizing the coexistence of multiple forms of "communitarianism" in the African community, from the *soninké* (Mali, Senegal, and Mauritania) to the *bamiléké* (Cameroon).[29] Naturally, *Black France* is located within a francophone context, in which the term itself serves to underline the historical connections and intersections between the Hexagon and areas of the world that were once colonized, that remain occupied—the Départements d'Outre-mer (Overseas French Departments, DOM) and Territoires d'Outre-mer (Overseas French Territories, TOM)—and that continue to be subjected to French hegemonic practices under the aegis of Francophonie.[30]

In many ways, the historical links between French literature and francophone literature in general reproduce the overall structure of this book, and only disciplinary shortsightedness has decoupled these fields of research.[31] For example, Hafid Gafaiti has argued that "it is necessary to stress that there is a structural link between the eighteenth-century universalistic ideal and the Enlightenment's racist classifications that later justified the European colonial enterprise"; this framework informs Christopher L. Miller's book *The French Atlantic Triangle: Literature and Culture of the Slave Trade,* in which slavery is explored in works by authors as diverse as Voltaire, Mérimée, Maryse Condé, and Edouard Glissant.[32] William B. Cohen underscored the longevity of French contact with Africa in his book *The French Encounter with Africans: White Response to Blacks, 1530–1880,* a legacy also addressed by Patrick Manning in his exploration of the historical period following Cohen's analysis in *Francophone Sub-Saharan Africa: 1880–1985.*[33] In fact, eighteenth-century representations of Africans had provided much of the justification for colonial expansionism, increased missionary activity, and of course the *mission civilisatrice* (civilizing mission) as an ideological project.[34] These constructs were subsequently challenged through the responses of African and Caribbean cultural and political practitioners, exemplified in the cultural, social, and political agendas of negritude and its leading intellectuals (Léopold Sédar Senghor and Aimé Césaire), anticolonial writings, nationalist ideologies, and postcolonial productions.[35] Therefore, throughout *Black France,* I have insisted upon the necessity of adopting both a transcolonial and transnational approach as a way of accounting for the transversal nature of relations.[36]

"Thinking about the *longue durée* of colonial history," Françoise Lionnet maintains, "one feels more acutely the urgency of re-articulating that history in terms of geography, of theorizing networks of power and influence in terms of a transcolonial consciousness that restitutes both memory and space, a space filled with different forms of memory and with alternative modes of feeling and apprehending the social world—in other words, with a different sensibility . . . Transcolonial subjectivity exists in tension with multiple epistemological locations, including traditional centers of power—political or economic institutions, the culture industry, the disciplines—and the maps of knowledge they produce."[37] This kind of approach is essential in order to better contextualize the links between the concerns of colonial and postcolonial writers. Additionally, the bilateralism of cultural, social, and political relations requires a departure from the insistence on the analysis of what Lionnet and Shu-mei Shih have described in *Minor Transnationalism* as "the vertical power relationship between the colonizer and the colonized," and accordingly "this transversalism also produces new forms of identification that negotiate with national, ethnic, and cultural boundaries."[38] These frameworks are crucial as we think about the colonies and the metropole, the social treatment of Africans under colonial rule and in turn in postcolonial France. For this reason, we can begin to explore what might be at stake in contextualizing contemporary France within the new parameters of globalization, wherein the "transnational designates spaces and practices acted upon by border-crossing agents, be they dominant or marginal. The logic of globalization is centripetal and centrifugal at the same time and assumes a universal core or norm, which spreads out across the world while pulling into its vortex other forms of culture to be tested by its norm" (Lionnet and Shih, "Thinking through the Mirror," 5). Invariably, these questions connect with broader sociopolitical issues that concern the manner in which French Republican ideals are deployed in the context of immigration politics to preserve the status quo and secure the dominance of a monolithic vision of history, while Africans in France remain the locus of colonial anxieties that are recuperated and capitalized upon by extreme right-wing ideologues as political currency.[39]

Colonial and imperial expansionism provided some of the more striking historical examples of the totalitarian impulses of universalizing tendencies—that is, measures adopted by the dominant socioeconomic powers at the 1884–1885 Berlin Congress that ignored the local because of the imperative to impose Western "universalist" standards on the communities they indiscriminately engaged in fracturing. Assimilation seems inadequate in its attempt at describing colonizing mechanisms whose objectives were in fact closer to the reduction of the other toward sameness.[40] For the rationale behind the actual merging of cultural elements contains the implication that métissage would be theoretically possible, a dimension that would of course run contrary to the ideals of French assimilation, itself founded on a civilizing imperative whose foundational tenets are situated in the act of compensating for perceived cultural, linguistic, political, religious, and social inadequacies. French colonial mechanisms were erected on an ethnocentric assimilationist paradigm that refused to interpret culture as a dynamic process and, accordingly, to incorporate African cultural elements, preferring instead to dismiss, repudiate, and systematically erase African contributions to some kind of universal entity. This refusal to incorporate African culture and values into the assimilationist paradigm in the colonial context has also been a key component of immigration debates and discourse in contemporary France. In fact, as Lionnet and Shih have argued, "to be 'French' is to relate vertically to an ideal image of the French nation, not to find common ground with other immigrants who have embarked on this process of 'becoming French.' There is a clear lack of proliferation of relational discourses among different minority groups, a legacy from the colonial ideology of divide and conquer that has historically pitted different ethnic groups against each other" (Lionnet and Shih, "Thinking through the Mirror," 2).

Whether or not official governmental organizations accept concrete sociocultural changes, France has been and continues to be transformed through its membership in the European Union, by Francophonie, Americanization, immigration, the socioeconomic determinants of the global economy, and other cultural, political, and social phenomena that transcend sovereign borders and boundaries. Paris itself has been the subject of several studies that have accentuated the importance of the capital city in literary historiography in general, and in Black historiography in particular. Tyler Stovall's *Paris Noir: African Americans in the City of Light* and Michel Fabre's *La rive noire* provided incisive readings of the Black American experience in France. In turn, Bennetta Jules-Rosette's *Black Paris: The African Writers' Landscape* has played an important role in locating the symbiotic connections between Paris and African writers (negritude, *Présence africaine,* and so on), and the African presence in France has also been extensively documented through photography and graphic design projects such as *Le Paris noir* by Pascal Blanchard, Eric Deroo, and Gilles Manceron.[41] Finally, Pascale Casanova's *The World Republic of Letters* conclusively demonstrated the centrality of Paris in the European context.[42] In turn, *Black France* explores the bilateralism and transversal nature of African and French relations and acknowledges the centrality of Paris, but also broadens and decenters the symbolic territory to provincial sites, simultaneously refuting any notion of cultural homogeneity that may be suggested or implied by such a diasporic space. Of course, to talk about the question of blackness in France is to consider a plethora of influences, including the African American presence, the negritude movement, important cultural figures such as Senghor, Césaire, Léon-Gontran Damas, and Frantz Fanon, the emergence of African student organizations and unions, France's connection with its Overseas Departments and Territories, migrant and clandestine workers, the *sapeurs,* and contemporary African writers.[43]

In his consideration of texts produced by Black authors in Africa, African America, and the Caribbean, Irele identifies

> the testimony they provide of the black self emerging across the world as the product of a growing consciousness and of the black experience deriving from a common relation to the white world as a function of a common association with Africa . . . In the literature of Blacks from the Diaspora, this association plays an important role both as focus of consciousness and, increasingly, as reference for self-expression. The controlling idea here is the awareness of a particularized experience—historical, social, and cultural—which gives rise to the sentiment of a distinctive identity. (Irele, *The African Imagination,* 19–20)

Paris played a defining role in the elaboration of the "African experience," in the formulation and reformulation of a global blackness. "Contacts between France and black Americans go back to the beginnings of the history of the United States," Stovall has shown (*Paris Noir,* xiii), and Paris was unusually receptive to African American culture. This dimension is accorded greater attention in chapter 3, in which textual mediations between Ousmane Sembene and Richard Wright are addressed. Whereas segregation was practiced in the United States, "racism," as Edmund White has pointed out, "had never been *institutionalized* in modern France, never confirmed and upheld by the law."[44] This is not emphasized in order to obfuscate the racial origins of French colonial practices, but rather to show how African Americans circulated in different ways than their colonized African counterparts. Brent Hayes Edwards has explored the Black transnational culture of the 1920s and 1930s in *The Practice of Diaspora: Literature, Translation, and the Rise of Black Internationalism,* arguing that

> if a discourse of diaspora articulates difference, then one must consider the status of that difference—not just linguistic difference but, more broadly, the trace or the residue, perhaps, of what resists or escapes translation . . . Such an unevenness or differentiation marks a constitutive *décalage* in the very weave of culture . . . The black diasporic *décalage* among African Americans and Africans, then, is not simply geographical distance, nor is it simply difference in evolution or consciousness; instead it is a different kind of interface that might not be susceptible to expression in the oppositional terminology of the "vanguard" or the "backward."[45]

On the contrary, though, African American writers were not silent about the exploitative colonial practices. Fanon, Wright, Langston Hughes, Césaire, and Senghor gathered at the Sorbonne for the First Congress of Black Writers and Artists, September 19–22, 1956 (Premier Congrès des écrivains et artistes noirs), and many were later to be present in Rome in 1959, and then at the First World Festival of Negro Arts in Dakar in 1966.[46] As Fabre wrote, "Guidebooks are keys to museums and monuments of the past more than to living places where everything is in constant change, and with time Paris has become a vast monument that new generations of black visitors come to sample" (Fabre, *From Harlem to Paris,* 338).[47] Gradually, Paris would also become the vibrant jazz and entertainment capital in which Josephine Baker had arrived in 1925 with *La revue nègre,* only to perform later at the Folies-Bergères.[48]

Initially in *There Ain't No Black in the Union Jack: The Cultural Politics of Race and Nation* (a text that is unfortunately less discussed than his later contributions) and subsequently in *The Black Atlantic: Modernity and Double Consciousness,* Paul Gilroy elaborated upon the specificity of British blackness, "produced in a syncretic pattern in which the styles and forms of the Caribbean, the United States, and Africa have been reworked and reinscribed in the novel context of Britain's own ensemble of regional and class-oriented conflicts."[49] In turn, the concept of a Black Atlantic allowed us to look beyond this model in order to "transcend both the structures of the nation state and the constraints of ethnicity and national particularity" (Gilroy, *The Black Atlantic,* 19). The theoretical specificity of a "Black France" only makes sense when we explore its links with a global blackness and recognize that certain vectors are nevertheless specific to the French and francophone sub-Saharan African experience. In each case, these terms parallel other examples of identity formation among minority groups, as for example the case of Asian American culture, which, as Lisa Lowe has shown, attempts to "disrupt the current hegemonic relationship between the 'dominant' and 'minority' positions," and in which we can substitute the notion of "heterogeneity" to describe "the existence of differences and differential relationships within a bounded category."[50]

In France, the influence of American and British culture has been particularly obvious in language, since the "in" term employed to refer to some contributions (art, world music, rap and hip-hop, urban dance, sport, film, fashion) made by sub-Saharan Africans, Caribbeans, and immigrant youth in France today is the English "black" rather than *noir,* a term that in turn is inextricably linked to reductive colonial stereotypes. In some ways, then, these constructs inaugurate another kind of allegiance, with their use of American and British signifiers. Blanchard, Deroo, and Manceron, in a superb visual study of blackness in France (that includes photographs, posters, and urban art) entitled *Le Paris noir,* have traced the genealogy of these terms and the historiography of race in France. The term or label *nègre* was initially interchangeable with the word "slave." *Noir* became common as early as the eighteenth century, when it was adopted in 1788 by the abolitionist Société des amis des Noirs, and "black" has been in usage in France since the 1980s.[51] An article by Valérie Zerguine published in France during the summer of 2002 indicated this shift, yet nevertheless signaled certain behavioral patterns that were accorded more value through the attribution of the distinctive labels "black" and *nègre:* "You're a black when you kick a ball or rap into a mic and a Negro when you look for a job."[52]

Somatic features are of course inescapable, indelibly marking the minority subject as an outsider to perceived and widely accepted identitarian norms linked to whiteness. Didier Gondola has in fact convincingly argued that the French authorities have been "preoccupied with forging and delineating a national identity that conflated race with citizenship. In this respect, foreign immigrants afforded France to create a racial identity: 'Frenchness' or 'whiteness.'"[53] Much like their Beur counterparts (the children of North African immigrants), sub-Saharan Africans in France find themselves in what Homi Bhabha has called a "third space," that is, "the 'inter'—the cutting edge of translation and negotiation, the in-between space—that carries the burden of meaning in culture."[54] Unable to fully integrate into French society, and considered outsiders by the countries from which their parents have migrated, they find that the unsettling experience of "double-unbelonging" evoked by Salman Rushdie is a problem to be constantly negotiated.[55] Paradoxically, it also constitutes a threat to the French Republic. "'French' culture," Rosello argues, "can conceive of itself as an autonomous entity only because its foundational discourses foster a sort of amnesia about its origins."[56] And so, having recourse to a neologism to explore this further, Rosello asks "what might be entailed in a case of 'departenance'":

> [The word can be used] as a way of talking about the encounter between changing bodies and collectivities, bodies and nations, bodies and communities, individuals and groups. It sounds and looks like it could be a French word, although it is not. One might say that it "belongs to the family" of words such as "départ" (leave), "appartenance" (belonging), and its questionable antonym "dés-appartenance" (un-belonging), but it remains an illegitimate offspring, a bizarre linguistic cyborg that is somehow related to parts, parties, and partners. (Rosello, "The 'Beur' Nation," 23)

"New hybrid identities" can constitute "local and transnational identifications, including primordial as well as postidentitarian conceptions of the nation."[57] As such, hybridity can "destabilize authoritarian forms of control, while interrogating the parameters and limits of the democratic state. Instead of working within the narrow boundaries of the state, these theories of hybridity pose a challenge to the limits of sovereignty" (Joseph,

10), paradoxically reversing the very process of projection exemplified in Bonnie Honig's characterization of "cultural organization and foreignness as threat and/or supplement."[58] Returning to this argument some years later, Rosello argues that

> one of the eminently problematic consequences of the analogy between what we think of as state hospitality and private hospitality is that each citizen is implicitly required to abide by the laws of (in)hospitality dictated by the current philosophy of the nation, regardless of whether they correspond to his or her personal set of ethics. Recent episodes have revealed the vulnerability of foreigners and nationals who find themselves caught between their own sense of hospitality and the logic of immigration policies. (Rosello, *Postcolonial Hospitality*, 35)

For these reasons, "transnational connections break the binary relation of 'minority' communities with 'majority' societies—a dependency that structures projects of both assimilation and resistance, " James Clifford has persuasively argued, generating "diasporic cultural norms [that] are deployed in transnational networks built from multiple attachments . . . Diaspora discourse articulates, or bends together, both roots and routes . . . the term 'diaspora' is a signifier not simply of transnationality and movement but of political struggles to define the local, as distinctive community, in historical contexts of displacement."[59]

Jean-Loup Amselle's early work—in particular *Au cœur de l'ethnie* and *Logiques métisses*—foregrounded the usefulness of métissage and examined the "englobing" characteristics of dominant socioeconomic entities.[60] Yet he himself has recently acknowledged, in his groundbreaking book *Branchements: Anthropologie de l'universalité des cultures,* that métissage may no longer be sufficient to allow us to comprehend the full impact of globalization:

> This work is organized around the notion of "connections." The objective was to distance oneself from the concept of métissage that had once been useful but that seems today too closely linked to a biological component. Through recourse to an electronic or computational metaphor, that of the connection, a framework emerges in which local signifiers are juxtaposed with a network of planetary signifiers, thereby allowing one to move away from an approach that understands our global world as the product of a mixing of cultures that are themselves seen as separate universes, and foregrounding instead the idea of triangulation, that is to say recourse to a third component in order to establish one's identity. (Amselle, *Branchements,* 7)

The third component draws proximity to Bhabha's understanding of "third space." Amselle effectively and compellingly proposes that the process of Islamic expansion in the tenth century be seen as a precursor to the phenomenon that is commonly understood today as globalization. According to this way of interpreting intercultural dynamics, colonialism finds itself relocated as a mechanism that proceeds from globalization, rather than the other way round. In turn, this framework offers us the occasion to adequately assess the complex manner in which populations and histories have become imbricated or creolized, rather than analyzing these entities as somehow autonomous, closed, and threatened with eradication by globalization. Amselle has advocated that we think instead in terms of *branchements*:

> In this context, perhaps more than ever before, Africa must be conceived of as a deterritorialized entity. As a floating signifier, Africa is a concept with a variable geometry that belongs as much to the French *banlieues* as it does to North American ghettos, to Brazilian favelas and African villages. Africa is thus an essential element of the planetary imaginary, to be found in a broad series of figures that are integral components of contemporary globalization . . . Africa then represents a construct, a concept that obeys a semantic logic that is totally independent of territorial roots. The Africa-concept belongs to all those who choose to take hold of it, to connect to it. (Amselle, *Branchements,* 15)

These ways of conceiving and reconceiving of both concrete and imaginative spaces are particularly well suited to the framework of this book, because they emphasize the importance of considering simultaneously a multitude of spaces prior to elaborating or formulating conclusions. Blackness can therefore contain simultaneously the potentiality of a fixed and mobile identity, available in the circulation of satellite broadcasts, the Internet, radio, television, cinema, world music, international sport, writers, artists, the Mourides, forms of trade and population movements that have no interest in abandoning nomadic existence, and so on. With the model provided by William Safran,[61] Clifford underlines the importance of relinquishing reductive classificatory frameworks:

> This overlap of border and diaspora experiences in late twentieth-century everyday life suggests the difficulty of maintaining exclusivist paradigms in our attempts to account for transnational identity formations . . . These, then, are the main features of diaspora: a history of dispersal, myths/memories of the homeland, alienation in the host (bad host?) country, desire for eventual return, ongoing support of the homeland, and a collective identity importantly defined by this relationship. (Clifford, *Routes,* 247)

History is thus a process of population dispersal, but also of reconfiguring a range of myths and individual and collective memories, of the experience of alienation, of nostalgia, even of melancholia.[62] One factor that remains constant is that globalization is not exclusively "homogenizing/hegemonic" or "heterogenetic/interpenetrating," but rather a process in which individuals and groups are "transformed by diasporas and intercommunication."[63] This process of "intercommunication" has tremendous implications for the bilateralism of exchanges between populations in Africa and those in France, exchanges that contain the possibility of operating outside of normative, hegemonic hexagonal influences. At a cultural level, the plural notion of a Francophonie in France has much to reveal.

If *antillanité* (Caribbeanness) is concerned with foregrounding the cultural specificity of the Caribbean outside of metropolitan influences and *créolité* (creoleness) relocates the centrality of the multiple cultural and linguistic influences generated by slavery to identity formation, then surely the theorization of the African Diaspora in France has a dimension to add to the discussion of identity formation inside and outside of empire.[64] For the Somali writer Nurrudin Farah, the search for an understanding of the Somali Diaspora involved an assessment of the cultural, economic, political, and social circumstances in which Somalis live, and paradoxically led him as the author-investigator to confront his own range of experiences as he navigated—and negotiated—his way through the new transnational zones that are borders, customs, and international departure terminals.[65]

The *New York Times* published a telling article on October 8, 1996, entitled "Neocolonialists Seize the *French* Language." The italicization of the word "French" in the headline seemed to suggest that various intercultural dynamics were altering the French language in such a manner as to render it unrecognizable, and that these influences were perhaps closer to contaminating rather than enriching the language, particularly since the article evoked a "crisis." However, the author nevertheless did acknowledge that France, while continuing to serve as the publishing capital of the francophone world, is almost exclusively being recognized for those works published in French by francophone authors (that is, essentially, those authors writing in French from within France's postcolonial communities or from beyond the Hexagon). This is confirmed by a cursory glance at recent winners of what are arguably France's most prestigious literary awards, namely the Goncourt Prize and the Renaudot Prize: Tahar Ben Jelloun from Morocco, Patrick Chamoiseau from Martinique, Amin Maalouf from Lebanon, and Ahmadou Kourouma of the Ivory Coast.[66] Significantly, similar mechanisms are to be evidenced in the anglophone world, although the discourse this has generated is strikingly different in the absence of an "anglophone" movement attempting to maintain London as the cultural center for productions in English (there is, for example, no Minister of Anglophony sitting in Westminster). Most critically acclaimed writers in the English language today are from the so-called Commonwealth or former British colonial territories: Salman Rushdie, Caryl Phillips, J. M. Coetzee, Nadine Gordimer, V. S. Naipaul, Ben Okri, Wole Soyinka, Derek Walcott, and so forth. And, of course, this situation is further problematized by those writers whose roots are located outside the metropole, but who are living within the metropole. As Lionnet has argued, "these practices thus serve to delegitimate the cultural hegemony of 'French' culture over 'francophone' realities."[67]

In Calixthe Beyala's novel *Les honneurs perdus,* for example, the epigraph explores the tenuous relationship between *francité* (Frenchness) and Francophonie, *français* (French) and francophone.[68] "Le Français est francophone mais la francophonie n'est pas française," we read. This sentence may seem relatively straightforward when it is read aloud: one translation could be "The French language is francophone but francophonie is not French." This interpretation would emphasize, or perhaps reject, those attempts that have been made to gather francophone countries under the aegis of the Hexagon, thus maintaining Paris as the ex-colonial "center."[69] Paradoxically, "critiquing the center, when it stands as an end in itself, seems only to enhance it; the center remains the focus and the main object of study. The deconstructive dyad center/margin thus appears to privilege marginality only to end up containing it" (Lionnet and Shih, "Thinking through the Mirror," 3). However, the capitalization of the word *Français* problematizes and destabilizes that meaning, and the translation then becomes "A French person is [or "the French people are"] francophone, but francophonie is not French." Of course, either way, the fact remains that "francophonie" is not French, and Beyala, along with other francophone authors, underlines the plurality of francophone cultural contributions.

A study of France that treated it as a monolithic entity would today be both inaccurate and irresponsible. While immigrants struggle to achieve integration, the monocultural perspective has been displaced, and it is, as Bhabha has argued, all the more essential "to think beyond narratives of originary and initial subjectivities and to focus on those moments or processes that are produced in the articulation of cultural differences" as we attempt to "locate" culture in spaces that are never readily identifiable (Bhabha, 1). Within the particular context of *Black France,* in which issues of immigration, transnationalism, and the intercultural dynamics of the francophone sub-Saharan African Diaspora are explored, shared points of memory are introduced by literatures produced in Africa, and in France by immigrants or the children of immigrants, but also by writers who live or publish in France while not considering themselves immigrants. The experiences narrated rejoin the epigraph to Beyala's novel, and the universal sameness that is contained in the singular "francophonie" no longer sufficiently incorporates the plurality and multiplicity of perspectives contained in the experiences of protagonists. Instead, the monolithic, hegemonic discourse of the former colonial center is transformed through the inscription of a transnational dimension that continues to define the inextricable links between French and francophone cultural politics and productions. Returning to the colonial era as a point of entry to recent debates on questions of immigration and national identity in contemporary France seems a necessary gesture, one that allows for the relocation of the origins of immigration discourse and migratory flows according to a specific set of economic, political, and social coordinates that are indissociable from a colonial, postcolonial, and global geometry.

The British context allows for a comparative perspective even if the colonial and postcolonial histories are quite different.[70] One should note that "Black" as a category in Britain is often used to describe Africans, Caribbeans, and South Asians. "And still," Rushdie writes, the word 'immigrant' means 'black immigrant.'"[71] The kind of space Rushdie has in mind, as it pertains to the process of decolonization and the redefinition of the parameters of Britishness (or Englishness, for that matter), is not unrelated to debates that have taken place in France over the future of secularism and perceived threats to Frenchness.[72] If we follow the manner in which Gilroy has continued to monitor this discursive realm in his book *Postcolonial Melancholia,* we see that while

> it has become necessary to take political discussions of citizenship, belonging, and nationality beyond the dual prescription of assimilation and immigration control . . . all these changes can be used to point to the enduring significance of "race" and racism and their historic place in the long and slow transformation of Britain, its changing relationships with itself, with Europe, with the United States, and the wider postcolonial world. (123–124)

To this end, Mark Stein's book *Black British Literature: Novels of Transformation* is useful in thinking about blackness in France in that he highlights how "black Britain is distinct from other postcolonial cultures: It lays claim to post-colonial and to British cultures in Britain" and "this tension is a reciprocal one in that 'blackness' redefines 'Britishness' and 'Britishness' redefines 'blackness.'"[73] The "transformative" potential and component of relations between Africa and France and Africans in France interest me.

The juxtaposition of "Black" and "France" in the title to this book deliberately aims to underscore the tenuousness and apparent oxymoronic dimension intrinsic to this construct. In fact, these autonomous entities have become symbiotic, mutually constitutive markers of African-French bilateral relations and histories that are forever imbricated.[74] The racial signifier is foregrounded in a deliberate rejection of official French arguments in favor of an undifferentiated community, so that "cultural" (Islam, language, family structure) rather than essentialized racial factors are invoked in immigrant discourse. Susan Peabody and Tyler Stovall, in *The Color of Liberty: Histories of Race in France,* insist that "one cannot understand questions of race in France without taking the colonial experience into consideration . . . race has been a significant factor in French life over the past three centuries; it is not something that suddenly happened in France with the rise of the so-called second-generation immigrants of the 1980s."[75] Even the reluctance of French authorities to address race serves to reinforce its centrality and validity as a category of analysis. Cen-

tral to my framework and contextualization of a Black France has been
Mbembe's distinction between "territory" and "place":

> In dealing with these questions, we will draw a distinction between Africa as
> a "place" and Africa as a "territory." In fact, a place is the order according to
> which elements are distributed in relationships of coexistence. A place, as
> Michel de Certeau points out, is an instantaneous configuration of positions.
> It implies a stability. As for a territory, it is fundamentally an intersection of
> moving bodies. It is defined essentially by the set of movements that take
> place within it. Seen in this way, it is a set of possibilities that historically sit-
> uated actors constantly resist or realize.[76]

Both Africa and France must be understood in these terms in order to capture the nature of cultural, economic, political, and social dynamics within, beyond, among, and of course in between these fluid territories.

   The term "Afro-Parisian" has gained increasing currency, being used to
describe the literary productions of francophone sub-Saharan African authors residing in France.[77] Jules-Rosette developed this concept in her
1998 book *Black Paris: The African Writer's Landscape*, in which she argues that "Parisianism refers to a literary interest in Paris as the social context for the author's works, the subject matter of their writings, and the
source of their focal audience" (7).[78] Accordingly,

> Black Paris is not an American-style ghetto. It consists of many communities
> sprinkled across the city, creating an exotic subculture that lurks behind the
> official monuments. As new immigrants pour into the city, Paris reluctantly
> makes room for them. This alternative environment has become the incuba-
> tion cubicle for a new style of African writing. (147)[79]

Having identified the emergence of a corpus of works by African authors
exhibiting common features that include residence in Paris and an engagement with the circumstances of that residency, Jules-Rosette's study insists
on the mutually constitutive nature of the African-French relations that
are at the center of these writers' concerns: "The Parisianism of the 1980s
would not have been possible without political pressure to liberalize legal
and social attitudes toward immigration in France and to combat xeno-
phobic sentiments" (48). As Boniface Mongo-Mboussa has shown, "ne-
gropolitan (as some have called them) writers emerge at the time when the
French Left came to power and when some Africans and Africanists were
dreaming of changes in French-African relations."[80] Aware of the originality of her sociological findings ("The term 'Parisianism' is not a genre description current among literary theorists. There is little critical work on
this relatively new genre, but the quantity of new works and their thematic
similarities warrant classification and recognition" [Jules-Rosette, *Black
Paris*, 148]), Jules-Rosette suggests what a study of these works might
yield: "As a collective physical and ideological space, black Paris is a landscape of memory that encompasses the subjective perspectives of African

writers. Through the environment of black Paris, experiences are communicated and memories reinvented" (149). Similar questions were raised in addressing the rise to centrality of Beur writers in the 1980s.

In his groundbreaking study of the Beurs, *Voices from the North African Community in France: Immigration and Identity in Beur Fiction,* Alec Hargreaves argued that "the key problematic which has preoccupied Beur writers" consisted in "the articulation of a sense of personal identity, forged in the particular circumstances which are those of an ethnic minority in France."[81] "Unlike the older generation of North African writers," Hargreaves continues, "the Beurs have undergone their formative experiences as part of an ethnic minority within France, where they have shared through family home in both the material disadvantages of the cultural traditions associated with first-generation immigrants. Beur authors have in this sense been the first to write from within the immigrant community itself" (Hargreaves, *Voices,* 4).[82] These processes are at work and analogous questions raised when one employs the term "Afro-Parisian" to describe the relatively new corpus of literary works produced by sub-Saharan African writers.

In her book *Afrique sur Seine: A New Generation of African Writers in Paris,* Odile Cazenave performs a useful expository task in documenting the substantial corpus of works produced by African writers in or on Paris predominantly since the 1990s, underscoring the innovative stylistic dimension of the writing, and certainly signals numerous pedagogic approaches that could result from exploring these works through questions relating to identity, diasporic community formation, reflections on the etymology of the concept of Diaspora, autobiography, and gender issues.[83] However, in her obsessive concern with distinguishing her book from Jules-Rosette's, she ends up, somewhat paradoxically, reaffirming the very centrality of Paris from which she sought to distance herself. "Jules-Rosette's taxonomy of their writing as Parisianist," Cazenave argues, "limits them to the periphery, both with regards to French literature and to Francophone literature, especially the African novel from the continent" (*Afrique sur Seine,* 3). The "Paris-centrism" of her own book is announced as early as the title itself, "Afrique sur Seine," as is the accompanying insistence on "generation" as a category of inquiry, for which she had critiqued Jules-Rosette: "Taking Jules-Rosette's definition of a 'Parisianist' genre, we raise the question whether such a categorization is wholly applicable to these newer narratives, and consider the risks of classification and of ghettoization in this literature" (4). I prefer to think of generation in terms of the entry into writing or publication rather than as an arbitrary category linked to age (a classificatory mode easily challenged by numerous writers, such as Sembene, Kourouma, and Mongo Beti, who produced texts with dramatically shifting concerns and contents over several decades both during and after the colonial period).[84] This problematic remains unresolved, as we read about "the Afro-Parisian novel" (151) and as "the characters in the new African writings of self in Paris display a variety of occupations" (153). The point in *Black France* is to acknowledge how earlier scholarly contributions to the interdisciplinary study of Africans and African Americans in France have allowed such projects to be undertaken, but also to expand the field of discourse in order to illustrate the ways in which Black Paris and France are often mutable in the imaginations of writers in texts whose sociological content applies equally to the metropole and to the Hexagon as a whole. Let us consider a range of other critical readings of these questions to further elucidate my position.

Bernard Magnier was one of the first critics to evaluate this corpus of works in an essay he published in 1990, "Beurs noirs à Black Babel." He identified a continuity with Beur literature, but also established certain organizational principles that included locality—"They live and write in Paris," "Parisian blacks"—and ethnicity—"They are 'blacks beurs' or 'beurs noirs' for some, 'negropolitans' or 'Gallo-negroes' for others. They live and write in Babylone-sur-Seine, in the 'black Babel' of Paris or its banlieue":

> The pioneering writers of "Parisian life" experienced the trauma of being elsewhere and discovered the difficulties of exile, but they knew their stays were limited and they could find comfort knowing that sooner or later they would return to the native land. But the "new heroes" don't have this perspective—one they may not automatically even wish for—and they often live adventures that are also not without ambiguity, in a land that is not entirely foreign to them and yet does not entirely belong to them.[85]

Abdourahman A. Waberi (from Djibouti but living in France) has also addressed this issue in an article, "Les enfants de la postcolonie: Esquisse d'une nouvelle génération d'écrivains francophones d'Afrique noire." His analysis concentrates on the decade after Jules-Rosette's initial study, but for him "the children of the postcolony or the transcontinental generation" are also a "generational phenomenon." He describes the generation he has in mind as the "fourth generation," the first three being the pioneer writers of 1920–1930, the negritude movement from 1930 to 1960, and finally decolonization and postcolonial disillusionment from the 1970s onward.[86] In "Littérature et postcolonie," Lydie Moudileno succinctly challenges this attempt to categorize these writers: "Recourse to a historical understanding of the 'postcolony' to account for literary production ends up reproducing an arbitrary and reductive parallel between the reading of history and the reading of a literary corpus."[87] I wholeheartedly embrace this position, one that I argued in favor of in *Nation-Building, Propaganda, and Literature in Francophone Africa* in highlighting the importance of Guy Ossito Midiohouan's 1986 revised historiography in *L'idé-*

ologie dans la littérature négro-africaine d'expression française.[88] The kind of homogeneity implied by these attempts at categorization must be resisted at all costs, since it is precisely the bilateralism of French-African relations that continues to inform literary works. Cazenave's own generational model rejoins Waberi's, and in aligning myself with Moudileno's warning, I also subscribe to Stein's argument that

> the term generation needs to be problematized; like the term literary history, it suggests neat separations and an idea of organic growth which does not accurately describe the literary texts in question . . . I'm problematizing the term generation because writers and texts cannot be readily taxonomized according to their age or the date of the authors' . . . arrival in their country of residence. (Stein, 5–6)

Having said this, I am not convinced Waberi himself fully subscribes to this notion of "generation," particularly since his own status and the remarkable originality of his writings come from precisely his capacity to exceed the kind of restrictive categorizations implied by the "generational" model. The contradictory nature of his position is indicated when he argues that

> The postcolonial process has by all evidence accelerated the circulation of extra-European cultural references, and recourse to these references has profoundly influenced both the artistic forms and practices of intellectuals located in the West. The great cultural centers of the former colonies no longer have the monopoly over the dynamism of artistic creativity. (Waberi, "Les enfants de la postcolonie," 14)

Three principles inform the framework of Cazenave's analysis: "a novel marked by the lack of focus on Africa/Africas . . . an axis of reflection over the implications of departure from a particular place and culture in favor of others on an individual level in terms of alienation and of the dislocation of acquired reference points . . . [and] the phenomenon of migration" (Cazenave, *Afrique sur Seine,* 161–162). Many of the novels under consideration can be considered under these rubrics. However, I disagree fundamentally with her on a particular point, and that disagreement is located in my own adherence to the model of "territoriality" discussed earlier: namely, the reduced importance Cazenave accords to Africa:

> These writers, both male and female, contribute to the formation of a new literature. Often their work, *only slightly preoccupied with Africa itself,* addresses questions of displacement, migration, and in this regard, poses new questions about postcolonial cultures and identities, as perceived by those living in France. But they don't simply subscribe to notions of immigration literature . . . they show the possibility of writing and thinking about oneself outside the prescriptions of the West—the former colonizing power. (Cazenave, *Afrique sur Seine,* 1, emphasis mine)[89]

The point is that these writers have transformed Africa into a global territorial signifier, one that exceeds Africa as "place" in arriving at an alternative understanding and designation of territory as fluid and mobile—but one from which Africa itself is never absent. Furthermore, as Moudileno has also argued, these writers "challenge literary historiography as it has been practiced up until now through their very position at the intersection of several geographic and intellectual territorialities" (Moudileno, "Littérature et postcolonie," 10). For this reason, I have accorded tremendous importance to the transcolonial nature of French-African relations in order to account for the polyvocal nature of African literary productions. The notion of territory allows for a consideration of the diversity that characterizes the African diasporic community in France, in which there are differences between the circumstances and experiences of individuals and groups according to national (Congolese, Malian, Senegalese) and ethnic (Mourides, Soninké) identities, but also more importantly in terms of the nature of relations between Africa and France and authors themselves, as well as the broader geographic multisited framework key to a contextualization of Black France in the twenty-first century (Caen, Lyon, Marseilles, Paris, Strasbourg, Toulon).

How then can one begin to account for the mediation that is at work between African writers in France and those in Africa? How do Communism and racism inform anticolonial and decolonizing imperatives, and how in turn do these operate transnationally in a context that might simultaneously include Africa, African America, Europe, France, and both Black and white consciousness at a given historical juncture? Furthermore, how can one possibly begin to understand the works of Alain Mabanckou, Daniel Biyaoula, Fatou Keïta, Henriette Akofa, Calixthe Beyala, or Fatou Diome (among others) without considering the ways in which Ousmane Sembene, Laye Camara, Cheikh Hamidou Kane, Ousmane Socé, and Bernard Dadié were always already "immigrant" writers?[90] Without the discursive transterritorial fields of Africa and France contained in the works of earlier African writers, how can we begin to comprehend complex gender issues as they pertain to the masculinist codes of La sape or the controversial question of female excision? For that matter, how can we decode the dialogue between national subjects and diasporic communities, internal and external African voices? And finally, how does the consecration of the migrant subject operate in France through the acquisition of cultural and economic capital alongside consecration linked to a "return" to Africa? For me, these kinds of factors are more relevant than an author's qualification for an analytic category that can invariably only be challenged or exceeded; the scholarship of Hargreaves on the Beurs has shown us that while the category itself was initially useful to account for a new phenomenon, it could only ultimately be limited by history.[91] Mamadou Diouf has eloquently captured the need for a pluralistic interpretation of Diaspora:

One must also speak of the emergence of a new, extraordinary literature, that of novelists who are no longer novelists of the in-between, of Africa and France, but rather novelists of Africa in France. This brings us back to the idea of tension, of movements that are not unidirectional but rather that go off in all kinds of directions. Young writers are today speaking about Africa and about France, and also about Africa in France. They present a history and forms of modernity that are quite different from colonial and post-colonial modernities; and these modernities give birth to a different Africa, whose line of questioning and problems—whatever the tragedy experienced—lead to the only important question, namely the need for a cosmopolitanism.[92]

That Paris remains a privileged site for a broad range of African interlocutors is indisputable—but beyond the fact of residency, analogous subject matter, and the common findings of a kind of new historicist approach to the works of African writers in Paris and France in general, one must not ignore the dynamic nature of African writing in Africa itself, and also by African writers living in other regions of the world, such as America (Assia Djebar, Chris Abani, Chinua Achebe, Emmanuel Dongala, Alain Mabanckou, Ngùgù wa Thiong'o, and others). If anything, the exclusionary nature of categorization is all the more dangerous in the European context where, as Etienne Balibar has convincingly demonstrated, the "tautology" that defines "others" as "not us" is intrinsic to the resulting concept of *préférence nationale* (national preference), one that Diome addressed in her first published collection of short stories, entitled *La préférence nationale*.[93] In fact, in her book *The World Republic of Letters*, Casanova has highlighted an often overlooked factor that concerns Paris's role as center of the colonial empire in this network of relations, and how it might operate differently for francophone authors:

> The position of Francophone writers, on the other hand, is paradoxical if not tragic as well. Since for them Paris is not merely the capital of world literary space, as historically it has been for writers everywhere, but also the very source of the political and/or literary domination under which they labor. . . . Making matters worse, the power of Paris is still more domineering and more keenly felt by Francophone writers for being incessantly denied in the name of the universal belief in the universality of French letters and on behalf of the values of liberty promoted and monopolized by France itself. (124)

Because of this, these notions, organized around *appartenance* (belonging) and such terms as *adhérence* (adherence) and *adhésion* (adhesion), serve to denote "on the one hand that to which one attaches," Balibar suggests, and "that to which one is attached, and on the other hand the community that one chooses" (Balibar, "De la préférence nationale," 115). This is perhaps what Lionnet suggested when she demonstrated that many postcolonial women writers

> insist on the relational nature of identity and difference, on the productive
> tensions between the two, and on the intricate and interdependent ways in
> which human agents function . . . The aim, in the end, is to reconstruct new
> imaginative spaces where power configurations, inevitable as they are, may
> be reorganized to allow fewer dissymmetries in the production and circula-
> tion of knowledge. (Lionnet, *Postcolonial Representations,* 5–6)

The fact that African writers have chosen to situate their narratives in both
Africa and France and to explore the various ways in which communities
are organized outside of the homeland in the diasporic context is of
course particularly striking. Additionally, the manner in which cultural
practices are maintained, challenged, and transformed, subjected to multiple influences, and in turn how ethnic, national, and regional rivalries are
exacerbated, is also highly significant in gauging the extent to which
French society itself is being systematically reorganized according to a set
of new coordinates. A transnational approach to these questions provides
a better contextual framework, one that permits the incorporation of
questions of labor mobility, immigration laws, youth culture, and so forth,
in an attempt to uncover some of the intercultural dynamics evidenced in
the literary productions of francophone sub-Saharan authors in general.
Jules-Rosette's notion of "Parisianism" has of course been useful in cir-
cumscribing recent developments in African-French relations and the ongoing centrality of Paris in this discourse. But Paris alone cannot serve to
completely delimit broader questions pertaining to reflection on blackness
in France in general. *Black France* extends the analysis from the colonial
era to the contemporary moment of postcoloniality, recognizes the importance of Paris, but also provincializes the immigrant experience while insisting upon a supranational dimension. All of these factors are of course
important in assessing the African presence in France and in establishing a
statistical record.

   Calculating the number of sub-Saharan Africans in France involves a
concerted analysis of the mechanisms employed in such calculations—
mechanisms that in turn have much to reveal concerning the politics of
immigration and the demands of the French Republic.[94] As Michel Wieviorka has shown, there has been a significant shift from the early category
of *travailleurs immigrés* (immigrant workers) to "Arabs," "Beurs," and
"Blacks," introducing the idea that "the transition from a social definition
of immigration to an ethnic, national, religious, or racial one is a complex
phenomenon that owes much to exclusion, stigmatization, or racism,"[95] in
what constitutes a classic example of what Rey Chow has characterized as
"the ever-renewable government efforts to fabricate and stabilize."[96] Official definitions and criteria have been deployed in order to ascertain who
is classified as an immigrant or a foreigner, and these are outlined and reported annually by the Haut conseil à l'intégration (High Council for Integration, HCI) to the prime minister. Current definitions are as follows:

Etrangers: Persons who cannot claim French nationality no matter where they were born.

Immigrés: Foreigners born overseas who have settled in France. The *immigré* may at some time in his or her life acquire French nationality.

Immigrants: Foreigners who have received an initial authorization to stay in France for at least one year. This category is only for the purpose of monitoring immigration flows.[97]

The government census of 1999 uses the criteria outlined by the HCI and includes no categories for ethnic criteria or information. The population of metropolitan France is categorized according to nationality and place of birth, and methods of calculation are both confusing and complicated. In a total population of approximately 58,520,688, there were 4,308,527 immigrants (7.36 percent of the total), comprising non-French born overseas who either resided in France as foreigners (2,753,588) or had acquired French nationality (1,554,939). Foreigners born in France (of whom there were 800,354) are not considered immigrants, regardless of whether they have acquired French nationality (509,598 of them had not done so), which dramatically reduces the official numbers.[98]

With these considerations in mind, one can make the following assumptions about the numbers of sub-Saharan Africans in France today. Recourse to statistics is extremely important in order to counter, on the one hand, popular misconceptions concerning definitions of "foreignness" and, on the other, perceptions that France is being "invaded" and "contaminated" by outsiders.[99] The fundamental reorientation that Gérard Noiriel proposed in his book *Le creuset français: Histoire de l'immigration, XIXe–XXe siècles* came from his commitment to demonstrating that France had a long history of immigration from many regions of the world, and accordingly to dispelling and countering stereotypes and myths through statistical facts: "If one takes seriously the statistic that establishes that one-third of the people living in France today have foreign 'roots,' then the centrality of the family as the explanatory principle of 'permanence' and 'tradition' collapses" (64). Peabody and Stovall suggest that "there were about 4,000 blacks living among the 25 million French at the time of the revolution" ("Race, France, Histories," 2). In 1936, according to Noiriel, non-naturalized foreigners were estimated at 2,198,236 and included 720,926 Italians, 422,694 Polish, 28,290 Portuguese, and 253,599 Spanish. By 1982, the total had risen to 3,680,100, and included 333,740 Italians, 764,860 Portuguese, 321,440 Spanish, and a substantial addition of 795,920 Algerians and 431,120 Moroccans (Noiriel, *Le creuset français,* 417–418).[100] The real nature of the perceived problem (one that has been well documented) concerns more recent transitions in the demographics of immigrants. For, in reality, in figures mostly gathered by the Institut national de la statistique et des études économiques (INSEE), the percentage of foreigners in the total French population has remained relatively constant since the 1930s: 1.06 in 1851, 2.97 in 1886, 6.58 in 1931, 5.28 in 1968, and 6.35 in 1990.[101] According to approximate statistics gathered by the Ministry for the Colonies in 1926, there were 1,685 Africans from Afrique occidentale française (AOF, French West Africa) and 230 from Afrique équatoriale française (AEF, French Equatorial Africa) living in France in 1926.[102] But the main nationality groups in France's foreign population have changed dramatically: in 1946 88.7 percent of foreigners were Europeans, 2.3 percent Maghrebis, and 0.8 percent other Africans; in 1962 72.2 percent were Europeans, 18.9 percent Maghrebis, and 0.8 percent other Africans; in 1975 60.7 percent were Europeans, 32.3 percent Maghrebis, and 2.3 percent other Africans; and in 1990 40.6 percent were Europeans, 38.7 percent Maghrebis, and 11.8 percent other Africans, constituting a total of 3,596,602 foreign nationals in a total population of 56,651,955 (Hargreaves, *Immigration, "Race," and Ethnicity,* 11, 26). Methodological issues and population estimates are complicated when all Africans are aggregated. While Todd estimates that there were approximately 28,000 Africans in France in 1968 and 176,745 in 1990 (406), and Michelle Guillon claims that there were 177,871 sub-Saharan Africans in France in 1982, 307,902 in 1990, and 447,521 in 1999,[103] the main point to underline is that their numbers grew exponentially at the end of the twentieth century, thereby transforming the cultural, political, and social landscape of Black France, while accelerating all kinds of transversal movements between and from Africa and the metropole. Many countries are now represented: Senegal (43,692), Mali (37,693), the Democratic Republic of the Congo (22,740), Cameroon (18,037), the Ivory Coast (16,711), and Congo (12,755).[104]

"The use of the word 'immigration' to encompass what are in many respects post-migratory processes," as Hargreaves has shown, "is itself symptomatic of the difficulties experienced by the French in coming to terms—both literally and ontologically—with the settlement of people of immigrant origin . . . such people are commonly referred to as 'ethnic minorities' or 'minority ethnic groups,' and a large part of what the French call 'immigration' is commonly known as 'race relations.'"[105] In the French context, the term *immigré* (that is, the social status accorded to an immigrant)—as opposed to "immigrant," "migrant," or "emigrant"—"has a tendency to fix the individual in a given condition . . . named as such s/he will always carry the trace of a stigmatized past." The term is even applied "to a whole category of people who have never migrated (the 'second' and 'third generation')."[106] Balibar has, in turn, insisted upon the fact that the official rhetoric is organized around the figure of the "foreigner" (*étranger*)—the "immigrant" functions as signifier for a broad range of cultural, political, and social issues, and "the less the social problems of the 'immigrants,' or the social problems which massively affect immigrants, are specific, the more their existence is made responsible for them."[107] As we shall see, this "capacity to lump together all the dimensions of 'social pathology' as effects of a single cause, which is defined with the aid of a series of signifiers derived from race or its more recent equivalents" (Balibar, "Racism and Crisis," 220), was deployed during the colonial period, as documented in Sembene's novel *Le docker noir* (*Black Docker*), as effectively as it was in postcolonial France during the 1990s with the "affaire des *sans-papiers.*" These discursive patterns duplicated earlier ones, as for example the Abbé Grégoire's own antislavery writings, such as *De la littérature des nègres* (1808), and Gobineau's *Essai sur l'inégalité des races humaines* (published between 1853 and 1855) which, though not widely read during his lifetime, nevertheless "remains the most comprehensive statement on and the master synthesis of nineteenth-century French racial thought" (Cohen, 218).[108]

Pascal Blanchard, Nicolas Bancel, and Sandrine Lemaire have, arguably, collectively edited the most significant contribution to French scholarship on (post)colonial studies, namely *La fracture coloniale: La société française au prisme de l'héritage colonial.*[109] Blanchard and Bancel have argued, in an essay entitled "Les origines républicaines de la fracture coloniale" ("The Republican Origins of the Colonial Fracture"), that although ideals of liberty and equality were fundamental in the founding of the French Republic, they were strategically adopted within a more strictly "culturalist" discourse," and in fact "racial inequality is at the heart of the colonial Republican mechanism."[110] This attempt to deracialize the colonial project and adopt a more culturalist agenda allowed for the civilizing mission while simultaneously deferring assimilation indefinitely, and this colonial discourse informs to this day official thinking on the question of immigration in France (Blanchard and Bancel, "Les origines républicaines," 38–39) as it has mutated across various paradigms from "le droit à la différence" ("the right to be different"/"the right to difference") to "le seuil de tolérance" ("the threshold of tolerance"), "la préférence nationale" ("national preference"), universalism, particularism, communitarianism, hyperpluralism, and multicommunitarianism.[111] This is precisely the kind of transcolonial vector I have alluded to, in which, as Balibar has shown, "the equivocal interiority-exteriority configuration which had, since the period of colonial conquest, formed one of the structuring dimensions of racism, finds itself reproduced, expanded or re-activated"[112] and has now triggered new forms of racism, "a racism of the era of 'decolonization' . . . whose dominant theme is not biological heredity but the insurmountability of cultural differences, a racism which, at first sight, does not postulate the superiority of certain groups or peoples in relation to others but 'only' the harmfulness of abolishing frontiers, the incompatibility of life-styles and traditions."[113]

In reality, France's rejection of multiculturalism is due to what it perceives as the term's historical indebtedness to and indissociability from the

American context in which the accompanying discourses on civil and individual rights are considered to protect citizens above and beyond the
communitarian imperatives of the Republican state.[114] Paradoxically,
Memmi points to the circularity of the argument in which communitarianism "is seen as proof of resistance by immigrants to integration into the
collective body of the nation," and the ghetto, while "feeding the idea of
separation, also stands as the expression of it"; accordingly, the "constitution of small communities at the heart of the national entity is not the outcome of some perverse gesture aimed at its destruction . . . but rather a
spontaneous and utilitarian agglomeration of minorities who have been
unable to identify themselves fully with the majority" (Memmi, *Portrait
du décolonisé*, 104). In France, the primary concern remains the integrational, assimilationist drive toward that ambiguous ideal that is Frenchness. Because of this, according to David Blatt, "the increased political
saliency of immigration issues helped revive a traditional French discourse
on integration and the nation-state that insists on the preservation of republican principles of undifferentiated citizenship and a firm rejection of
any public recognition of ethnic or cultural identities."[115]

The colonial civilizing mission was premised on the attempt to create
French cultural prototypes. Newly formed French-Africans soon realized
that that stated objective was unattainable. Their status as colonized subjects and constructs inscribed by a hyphenated identity forever precluded
their access to some distant evolutionary point, much in the same way
as today's ethnic minorities are relegated to topographic zones in the
banlieues (housing projects) outside of the parameters of Frenchness.
Ironically, of course, the marginalization of these groups creates the very
ghettos that the French perceive as the inevitable outcome of U.S. multicultural politics. The end result of these disparate policies is similar,
though, thus reducing the validity of French critiques of U.S. multiculturalism. Fanon underscored how linguistic and even broader cultural identification with France was insufficient to confer full Frenchness, a dimension Cohen addressed in his book *The French Encounter with Africans*:
"The black migrants from the Antilles, however, should not have suffered
most of these problems: they knew French and French culture, they were
French citizens, and their lifestyle was not significantly at variance from
that of their white compatriots. To the extent that they suffered ostracism,
they were victims not of xenophobia but of racism, for race seemed to be
the only characteristic that distinguished them from countless other
Frenchmen" (Cohen, 287). My own analysis, without claiming to be exhaustive, nevertheless attempts to explore the pluridimensionality of migration to achieve a more accurate rendition of population flows and the
bilateralism of French-African relations. To this end, the analysis extends
to African soldiers, students, intellectuals, victims of modern servitude
and gender oppression, political refugees, *sapeurs,* asylum seekers, and

sans-papiers. In order to extrapolate with a degree of accuracy the significance of African contributions to public discourse in France, it remains crucial to correct false assumptions and to denounce the reductive discourse that occludes African contributions (among others) to the cultural, social, and political landscape of the Hexagon today.[116]

For example, African soldiers made immeasurable contributions to France's military forces during both the First and the Second World Wars. In fact, as Miller has shown, the decade of the 1920s "has long been excluded from histories of francophone literature [and it] is in fact remarkably contemporary. It was in the 1920s that the question of African immigration (now such a pressing issue) was first posed."[117] Furthermore, as a point of contact for colonial subjects, Paris itself became a privileged site, and "almost all the great political leaders of Indochina, sub-Saharan Africa, the Antilles, and Madagascar either visited or lived in Paris at some time between the two wars."[118] Immigrant populations from Africa and Asia transformed the Parisian landscape during the twentieth century (one only has to think of the neighborhoods around La place d'Italie, Barbès Rochechouart, and Belleville), but only rarely is the longevity of this influence understood: "In France, immigrants from the colonies became 'visible' at the beginning of the 1930s, in particular in Paris . . . this reality has as much to do with colonialism as it does with the history of immigration, although only rarely is it linked specifically to colonial history" (Blanchard and Deroo, "Contrôler," 107).[119] Most notably, the Paris Mosque opened in 1926, and "a new generation settled in Paris and its suburbs. In addition to immigrant laborers, a significant number of political leaders, artists, and students began to arrive . . . and as for 'illegal' immigration, it represented up to one-third of all workers in the metropole" (111–112). Literary magazines and journals began to be published, such as *La revue du monde noir* in 1931 and *Légitime défense* in 1932, among others including *Le paria, La voix des nègres,* and *La race nègre;* most are rarely discussed today.[120] Black political organizations were created, most notably Le comité de défense de la race nègre (CDRN), founded in 1926 by Lamine Senghor.[121] An active Black intelligentsia established itself and was critical of the first African deputy elected to the French National Assembly, Blaise Diagne. The discourse at the time surrounding African and French bilateral relations was truly symbiotic because the French authorities made concerted efforts to interrupt the flow of ideas between France and Africa. Already, "blackness" had become a defining concept, one that served to organize and mobilize individuals.

Estimates are that some 189,000 soldiers from the AEF and AOF fought in the First World War, and that approximately 30,000 were killed.[122] During the Second World War, 178,000 sub-Saharan African and Malagasy soldiers fought, and some 21,500 lost their lives (Dewitte, *Deux siècles d'immigration,* 51).[123] In addition to these African soldiers, Stovall has claimed that about 200,000 African Americans "saw duty in France" during the First World War (*Paris noir,* 5). This moment in history was absolutely critical in raising the political consciousness of colonized subjects: "The milieu that these veterans formed during the 1920s was one in which the most fundamental premises of colonialism were called into question, critiqued and attacked—in organizations whose newspapers circulated back to Africa, threatening colonial order" (Miller, *Nationalists and Nomads,* 10). Much has been said and written about the invaluable contributions made by the now-famous *tirailleurs sénégalais*—in 1994, the French government was heavily criticized for "its relative silence during commemorative events in August 1994 with regard to the role played by African troops in the landings on the Provence coast."[124] Of course, there were significant political developments from World War II onward, legal changes and decrees enacted to redefine relations between France and Africa, from the 1944 French Conference in Brazzaville to the 1946 debates on the French Union. Their ultimate objective was to keep the Union française as a functioning organism under the aegis of the *loi-cadre* of 1956, but the September 28, 1958, referendum paved the way for independence—or rather the beginning of new alignments for a French-African community. Guinea had voted "no" in the referendum and became independent on October 2 of that year,[125] and other AEF and AOF countries followed Guinea's lead during 1960. Governance was to have been conducted by the Ministry for Cooperation, focusing on sub-Saharan Africa, and "in this situation France devised the policy of cooperation in order to provide its former territories with the necessary financial aid, technical expertise, and personnel for administration and development. Through this policy, it also sought to maintain a privileged relationship with them despite their attainment of international sovereignty."[126] Only in 1998 did the French government finally change its official way of working with Africa by abandoning the model provided by the Ministry of Cooperation and incorporating African matters into the Ministry of Foreign Affairs. For Catherine Coquery-Vidrovitch, this was ultimately a conscious attempt to relinquish "bad habits linked to an unequal and paternalistic cooperation in favor of a partnership respectful of equality in difference" (Coquery-Vidrovitch, "Colonisation," 41).

In addition to the African soldiers on French soil, growing numbers of African students were coming to France as intellectual migrants. These students were designated interchangeably as *étudiants coloniaux* (colonial students), *étudiants d'outre-mer* (overseas students), and *étudiants noirs* (Black students).[127] According to Abdoulaye Gueye, there were as few as twenty African students in France in the 1920s.[128] As Guimont's extensive research has shown, "students in the '30s were the product of the ideals of assimilation . . . Those of the '50s were the students of action." (Guimont, 15). Yet there were tremendous disparities in formalized educational and literacy levels in colonial zones—for 1949–1950, Guimont reports average literacy rates of 4.2 percent in the AOF and 8.5 percent in the AEF sectors, with figures jumping to 22.9 percent and 20 percent in Cameroon and Togo respectively as a result of variations in administrative practices (22). In fact, prior to 1946, the number of African students in France was negligible; "education was prioritized in the process of developing the territories" (80), and the creation of bursaries radically altered this dynamic, such that by 1952–1953 there were some four thousand African students in France (72), a number that grew to eight thousand by 1965 (299). "At Independence," Guimont notes, "every francophone African country sent most if not all of its [qualified] students to the former metropole. Only Madagascar and Senegal had developed a higher education system prior to 1958, without of course keeping all their students in Africa because of a lack of space, the absence of certain fields of specialization, and of course because they could not compete with the appeal to students of studying in France" (37); "the motivations of non-bursary recipients to study in France reflected the prestige accorded to the metropole in the African imaginary" (299). In any case, by 1960–1961, only 2,674 students from the AOF were pursuing higher education in Africa (39). "After Independence, France's control over African students was of the greatest importance to its new policy on Africa, based on 'cooperation'" (155). While France's educational policy aimed to establish the "ideological continuity of the French colonial system based on assimilation and the idealization of the metropole" (300) and to create a sympathetic political elite, student mobilization in the metropole against colonialism was inevitable and inaugurated a complex process of mediation between Africa and France whereby the very "identity of African students oscillated between a long-term position as interlocutors for the French and African authorities and an immediate oppositional political force" (301).

Ultimately, student groups in the metropole proved to be powerful voices in articulating anticolonial positionalities. "Unlike their predecessors, post-FEANF intellectuals [Fédération des étudiants d'Afrique noire française, Federation of Students from French sub-Saharan Africa] have not felt it necessary to be in Africa in order to contribute to the elevation of the continent and in so doing manifest their African allegiance" (Gueye, *Les intellectuels africains en France,* 233). As we shall see in chapter 6 when the focus shifts to *La sape,* the characterization of "expatriates as role models" (235) is problematic given the harsh realities of immigrant circumstances in France.[129] The fact nevertheless remains that the dialogue between "expatriated intellectuals" and "Africans on the inside" (237) is not a closed entity, but rather one that, as Mbembe has shown, is "deployed from a foreign center, a third space, that is France" (quoted in Gueye, 237); accordingly, this "detour emerges as a structuring element in this relational discourse" (238). Mamadou Diouf summarizes this identitarian process by saying that the community "is no longer exclusively African and not yet definitively French. Either way, it can only be French differently."[130] After the dissolution of the FEANF, some kind of study experience in France remained essential, and cultural and social capital could be acquired through a sojourn in France that presented "itself as the opportunity to rehabilitate the African *milieu* of origin (whether the family, the neighborhood, or a larger group). This rehabilitation can just as well be material as psychological, allowing its authors to derive certain advantages" (Gueye, *Les intellectuels africains en France,* 87–88).[131] J.-P. N'Diaye, in his book *Enquête sur les étudiants noirs en France,* noted that in his interviews with students, they accounted for their preference for Paris by its "cultural prestige" and its "cosmopolitanism." In response to the question "What do you admire the most about France?" 30.6 percent mentioned technical and economic development and 27.4 percent the cultural component.[132] Such findings will be crucial in exploring "francocentrism" and the acquisition of cultural capital in chapter 2.

Numerous student associations were established, and the 1935 Association des étudiants noirs en France (AENF, Association of Black Students in France) published an important journal entitled *L'étudiant noir.* Other student networks and arrangements were to be evidenced, such as *L'étudiant guinéen, La voix des étudiants dahoméens,* and *L'étudiant malien.* Historically, at least, African "intellectuals have assigned themselves the geographical positions they would assume according to the historical context or more precisely according to the political status of Africa" (Gueye, *Les intellectuels africains en France,* 232). The first students came to France to prepare for service upon their return to Africa, particularly in the aftermath of Independence when the immediate imperative was to rebuild Africa. A central question concerns the links between "expatriation and the question of social legitimacy," according to which passage to France could be perceived as an "individualistic action aimed at socioeconomic self-promotion," and study abroad could be interpreted as opportunistic. Study abroad therefore contained the risk of "no longer being accepted in the society of origin," introducing a complex mediation with the Africans *du dedans* (at home in Africa) (131).[133] Naturally, this critical discourse has generated an adversarial mode through a counter-discourse that has stressed that "living in France and serving the interests of Africa are not essentially incompatible" (134). Paradoxically, the tenuous mediation between "home" and France has generated a Diaspora (a concept first applied to Africa by Irele in 1965)[134]—we have an "African Diaspora in France," Gueye claims (205)—constructed from an exclusionary framework: "recognizing the limitations on individual integration, expatriated intellectuals have been forced to conceive of and elaborate conditions conducive to ethno-communitarian mobilization" (205). As with other immigrant categories, the very structure of the French Republic is central to ethnic mobility and cultural and social belonging.

Clearly, as Mbembe has argued with regard to Africa, "new forms of territoriality and unexpected forms of locality have appeared. Their limits do not necessarily intersect with the official limits, norms, or language of states" ("At the Edge of the World," 24). For example, Brazzaville, the capital of the Republic of the Congo, stands as an example of "extraterritorialization," whereby "the capital itself has its center of gravity outside itself, in the relation the state maintains with the oil companies operating offshore" (Mbembe, "At the Edge of the World," 48). We are now dealing with what Chevrier has evoked as a kind of "extracontinental Africa."[135] Whether dealing with France's former colonies or its Republican tradition, the kind of "shared culture" Sassen had in mind that "provided the experience through which nationhood could be constituted and assimilated," while feeling threatened in the French context, has not actually put into question the institution itself.[136] As Nicolas Bancel, Pascal Blanchard, and Françoise Vergès have argued in *La République coloniale: Essai sur une utopie,* the Republic can be "rebuilt, modernized, democratized starting from a number of projects that have been in place for a few years now and a number of transformations that are under way."[137] Historically, then, the French Republic has wrestled with a range of models aimed at the supposed assimilation or integration of outsiders under the aegis of the Republic.

Many studies in both the humanities and the social sciences have attempted to unpack these complex tautologies, most notably Amselle's *Affirmative Exclusion: Cultural Pluralism and the Rule of Custom in France* (in which he highlights the transcolonial nature of racial problems, ranging from the biological and differentialist foundations of the colonial project to contemporary widely disseminated views) and F. Gaspard and F. Khosrokhavar's *Le foulard et la République.*[138] As Blatt explains,

> the republican model conceives of integration as a process by which individuals subordinate their particularist origins and accept membership in a unitary nation-state defined by shared universalist values . . . ethnic origin is deemed unacceptable as a basis for organization and mobilization by political actors, or for conferring of rights, recognition, or entitlements by public authorities. (Blatt, 46)

There are striking differences to be recorded between other European attempts to deal with the question of greater inclusion of minority populations. Adrian Favell has shown how these issues are discussed as "race relations" in Britain and as "multiculturalism" in France, where *citoyenneté* (citizenship) and *intégration* (integration) are also determining factors.[139] Remarkable terminological shifts have occurred in France, from *assimilation* (reduction of difference in order to secure the homogeneity of dominant cultural and social norms), to *insertion* (a mechanism to foster participation in the "general" population while maintaining the specificity of various cultural and religious practices), and finally to *integration* (ultimately "predicated on the assumption that social differentiation is or should be in the process of being reduced" [Hargreaves, *Immigration, "Race," and Ethnicity*, 2]). In the French context, these categories are inseparable from the concerted attempts at securing and safeguarding the cultural and social homeostasis of French normativism and universalism. In his analysis, Dewitte includes the HCI's official definition:

> integration should not be conceived of as the middle ground between assimilation and insertion, but rather as a specific process: the objective is to encourage through this process the active participation in national society of varied and different elements, while accepting the subsistence of cultural, social, and moral specificities and in believing that this variety and complexity enriches everyone. Without denying differences, finding ways to take them into consideration without exalting them, a policy of integration emphasizes resemblances and points of convergence in order, through equal rights and obligations, to achieve solidarity between the different ethnic and cultural constituencies that make up our society and to give each and every one of us, no matter what our origins may be, the possibility of living together in this society whose rules we have accepted and which we are a constitutive element of. (Dewitte, *Deux siècles d'immigration*, 88)

The central problem comes from the fact that "the ideology of assimilation is indeed deeply ethnocentric."[140] "To become French," the authors of *La République coloniale* demonstrate, "implies abandoning all that differentiates—regional language, religion, desire for autonomy. The Republic is one and indivisible, and refuses on its territory any breach of this principle . . . The idea of race—understood as the hierarchical difference between groups—concerns Republican citizenship. Some are more citizens than others: the creation of a *colonial citizenship* in 1946 that was different from the citizenship applied in the metropole was the most striking example of this" (Bancel, Blanchard, and Vergès, 122–123). Republican ideological imperatives have been reflected in the repeated changes made to French immigration policy since the early days of decolonization, most significantly in 1974 and 1993 when tougher legislation was introduced to make entry into France from the former colonies as well as the acquisition of citizenship by those individuals residing on French soil all the more difficult.[141]

Jean-Paul Sartre was an astute observer of African-French relations, and his awareness of this bilateralism informed his contextualization of the links between Africa and France. Yet his entry "Présence noire" in the inaugural issue of *Présence africaine* evoked the notions of *ici* (here in France) and *là-bas* (there in Africa) to characterize this relationship, and this evocation was highly problematic; for example, he argued that "each time we shake the hand of a black person here, it erases the violence we committed there."[142] *Nothing* of course erases French culpability overseas, and the realities of French racism in the metropole during the colonial era (as "documented" in Sembene's novel *Black Docker*) should not be obfuscated either. Furthermore, while it is important to underline the symbiotic nature of African-French relations, the central point here is to recognize the presence of the *là-bas ici*—the there here. The permanence of a Black France is a reality today, although prevailing discourse regularly undermines this factor. In fact, the official website for the Cité nationale de l'histoire de l'immigration (CNHI) project potentially voids its positive dimension by employing an ambiguous phrase to characterize its mission— "Leur histoire est notre histoire" ("Their history is our history"; see http://www.histoire-immigration.fr)—attributing value to the constitutive dimension of bilateral relations while simultaneously demarcating divisions through the recuperation of a discourse of separateness and ownership in which one is left with the uncomfortable realization that "they" remain other (them) while "we" comfortably occupy the space reserved for us. Lorenzo Prencipe has underscored how the "spatial and relational exteriority of an individual . . . have respectively led to a confusion between the terms 'foreigner' and *immigré*, and then widened the modalities of exclusion and reinforced the barrier between the 'them' and the 'us'" (Prencipe, "Médias et immigration," 140).[143] The point surely should have been to abandon such constructs, to multiply the sites of memory through the delineation of new coordinates that render such arbitrary divisions redundant and insignificant. Effectively, such conscious or unconscious linguistic constructs reveal the degree of concern pertaining to what could be described as a "colonization of the Hexagon." This is a pan-European phenomenon, because "every European power contributed to the expansion of Europe's borders overseas. Every European power is experiencing today the 'return of empire' on its soil" (Bancel, Blanchard, and Vergès, 161).[144]

In 2001, the French prime minister commissioned Driss El Yazami (vice-president of the Human Rights League) and Rémy Schwartz (Maître des requêtes au Conseil d'Etat) to report on the possibility of creating a national center for the history and cultures of immigration. On March 10, 2003, the newly appointed prime minister Jean-Pierre Raffarin appointed former minister of culture Jacques Toubon to head the Mission de préfiguration du Centre de ressources et de mémoire de l'immigration, whose completed report was published in May 2004.[145] On July 8, 2004, Raffarin announced that the CNHI would open in 2006 at the site of the Palais de la porte dorée in Paris, saying (as quoted on the project's website, http://www.histoire-immigration.fr), "This new cultural site has been conceived as much as a museum as as a cultural center, with live performances, and for film screenings, conferences and colloquia." The project declares its adherence to the definition of a museum provided by the International Council of Museums (ICOM):

> A museum is a non-profit-making permanent institution in the service of society and of its development, open to the public, which acquires, conserves, researches, communicates, and exhibits, for purposes of study, education,

and enjoyment, the tangible and intangible evidence of people and their environment. (Toubon, 18)

The projected configuration of the permanent installation includes a number of categories relevant to the memorialization of a Black France: "The Republican school," "1914–1918: Foreigners and Colonials in the Great War," "Immigration Policy through the Decades," "African Intellectuals and Politicians in France," "Religion and the Republic," "The Port of Marseilles," "Colonials in the Metropole," "Women in Immigration," "Belleville," "How to Become French," and "Colonization and Decolonization." Toubon believes that immigration must be privileged as an "integral part of French History" (13), and that providing for a "necessary recognition of the place immigrant populations have in the destiny of the Republic should help every French person to cast a truthful look at French identity today, and reconcile the multiple parts whose values make the nation so strong" (9).

Other commentators on contemporary French attempts at exploring memory have been more skeptical, particularly since the French National Assembly has signed into law two bills, the first (no. 667, Proposition de loi visant à la reconnaissance de l'œuvre positive de l'ensemble de nos concitoyens qui ont vécu en Algérie pendant la période de la presence française, passed on March 5, 2003) aimed at recognizing the "positive" contributions of French citizens in Algeria, and the second (no. 389, Reconnaissance de la Nation et contribution nationale en faveur des Français rapatriés, passed on February 23, 2005 [amended in 2006]) recognizing "national contributions" made by "repatriated French citizens." (I discuss these further in chapter 2.) This phenomenon is not, of course, unique to France, as Ali Behdad powerfully illustrates in the American context in his book *A Forgetful Nation: On Immigration and Cultural Identity in the United States*: "I use the notion of amnesia throughout my discussion to mean a form of cultural disavowal that simultaneously denies certain historical facts and produces a pseudo-historical consciousness of the present."[146] Similarly, the title of Marc Augé's essay *Oblivion* speaks for itself. "Oblivion is a necessity both to society and to the individual. One must know how to forget to taste the full flavor of the present, of the moment, and of expectation, but memory itself needs forgetfulness: one must forget the present past in order to find the ancient past again."[147]

Similar projects have already been undertaken in France, but none with the same degree of state support. The Association pour la connaissance de l'histoire de l'Afrique contemporaine (ACHAC), directed by Pascal Blanchard, has as its objective the study of colonial culture in all its manifestations, and the association has produced several very important works. Naturally, with a museum project of the nature and scope proposed, the question will be to see not so much what will be remembered, but rather what may be silenced. In 2002, the memorialization of the fortieth anniversary of the end of official conflict between Algeria and France was heavily criticized.[148] For this new museum to perform a useful task, one can only hope that "conservation" of memory will be secondary, so that the museum emerges not so much as a repository for the past, but rather as a site at which the past and the present can operate as a dynamic ongoing process of productive dialogue and reimaginings of human communities. As Clifford has argued in "Museums as Contact Zones," "Within broad limits, a museum can accommodate different systems of accumulation and circulation, secrecy and communication, aesthetic, spiritual, and economic value . . . Aspirations of both dominant and subaltern populations can be articulated through this structure, along with the material interests of national and transnational tourism" (218).[149]

Perhaps the fundamental problem exemplified by this project is its failure to recognize that, as Wieviorka points out, history and memory are very different projects, and that, according to Patrick Weil, "too little history is compensated for by an excess of memory";[150] this is the "colonial fracture" that must be addressed, the historical void evoked by Blanchard, Bancel, and Lemaire, from which the most urgent action "consists in bringing France's colonial past to the forefront of national thinking and historiography, in order to produce perspectives that make postcolonial situations intelligible."[151] Furthermore, when it comes to the context of France and Africa in particular, the shared historical experience needs to be foregrounded:

> France and Africa share a common history, expressed jointly by the role France has played for centuries in Africa north and south of the Sahara, and by the more recent presence in the Hexagon of Africans who have, in turn, through their actions, their work, their thinking, had a concrete impact on the course of French history. (Bancel, Blanchard, and Vergès, 30)

These questions are even more important today as the European Union itself has been forced to think carefully about what a future European identity might correspond to, reflection whose urgency has been accelerated by debates concerning extreme right-wing politics in Belgium, Britain, France, Germany, Italy, and the Netherlands, the expansion of Islam in Europe, and the so-called war on global terror. These factors are all connected to the debate on whether or not to extend membership to Turkey as an Islamic state, as if the 40 million Muslims in Europe were not already integral components of European identity.[152]

There is a global fascination with events in Africa that are perceived on the one hand as external, epitomized through the spectacle of suffering (so brilliantly captured by Susan Sontag in her book *Regarding the Pain of Others*) and organized around genocide, civil conflict, the AIDS epidemic, and corrupt governance,[153] as examples of African "savagery," and on the other those that are perceived as internal to France and Europe, organized around immigration, excision, polygamy, Islam, and the *sans-*

papiers affair, as signifiers of "African barbarism." These constructs simultaneously recuperate colonial discourse, remapping these new coordinates in order to arrive at analogous conclusions, in a process Blanchard and Bancel have shown inaugurates a perfect example of the transcolonial circulation of discourse in the careful transition from the justificatory language of the civilizing mission to the humanitarian imperative that serves to further consolidate the tenuously constitutive vectors of nurture and exploitation.[154] The focus on the analysis of a range of cultural, economic, political, and social issues in Africa that have received global attention is crucial in order to counter the manner in which these questions have entered the popular imagination and generated widespread cynicism and disillusionment, belief that activism is futile and problems insurmountable.

We have every right to be skeptical about and suspicious of the discourse on the connections between France and the "other." Perhaps the museum project constitutes at the very least a step in the right direction, an indication as to how former colonial powers are addressing and redrawing national boundaries, exploring the various ways in which cultural and social phenomena are transcolonial in nature, and how transnational and post-sovereign paradigms are acquiring currency in contemporary negotiations and renegotiations of a global understanding of humanity. With this thought in mind, it may one day become possible, as Seyla Benhabib has suggested, to "view human cultures as constant creations, recreations, and negotiations of imaginary boundaries between 'we' and the 'other(s).'"[155] Certainly, *Black France* navigates with caution through this challenging landscape. Ultimately, in this process, the agendas of those "doing" the remembering must be scrutinized. This will be a test of France's capacity to reimagine community in the Hexagon, to reimagine a Hexagon and a Europe at the crossroads of cultural navigations that ignore borders and nationalisms, fostering a global citizenry engaged with human rights, and in which centers and peripheries are constantly being reformulated, redrawn.

Black France's claim to originality comes from its attempt to broaden the category of immigrant literature by consulting existing research on minority cultures and diasporic texts, and extending the parameters of research beyond the tradition that has tended to locate immigrant narratives as intrinsically post-Independence or postcolonial phenomena. Sub-Saharan African works published prior to political independence by such diverse authors as Ousmane Socé (*Mirage de Paris,* 1937), Laye Camara (*L'enfant noir,* 1954), Bernard Dadié (*Un nègre à Paris,* 1959), Ferdinand Oyono (*Chemin d'Europe,* 1960), and Cheikh Hamidou Kane (*L'aventure ambiguë,* 1961), are considered in chapter 2 as immigrant narratives, given their treatment of the circumstances of socioeconomic and cultural displacement between Africa and the metropole.[156] Focus on these texts will provide a more historically accurate framework with which to explore works that have emerged both in Africa and from within France's postcolonial communities since official independence. This analysis is carried through to chapter 3, but the framework is broadened to a consideration of global blackness that allows for a reading of Ousmane Sembene's novel *Le docker noir* (1956) and Richard Wright's *Native Son* (1940).[157]

Strategically situated at the juncture between the colonial and postcolonial eras, chapter 4 examines the short story "La noire de . . . " ("Black Girl"), published in 1962 (but set just before Independence) by the Senegalese writer and filmmaker Ousmane Sembene, and juxtaposes this text with a more contemporary work, *Une esclave moderne* (2000), written by a Togolese woman, Henriette Akofa.[158] Whereas colonial practices had traditionally been denounced in works set in Africa, Sembene's short story is particularly original since the transplantation of the central protagonist, Diouana, from Senegal to France simultaneously displaces and relocates the indictment of colonial ideology for its racial and discriminatory characteristics from Africa to France. While Diouana's status as a colonized subject in the African context was essentially unquestioned in the rigorous separation enacted by the colonial hierarchy, in France she becomes increasingly conscious of her ethnic identity and of the multiple ways in which she is exploited. An important parallel is therefore drawn between the roots of colonial ideology in the metropole, its dissemination in the colonies, and its subsequent survival into contemporary immigrant discourses. Sembene's text then has a particular resonance with a plethora of more recent works, and much can be gauged by considering contemporary forms of slavery and servitude, as evidenced in Akofa's account of her experiences. This chapter introduces an interesting dynamic, since Sembene's "fictional" short story is structured around a *fait divers* (a news item), while Akofa's work is an autobiographical or testimonial narrative that is read alongside actual court proceedings pertaining to her experience drawn from the registry of the European Court of Human Rights in Strasbourg, France. In chapters 4 and 5, the question of audience becomes critical; I argue and attempt to demonstrate that both Akofa's and Fatou Keïta's texts constitute important testimonies, and then highlight how upon entry into the public domain of the Hexagon these narratives are recuperated by the French authorities in the service of culturalist and exclusionary agendas.

Keïta's novel *Rebelle* (1998) and Calixthe Beyala's *Lettre d'une Africaine à ses sœurs occidentale* and *Lettre d'une Afro-française à ses compatriotes* provide the focus of chapter 5.[159] In this instance, the controversial question of female excision is addressed through a consideration of the sociocultural circumstances of African women both in francophone sub-Saharan Africa and in the African Diaspora in France, framed in close dialogue with several key theorizations of these questions. The universalizing exigencies of Frenchness are foregrounded in order to address the potentialities of a multicultural society and the implications for the future of ethnic relations in the Hexagon.[160] Key to this discussion is the issue of location and the bilateral exchanges that take place between insiders and outsiders, and examination of the interpenetrative nature of discourse. Whereas African feminists are often criticized for embracing European feminist thought, the phenomenon of the *sapeurs* (explored in chapter 6), who embrace European aesthetic codes, provides an interesting point of comparison that ultimately allows us to better understand gender issues in the postcolony and Diaspora along with multiple forms of social marginalization. For example, even through *La sape* is a strictly masculinist practice, writers have been critical of its superficial connection to material culture; further analysis of the homosocial and homoerotic dimension of the practice will also help to advance the argument.

The phenomenon of the *sapeurs* is explored in chapter 6 through a consideration of novels by Alain Mabanckou (*Bleu-Blanc-Rouge,* 1998) and Daniel Biyaoula (*L'impasse,* 1996, and *Agonies,* 1998).[161] (The word *sape* originated as an acronym for the Société des ambianceurs et des personnes élégantes [Society of *Ambianceurs* and Persons of Elegance] and designates young people who travel to France to acquire designer clothes.) This chapter provides a cultural history of the way dress codes have marked the experiences of Congolese Diasporas in France, using a theoretical context inspired by a transnational understanding of performance and identity, but also informed by a broader discussion of the construction of gender and identity. This section also explores the way Paris and France continue to serve as a mythic space for sub-Saharan Africans intent on the acquisition of secular capital. Chapter 7 builds on this material to consider other migratory developments within the global economy, and the focus shifts to Fatou Diome's 2003 novel *Le ventre de l'Atlantique,* which offers an innovative challenge to the migration myth discussed in the *sapeurs'* quest.[162] Diome's protagonists distance themselves from the portrait gallery of dislocated sub-Saharan African protagonists who constituted the earlier demographics of migration, and effectively map out the new coordinates of a transnational geometry in which the periphery is repositioned as another center, one that questions development politics, structural adjustment policies, and globalization's impact on sub-Saharan Africans.

TWO

Francocentrism and the Acquisition of Cultural Capital

I felt such a strong affinity for this
country that I did not know, and whose
genius and beauty I had been taught to
sing since childhood, that I wondered
whether I had not perhaps been French
in a previous life.

Ferdinand Oyono[1]

The European elite undertook to
manufacture a native elite. They
picked out promising adolescents;
they branded them, as with a red-hot
iron, with the principles of western
culture; they stuffed their mouths
full with high-sounding phrases,
grand glutinous words that stuck to
their teeth. After a short stay in the
mother country they were sent home,
white-washed. These walking lies had
nothing left to say to their brothers;
they only echoed.

Jean-Paul Sartre[2]

The return to the colonial era as a point of entry to recent debates on
questions of immigration and national identity in contemporary France
seems a necessary gesture. Such a return offers the opportunity to carefully
delineate the advantages of a transcolonial approach, but, more importantly, to relocate the origins of immigration discourse and migratory
flows according to a specific set of cultural, economic, political, and social coordinates that are indissociable from a colonial, postcolonial, and
global geometry. The discussion of immigration has tended to locate it as

a post-Independence practice associated with the politics of decolonization, when in fact population flows were central to the colonial project as
sub-Saharan Africans migrated to the metropole to pursue educational
training, serve in the French military, or enter global labor markets. In
fact, not only has this dimension not received the concerted analysis it deserves, but further consideration of these issues has much to reveal about
the manner in which the French civilizing mission was deployed, and early
assimilationist models constructed under direct rule.

Immigration legislation has certainly been central to the politics of
postcoloniality, as once-colonized peoples and the former colonial powers
have attempted to redefine the parameters of their relations and adjust, accordingly, population movement between these topographic spaces. Indeed, as the authors of *La République coloniale: Essai sur une utopie* have
insisted, "The reconsideration of the legacy of the colonial Republic concerns France as much as it does its former colonies."[3] The voluntary or
forced displacement of African subjects has a long history that we can begin to address only by extending our analysis to a consideration of texts
produced in the colonial era that enact a mediation between fiction and
the evidential component of a given sociopolitical time frame; this will allow us to assess the symbiotic network of constitutive historical trajectories.

Central to the discussion in this chapter will be a consideration of the
particularities of French direct rule and colonial education as the markers
of both a theorization of assimilation and the resulting counter-discourse
produced by African writers. To this end, Pascale Casanova's consideration
of the centrality of Paris is pertinent to the question of francocentrism,[4]
since "innumerable descriptions in novels and poems of Paris in the nineteenth century and, especially, the twentieth century made the city's literariness manifest," and naturally it is this construct that in turn circulated
in colonial pedagogy and curricular orientation.[5] "These countless descriptions of Paris—a literary genre inaugurated in the late eighteenth century—were gradually codified, so that over time they amounted . . . to a
'recitation'—an immutable leitmotif, obligatory in form and content"
(Casanova, 26). Naturally, given the colonial education received by African writers, such findings are to be found in the work of Ousmane Socé,
for example, but they also, of course, provide the source of engagement
for Bernard Dadié's challenge to this myth of universalism, according to
which "Paris was thus doubly universal, by virtue both of the belief in its
universality and of the real effects that this belief produced" (Casanova,
30). Paris is the key topographic site to which protagonists travel, but also
operates as an interchangeable metaphor for France itself.

Accordingly, the myth of Occidental superiority as an intrinsic component of the expansionist project must be scrutinized in order to better locate contemporary immigration discourse and to delineate the transcolo-

nial nature of African and French relations. The focus will be provided by francophone sub-Saharan African novels published between 1937 and 1961 that address various tenets of French colonial rule and that are anchored in that historical moment. The authors selected for extended critical attention originate in three different countries, and, in terms of their critical reception and the broader impact their works have had on subsequent generations of African authors, they can be considered representative of the most significant aesthetic and ideological positionalities of the era. They are Laye Camara (Guinea), Cheikh Hamidou Kane and Ousmane Socé (Senegal), and Bernard Dadié (Ivory Coast). While these writers have produced numerous works, those considered for the purpose of this chapter are *L'enfant noir* (*The Dark Child/The African Child*), *L'aventure ambiguë* (*Ambiguous Adventure*), *Mirages de Paris* (*Mirages of Paris*), and *Un nègre à Paris* (*An African in Paris*).[6] This period coincides with an unusual degree of literary productivity and this analysis cannot therefore claim to be exhaustive.[7] The specificity is therefore provided by the cultural, economic, and political context of colonialism, but of course will have much to reveal concerning the politics of multiculturalism in France today and the prevailing dictates and imperatives of assimilationist and integrational policies.[8]

In 1947, the Presses Universitaires de France inaugurated a new series under the rubric "Colonies et empires: Collection internationale de documentation coloniale" ("Colonies and Empires: International Collection of Colonial Documentation"), devoted to colonial studies, with Ch.-André Julien as the series editor, himself a professor of the history of colonization at the University of Paris and, perhaps more importantly, a *conseiller de l'union française* (councilor of the French union). This cohabitation of the governmental and educational branches of the French civil service is of course indicative of the ideological agenda of the colonial state that informed the civilizing mission and that was disseminated through colonial education. The inaugural volume of the series was entitled *Les techniciens de la colonisation* (*The Technicians of Colonization*), and a subsequent volume featured an essay by Robert Delavignette, the governor of the colonies and honorary director of the National School of France Overseas, in which he hailed Maurice Delafosse, a former governor, as "one of our best Africanists."[9] As Bernard Mouralis has argued in his book *République et colonies: Entre histoire et mémoire; La République française et l'Afrique,* Delavignette was "directly implicated in this process of social transformation, on the ground as an administrator or at the very highest level as director of political affairs with the Ministry of France Overseas."[10] As we shall see, convincing colonized subjects that their ancestors were also "the Gauls" was central to the French imperial ambition and therefore an intrinsic component of the works written by francophone sub-Saharan African authors who were the products of these ideological experiments.[11] Reading these texts as a collective body produced in various sectors of the French colonies, from French West Africa (AOF, established in 1904 and made up of the Ivory Coast, Dahomey, French Guinea, Upper Volta, Mauritania, Niger, Senegal, and French Sudan) to French Equatorial Africa (AEF, founded in 1910 and made up of Congo, Gabon, Oubangui-Chari, and Chad), provides the occasion to explore a multiplicity of responses to colonial experiences, at some times analogous and at others quite different.[12] Simultaneously, such a framework allows for discrimination between some of the ways in which writers have responded in order to highlight points of commonality and distinctions both within French colonies and in relation to Belgian, English, German, and Portuguese imperialism, among others.[13]

It remains of paramount importance to underline the economic, humanitarian, political, and scientific organizational principles of the colonial project that served to "conceal the true foundations of the colonial phenomenon," since these were recuperated in the process of formulating "humanitarian arguments or arguments that claimed a scientific basis, thereby allowing for passage from the stage of *explanation* to that of *justification*."[14] Similarly, the centrality of the pedagogic component as early as 1817 in certain areas is crucial in understanding the legacy of colonialism, the engagement of African writers with ensuing cultural and sociopolitical circumstances, and of course the impact of francocentrism.[15] Central mechanisms for defining colonial educational policy were the *Bulletin de l'enseignement en A.O.F.,* which was founded in 1913 and which became *L'éducation africaine* in 1934, and the *Journal officiel de l'A.O.F.,* in which "the great events in French history and France's relations with various West African countries [and] French geography and that of its colonies, particularly those in West Africa," were outlined (Midiohouan, *L'idéologie dans la littérature,* 46). As Alice Conklin has shown in her superb study of the French civilizing mission, *A Mission to Civilize: The Republican Ideal of Empire in France and West Africa, 1895–1930,* the concept of civilization was not only invented by the French in the eighteenth century, but subsequently "elevated to the realm of official imperial doctrine."[16] As such, "the notion of a civilizing mission rested upon certain fundamental assumptions about the superiority of French culture and the perfectibility of humankind" (Conklin, *A Mission to Civilize,* 1) and, as Conklin argues,

> Republican France invested the notion of a civilizing mission with a fairly specific set of meanings that set limits on what the government could and could not do in the colonies. By officially acting within these limits, the French managed to obscure the fundamental contradiction between democracy and the forcible acquisition of an empire. (2)

Colonial expansion was, as Hans-Jürgen Lüsebrink has suggested, concerned with "the acculturation of the conquered populations: their institutional, cultural, and administrative supervision; their training, and therefore with the transmission, essentially by means of schooling and textbooks, of the political and cultural ideology of the metropole."[17] When William Ponty assumed the position of governor general of French West Africa in 1907, as Conklin informs us, "instruction was identified as the new administration's foremost social measure . . . Ponty was driven by a conviction that it was France's responsibility to direct the emergence of a new social order in West Africa, which, without becoming French, would better conform to prevailing French mores" (Conklin, *A Mission to Civilize,* 108). Accordingly, Ponty

> took several steps designed to clarify the content and pedagogical methods of education and to increase the number of schools available to Africans. Under his administration, French became the official language of the federation; the first comprehensive course plan applicable to the entire federation was drawn up, and the first manuals began to be published. (131)

To this end, Georges Hardy, the *inspecteur général de l'enseignement en Afrique occidentale française* (chief inspector for education in French West Africa) from 1913 to 1931, authored a book entitled *Une conquête morale: L'enseignement en A.O.F.* that carefully delineated the moral foundations of the colonial project, and, as chief inspector, "outlined through several texts the contours of the textbooks that would be used in African schools" (Lüsebrink, "Acculturation coloniale," 118).[18] The transcoloniality of these issues is particularly striking given that the French authorities have been actively involved in several potentially revisionist projects since the beginning of the twenty-first century specifically designed to address France's colonial legacy at both the educational and national levels. First of all, one should point out that the Centre national de l'histoire et des cultures de l'immigration (CNHI) "will suggest modifications of school textbooks and programs so as to accord the history of immigration the place it deserves in the history of the nation."[19] And secondly, as mentioned in chapter 1, two significant bills have been signed into law by the French National Assembly, one recognizing the "positive" contributions of "French citizens who resided in Algeria during the French presence" and the other recognizing "national contributions" made by "repatriated French citizens."[20] These developments systematically ignore the symbiotic connection between state propaganda and the colonial project and refuse to acknowledge colonialism as an oppressive practice. Sandrine Lemaire has carefully documented this history, and addressed its lasting impact on the fabric of French society:

> During the colonial period, authors of school textbooks were the active promoters, as they illustrated it, of colonialism. History and geography textbooks, as well as those in literature and philosophy, reflected imperial sentiments and preached the *gospel* of Empire that was already making its way into the popular press . . . School discourse during the colonial period played

an essential role in assisting the penetration of colonial ideology throughout the social body, and functioned as a crucial tool aimed at building and perpetuating a French identity . . . This valorizing history of the French and of their actions simultaneously served to spread a broad range of stereotypes about the colonized.[21]

These mechanisms were enacted as programmatic changes under the supervision of Hardy, whose contribution to the conceptualization of colonial education was tangible. He was particularly effective in establishing French influence because he recognized the potential pitfalls of a unilateral educational model, preferring instead to identify the specificities of the local context, in which the adaptation of "colonial teaching to the cultural space of indigenous populations" (Lüsebrink, "Acculturation coloniale," 115) would be of paramount importance. In the same way that diasporic communities are not homogeneous—although they are often treated as such by the authorities—colonial ideology was also naturally reconfigured depending on each specific context: "The challenge to the unitarian concept of civilization and gradual recognition of the specificity of African cultures forced colonial ideology to undergo adjustments."[22] Accordingly, this "educational strategy . . . transformed Western cultural and moral values into accepted norms . . . that were intrinsically linked to the colonial project of acculturation intent on making Republican ideology coincide with the desire to expand into countries overseas" (Lüsebrink, "Acculturation coloniale," 121).[23] Naturally, we must be careful not to place too much faith in Hardy's understanding of what constitutes local culture, since, as will become only too apparent, such constructs are invariably mediated through a complex set of projections and stereotypes. Nevertheless, the cross-pollination, the "objective of anchoring colonial education within an intercultural perspective rather than in simple imported metropolitan models" (Lüsebrink, "Acculturation coloniale," 118), would indelibly mark francophone literary production.

Mouralis has shown that the development of colonial schooling can be divided into three broad stages: "an initial period beginning with the origins of colonization up until 1903; a second one from 1903 to 1944, when the Brazzaville Conference was held; and finally a third running from 1944 to 1960, the year when most territories located in the two Federations acceded to Independence" (Mouralis, *Littérature et développement,* 59). Within this framework, schools were not established with any degree of uniformity—some areas that had concentrated contact with the colonial authorities, such as Brazzaville and Dakar, made considerable inroads into education, whereas others were relatively ignored. This was in part because of two general strategic concerns. The first, as Midiohouan has indicated, pertains to concerns with delaying the indigenous consciousness of sociopolitical arrangements: "whereas primary education was well organized by various administrative mechanisms, the same was not true for secondary education, where the colonizer deliberately slowed things down as a way of maintaining intellectual and political asthenia and preventing any kind of broader consciousness" (Midiohouan, *L'idéologie,* 50); the second emerged from a need to incorporate a collaborative elite into the administrative colonial structures: "the artisans and theoreticians of colonial policy are just about unanimous in acknowledging that . . . education in Africa should above all have practical goals and, as its main function, the task of training the subaltern personnel necessary for the smooth operation of the colonial system" (Mouralis, *Littérature et développement,* 80). Schoolchildren were motivated toward a forced complicity in the dissemination of colonial propagandist ideology and therefore assisted in the promotion of the idea of *La grande France* (France the Great) when they completed research projects that "underscored and criticized negative aspects [of Africa], thereby allowing them to present colonization as the only means by which Africa could accede to modernity."[24] As Sayouba Traoré, a novelist from Burkina Faso, recently stated in an interview, "With all the changes engendered on our way of life and thinking, colonialism paved the way for immigration."[25]

A "definitive consolidation of the Republican Regime" occurred during the Third Republic (1870–1914), in particular after the 1884–1885 Berlin Conference, and, as Mouralis has argued, "was followed shortly thereafter by the conquest of an empire that was to turn France into one of the world's principal colonial powers" (Mouralis, *République et colonies,* 10).[26] Republican ideals are crucial in this context since they introduce a contradiction between the broader claims upon which they are founded (namely a "humanistic discourse") and the realities on the ground in the colonies ("a set of mechanisms that in reality deny the very possibility of the proclaimed ideals being achieved") (Mouralis, *République et colonies,* 11). "Liberty, equality, and the educational mission," as Bancel, Blanchard, and Vergès have argued, "end up emptied of their universal revolutionary potential" because they are infused with "a discourse of racial inequality" (54–57). Only by considering the image of the colonized subject can we understand how the foundations of colonial discourse— economic, political, humanitarian, and scientific—that I mentioned earlier help to justify colonial expansionism. This image is a central component of colonial discourse and one that francophone sub-Saharan African authors and theoreticians have been forced to address in order to rescue identities from the various distortions. In the context of this book, writers such as Kane, Dadié, and Sembene, for example, have these concerns at the forefront of their thinking. As Albert Memmi has shown in his incisive reading of the relations between the colonizer and the colonized,

> Just as the bourgeoisie proposes an image of the proletariat, the existence of the colonizer requires that an image of the colonized be suggested. These images become excuses without which the presence and conduct of a colo-

nizer, and that of a bourgeois, would seem shocking. But the favored image becomes a myth precisely because it suits them all too well.[27]

Memmi fastens on the constitutive dimension of these relations, and this gesture is necessary in order to comprehend the ways in which French civilizationist discourse operated. "At the basis of the entire construction," Memmi argues, "one finally finds a common motive; the colonizer's economic and basic needs, which he substitutes for logic, and which shape and explain each of the traits he assigns to the colonized" (Memmi, *The Colonizer and the Colonized,* 83). However, the "substitution" of the colonizer's logic is not sufficient in and of itself; it also necessitates the colonized's participation: "In order for the colonizer to be the complete master, it is not enough for him to be so in actual fact, but he must also believe in its legitimacy. In order for that legitimacy to be complete, it is not enough for the colonized to be a slave, he must also accept this role" (88–89). These are the realities that writers had to confront as they endeavored to negotiate a space for themselves in a field of discourse in which their voices had hitherto been silenced or alternatively ventriloquized through the disjointed and distorted medium of colonial "voice boxes" in which there was no correlation between their experience and that being articulated.

In his book *Ecrire en pays colonisé,* Midiohouan continues the project he started in 1986 with *L'idéologie dans la littérature négro-africaine d'expression française,* in order to underline how early francophone sub-Saharan texts constituted "a colonial literature, given that they participated objectively and often even explicitly in the colonial project" (Midiohouan, *Ecrire,* 33). As we shall see, the question of participation through literature in a broader ideological context continues to be a determining issue in any discussion of francophone sub-Saharan African writing.[28] Whereas in his work on ideology he formulated a revised historiography that questioned the insistence on engagement as a category of analysis, Midiohouan now turns his attention to questioning the way in which "dominant historiography came to characterize globally the writings of black writers during the colonial period" (Midiohouan, *Ecrire,* 81). The challenge to this historiography comes from an illustration of differences at the level of both aesthetics and ideology among texts published by Africans between 1920 and 1945. In issuing this challenge, he rejoins the work of Miller in *Nationalists and Nomads: Essays on Francophone African Literature and Culture,* who extensively addressed these distinctions through categories of "revolution" and "involution." For Miller, these categories apply to the assumed positionality of authors in response to the demands and exigencies of the colonial order with which their texts are necessarily in mediation. On the one hand, writers can explore the revolutionary potential of their writings in order "to resist and critique European power," or alternatively they can embrace the involutionary, whose objective is "to enfold all souls and all civilizations within a universalism that remains somehow French" (Miller, *Nationalists and Nomads,* 10). As Miller points out, this is "an apparently binary opposition that serves merely as a convenience here, a device for describing the fluid negotiations of identity and culture engaged in by colonized Africans in this period" (10). Indeed, I previously explored similar mechanisms in the postcolonial context through state involvement in the process of "engineering" history and literature, whereby distinctions between "official" and "nationalist" writers were possible in a context in which "official writers defended a specific vision of society and dedicated their creative activities toward achieving those ends," while "a competing cultural elite represented by *avant-garde* resistance authors (sometimes censored, and almost exclusively published abroad) menaced this monolithic construct."[29]

A number of texts published in the colonial context exemplify the problematic raised by Midiohouan and Miller, and are important in order to gauge how the texts I shall consider in detail in this chapter deviate from these early concerns. The three most important are Ahmadou Mapaté Diagne's *Les trois volontés de Malic* (1920), Bakary Diallo's *Force-Bonté* (1926), and Lamine Senghor's *La violation d'un pays* (1927).[30] Diagne's protagonist praises the colonial educational system, and because of this his work "stands in this literary history as both the original fictional text and as one of the most naively procolonial and pro-French documents" (Miller, *Nationalists and Nomads,* 48); in turn, Diallo's autobiographical narrative about a *tirailleur sénégalais* who returns to Africa, which was "favorably received" (Midiohouan, *L'idéologie,* 67), vacillates between praise for the colonial mission and a seeming disillusionment with it; both Midiohouan and Miller devote considerable attention to Lamine Senghor's work and insist on the importance of its anticolonial stance.[31] For Miller, *La violation d'un pays* stands as a "counterpart to the equally propagandist *Les Trois Volontés de Malic,* which told a diametrically opposed version of events and which contained a wholesale mystification of French-language literacy" (Miller, *Nationalists and Nomads,* 25), and Midiohouan seemingly concurs, since "at an ideological level, *La violation d'un pays* constitutes a systematic refutation of Mapaté Diagne's arguments" (Midiohouan, *Ecrire,* 55). As both critics have emphasized, these relatively ignored texts have much to teach us about the history of francophone sub-Saharan African writing. The construct of the idea of the colonial subject evoked by Memmi had been challenged as early as 1927 by Lamine Senghor, who was "far from ignoring the false and generally negative images that whites provided of Africa through literature and in newspapers. In several articles and speeches, he denounced the lies, clichés, and myths that circulated concerning blacks in Europe" (Midiohouan, *Ecrire,* 54). As Memmi writes, Lamine Senghor came to realize that "revolt is the only way out of the colonial situation . . . His condition is absolute and cries for an absolute solution; a break and not a compromise," while for Diagne, "the mythical and degrading portrait ends up by being accepted and lived with to a certain extent" (Memmi, *The Colonizer and the Colonized,* 127, 87).

The advancement of this dialogue and of anticolonial discourse was of course to be evidenced in both Africa and France, but in the latter, "black metropolitan intellectuals bathed in the same climate of anticolonialism," and the minister for the colonies, only too aware that a continued presence in Africa was necessary to preserve France's position as a global power, actively worked toward "slowing their momentum and avoiding any propagation of subversive ideas that might reach Africa" (Midiohouan, *L'idéologie,* 89). Because the Hexagon's frontiers were porous, potentially admitting broader consciousness of a global blackness that would include the influence of the Harlem Renaissance, student organizations, trade unions, and political groups, interference with and interruption of the flow of information was crucial to avoid the undermining of the colonial agenda. Having enlisted the support of a newly emerging class of évolués (educated Africans) that would disseminate colonial ideology, working assiduously to promote these empathetic and collaborative voices through distribution networks and favorable prefaces, colonial repression and censorship offered an early indication of the kinds of circumstances postcolonial writers would be confronted with at the hands of authoritative regimes determined to silence all forms of oppositionality.[32] Somewhat paradoxically, though, "the cultural and political geography suggested by Africans' activities in this period lends some credence to the old image of the French hexagon as a space of refuge for its own colonized peoples—as a place where draconian French colonial rule could be escaped—ironically, in France itself" (Miller, *Nationalists and Nomads,* 10). As we shall see in the next chapter, the same ambiguity would be evidenced after the Second World War, when African American artists and authors "escaped" racism and anti-Communist sentiment in America by coming to France. A number of measures, such as the creation of the French Union in 1946, the enactment of the *loi-cadre* of June 23, 1956, by the French Ministry for France Overseas, under the leadership of Gaston Defferre, as a reform of the colonial administration, and the creation of the Franco-African Community in 1958, were all accompanied by provisions for elections and guidelines for local governance and African representation in the colonies.[33] These were combined with educational reform that yielded a new generation of "intellectuals, trade union leaders, and politicians who had no intention of serving as either the instruments or the auxiliaries of colonial policies, but instead endeavored to do all that they could in the struggle toward the emancipation and self-determination of the African people" (Midiohouan, *Ecrire,* 63–64). Furthermore, the First Congress of Black Writers and Artists, September 19–22, 1956, in Paris furnished an "occasion to consider the problem of the existing relationship between the cultural and the political and to define in particular the newfound responsibility of the black writer and artist in the inescapable path to decolonization" (Mouralis, *Littérature et développement*, 31). The process of decentralization was well under way—including numerous examples and symbols of population mobilization in Algeria, Indochina, Morocco, and Tunisia—and the "technicians of colonization" would now have to confront the realities imposed on them by the "architects" of decolonization.

All of these factors provide the backdrop to the works of Camara, Kane, Socé, and Dadié, authors who turned their attention to the exploration of the limits and potentialities of acculturation.[34] Colonial education and the dissemination of the myth of French universalism and cultural superiority created a logical desire among colonial subjects to travel to the metropole, the result of an acquired francocentrism that in turn contained the promise of cultural capital. As I argued earlier, the return to the colonial period and to an analysis of the narratives of young African students has much to offer, because they were among the first to live out as practice the theories of colonial ideology advanced through colonial education, and thus became the representatives of a different facet of migration. They traveled as a carefully selected elite to engage in advanced study at a time when formalized university education was not available in either French West Africa or French Equatorial Africa, and their reception and field of discourse were radically different from those of economic migrants. As Mouralis has insisted, the study of African-French relations should be undertaken according to an approach that emphasizes "the *continuum* that links the metropole with the colonies, the colonial period with the postcolonial one, rather than a logic of disjunction" (Mouralis, *République et colonies*, 26). For the purposes of this chapter, though, the process of demystifying the colonial project in general and the civilizing mission in particular is foregrounded, and therefore of course the resulting experiences of alienation, disillusionment, and exile that are intrinsic to the broader experience of transnational mobility. Unexpectedly, perhaps, the conclusions of these narratives pertain as much to Africa as they do to France, since "an understanding of Africa is an indispensable point of entry to an understanding of France" (Mouralis, *République et colonies*, 88), and thus they further underline the ways in which the histories of France and Africa have become forever imbricated.

"Yes, I want you to go to France. I want that now, just as much as you do. Soon we'll be needing men like you here," says the father of Laye, the protagonist of Camara's novel *L'enfant noir* (Camara, *The Dark Child*, 182). Recognizing the coordinates for success under the new social order and the pragmatic validity of enlisting his son in advanced study overseas in the metropole as a logical outcome of his colonial schooling, Laye's father condones his upcoming migration. Of course, as Midiohouan has pointed out, this decision comes in response to very powerful social forces:

"William Ponty's ideological mission consisted in making the first African intellectuals feel that their interests, their destiny, their hopes depended on the colonial system" (Midiohouan, *L'idéologie*, 72). In the original French text, the shift from the personalized "je" (I) to the subject "tu" (you) he is addressing—"je veux que tu ailles en France, je le veux aujourd'hui autant que toi-même" (Camara, *L'enfant noir*, 213)—is all the more significant since this directionality underscores the reality of the situation, in which it is the son who has the perceived opportunity to go to France and advance in the system, while the father's awareness of his son's potential coincides with his own consciousness of the fact that this trajectory is not available to him and that this exclusion is indicative of a broader process of marginalization as a result of colonial policy. The son represents the future of Africa, we are led to believe, while the father is gradually relegated to the position of repository for the declining cultural and social values of the previous social order. Furthermore, use of the verb *vouloir* on two occasions in the same sentence reveals the ambiguity of the situation; Laye's father is above all generous in his patriarchal endorsement and encouragement, but the first instance of "je veux" (I want) is closer to an instruction, while the second hints at an element of desire that reinforces his own marginalization: "je le veux aujourd'hui autant que toi-même" ("I want that now, just as much as you do"), understanding of course that his son's trajectory is not available to him. To this extent, Camara's novel emerges as a circular narrative, both because the central protagonist travels away from and then back to the originary point and because his own experience connects at a psychological level with his father's.

Published in 1954, the text introduces its narrative of displacement in the opening sequence, as Laye's father prophesies the outcome of his son's encounter with colonial education and anticipates his future trajectory: "I fear, I very much fear, little one, that you are not often enough in my company. You are all day at school, and one day you will depart from that school for a greater one. You will leave me, little one . . ." (Camara, *The Dark Child*, 27). This is, of course, an extremely powerful indictment of colonial education, since Laye's inability to complete his training in Africa effectively denies Mande culture the opportunity to reproduce itself in a dynamic process contained in the duplication of his father's heritage. The consequence of this, as Miller has shown in his exhaustive reading of *The Dark Child*, is "a future outside of the coherence of local culture."[35] Writing retrospectively, Camara is able to articulate this loss as he addresses his own incapacity to fully comprehend and discuss Mande culture since "I did not know: I had left my father's house too soon" (*The Dark Child*, 11). Expressing his awareness of this loss, the novel analyzes the mechanisms implemented that have brought about these conclusions.

As in so many works by African authors of this generation, the central protagonists are either children or young men. For example, in Charles

Nokan's *Le soleil noir point,* Tanou evokes the poor living conditions in France and the constant struggle to keep abreast of his studies in combination with the work that he does to support himself: "I can no longer find the France of my dreams of yesteryear looking into the starlit night. This is for me the era of disillusionment."[36] Likewise in Ouologuem's novel *Le devoir de violence (Bound to Violence),* Kassoumi's experience in France is epitomized by his failure to adapt.[37] Because of their respective cumulative biographies at this juncture in their lives, education is of course a determining factor, but it is all the more so given the requirements of schooling under French direct rule as a propagandist and assimilationist device. In *The Dark Child,* this factor is underlined immediately when Laye declares, "I was a little boy" (17). Traditionally, at least, this developmental period is associated with a certain innocence, and Laye engages with this assumption in order to further emphasize the nature of the process of corruption that begins with the malleable child. Whereas Laye initially attended Koranic school, the French school is explicitly privileged. The new order has replaced the biological parents with the surrogate paternalism of the "new school," thereby inaugurating the lengthy process that will gradually distance the child from the African contribution to his intellectual and moral development. In this new equation, the French colonial order refuses to validate experience outside of the school system, thereby fracturing the link between the private and the public space and introducing a gap between domestic values and training and those acquired at school. As we will see in greater detail later (and indeed throughout the book this will function as a connecting topos), this kind of disconnect between home and school has also been characteristic of the uncompromising ideals of the French Republic in its relation with the politics of multiculturalism in France today. In Laye's case, the potential for achieving a formative relationship with his father is curtailed by the demands of the new order, in which his father's influence and legacy are relegated to the margins as both he and his child defer to the colonial educational system and its active dissemination of colonial ideology, the assimilationist program, and the myth of Occidental superiority. "The relation to the totemic snake, so closely linked to the notion of identity here," as Miller argues, "will follow a path of divergence and alienation, leading back cyclically to nostalgia, recollection, and narration" (Miller, *Theories of Africans,* 159).

While colonial education dominates, the circumstances on the ground are far more complex, given that several cultural models are forced to cohabit—in the case of Laye, his ethnic affiliation is located in Mande culture and Islam. The colonizer refuses to acknowledge or accord any validity to alternative educational models and carefully coded practices, such as the Kondén Diara lion ceremony (which is accompanied by the circumcision of young boys), the Koranic school, and formative training delivered by both parents and extended family. These practices emphasize civic responsibility, yield an enhanced social status among the Mande, and are intrinsic to the fabric of the local society. They serve to challenge the Western construct of Africa as a cultural void in need of colonization, a construct upon which the civilizing mission is erected. The challenge with which Laye's father is confronted is, therefore, to somehow reconcile his family's position and heritage with the new school, a challenge shared by the children of immigrants in France today.[38] The significance of the nature and scope of the choices Laye has to make at such a young age are underscored by the vocabulary of anxiety Camara employs and the directionless status of the boy: "And I was no longer sure whether I ought to continue to attend school or whether I ought to remain in the workshop: I felt unutterably confused . . . My perplexity was boundless as the sky, and mine was a sky, alas, without any stars" (*The Dark Child,* 27) ("Et je ne savais plus si je devais continuer d'aller à l'école ou si je devais demeurer dans l'atelier: j'étais dans un *trouble inexprimable* . . . Mon *désarroi* était à l'image du ciel: sans limites; mais ce ciel, hélas! Etait sans étoiles" [*L'enfant noir,* 21, emphasis mine]). The final choice between the father's workshop and the colonial school juxtaposes diametrically opposed and irreversible trajectories. To follow in his father's footsteps would offer Laye the opportunity to continue his lineage and embrace a highly respected vocation in the Mande community, whereas attendance at the French school symbolizes adherence to the coordinates of the new order. Both are pragmatic choices, of course, each in favor of a certain power structure, but the new school is designed with the specific intention of systematically dismantling, erasing, and replacing the old order. The paradox is that Laye's community does not exist in a political and social vacuum, and that the dilemma with which he is faced is ultimately only rhetorical since, had Laye opted for advanced training and initiation under his father's supervision, it is unlikely that such activities would have carried the same prestige for much longer in any case. In fact, the lengthy descriptions he gives of his father's practices in his workshop anticipate the Cartesian, dismissive, and reductive discourse of the colonizer for whom these activities are only technical operations: "The operation going on before my eyes was certainly the smelting of gold, yet something more than that: a magical operation that the guiding spirits could regard with favor or disfavor" (*The Dark Child,* 35).

Having expressed the manner in which he is "unutterably confused" (the French *trouble inexprimable* is a more powerful evocation of the sensation of disorientation), Laye wrestles with his decision: "My perplexity was boundless as the sky, and mine was a sky, alas, without any stars" (27). The absence of stars here serves as a symbolic indication of the extent to which Laye is directionless, literally without a compass (the French would say *déboussolé*). Reinforcing his status as child and abnegating the responsibilities of adulthood that he is neither culturally (he is not yet circumcised) nor psycho-emotionally prepared for, Laye turns to his father for an appropriate decision: "'Father! . . . Father! . . . !' I kept repeating. 'What must I do if I am to do the right thing?' And I wept silently and fell asleep still weeping" (28). The question of what constitutes the "right thing" is of course a complex one, one that the colonial order has unjustly asked of the young boy who is already troubled by his awareness of the contradictory nature of the demand that is being made of him: that he individuate from his biological parents and reject a cultural heritage he was growing to respect unquestioningly. Indeed, "the unity between father and totem, excluding the son, at the end of the first chapter," as Miller has suggested, "is symbolic of the individuation and differentiation without which the writing of a novel seems impossible" (Miller, *Theories of Africans,* 160). Not surprisingly, this process has triggered a range of clinically diagnosable symptoms of anxiety disorders and psychological malaise, early indicators of the separation anxiety and post-traumatic stress disorder that will manifest itself later in the text. Indications of these include "my distress," "sleep did not come and I tossed restlessly on my bed," "I wept silently and fell asleep still weeping," and "inexpressible confusion" (*The Dark Child,* 28). The question of choice is rather limited, of course, since the implanted colonial school emerges as a powerful institution, one that rapidly voids the potentiality for resistance and rejection in favor of collaboration and participation; this is unambiguously confirmed by Laye's father's insistence that "soon we'll be needing men like you here" —namely African men who will perform important sociopolitical functions, but also perhaps provide a degree of subversive objectivity as insiders.

Once Laye begins to attend the new school, Camara juxtaposes the rural village of Tindican where Laye's grandmother resides with the urban context of Kouroussa where colonial inroads have been greater (the presence of the colonial school and of railway tracks emphasizes this point). As Miller has argued, "It would be pointless to resist interpreting the train as a sign and symbol of colonial penetration; the relation is synecdochal in that the railroad was the principal tool of colonial occupation and exploitation in the interior of West Africa—it is part and parcel of the political phenomenon that it represents here" (Miller, *Theories of Africans,* 135). This construct is of course relative, but serves to underline the manner in which colonial influences become equated with technological modernity and therefore also underlines the need for Africans to be incorporated into this new global capitalistic order. Laye's arrival in the rural village provides the occasion to gauge the distance that is already in evidence between his progress in the colonial system and the distance he has traveled in comparison to other young Africans of his generation. Laye rapidly acquires considerable cultural and social capital; we are told that "in deference to the city boy sharing their country games, [the young country boys] gladly kept their high spirits in control. Furthermore, they were full of admiration for my school clothes" (*The Dark Child*, 52). Laye himself articulates his awareness of his enhanced status: "Filled with envy, my playmates watched me put on my short-sleeved khaki shirt, shorts of the same color, and sandals. I also had a beret, which I hardly ever wore" (52). Indeed, as we shall see later, these constructs, which emerged during the colonial era, have survived into the contemporary period, in which the term *paysans* (peasants) is widely used in the discourse of the *sapeurs* to denigrate economic migrants.[39] This realization of apparent cultural and social capital contains its own contradictions, since Laye's envy of what the other young boys enjoy is reciprocal. While the other boys may be drawn to the symbols (material and educational) of colonial urban culture, Laye remarks on their constraints and their symbolic incompatibility with the surrounding environment—those clothes "were a great nuisance" (53)—and he "envied [the other boys] their freedom of movement" (52). The new order is accompanied by certain constraints that serve metaphorically as a commentary on the colonial system's organization and ordering of the colonial subject, so that Laye says, "I would have liked to have rid myself of those clothes fit only for city wear" (53). Laye relishes the opportunity to escape from the city and the pressures associated with colonial schooling: "I had come to the country to run about, to play, to scale the lookout posts, and to lose myself in the tall grass with the herds of cattle, and of course I could not do any of these things without spoiling my precious clothes" (53). This is more than a simple statement concerning the pleasure all young people have in spending time away from school; it has to do with the regimented component of colonial school that is concerned with shaping and molding a new generation of Africans. In fact, the initial encounter with colonial education is conceived outside of any specific time frame, and there is no notion of the longevity of the contact or indeed, for that matter, of its permanence: "Neither my mother nor I had the slightest suspicion how long I would be a student in the latter" (77). Laye's father realizes the necessity of working with the new power, and when the mother expresses her resistance and skepticism, she is ultimately silenced by his patriarchal authority.

Camara devotes considerable attention to the curriculum, and calls attention to the near complete disconnect between the public component (delivered in the colonial school) and the private (cultural paradigms of the home): "Nothing that we learned was old or expected; all came through from another planet, and we never tired of listening" (*The Dark Child*, 79). In fact, the transcontinental voyage Laye takes to France at the end of the novel is, in many ways, tantamount to a trip to another planet. An analogous violence is established within the text between the curriculum and the school environment itself, in which a disturbing hierarchy between pupils and teachers is evident. Camara has delineated a careful analogy between the school environment and the broader colonial one, in which it becomes clear that the behavioral patterns of the children reflect those of the colonial order. The vocabulary of aggression, submission, and dominance is organized around such references as "a beating" (80), "caning" (80), "blows" (80), "punishments" (80), "deliberate cruelty" (83), "a brutal beating" (84), and "sweeping the schoolyard" (80), thereby rejoining Dadié's novel *Climbié,* in which schoolchildren are punished for using indigenous languages with the "symbol" in the school compound as a way of foregrounding the privilege and forced imposition of new cultural codes.[40] Camara recounts how older pupils—"less strictly supervised— persecuted us in every conceivable way. They were a haughty lot, and with reason, since no doubt they were repaying the treatment they had themselves received" (82). The system perpetuates itself in this manner, delegating violence according to a strict hierarchy in which the schoolyard emerges as microcosm of the colony itself. Accordingly, we learn of how the young boys "worked like galley slaves" (83); "the only tools we had were our hands—our hands, and our fingers, and our fingernails" (82); "the whips whistled as they moved through the air; our backs felt as though they were on fire. Our flesh smarted, and tears fell from our eyes" (83). They endured "deliberate cruelty" (83), often in the form of "a dreadful beating. It was administered so violently, in such a diabolical rhythm, that even a deaf man would have understood that these blows were given not to speed up the work but to extort food and money" (83). The slavery topos emerges again as the father of one of the pupils finally protests against this violence: "I am not sending my son to school for you to make a slave out of him" (86). Eventually, the analogy that inextricably links the violence to the broader colonial project is unambiguously established in the nationalist discourse of the 1950s: "Such beatings were utterly alien to my people's passion for independence and equality" (84). This is a striking example of the mediation between fiction and the evidentiary component, since this rhetoric cannot be seen as neutral in the sociopolitical context in which it was conceived in the last years before Independence.

The gradual process that transports Laye from childhood to adulthood coincides with the parallel course that leads him away from the sociocultural framework of his parents' culture. The moment at which Laye becomes a "man" according to Mande culture—that is, the moment of circumcision—and identifies with his community is ruptured by his departure for Conakry. As he progresses through the colonial education system, his trajectory is progressively centralized through steps that lead him from the local school to the regional one and ultimately to the very center of the metropole. At this juncture, the colonial process coincides metaphorically and literally with the boundary that is established between Laye and his heritage and between Laye and Africa itself. The colonial ed-

ucational process has completed its mission of transporting the educated
individual away from his continental affiliation toward the parameters of
the new order—the évolué French cultural prototype now mediates his relationship with Africa and Africans through the lens configured by colonialism. Indeed, Laye expresses some incredulity at the rapidity with
which his formation has culminated in the transnational experience: "Am
I really going away?" he asks, to which his father responds, "What else
can you do? You know that you must" (141). At this point, it would seem
that Laye has realized something that his parents had struggled to come to
terms with long before, namely that entry into colonial education was a
one-way route. In many ways, then, the work of sub-Saharan African writers of this generation contains a theorization of the ambiguity, not so
much of cross- or intercultural contact, but rather of the implications of
contact with a hegemonic and monolithic system that works toward the
eradication of the potentialities of hybridity or métissage. As the protagonists navigate through the system, they are confronted with the complexity of their circumstances.

Once in Conakry, Laye is struck by the substantive reorganization that
has taken place as he comes into contact with the advanced stages of colonial expansionism in the urban center. Both Laye and Check Omar, his
fellow traveler on "the temporary highways of exile" (178), experience
physical symptoms as a consequence of study away from home and of exile within the boundaries of their own continent. "Check Omar is seriously ill" (175), we learn, and even dies prematurely. However, much like
his uncle, Laye dreams of what lies "beyond" and has a sense of adventure. When he returns to Kouroussa for a short vacation, he is always
greeted with praise, and he enjoys the company of other évolué children
who have returned from schooling away from home. As conflicted as they
may be about the challenges of exile, they are nevertheless seduced by the
prestige bestowed upon them as a direct consequence of the cultural capital they have acquired and that is inseparable from a broader cumulative
process that contains the promise of travel to France. Having become
aware of the latest link in this movement toward France, Laye's mother articulates her firm opposition to his further studies: "You're not going!"
(180). The tenuousness of the circumstances ultimately emerges when
Laye's father is compelled to encourage his son to go to France as an essential step in the new power structure: "Then you agree I should go?"
asks the boy, to which the father responds "Yes. . . . Yes, I'm willing. For
your sake. For your own good" (181). His father's paradoxical decision to
condone the upcoming migration is imprecise and uncertain, and its positive dimension will, naturally, only be addressed retroactively through
concerted analysis of the colonial project as a whole.

Laye's father invokes the benefits of the journey for his son, but, in refusing to ignore the detrimental impact of colonialism on local culture, he

perhaps suggests an unanticipated aspect of colonial culture, namely that the consciousness of oppression that the colonized subject will acquire along the road to formulating an anticolonial stance may just alleviate colonialism's broader impact and assist in preserving local cultural elements: "This opportunity is within your reach. You must seize it . . . Yes, I want you to go to France. I want that now, just as much as you do. Soon, we'll be needing men like you here" (182). It is crucial to generate an African elite poised to assume responsibility alongside the colonial forces, but, perhaps more importantly, Laye's father alludes here to the imminence of political independence. Furthermore, he clearly understands the direction in which his son is heading. "I knew quite well that eventually you would leave us. I knew it the very first time you set foot in school. I watched you studying with such eagerness, such passionate eagerness! . . . Yes, since that day I have known how it would be. And I gradually resigned myself to it" (181–182). This is all the more remarkable considering that both Laye and his mother had not the "slightest suspicion" (77), while also echoing his prediction in the opening section of the novel: "You will leave me" (27). As soon as Laye learns that he will begin his French experience in Argenteuil on the outskirts of Paris, his attention shifts back to the myth of Paris he has embraced: "And I began to dream about Paris. I had heard about Paris for so long!" (183). Laye's mother finds little solace in the fractured family with which she is left: "Yesterday it was the school in Conakry; today it's the school in France; tomorrow . . . What will it be tomorrow? Every day there's some mad scheme to take my son away from me! . . . And now they want to take him away to their own land!" (184–185). Once again, given that Laye has come to represent the most valuable human capital of his generation, the association with slavery is hard to ignore: "All the time she had been talking and fighting against them she must have been watching the wheels going round and round: first this wheel, then that, and then a third and greater wheel, then still more, many more, perhaps, which no one could see. And how could they be stopped? We could only watch them turning and turning, the wheels of destiny turning and turning" (186). He recognizes the futility of questioning the powerful nature of the organized colonial project and its ability to disseminate its ideology, rejoining perhaps the subversive quality of his father's faith in "men like him" in a newly decolonized national space. As he boards the plane for France, however, Laye evokes the degree to which he is disrupted by his departure: "Oh! it was a terrible parting! I do not like to think of it. I can still hear my mother wailing. I can still see my father, unable to hide his tears . . . No, I do not like to remember that parting. It was as if I were being torn apart" (186–187). The English translation does not adequately convey the forcefulness of the French vocabulary: both *déchirement* and *arraché à moi-même* (*L'enfant noir,* 219) are stronger than "terrible parting" and "being torn apart," conveying the existential anguish and trauma sustained at this moment by the young man. As F. Abiola Irele has suggested, "At the same time, we are conscious of the irreversible nature of the transformations the impact of Europe has effected in our midst and which are so extensive as to define the really significant frame of reference of our contemporary existence."[41] The apparent irreconcilability of his childhood with colonial schooling is underlined as he describes his disjointed identity in concert with the hegemonic construct of French colonialism, one that is ultimately organized around the use of French language literacy as the marker of exclusion. As Miller has shown, "French, simply put, is the medium of alienation, the perfect synecdoche for Camara's exile, his imperfect knowledge of his own culture, and his inability to tell the reader what is what" (Miller, *Theories of Africans,* 178).

The lure of advancement in the colonial order is always present, though, thereby rejoining an analogous metaphor in the repeated allusion to Toundi's *gourmandise* (greed) in Ferdinand Oyono's novel *Une vie de boy* (*Houseboy*), which is insisted upon not to exculpate or exonerate the colonizer, but rather to underline the fact "that the postcolonial relationship is not primarily a relationship of resistance or collaboration but can be best characterized as convivial, a relationship fraught by the fact that the *commandement* and its 'subjects' having to share the same living space."[42] This is powerfully illustrated in the concluding words to Camara's novel, where the sexual overtones serve to confirm the extent to which Laye's own complex relationship with France is realigned with a desire expressed through sexual arousal or stimulus, triggered by Paris (transmuted here into a map of the métro) as the signifier responsible for what might well be an erection causing the uncontrolled swelling in his pocket: "Later I felt something hard when I put my hand in my pocket. It was the map of the *métro*" (Camara, *The Dark Child,* 188; "Plus tard, je sentis une épaisseur sous ma main: le plan du métro gonflait ma poche" [Camara, *L'enfant noir,* 221]). Camara's novel provides a powerful exploration of the impact of colonial education on a colonized African community and reveals the aptitude and efficiency of ideological mechanisms in disseminating the policies of assimilation. The work of Cheikh Hamidou Kane has much to contribute to this subject, since it provides a further example of the manner in which the myth of Western superiority is deployed, but simultaneously engages in an extensive analysis of the philosophical foundations of this project.[43]

Kane's novel *L'aventure ambiguë* (*Ambiguous Adventure*) is explicitly anchored in the context of Islam, and it is within this framework that the response to colonialism is addressed. The central protagonist, Samba Diallo, is observed at a Koranic school, where he is learning to recite verses from the Koran. As Mildred Mortimer has explained, "for the duration of his apprenticeship, Samba . . . will be removed from his biological parents and have a foster father, a spiritual guide, to initiate him."[44] The Master,

Thierno, appears excessively harsh in his reaction to his student's mistakes. However, this violence needs to be contextualized, and colonial education must also be understood as an aggressive violation of local practice, given its hegemonic character. "Thierno's violence toward Samba," as Mortimer has argued, "may originate in frustration and fear that he will not have the time to prepare Samba as his suitable successor" (Mortimer, 57). Concerned with the pernicious advances of the colonial school, Thierno redoubles his efforts at delivering his Islamic training as a necessary response to preserve the centrality of the Koran to his community. Like Laye, young Samba comes from a well-established and respected elite local family that initiates a dialogue with the larger community in order to determine its response to the arrival of the new Western school. Significantly, "both Samba and Laye are cut off from the rational comprehension of their culture of origin by their transfer to the French school. They become cultural hybrids largely because both Toucouleur and Malinké traditions call for a maturation process" (Mortimer, 56). Initially, the importance of foregrounding Islam over the colonial school is insisted upon: "We reject the foreign school in order to remain ourselves, and to preserve for God the place He holds in our hearts. But have we still enough force to resist the school, and enough substance to remain ourselves?" (Kane, *Ambiguous Adventure*, 10). As Kane rightly signals, there is considerably more at stake here than simply countering the new school, since the struggle is not so much to preserve one cultural and educational paradigm over another but rather to resist the colonial school precisely because of its project of erasing vestiges of Islam alongside other local sociocultural practices and models. As Conklin has shown, Governor-General Ponty had insisted that "the spread of French was a means to counter Islam as well, 'for experience has taught us that Muslims who know our language are less prejudiced'" (Conklin, *A Mission to Civilize*, 132). The primacy that is ultimately accorded to the colonial school comes from its technological advances, and even the Master is compelled to acknowledge this: "It is certain that their school is the better teacher of how to join wood to wood, and that men should learn how to construct dwelling houses that resist the weather" (Kane, *Ambiguous Adventure*, 11). Once this has been recognized, the incompatibility of the two educational models—Koranic and colonial—is underscored precisely because of the refusal of French direct rule to accommodate other paradigms. In fact, the Master's death serves as a metaphor for the broader social death of an old system that is to be replaced by a new one, not because of some necessary progressive gesture, but because the latter is all-encompassing: "he was now near death. But at the same time as himself, he felt that the country of the Diallobé was dying from the assault of strangers come from beyond the sea" (Kane, *Ambiguous Adventure*, 23). The very premise of French presence and dominance is located in its ideological expansionist project based on a universalizing

imperative. However, as Irele has shown, it would be a mistake to underestimate the capacity of the cultural system that is menaced to reformulate
itself and to grant the colonial system the absolute power to function as
what Jean-Loup Amselle and Elikia M'Bokolo have described as a *société
englobante* (englobing society):

> The notion of the universality of human experience does not, however, im-
> ply uniformity—quite the contrary—but it does mean that cultures maintain
> their dynamism only through their degree of tension between the particular
> and the universal. Alienation, in this view, cannot mean loss; the fulfillment
> it promises resides precisely in the degree of integration it helps us to
> achieve. In its creative potential, alienation signifies the sensitive tension be-
> tween the immediate closeness of the self and the reflected distance of the
> other. (Irele, "In Praise of Alienation," 223–224)[45]

The chief of the Diallobé pays careful attention to what is at stake in
sending young men to the colonial school. Indeed, this perspective was
not provided in Camara's novel, beyond the skepticism expressed by
Laye's mother on the matter. The chief of the Diallobé ponders the opportunity cost of the new system, asking, "But, learning, they would also
forget. Would what they would learn be worth as much as what they
would forget? I should like to ask you: can one learn *this* without forgetting *that,* and is what one learns worth what one forgets?" (Kane, *Ambiguous Adventure,* 34). He identifies the very problem that is at the heart
of the dilemma and recognizes the all-inclusive nature of the colonial
school, within whose structure any bilateralism is voided. "The Grande
Royale" (Samba's aunt), as Mortimer demonstrates, "offers a pragmatic
approach to solving political and cultural dilemmas in a rapidly changing
society" (Mortimer, 58). Her decision to support the colonial project is
due more to the expediency of involvement, the opportunism of the new
order, and also has a more subversive component that alludes to the possibility of mastering and conquering the emerging power structures in favor of the Diallobé people and community La Grande Royale represents:
"we must go to learn from them the art of conquering without being in
the right. Furthermore, the conflict has not yet ceased. The foreign school
is the new form of the war which those who have come here are waging,
and we must send our elite there, expecting that all the country will follow them" (Kane, *Ambiguous Adventure,* 37). This also functions as a
point of intertextuality with Camara's novel, in which his father argues
along similar lines. The paradox, of course, is that while the colonial
school instills the myth of French superiority by denigrating local culture,
the same local elite are nevertheless privileged in the new order, albeit by
delineating and resignifying the coordinates for cultural and social capital.

La Grande Royale's rhetorical agency is quite striking, as she proceeds
to demonstrate why the choice of the new school is unavoidable:

more and more we shall have to do things which we hate doing . . . I, the Most Royal Lady, do not like the foreign school. I detest it. My opinion, nevertheless, is that we should send our children there . . . The school in which I would place our children will kill in them what today we love and rightly conserve with care. Perhaps the very memory of us will die in them. When they return from the school, there may be those who will not recognize us. What I am proposing is that we should agree to die in our children's hearts and that the foreigners who have defeated us should fill the place, wholly, which we shall have left free. (Kane, *Ambiguous Adventure,* 45–46)

This approach is eventually embraced by the collectivity as an essential step toward a type of modernity delineated by colonial ideology. Of significance, however, is La Grande Royale's lucidity in highlighting the inevitable loss that such a measure will entail, as young people adopt alternative identitarian models that will ultimately distance them from their community of origin while also dismantling the local memory that had been reproduced by each successive generation. Kane explores this process in some detail by providing a rapid historical overview of France's successful conquest of the region. This provides us with an important insight into Kane's own attempt at theorizing this exercise in dominance over the Diallobé and clearly connects with analogous colonial experiences in francophone sub-Saharan Africa:

Strange dawn! The morning of the Occident in black Africa was spangled over with smiles, with cannon shots, with shining glass beads. Those who had no history were encountering those who carried the world on their shoulders. It was a morning of accouchement; the known world was enriching itself by a birth that took place in mire and blood. From shock, the one side made no resistance. They were a people without a past, therefore without memory. The men who were landing on their shores were white, and mad. Nothing like them had ever been known. The deed was accomplished before the people were even conscious of what had happened. Some among the Africans, such as the Diallobé, brandished their shields, pointed their lances, and aimed their guns. They were allowed to come close, then the cannon were fired. The vanquished did not understand . . . Others wanted to parley. They were given a choice: friendship or war. Very sensibly, they chose friendship. They had no experience at all. (Kane, *Ambiguous Adventure,* 48)

The discourse and vocabulary recuperated by Kane in this instance reveals his own ambiguous role as mediator between two cultural domains he knows intimately, as he combines French opinions of Africans ("Those who had no history were encountering those who carried the world on their shoulders") with exempla of ultimately futile African resistance. In the previous section, La Grande Royale alluded to the colonial process of erasing local memory, and now the colonial view that Africa is ahistorical is put in evidence. What this discourse reveals is the colonizer's point of entry in which the African subject was characterized as being devoid of

culture and therefore logically receptive to a civilizing matrix, one that
would culminate in a carefully coded process in which subjects were
"checked by census, divided up, classified, labeled, conscripted, adminis-
trated" (49). Corporal and mental control become synonymous in their
function of dictating the behavior of the colonial subject: "The new school
shares at the same time the characteristics of cannon and magnet. From the
cannon it draws its efficacy as an arm of combat. Better than the cannon, it
makes conquest permanent. The cannon compels the body, the school be-
witches the soul" (49). Samba, then, following in the footsteps of Laye, is
compelled to accept these new circumstances in order to secure an advan-
tageous position for his son in the new society: "'this future—I accept it,'
he said. 'My son is the pledge of that. He will contribute to its building. It
is my wish that he contribute, not as a stranger come from distant regions,
but as an artisan responsible for the destinies of the citadel'" (80).

Whereas Laye's gradual displacement through the colonial school system generates the feeling of "being torn apart," Samba's own experience is
embodied in terms of "ambiguity": "It suddenly occurs to us that, all
along our road, we have not ceased to metamorphose ourselves, and we
see ourselves as other than what we were. Sometimes the metamorphosis
is not even finished. We have turned ourselves into hybrids" (112–113).[46]
As Mortimer has indicated, though, "he fears becoming a hybrid" (Mortimer, 63). This analysis of the resulting metamorphosis and hybridity of
the colonial subject gains proximity to the experience of so many African
protagonists for whom only failed hybridities are evidenced: namely, the
realization that the promise of acculturation is only a promise, so that the
hyphen in the newly created "French-African" identity (as the conclusion
to Oyono's novel *Houseboy* confirms) emerges merely as an indelible
symbol of the dividing marker between the domesticated French cultural
prototype and the dream of actual Frenchness itself. Ambiguity emerges
from the irreconcilability of the two parts, and therefore stands as an indictment of the potentialities of métissage. The reorganization of the cultural and social sphere destabilizes the colonial subject, transforms the
customary points of reference (Laye described this situation in terms of a
"sky without stars"); "The point is not that the culture does not have a
reality for him," Irele signals; "it does, but that precisely is the problem;
he knows that it is a precarious reality, that the axis of the world in which
he is living is shifting from its grounding in the institutions and values of
the traditional culture toward a new point of orientation determined by
the impact of an alien culture, specifically Western civilization" (Irele, "In
Praise of Alienation," 207).

Kane approaches these questions from an original perspective, one
that intersects in many ways, at least historically, with seminal works produced by such Senegalese contemporaries as Léopold Sédar Senghor (*Liberté I: Négritude et humanisme* [1964]), and Cheikh Anta Diop (*Nations*

nègres et cultures [1954], *L'Afrique noire précoloniale* [1960], and *L'unité culturelle de l'Afrique noire* [1960]).[47] This philosophical attempt at exploring the myth of Occidental superiority can therefore be seen as a further attempt to theorize, through literature, the colonizer/colonized relationship that is so crucial to our understanding of the migration myth, or at least the ambiguity of that relationship. Indeed, while some texts continue to receive critical attention, others are being ignored, or at the very least insufficiently exploited in curricular offerings or overlooked in scholarly work. This is especially evident when one considers the remarkable body of research that has been devoted to the content and form of the Caribbean experience, including Aimé Césaire's *Discours sur le colonialisme* (*Discourse on Colonialism*), Frantz Fanon's *Peau noire, masques blancs* (*Black Skin, White Masks*), Edouard Glissant's *Le discours antillais* (*Caribbean Discourse*), and Jean Bernabé, Patrick Chamoiseau, and Raphaël Confiant's *Eloge de la créolité* (*In Praise of Creoleness*).[48]

Samba's ambiguous status emerges from the colonial system itself, which creates at least two distinct categories of thought by insisting on the centrality and prominence of the Western component: "I am not a distinct country of the Diallobé facing a distinct Occident, and appreciating with a cool head what I must take from it and what I must leave with it by way of counterbalance. I have become the two" (Kane, *Ambiguous Adventure,* 150–151). As Irele has argued, "Samba Diallo is the archetype of the divided consciousness, of the African who suffers in his mind the effects of cultural dispossession. His agony is that of his dual nature, marked by a cleavage rather than an integration of its two frames of reference" (Irele, "In Praise of Alienation," 203). Once in France, the initial logic informing entry into the new school is challenged, tested: "You claim that the great need we have of the West leaves us no further choice, and merely authorizes submission, until the day when we shall have acquired mastery of them ... if we accept it and accommodate ourselves to it, we shall never have the mastery of the object. For we shall have no more dignity than it has. We shall not dominate it" (Kane, *Ambiguous Adventure,* 153–154). However, the ultimate outcome leads Samba, as it does Laye, to confront his own responsibility for the ease with which the colonial seduction took place: "My hatred is a re-inhibition, if I may use that word, an annulment, of love ... No one should ally himself with them without having observed them well beforehand ... The most poisoned hatreds are those born of old loves" (160–161). His initial desire for advancement in the system forces him to accept a degree of responsibility as well: "Perhaps it was with their alphabet. With it they struck the first hard blow at the country of the Diallobé. I remained for a long time under the spell of those signs and sounds which constitute the structure and the music of their language" (159).[49] Further parallels with Laye are evidenced as Samba evokes the crucial moment at which colonial education intervened and transported him away from the teachings of the Master: "I had interrupted my studies with the teacher of the Diallobé at the very moment when he was about to initiate me at last into the rational understanding of what up to then I had done no more than recite" (160).

The colonial project is concerned with reproducing cultural proto-types according to carefully delineated parameters that have nothing to do with the local culture: "But they—they interposed themselves, and under-took to transform me in their image" (160). Kane concludes with a de-nunciation of the emptiness of Occidental material culture. His escape into death when the Fool murders him after he is unable to perform as substitute for the old Master coincides with the distance he also achieves from the myth of France itself. As in so many narratives that have ex-plored displaced African subjects (Mildred Mortimer notes that "Samba uses metaphors of journey—road, adventure, itinerary . . . in expressing his sense of loss and confusion" [63]), death emerges as the only suitable repository for a fractured identity: "You are entering the place where there is no more ambiguity" (Kane, *Ambiguous Adventure,* 177). Return to Africa is not accompanied by reinsertion into the social order. Colonial education is a unidirectional mode of cultural transportation, and as Mortimer has claimed in her dismissal of the possibilities of social reinte-gration, "Although Samba has not been seduced by the bright light of Western materialism, he has become exhausted in his struggle against it, a lonely struggle to preserve his religious values and African identity in a sterile and mechanized world from which God seems to have disappeared" (Mortimer, 62). Accordingly, Samba and Laye share in the trauma of exile, and writing provides the space in which to reflect on the experi-ence itself while also articulating it as a way of terminating its repetition: "The very expansion of his vision upon the world becomes for him his dilemma, his existential plight," concludes Irele, and "he is no longer able to relate to the world because that world is no longer coherent, no longer offers him a stable and compact order of values" (Irele, "In Praise of Alienation," 203). "I am like a broken balafong," Samba claims, "like a musical instrument that has gone dead. I have the impression that nothing touches me anymore" (Kane, *Ambiguous Adventure,* 150). Colonial edu-cation promised cultural capital to the attentive subject; Kane's novel con-vincingly exposes the shortcomings inherent in an uncompromising bi-nary system used as the basis for defining and expanding human relations. Similarly, the works of Ousmane Socé and Bernard Dadié provide excel-lent examples of the ways in which the myth of French cultural superior-ity operates as a strategic device for imposing colonial rule, and how in turn it can be unpacked and demystified by an attentive observer of these elaborate dynamics.

A new architecture and topography characterize Socé's initial discus-sion of colonialism in *Mirages de Paris.* The text is constructed as the narration of a story, an adventure: "One day, the whites made their appearance; they built a railroad that transported tools; then the white men built a new village next to the old one that ruled over the first" (Socé, *Mirages de Paris*, 7). Central to the analysis is the emphasis on the politics of separateness, as the colonial forces distance themselves from the colonized subjects. While the young protagonist, Fara, attends Koranic school from the age of six onward, the colonial order will have successfully intervened and altered his itinerary by the time he is nine, enrolling him in the "white man's school" (12). Fara's experiences are like those of Laye and Samba, who, while originating in different regions of the AOF, nevertheless share points of commonality—certainly they all experience the colonial imperative of foregrounding the colonial school over the Koranic one and also of course the attempted standardization of French-language acquisition. Fara proves to be particularly adept at both recognizing and learning the new symbols of the French alphabet, and he is rewarded for this assimilationist aptitude: "The lady with the 'rosy ears' gave Fara two mandarins and a friendly pat on the cheek" (13). The very reference to the pigmentation of the teacher's ears so early in the novel prefigures the centrality of ethnocentrism, Orientalism, and reverse Orientalism in this novel, as we witness Fara's exposure to a range of images and stereotypes of Africa.[50] As Edwin Hill has shown, "Since the heart of the story does not begin in earnest until Fara arrives in Paris, the fact that Socé opens with the main protagonist in a classroom in Africa suggests the importance of Fara's identity as a subject of colonial education."[51] Indeed, these passages are important since they allow us to assess and confirm the content of the colonial curriculum:

> In this way a dangerous love for the exotic was taking shape in his young soul, susceptible to golden illusions. Distant lands beyond the horizon had an irresistible hold on him. And to see Paris, which all agreed was an El Dorado, Paris, with its beautiful monuments, magical spectacles, its elegance, its powerful life that we so admired at the cinema. (Socé, *Mirages de Paris*, 15)

A reversed "exoticism" is at work, since traditionally, at least, the discourse of the exotic is linked to Western "Orientalizing." A visual and textual process contributes to the construction of the Other, and significantly Fara is drawn to multiple narratives that deal with the African experience in a more general manner: "And he sought out any source that could provide his imagination with something additional that he could use in the architecture of this wonderful world, built and placed beyond the seas: tales of black sailors, those of Senegalese war veterans, even those of colonials who, in their nostalgia, embellished their memories" (15).[52] Fara is gradually seduced by the colonial project's promise of advancement and reward, and reconditioned to admire French culture. Accordingly, his newly acquired francocentrism leads him naturally to aspire to greater proximity to France itself: "Fara's greatest wish was to see this France, whose language, history, and geography he had learned with complete devotion" (15). Passage to France and to its capital city, Paris, becomes imperative to Fara, and confirms his attachment to a new national memory located in a purely French context. Socé astutely structures his narrative around this initial point of contact through colonial education in order to subsequently transport the young protagonist to France, where he can apply this theoretical apparatus through an experiential mode of living in the metropole. However, "what constitutes *seeing,*" Miller warns us, "becomes a troubling issue. Seeing becomes *hallucinating,* in a process of false identification with the Other" (Miller, *Nationalists and Nomads,* 64). The experience on the ground in the French capital redirects ethnographic fieldwork toward Africa. This is a gesture that, as we shall see, is also undertaken—but with radically different conclusions—in Dadié's novel *Un nègre à Paris (An African in Paris).* "Today," we learn, "Fara would fulfill his dream; he would set sail for France on one of those steamers that exhaled the air of distant oceans and that awakened mirages of countries of inconceivable beauty" (Socé, *Mirages de Paris,* 16). Not surprisingly, such constructs echo the findings and observations that are intrinsic to Casanova's book, in which "the existence of a literary center is therefore twofold: it exists both in the imaginations of those who inhabit it and in the reality of the measurable effects it produces" (Casanova, *The World Republic of Letters,* 24).

Somewhat paradoxically, Fara is selected to attend the 1931 Exposition coloniale (The International Colonial and Overseas Exposition), further emphasizing earlier analogies established in the text to the question of ethnography and the complex process of structuring and constructing the other.[53] "The *Exposition,*" as Hill points out, "inverses the conventional travel paradigms by bringing the empire 'home' to the nation" (Hill, 628). As Fara leaves the port of Dakar he, like so many of his African predecessors, passes the island of Gorée, thereby reintroducing the slavery topos that connects with so many of the texts considered in this book (from Sembene's "Black Girl" to Diome's *Le ventre de l'Atlantique*) and reminding the reader of the transhistorical nature of European-African exploitative relations. From the deck of the ship, Fara reflects on the journey that has resulted in this departure: "with each turn of the propeller he grew more and more distant from his homeland, his parents, and his childhood friends . . . each turn of the propeller brought him closer to an immense and prestigious country that he both loved and feared at the same time . . ." (Socé, *Mirages de Paris,* 17). Much as Laye's father recognized early on that his son would ultimately only further distance himself from his heritage, Fara himself expresses a certain reservation and foreboding about the journey that lies ahead: "Fara couldn't help but somehow feel that he would never see those things again" (20).

Fara's fieldwork begins during the passage to France. Much in the same way as the houseboy Toundi in Oyono's novel *Houseboy* overhears conversations between colonials at the European Club, so too does Fara witness discussions and exchanges among white passengers returning to France from the colonies. These conversations are all the more striking given that they occur in a seeming vacuum in which the present African is ignored. From these exchanges, Fara is able to more accurately and authentically gauge sentiment regarding the colonized "natives": "one must be careful not to open their eyes too wide," he learns, "because you'd only turn them into 'dangerous elements' and the day will come when they will kick us out . . . the French administration is misguided in its insistence on educating the natives. One can't do a thing there anymore with emancipated blacks . . . Blacks should be left alone in their ignorance!" (22–23). Considering that Fara has recently completed his educational training and emerged as the representative of an African évolué class, this kind of discourse is of course confusing. While a gentleman from Perpignan reminds his interlocutors, almost as an afterthought, of their mission—"We are in Africa to civilize them, so you have to give them some instruction, just not too much" (23)—the economic component that is of primary importance and the accompanying need to maintain a trade imbalance favorable to the colonizer are discussed: "the natives would buy without grumbling so long as the junk they bought was 'shiny,' 'sparkly,' or 'flashy'" (22–23). In fact, having arrived in France, he is addressed by the same gentleman from Perpignan:

> "Well, this must be quite a change for you from Dakar, eh?" the trader from Perpignan said to him. "Yes," answered Fara, "what I see here is really beautiful . . . the architecture, transportation, the comfort, hygiene, order, activity, everything is on a superior level to what you find in Africa." . . . The Syrian trader, his eyes wide open with surprise, exclaimed, "He sounds like a book, that one! Well, mister, you must have been educated?" (25)

Clearly, he places little faith in the pedagogic component of the colonial mission, since he seems surprised that Fara is so articulate, thereby contradicting, of course, his own sentiments concerning the inferiority of the colonized subject.[54] When Fara responds, the Perpignan trader switches from the familiar *tu* to the more formal *vous* ("Vous avez donc fait des études?" [25]), indicating that Fara commands respect only through the demonstration of French-language literacy and the performance and exhibition of assimilation and therefore distantiation from the African component of his identity, which is perceived only in negative terms.

Once in Paris, Fara is able to begin the task of observing "French behavior." However, while one might assume that this would invest him with narrative authority, the situation is rendered more complex because of the fact that Fara mediates his encounter with the Other through his

colonial education—in other words, Fara has been so assimilated that he
is not equipped with the kind of lucidity invested in Dadié's protagonist
Tanhoe, who has achieved the degree of consciousness associated with
Memmi's colonized subject, who no longer "accepts," by the time he arrives in the metropole. Years before Fanon would formulate similar com-
mentaries in *Black Skin, White Masks,* Fara describes the popular response to his pigmentation, delivered through "the cinema and fantastic
tales in which the lesson was that a black person was a living puppet"
(Socé, *Mirages de Paris,* 64): "This vast crowd of white people perturbed
him. It was the very first time in his life he had had such an overwhelming
sensation of his being and of his color" (30) and "Look at that man,
Mom, he forgot to wipe his make-up off!" (34). As Fara navigates his way
through the streets of Paris, he provides a comparative account of behavior and lifestyle and tests the geography and history he learned about in
Africa. These are now available to him in their commemorative forms as
monuments and street names (the Place de la Bastille, the mayoral office at
the Hôtel-de-Ville, the Cathedral of Notre-Dame, the Latin Quarter, the
University of the Sorbonne, the Luxembourg gardens, and the Pantheon)—namely the kind of *lieux de mémoire* (realms of memory, memory
sites) assembled by Pierre Nora in his multivolume study of the parameters of Frenchness and French identity.[55] The fact that Fara concentrates
on the topography of Paris prior to addressing the Exposition itself is important since it further complicates any assumptions one might have
about that which effectively constitutes the Other from Fara's perspective.
In actuality, Fara's francocentrism is central to this dynamic in which both
structural frameworks—Paris and Africa within Paris (the Exposition itself)—collapse in a complex network of closely intertwined referents and
signifiers, so that "if the city of Paris has failed to conform to Fara's literary
expectations, the exposition, in contrast, harmonizes perfectly with his old
mirages" (Miller, *Nationalists and Nomads,* 81). Accordingly, "the pavil-
ions of the exposition were designed to offer a mirage of the colonies, per-
mitting a new and fantastic kind of trip" (67).[56]

   Juxtaposed with the virtual ethnography of Paris Fara provides is the
Exposition itself. Having traversed the streets of Paris, Fara now comes
face to face with an official state-sponsored reconfiguration of the colonial
space (what Miller has described as a "state-sponsored hallucination"
[*Nationalists and Nomads,* 65]): "He made his way down the Grand Avenue of French Colonies. To his right, Martinique, Reunion, Guadeloupe"
(Socé, *Mirages de Paris,* 35). The fact that a francophone sub-Saharan African writer chose to discuss the Exposition is crucial to our understanding of French colonialism, and the centrality of this event in the history of
African-French relations cannot be underestimated. Indeed, the Exposition of 1931 can be said to represent "the apogee and the apotheosis of
French colonial mythmaking efforts; it seemed to express the greatest con-

fidence the French would ever have in their superiority and in the benevo-
lence of their mission to civilize" (Miller, *Nationalists and Nomads,* 65),
and "the exposition staged the colonial Republican project right in the
heart of Paris, a project at once claimed, glorified, and magnified" (Bancel,
Blanchard, and Vergès, 110). Furthermore, the Exposition was an important component of colonial propaganda, designed specifically with the intention of unifying French public opinion in favor of further consolidating
imperial power:

> The Exposition signaled the advent of a resolutely modern and planned con-
> ception of colonial propaganda: an immense media campaign was launched
> a year before its opening, and week after week every newspaper related the
> progress that had been made . . . It was conceived with the specific goal of
> endearing the colonial empire to the French people and of bringing together
> Western colonial powers through a shared glorification of the grandeur of
> the Occident. (Bancel, Blanchard, and Vergès, 111–112)[57]

Colonial education has afforded Fara a privileged understanding of
French culture and also familiarized him with the prevailing idea of Africa, one that he recuperates and performs—indeed, he is able to market
himself at the Exposition as a native informant: "I'm from there; I was
only captured two months ago! Ladies and gentleman, come closer! . . . To
see a real authentic negro close up, now that was really something . . . "
(Socé, *Mirages de Paris,* 36). From the sequential set of mirages (the Colonial Exposition) in which the bilateralism of Africa in France becomes indissociable from France in Africa itself (the colonial project), Fara's very
presence in France is of course a logical outcome of the colonial mission's
nature as an enterprise infused with mutually constitutive discourses. This
is a product of colonial discourse itself that ends up, as Mbembe has indicated, "producing a closed, solitary totality that it elevates to the rank of
generality . . . How could it be otherwise, since the actual is no longer perceived except through the mirror of a perversity that is, in truth, that of the
subject uttering this discourse? Colonial language thus advances, deaf to
its silent vibrations and endlessly repeating itself" (Mbembe, *On the Postcolony,* 178). Fara's most significant encounters in France emerge as a result of his presumed authority on Africa (wrongly presumed, as we shall
see), upon which he capitalizes in order to approach and initiate a conversation with two young French women, offering to serve as a guide: "I'm
from French West Africa . . . I could be your guide . . ." (Socé, *Mirages de
Paris,* 38). The relationship with Jacqueline that develops from this initial
encounter allows Fara to explore another facet of Paris as he shepherds
her through the vibrant nightlife, the intersection of a transnational global
blackness evidenced through Cuban music, the rumba, jazz, tam-tams,
clarinets, and trumpets. They attend the *bal nègre* (Negro ball) and the famous Cabane Cubaine nightclub in Montmartre. For Jacqueline, the club

becomes another version of the colonial exhibition: "In the throng of blacks gathered at the Cabane Cubaine, so similar in appearance, Fara introduced Jacqueline to Africans, Haitians, and Mauritians. People said this nightspot was an ethnographic museum of the black world, to which each nation had sent along a specimen" (55–56).

When the colonial exhibition ends, Fara decides to extend his stay in France in order to pursue his interest in Jacqueline, but also, of course, because of his francocentrism: "I have come to need the vertiginous perspectives of the capital, the multicolored enchantment of its evenings" (72–73). From this point on, he begins to uncover how French society really feels about him. He is well received by her parents when he is initially introduced to them as a friend, but ultimately their relationship is not acceptable to her social milieu, whose homeostasis is destabilized by their exogamous union. On the occasion of a dinner at her home, Fara is asked to provide them with his impressions of France. Rather than offering the anticipated answer, one that would endeavor to praise French society and thereby confirm their perceived notions of how a young African should express gratefulness for France's colonial generosity, he reverses the question by insisting instead on his surprise at French ignorance concerning Africans. This exposes the family's essentialism, but nevertheless in a less direct and confrontational manner than if he had simply accused them of racism:

> He evoked the ignorance of people here with regard to blacks. For the most part, their friends only talked about the faults and comicalness of the blacks, making these into their defining attributes by dwelling on them at length. In turn, cinema and literature come to their rescue, producing "exoticism" and "documentation" at the service of preconceived notions. (90)

Fara's own community in Paris is built around an African Diaspora that comes together in ways that would have been impossible in Africa: "This diverse world made up of blacks constituted Fara's guests. In Africa, they would have lived in different social spheres and would have set up hierarchies" (116). Through dialogue with other Africans, important thinking on colonialism takes place, and Fara articulates a position that effectively anticipates many of the problems of decolonization and the sociopolitical circumstances of the postcolony: "First, concluded Fara, must come economic emancipation, because a people in a state of economic inferiority will face enormous difficulty achieving political emancipation" (121). When Fara is confronted with the realities of racism in Paris and resistance to métissage, it is the music of Duke Ellington that provides the kind of therapeutic value it was to generate decades later in segregationist America during the struggle for civil rights, and that would be evoked in Emmanuel Dongala's *Jazz et vin de palme* through reference to the music of Coltrane: "Fara was transported into another world, one made of musical harmony and in which there was nothing to remind him of what had made him miserable" (166).[58] Socé's text is mediating some of the central debates of his era, and his novel can be seen as the "narrative of Ousmane Socé's positions on cultural métissage,"[59] a dimension evidenced in his first novel, *Karim,* which according to Midiohouan had "praised cultural métissage" (Midiohouan, *L'idéologie,* 72). As Alice Conklin argues,

> At the same time officials determined that Africans were too ethnically different ever to become culturally French, metropolitan publicists and colonial policymakers began to condemn the same sexual contact between the races that they had earlier tolerated; instead they endorsed white endogamy and traditional French family formation. Meanwhile, handbooks on life in the colonies not only reinforced this message but also spelled out more explicitly the degree of acceptable social mixing between the French and Africans . . . In the interwar years a variety of experts popularized the notion that the practice of interracial unions was dangerous for two reasons. First, the illegitimate offspring, the métis, of such unions were considered potentially as rebellious as the évolués with whom they were sometimes compared . . . The best way to avoid such a problem in the future, everyone agreed, was to ban *métissage* altogether. The second reason for the growing alarm about miscegenation was the fear that interracial sex might contribute to the degeneration of the white race. The very existence of métis children was proof of this degeneration.[60]

In this way, the Colonial Exposition plays a central role in its attempt at solidifying ethnic categories. "The *Exposition,*" as Hill argues, "works towards that hegemony in its underlying presupposition that colonial subjects are *definable* and *representable* . . . Here, difference, rather than simply posing a threat, becomes a constitutive element of empire. In fact, imperial *métissage* depends on the ability to define and represent in order to maintain the possibility of arbitrarily casting subjects in either a harmonious or menacing light" (Hill, 641–642). Ultimately, when Jacqueline dies at the end of her pregnancy, her parents recuperate the child. Fara's initial dream of Paris becomes a nightmare from which, as for many African protagonists, suicide provides the only escape. Yet, as Stovall has argued, "by bringing a central colonial anxiety, miscegenation, to the metropole, however, such contacts forecast the outlines of postcolonial conflicts in the late twentieth century."[61] Fara's francocentrism had led him to dream for years of the day he would walk the banks of the Seine in the mythic city of Paris; little did he know that from these very banks he would plunge to his death: "Delirious with happiness, Fara dived into the cold waters of the Seine River" (Socé, *Mirages de Paris,* 187).

The myth of Western superiority has rendered such unions contradictory to French interest—indeed, in the nineteenth century, Gobineau's thesis was organized around the supposition that the inequality of races was a reality. Many of these assumptions inform extreme right-wing politics in

Europe today in countries such as Belgium, France, Great Britain, Italy, and the Netherlands. The possibility of cohabitation is compromised precisely because the colonial system requires a hierarchical order that voids the potential of cross-cultural mixing between components that are perceived as unequal, much in the same way as multiculturalism is today rendered impossible by the monolithic imperatives of the French Republic.[62] However, as Lüsebrink has underlined, "as the colonial dream of a grand Euro-African empire was abandoned, the concept of métissage disintegrated shortly after making its initial appearance" ("Métissage et société coloniale," 218), and it would be some time before the question returned to the agenda of policymakers in the Hexagon. In *Mirages de Paris*, "*métissage* is thus given the appearance of a positive, life-affirming blend of cultures," but "is thus compromised by two kinds of problems: one is the political inequality governing relations; the other is the fog of illusions within which the exchanges take place" (Miller, *Nationalists and Nomads*, 86, 88). Accordingly, such transcolonial questions void the potential of métissage by highlighting that cultural and social synthesis are ultimately reciprocal, that is, founded through constitutive arrangements.[63]

Colonial education is a central issue in the work of Dadié, and was the subject of concerted analysis in his 1956 novel *Climbié,* in which the eponymous hero attends the famous Ecole Normale William Ponty.[64] The colonial school provides a contact zone between Africa and France, a privileged site for the dissemination of colonial propaganda and the fashioning of an imaginary space for the conditioning of colonial subjects. Dadié's *An African in Paris* shares numerous points of commonality with other francophone sub-Saharan African novels produced during the 1950s, principally, as Elisabeth Mudimbe-Boyi has remarked, the "triadic departure-adventure-return structure . . . which clearly identif[ies] it as a travel narrative," but it "is at the same time a novel of initiation and a didactic novel in which the narrator seeks to restore a pedagogical function to the journey. As in traditional folktales, the hero departs after he has been entrusted with a mission, one for which he will be accountable to his community."[65] As in the work of Camara, Kane, and Socé, among others, travel to France is also about the acquisition of cultural capital. "To go to Paris," Mudimbe-Boyi points out, "is to accomplish a rite of passage that transforms one into 'somebody' . . . departure implies a return to his starting point after he has completed a formative journey, the reward of which will be shared by the community" (Mudimbe-Boyi, "Travel Representation," 33–35). As we shall see in chapter 6, narrative circularity is a transcolonial phenomenon, one that can be compared to the equation of departure and descent that is inseparable from the secular quest of the postcolonial *sapeurs*. However, Dadié also treats this trajectory in a radically different manner. Whereas the novels of Socé, Camara, and Kane foreground displacement as the mode through which greater consciousness is achieved as a mechanism for deconditioning and questioning colonialism, Dadié's novel distances itself from this process in order to provide an unprecedented concentration on the foundations of the ideological project as a way of demystifying the fantasy of Occidental superiority.

In many ways, *An African in Paris* operates intertextually with *Mirages de Paris* to the extent that it claims to *see* Paris (and therefore, I would argue, France itself) through the eyes of a young African man in France for the first time. Both writers ultimately reach analogous conclusions concerning the contrived image of Paris crystallized in the minds of talented évolués, yet Dadié's novel aligns itself with a long tradition of travel diaries and narratives employed to formulate social critiques. This mediation with established literary conventions, achieved through the transposition of the young protagonist Tanhoe Bertin to France, is to be understood principally as confirmation of the acquired pedagogic accomplishments of the colonial subject, but also affords the writer the occasion to subvert the tradition. A considerable number of works have engaged in such practices—Ali Behdad, for example, considers some of these texts in the nineteenth century in his book *Belated Travelers: Orientalism in the Age of Colonial Dissolution,* and as we shall see in the next chapter, this intertextuality has also informed Sembene's novel *Black Docker.*[66] In the case of *An African in Paris,* it is achieved through recourse to a narrator who refuses to identify with and "accept" the distorted "portrait" the colonizer has drawn of him. "Willfully created and spread by the colonizer," Memmi writes, "this mythical and degrading portrait ends up by being accepted and lived with to a certain extent by the colonized. It thus acquires a certain amount of reality and contributes to the true portrait of the colonized" (Memmi, *The Colonizer and the Colonized,* 87–88), thereby competing with the myth itself and its imaginary life as it enters into circulation. Fara arrives in Paris with sublime confidence in his training yet blinded to the reality of his assimilated captivity; Tanhoe distinguishes between imitation and reality and acknowledges that colonial relations are stratified. With an enthusiasm comparable to that of Tanhoe's fellow African students, he learns that the topography is imminently shifting to the French capital: "Good news, my friend, good news! I have a ticket to Paris . . . yes, Paris! The very same Paris we've so often talked and dreamed about! I'll be leaving in a few days. Even I will be able to see Paris with my own eyes!" (Dadié, *An African in Paris,* 3). This opportunity provides Tanhoe with the structural framework to begin testing the earlier imaginative journey he had made to the land of his new ancestors the Gauls in the colonial classroom against the literal journey: "Soon I can stop thinking about the Paris I've only seen on postcards or in films, the Paris others wanted me to see" (4).

The first observations recorded for his interlocutor, to whom he writes the lengthy letter that constitutes the novel, concern the "constant movement," the way "the electric lights are left on during the day in restaurants and stores," and "the very nature" and "attitude" of the Parisians, who "enjoy their freedom. This is their city, and they know it. And to be a part of all this is irresistible" (17).[67] Tanhoe demonstrates his educational accomplishments, providing an official history of Paris structured around the French Revolution. The expressions, behaviors, mannerisms, codes, conventions, and etiquette of the French are contained in recurring descriptive modes and generalities that include observations on "the nature of the Parisians" (19). A plethora of information is also available on ethics, morality, marriage, divorce, religion, single motherhood, child-rearing conventions, eating and drinking practices, burial rites, café culture, the métro, and French women—in many ways, *An African in Paris* shares aspects with the kind of research undertaken by Pierre Bourdieu on "distinction,"[68] in which access to local culture requires "reading between the lines" (Dadié, *An African in Paris*, 52). Like other African protagonists, he becomes all too aware of ethnic identity: "Yes, it's true, I scare people—especially women and children. They see me coming and immediately try to escape; there's no getting beyond the initial expression—They must wonder what in the world possessed God to get the colors wrong and smear me with tar" (43). In this framework, the métro network becomes paradigmatic and symbolic of a broader commentary on French modernity:

> that enormous underground spider web which lures everyone is the perfect symbol of all those who built the marvels we're forever admiring . . . And it's when you're inside those corridors that you become most aware of the enormous love the Parisians have for what their machines have given them: the opportunity to play king. Machines do the work and have given the people the right to be lazy and enjoy life, the right to steal a bit of time, even from tomorrow. (56)

Of particular significance to the novel is Tanhoe's concerted effort to question his own methodology for critiquing France. Travel and colonial discourse on Africa had tended to formulate judgment and arrive at conclusions mediated exclusively through ethnocentrist constructs; aware of this tendency, Tanhoe attempts to avoid duplicating it by situating himself at the intersection of the training he has obtained in the colonial school and that he has received outside of it. This position allows him to navigate between multiple fields of discourse, and, thus equipped with greater objectivity, he can articulate a much more forceful critique of colonial ideology by exploring the inherently contradictory nature of colonial rhetoric against evidence acquired through fieldwork in the metropole. Instead of traveling outside of France, as Montesquieu had pretended to do in his book *Lettres persanes* (*Persian Letters*) in order to criticize French society, Tanhoe travels outside of empire—not to critique Africa, but rather to assess and measure French colonialism. Dadié ventriloquizes a new critique of the West in which his statement "I can safely say that one cannot get to know a people simply by reading what has been written about them"[69] clearly alludes to reductive ethnographic historiography. In so doing, Tanhoe recognizes the ironic component of his own discourse, and also of course its inherent limitations: "Parisians are like any other people; you can never say all there is to say about them. They overwhelm you, and it would be foolish to judge them as a group on the basis of only a few examples" (121). This acknowledgment and expression of awareness of the dangers of assuming a position of authority in the analysis of other cultures aligns Dadié's project with the concerns of a broad range of works produced by philosophers, sociologists, and cultural critics, most notably Jean-Loup Amselle's *Logiques métisses,* Christopher Miller's *Theories of Africans,* V. Y. Mudimbe's *The Idea of Africa,* and Françoise Lionnet's "*Logiques métisses:* Cultural Appropriation and Postcolonial Representation."[70]

As Mudimbe suggests, Amselle's *Mestizo Logics: Anthropology of Identity in Africa and Elsewhere* allows us

> to imagine the possibility of a reversal of anthropology's perspective. Essentially, *Mestizo Logics* is a critique of "ethnological reason," which, by definition, always extracts elements from their context, aestheticizes them, and then uses their presupposed differences for classifying types of political, economic, or religious ensembles.

Accordingly, Amselle's own "mestizo logics,"

> instead of distinguishing and separating, would bear witness to the "indistinction" or original syncretism of elements in a social totality and thus at least solve the dilemma opposing the "universality of human rights" and "cultural relativism," a dilemma which, in terms of political values, actualizes the tension and opposition between universality as totalitarianism and cultural relativism as an expression of democracy. (Mudimbe, *The Idea of Africa,* 52–53)

In the case of *An African in Paris,* the issue is not simply assuming the right to speak—that in and of itself would be a fairly redundant gesture—but also identifying what Dadié does not write as much as what he does. With this in mind, Dadié's project, rather than reproducing the "vertical axis of a hierarchical relationship" described by Mudimbe-Boyi, instead rethinks and reformulates the premise of the original foundational discourse erected around "value judgments, vocabulary with negative connotations, and normative binary oppositions" (Mudimbe-Boyi, "Travel Representation," 26, 32). As Mudimbe-Boyi shows, Dadié "resists a metonymic reduction," then "relativizes the results of his observation," and therefore ensures that the reader remains "on guard against overgeneralizations and categorical pronouncements" (33). The strength of the work and the analysis originates in the gesture of forfeiting the pitfalls of a repetitive formula, given that the central logic informing colonial expansion can be located in a complex set of projections that require demystification rather than a counter-discourse or oppositional narrative. In colonial discourse, "cultural differences are transformed into moral differences that justify and legitimize the missionary and colonizing enterprise" (31). This distancing from colonial narratives is central to the novel, since "Dadié's traveler has urged readers to accept alterity and difference in the acceptance of a shared humanity" (35)—the novel becomes a demonstration of this argument, and "Dadié's authoritative narrator expresses himself as the one who experienced what he is recording, and not as the inheritor of an intertextuality or of an ideology" (35). Tanhoe confirms this position when he writes to his friend, "Haven't we all—every single one of us—admitted to ourselves that all people are alike? We keep talking about different customs, different countries, different cultures, and different races, but in the final analysis isn't everyone the same?" (Dadié, *An African in Paris,* 128).[71]

Accordingly, *An African in Paris* goes beyond the parameters of the negritude project, which was primarily concerned with rehabilitating blackness and black culture. We are dealing with a complex network of carefully codified projections that, according to Mudimbe-Boyi, "creates, invents, and orders everything in terms of itself. In this context, the Other tends to become, in one way or another, a reflection of the Self" (Mudimbe-Boyi, "Travel Representation," 31), and the objectives of negritude become not so much futile but rather less productive than Dadié's unexpected attempt to engage directly with the anxieties, insecurities, needs, paranoia, or even the "hysteria" of the colonizing body.[72] "The civilizing project," André-Patient Bokiba argues in his book *Ecriture et identité dans la littérature africaine,* "implies the dislocation of all these stereotypes and the restructuring of the black psyche according to a new set of values"; necessarily, then, "the civilizer must form a reassuring image both of himself (or herself) and the other that is likely to provide ethical justification for his (or her) actions."[73] Jean-Pierre Makouta-Mboukou has devoted considerable attention to this question in *Introduction à l'étude du roman négro-africain de langue française,* underlining the centrality of such an action:

> Demystifying a phenomenon, an event, a crude fact, consists in demonstrating how both the images one has formed and the explanations one has provided are false, and admitting that one deliberately sought to deceive. Furthermore, the process of demystification, in order to effectively dispel the error or the lie, must also include a demythologizing component. For, once one has denounced the error, things must be brought back to their just dimensions, to their real value.[74]

The francophone writer must therefore endeavor to both "demystify" and "demythologize" those received attributes of blackness. Edward Said per-

formed an analogous task in his seminal work *Orientalism.*[75] As we saw in
the previous section, the Colonial Exposition itself "had allowed for a
popularization of an ethnocentrist vision" (Bancel, Blanchard, and Vèrges,
114) and served as a powerful agent in consolidating the "idea" of Africans. Dadié's novel is effective because it addresses the imperative of demystification, and "the irony of this situation," Mudimbe-Boyi argues, "resides in the inversion of the gaze: the West, formerly the sovereign gaze and
the master word, is now being identified as the Other" (Mudimbe-Boyi,
"Travel Representation," 29). This is a subversive gesture that serves in
turn to undermine the premise of the colonial project itself by demonstrating that the logic informing the stratification of imperial relations is un-
founded.

Dadié's original methodology is organized around formulations that
are more complex than simple irony, since his commentary specifically
functions as a result of the bilateral training he has received in a French
colonial school in Africa. The title of the novel naturally confirms the pejorative dimension of blackness itself as a colonial construct (one which
Sembene also fastens on in *Black Docker*), an inescapable somatic factor
that differentiates Tanhoe from the people around him in Paris: "There's
no disputing the fact that I'm different from the Parisian, and not simply
because my skin is darker. We think differently too. Moreover, they're surrounded by all those mechanical toys few of us have—refrigerators, tele-
phones . . . Perhaps I should try to imitate them, but in some things I don't
see any way we can close the gap that separates us" (Dadié, *An African in
Paris,* 151). Later, Tanhoe's formulations are hardly ambiguous: "These
people who'd never consent to put a man, much less a whole group of
men, in chains" (90) and, "In fact, if Paris were to decide to gain control of
another country, it would be to institute justice and liberty for everyone"
(119). In his discussion of Dadié's novel and its connections with Montesquieu's *Lettres persanes,* Jean Derive locates the intertextuality of *An
African in Paris* in French pedagogic practices: "What is absolutely certain
is that through his secondary education, he could not have failed to know
this work, at least sufficient excerpts of it to familiarize himself with the
principles according to which it functioned."[76] That Derive immediately
qualifies his remarks by adding "This reference to intertextuality is not an
attempt to either question or diminish the originality of Dadié's vision,
which in any case has nothing to with plagiarism" (Derive, "*Un nègre à
Paris,*" 196) is significant—indeed, questions of intertextuality, plagiarism,
and recycling will be central to the analysis of Sembene's novel *Black
Docker* in the next chapter. The fact that Dadié attended French colonial
school means that his frame of reference includes French historiography,
and therefore he positions himself in dialogue or mediation with this extensive corpus, particularly with what Derive calls the "negative intertextuality" that has "contributed to inscribing a negative image of the Negro

in French mentality" (198). Paradoxically, he emerges as a "francophone" writer because of this trajectory, revealing one of the central paradoxes of Francophonie itself: the text "is as much addressed to a French audience as it is to a francophone African one" (197).

The successful dismantling and demystification of the myth of French superiority of course depends on Dadié's ability to engage with the central principles of these works, and the originality comes from the fact that, in this case, the "foreigner" looking at France "is a colonized subject observing civilization from within its metropole" (Derive, "*Un nègre à Paris,*" 196). Tanhoe can operate in this domain because he is a dual insider, both colonized and educated, marked by colonial pedagogy but also an authoritative informant on the African component of his training, which the colonizer has been incapable of penetrating precisely because the reductive discourse of anthropology perceived itself as a "means of gaining local 'knowledge' and as a reflection of European preoccupations projected onto Africa" (Miller, *Theories of Africans,* 139). Tanhoe's claim that "to know, appreciate, and love a people, you must study their history" (Dadié, *An African in Paris,* 85) unambiguously indicts the French colonial project for its failure to do so, favoring instead a reductionist, uninformed view of Africa as the justificatory discourse for colonial expansionism. In this way, *An African in Paris* undertakes the crucial task of correcting negative constructs of Africans—Dadié is so effective at doing this that he does not even need to mention or designate the stereotype in question, since "he is well aware of its presence in the collective imaginary of his French and African readers" (Derive, "*Un nègre à Paris,*" 199). For this reason, the novel should be accorded more critical attention than it has hitherto received, particularly in light of contemporary debates on immigration in France in which such reductive images survive and inform right-wing political strategies and exclusionary discourses. The originality of *An African in Paris* comes not from an aggressive, direct attack on France, but rather from an uncompromising and carefully formulated engagement with stereotypes and projections, systematically unpacking one after the other and revealing their fallacious foundations: "his way of fighting against colonial ideology consists in exposing the futility of this perspective" (Derive, "*Un nègre à Paris,*" 208). *An African in Paris* is a text that provides the reader with a carefully formulated and insightful analysis of France on the eve of decolonization; but it is also a text that has survived its historical moment, and its formulations and observations have much to reveal to us today about the foundations of the Occidentalist discourse of cultural superiority that continues to inform immigration discourse in France at the beginning of the twenty-first century.

Laye, Samba, Fara, and Tanhoe are the symbols of a generation of young Africans who have explored the migration of memory and of the imagination. As Irele has concluded in his book *The African Imagination: Literature in Africa and the Black Diaspora,* the moral perceptions that inform the African sense of racial and historical grievance issue into a comprehensive critique of the West, a questioning of its assumptions about itself and of its vision of the world. Under the pressure of experience, our writers have had to undertake a critical reassessment of the colonizer, of the philosophy of life that is assumed to underlie his disposition toward the world, and anticipate in the course of this reassessment some of the key strategies of contemporary Western thought.[77]

In Oyono's *Chemin d'Europe,* a similar project is undertaken by the central protagonist, Barnabas, as he claims, "I felt such a strong affinity for this country that I did not know and whose genius and beauty I had been taught to sing since childhood, that I wondered whether I had not perhaps been French in a previous life" (45). Again, the community places its faith in a young man whose anticipated return to Africa, having acquired cultural and economic capital, is invested with a double meaning, both physical and economic: he is "determined to travel across the oceans to distant shores to conquer notoriety" (101). However, the broadening of the framework to include Europe as early as the work's title hinted at the kinds of migration networks that the era of postcoloniality would witness, as young Africans continue to this day to migrate from Africa to the North in pursuit of cultural, economic, and social capital. Protagonists who came to France and Europe during the colonial era in the spirit of discovery later evoked feelings of exile and nostalgia, and their displacement usually resulted in disillusionment, return, suicide, or death (physical and social), as the experiential and evidentiary modes rarely coincided with the mythic constructs they departed with. For the new generation of migrants, passage to Europe is a complex process, one that has introduced a new lexicon with terms such "detention centers," "refugee status," "camps," "clandestinity," and *sans-papiers.* Nevertheless, the conclusions and findings of subsequent chapters all point to the transcoloniality of the central problematic informing the migration process, whether the protagonists in question are students, travelers, *sapeurs,* workers, or clandestine subjects.

THREE

Textual Ownership and the Global Mediation of Blackness

But I am African. Why would I go
looking for something in the United
States? I don't have to search for an
identity. I'm an African. For me,
Africa is the centre of the world.
The United States and Europe are
on the periphery of my world.

Ousmane Sembene[1]

The two historically possible solutions
are then tried in succession or
simultaneously. He attempts either
to become different or to reconquer
all the dimensions which colonization
tore away from him.

Albert Memmi[2]

Will verify subject's residence and ascertain his activities upon his return
to the United States from France,
presumably in September, 1946.
If possible, secure the subject's
reason for his trip to France.

Federal Bureau of Investigation
file on Richard Wright[3]

Colonialism and the accompanying violence of Western language literacy,
which was indissociable from the pedagogic mechanisms of the French
imperial ambition, have left indelible marks on francophone literary production. In fact, francophone writers have by definition been compelled to
mediate their aesthetic and political projects through a linguistic domain

that is inextricably linked to this historical context. This mediation has led writers to align themselves with or distance themselves from existing models, inaugurating a paradoxical gesture, given that each choice has served to reinscribe the centrality of the very paradigm whose periphery they sought. Postcolonial theory has addressed these circumstances through concepts such as "abrogation" (which "involves a rejection of the metropolitan power over the means of communication") and "appropriation" (through which "language is adopted as a tool and utilized in various ways to express widely differing cultural practices").[4] As useful as this terminology may be, it does not explicitly incorporate the broader lexicon to which it is tangentially connected though categories such as intertextuality, plagiarism, and recycling.

Francophone writers have invariably found themselves ensnared in complex creative circumstances requiring a mediation with established aesthetic conventions. While innovation is of course a precondition for the transformation, mutation, and survival of literary genres—from Oulipo, the *nouveau roman,* and magic realism to reformulations of various postmodernist models—francophone texts have only rarely been embraced for their originality.[5] Critics have often generated the kinds of reductive readings epitomized by Jacques Chevrier, who argues, "One must agree that the novel is, to a great extent, a Western form imposed on Africa as the consequence of the brutal encounter between two cultures, and one can easily recognize Balzac and Zola in the literary models that have for the most part inspired Negro-African novelists of French expression."[6] The claim that African writers are merely Black variations of canonical authors has of course been denounced by a range of critics, who have insisted on the intrinsic originality of francophone texts by adopting anthropological approaches to the study of literature (Miller), explored the centrality of ideology (Irele), or maintained the validity of theorizing the national (Bjornson, Huannou, Midiohouan, Thomas) in order to account for the specificity of cultural and sociopolitical circumstances.[7] In turn, many francophone sub-Saharan African writers have challenged and even played with these assumptions in their attempt to confuse these power relations. Asking in his essay "Orphée noir" ("Black Orpheus") what negritude might be, Jean-Paul Sartre is paradoxically forced to acknowledge the incapacity of language to define the term: "European languages do not have the vocabulary with which to explain the term."[8] In turn, Sony Labou Tansi claimed, "I have never had recourse to French, it is rather French that has had recourse to me," insisting on the imperative of political engagement while foregrounding creative integrity.[9]

Fundamental questions pertaining to textual ownership remain central to critical readings of texts produced by francophone practitioners, and there is a strong record of scholarship on the most notable cases: those of Yambo Ouologuem, Calixthe Beyala, and Laye Camara.[10] In fact, these

considerations have been central to literary analysis and criticism for some
time now; for example, theoreticians such as Julia Kristeva and Roland
Barthes stressed the importance of considering intertextuality, and Jacques
Derrida's theory of deconstruction emerged from the concern with exploring the tenuous relationship of and the contradictions between the writer's consciousness and his or her projects, the various intertextual influences that invariably inform the process of creativity; and in doing so it
complicated questions of textual ownership.[11]

The objective of this chapter will be to consider Ousmane Sembene's
1956 novel *Black Docker* within a transcolonial and transnational framework that will attend to the connections between this work and a range of
other texts generated by African, African American, Caribbean, and European authors.[12] This case study of Sembene's novel will focus on a different facet of the question of textual ownership in order to highlight the
manner in which these questions are so often inextricably linked to colonial stereotyping. Although Sembene's text received relatively little detailed critical attention from the leading scholars among the generation of
critical pioneers in francophone sub-Saharan African studies (chronologically these would include Lilyan Kesteloot, Dorothy Blair, Jacques Chevrier, and Bernard Mouralis), this novel has been the subject of renewed
criticism organized around questions of intertextuality in essays by Wilfried Feuser (1986), János Riesz (1995), Anthère Nzabatzinda (1995), Sélom
Gbanou (1997), and David Murphy (2000).[13] This chapter builds on the
scholarly intertextuality currently available to us (as each critic further extends the parameters of the debate by building on earlier analyses), situates this discourse according to the coordinates provided by an African
and African American critical apparatus, and takes the debate in a new direction by demonstrating how the mediation between Sembene's work
and Richard Wright's 1940 novel *Native Son* complicates the neutrality of
terms such as "intertextuality" and "recycling."[14]

Much of the following discussion will be less concerned with the question of establishing "borrowings"—although this constitutes an integral
component of the argument I am formulating—than with exploring and
underscoring how writers with different national origins function intertextually to approach the evidentiary mode provided by analogous sociocultural circumstances. As a point of entry, I want to consider an interview
conducted by David Murphy in 1995 with Sembene:

Murphy: Your first novel, *Black Docker,* deals with the African commu-
          nity in Marseilles during the 1950s. The Jamaican writer, Claude
          McKay, also deals with the black community during an earlier
          period, the 1920s, in his novel, *Banjo.* Had you read this book
          before writing *Black Docker*?
Sembene: No, I hadn't read it. I still haven't read it either. I don't think it
          was available during the colonial period . . .

Murphy: During this period, did you identify more with the work of black
            writers from the United States like Richard Wright, James Bald-
            win, Ralph Ellison, than with the works of African writers who
            wrote about a mythical Africa of the past?

Sembene: But I *am* African. Why would I go looking for something in the
            United States? I don't have to search for an identity. I'm an Afri-
            can. For me, Africa is the centre of the world. The United States
            and Europe are on the periphery of my world. (Sembene, "Inter-
            view at Filmi Doomireew," 227–228)

Sembene is known for being rather direct during interviews, and I am not
suggesting that his dismissal of African American writers or even his reluctance to follow this line of questioning constitutes an attempt to conceal the role of intertextuality between his work and that of his transatlantic counterparts—in fact, as I will show, Sembene has acknowledged
elsewhere that he had read African American works. Furthermore, he reiterated a similar statement at the Cannes Film Festival in 2004, where his
film *Molaade* was screened: "Europeans don't care whether or not Africa
is represented. It's not their navel. Much in the same way that they are not
our center. Europe is our periphery."[15] In both instances, Sembene an-
nounces his sensitivity to the recuperation of African productions by the
former metropolitan center of empire. Nevertheless, the Afrocentrist tone
of his statements is striking, and raises important questions concerning
the influence of African American and diasporic writing on his work, and
also the nature of reciprocal influences between African and African
American writers. As Michel Fabre has argued in his book *From Harlem
to Paris: Black American Writers in France, 1840–1980,* "Of all the Afro-
American writers who resided in France between the two world wars,
Claude McKay remained there the longest and mixed most with all sorts
of people—black and white, American and French, European and African—in both Paris and the provinces. He also derives inspirations from
his French experience, not only in *Banjo,* in which Marseilles plays more
than a background role, but in a number of essays analyzing the complex
class and race relations in Western Europe."[16] Even though Sembene circulated outside the Parisian and Black intelligentsia during his stay in France
from 1948 to 1960, he could not have been immune to a broader public
discourse pertaining to the cultural and socioeconomic circumstances of a
global blackness. Prior to exploring in detail specific borrowings from
Wright's work, I want to consider this discursive realm in France during
Sembene's residency.

In the interview by Murphy, Sembene expresses doubt that Claude
McKay's *Banjo: A Story without a Plot* was available during the colonial
era. Initially published in 1929 in New York by Harper and Brothers, the
novel was translated as *Banjo* by Ida Treat and Paul Vaillant-Couturier
and published by Editions Rieder in 1931.[17] According to Kesteloot,

Banjo's success did not stop with the first "triumvirate" of black writers. Ousmane Socé pointed out during the same period in *Mirages de Paris* that *Banjo* was displayed in black-student bookshelves right next to books by Delafosse . . . Ousmane Sembene in *Le docker noir* was more influenced by *Banjo* than by the novels of Richard Wright, to which *Le docker noir* is occasionally compared. (Kesteloot, 72–73)

Murphy's essay on *Black Docker* and *Banjo* convincingly challenges Kesteloot's assumptions concerning Sembene's relationship to McKay's work, highlighting thematic commonalities but arguing that any so-called intertextuality has more to do with what I have called a broader public discourse on global blackness: "In spite of Lilyan Kesteloot's claim that *Black Docker* was influenced by *Banjo,* it would seem that Sembene had never read McKay's book, even if he was aware of its reputation and had met people who had known the Afro-American writer during his stay in Marseilles" (Murphy, "La danse et la parole," 464). While in both texts the central protagonists (Ray and Diaw) are writers in Marseilles, there are fundamental theoretical and political differences between the two projects. Murphy shows how a juxtaposition of these works "allows us to rethink the very notion of a 'black' identity that would bring together Africans and blacks in the diaspora under a single banner" (464). For example, "the celebration of an energetic and spontaneous black community one finds in McKay's work is a long way from the description of an oppressed and marginalized black community in Sembene's" (465), and for Sembene, "there is such a thing as a black identity, but it has its roots in a shared history and culture rather than in a black essence" (470). The transatlantic connection needs to be further theorized in order to recognize not just the obvious interhistoricity, but also the distinctive trajectories that new demands and exigencies have placed on the transplanted subject:

What distinguishes African and Afro-American writers is that the former were raised in a black culture which, in spite of the upheavals of the slave trade and colonization, continues to express an African cultural identity . . . On the other hand, Afro-American writers, severed from ancestral lands and cultures by slavery, are now in a precarious position between an African culture they no longer belong to and an American culture that rejects them. (468)

Manthia Diawara, in his book *In Search of Africa,* has also addressed the important question of "the mental and moral disposition of the racialized subject."[18] My point, however, is to follow up on Kesteloot's concluding remark in order to highlight how it is precisely to Wright's work that we should be looking for analogies.[19]

As Tyler Stovall has argued in his book *Paris Noir: African Americans in the City of Light,* "the perceived difference between racial attitudes in

France and the United States has given a singular political dimension to the history of African Americans in Paris that distinguishes it sharply from the experience of white expatriates" (xiii). Americans in general were able to do things in France they could not do in the United States under the prevailing climate of McCarthyism, anti-Communism, and the politics of racial segregation, although of course fascination with America itself existed in other cultural and economic domains.[20] Naturally, the characterization of France uniquely in terms of a discourse of salvation occluded a range of complex sociopolitical issues in France pertaining to the colonial project, including, of course, the rise of German fascism, which was itself very much informed by a discourse of white racial supremacy (most memorably during the 1936 Berlin Olympics at which, much to Hitler's dismay, the Black American athlete Jesse Owens won four gold medals). The imperative to signal such inherent contradictions between the way African Americans were received and welcomed and the way African colonial subjects were treated is very much a contemporary theme, since Black American culture (music, film, fashion, and literature) is accorded particular attention in France at a time when the reductive stereotyping of immigrant African populations continues to be symbiotically linked to colonial constructs.[21] The fact nevertheless remains that France, and Paris in particular, emerged as a vibrant and receptive site for the formulation of global blackness. According to Brent Hayes Edwards, in his book *The Practice of Diaspora: Literature, Translation, and the Rise of Black Internationalism,* "Paris is crucial because it allowed boundary crossing, conversations, and collaborations that were available nowhere else to the same degree," and "the larger point is that one can approach such a project only by attending to the ways that discourses of internationalism *travel,* the ways they are translated, disseminated, reformulated, and debated in transnational contexts marked by difference."[22] Given Sembene's own growing politicization after his arrival in France, the plight of African Americans would have been of particular interest and concern to him. My concern at this juncture is then with establishing the kinds of discourses Sembene would have been exposed to and drawn creative and political inspiration from.

In one of the epigraphs to this chapter, the FBI requests that its agent monitoring Wright's activities in France ascertain "the subject's reason for his trip to France." Although the request seems to have been written with no sense of irony, the "reasons" are obvious to an informed observer of post-1945 American society—in fact, to this day, even though these files are in the public domain, this material remains sensitive. As Fabre has insisted, "above and beyond the encounter of black America and France, Paris was becoming more and more a melting pot for the different groups of the black diaspora. An entire dimension of the intellectual history of the black world was formed in France," and Paris enjoyed its resulting reputa-

tion as "a cultural cradle where literary achievement was held in rever-
ence" (Fabre, *From Harlem to Paris,* 8, 175).[23] Major African American
writers arrived in Paris after the Second World War, including Richard
Wright in 1946, James Baldwin in 1949, and Chester Himes in 1953:
"Guidebooks are keys to museums and monuments of the past more than
to living places where everything is in constant change, and with time
Paris has become a vast monument that new generations of black visitors
come to sample" (Fabre, *From Harlem to Paris,* 338). As I have already insisted, criticism of France and of its colonial mission is also essential to
any claim to objectivity about the broader social context. As Miller has
noted concerning Claude McKay, who lived in France from 1922 to 1934,
"McKay attacks racial prejudice in several national forms, each of which
is shown to be self-blind; principally, he compares racism in the United
States and in France,"[24] a point underscored by Murphy, who says that
McKay "criticized his Afro-American *confrère* for refusing to acknowledge the realities of French colonialism and of the racism that existed in
France" (Murphy, "La danse et la parole," 466).[25]

Global blackness also needs to be considered by taking into account a
range of social forces contributing to the formation of diasporic communities. While obvious factors connect populations on the African continent
with African immigrants in France and African Americans, it remains of
paramount importance to avoid the temptation of reformulating these
analogies in terms of a homogeneous diasporic community. For example,
McKay's *Banjo* features a Café African, in which "the Negro-Negroid
population of the town divides sharply into groups" (McKay, *Banjo,* 45),
whereas Sembene's *Black Docker* "describes a black community in which
there are rigid hierarchies that place Antilleans above the Senegalese (a
name that has come to designate all Negro-Africans and that reveals the
disdainful attitude toward Africans)" (Murphy, "La danse et la parole,"
466), all of whom gather at the local "multicultural" café: "In this little Africa in the south of France, all the countries, all the different ethnic groups
were represented. In keeping with the customs of their native land, each
territory had its own boundaries: the cafés. Prejudices and origins were often the subject of argument" (Sembene, *Black Docker,* 41).

Banjo entered the field of discourse on global blackness in France very
early on. In fact, as Edwards has shown, "the glowing reception of *Banjo*
in metropolitan Francophone circles was cemented by the publication of a
section of the novel in the journal *Légitime Défense* in June 1932" (B. Edwards, 191). His work also appeared in an earlier journal, *La revue du
monde noire,* and "*Banjo* was just as indispensable for the students who
would go on to found the Négritude movement" (187). Significantly,
"Damas claimed that he, Césaire, and Léopold Sédar Senghor" shared the
book with "their fellow black students" (187–188). As we shall see, these
are just a few examples of the remarkable attention accorded to African

American and Caribbean writing and society in France at the time, a factor that is inextricably linked to broader intertextual processes and mechanisms.

Wright's work appeared in the very first volume of *Les temps modernes,* published October 1, 1945.[26] This was to be the beginning of an important collaborative relationship with the journal, one that was defined
by the serialization of his novel *Black Boy* (*Jeunesse noire*) in a translation
by Marcel Duhamel in issues 16–21 (January–June 1947). Some of Wright's
most important and provocative essays were also published in the journal,
including "Littérature noire américaine" ("Black American Literature,"
1948) and "J'ai essayé d'être communiste" ("I Tried to Be a Communist,"
1949).[27] *Les temps modernes* was an important medium for disseminating
the work of Black intellectuals and for thinking about blackness in general. Alongside Wright's work, one could find Edouard Glissant's "Terre à
Terre" ("Earth to Earth," 1948), Jean-Paul Sartre's essay "Orphée noir"
("Black Orpheus," 1948), and Michel Leiris's "Martinique, Guadeloupe,
Haiti" (1950), and the journal also featured a selection of francophone po-
ets (Léon Gontran Damas, Léopold Sédar Senghor, Aimé Césaire, Jacques
Roumain, Jean-Joseph Rabéarivelo, and Jacques Rabémanajara) from
Senghor's forthcoming anthology, *Anthologie de la nouvelle poésie nègre
et malgache de langue française* (*Anthology of New Black and Malagasy
Poetry in French*).[28]

These fertile cross-cultural exchanges were of course central to the mis-
sion of the journal and publishing house Présence Africaine. Indeed, the
Comité de patronage (editorial board) of the inaugural issue of *Présence
africaine* in 1947 included such figures as Albert Camus, Aimé Césaire,
Bernard Dadié, André Gide, Paul Hazoumé, Michel Leiris, Léopold Sédar
Senghor, and Richard Wright, thereby reinforcing the dialogue between
Africa, African America, the Caribbean, and France.[29] As in the first issue
of *Les temps modernes,* an excerpt from Wright's work[30] appeared alongside works by many other significant authors: a preface by André Gide
and contributions from Sartre ("Présence noire" ["Black Presence"]), sociologist Georges Balandier ("Le noir est un homme" ["The Black Is a
Man"]), and African writers such as Senghor, Dadié, and Birago Diop. In
addition to his own work, Wright also cotranslated with Thomas Diop the
closing essay by Alioune Diop, the founder of *Présence africaine:* "Niam
n'goura or Présence Africaine's Raison d'Etre." Perhaps even more significant is the inclusion of a review by Madeleine Gautier of Wright's novel
Native Son (*Un enfant du pays*).[31]

These collaborative ventures culminated in the organization of the
First Congress of Scholars of the Negro World, held in France September
19–22, 1956.[32] The importance of the event and its perceived menace to
transnational politics is perhaps confirmed by the attention accorded to
the project by the FBI:

> Subject: First Congress of the *Présence Africaine:* A Congress of Scholars of
> the Negro world, sponsored by the leftist *Présence Africaine* is scheduled to
> take place in Paris September 19–22, 1956 . . . The Embassy has been in-
> formed that *Présence Africaine* for a time received a subsidy from the French
> Government which was subsequently discontinued because of the leftist anti-
> colonial and generally irresponsible nature of its editorial policy. (FBI,
> Wright file, 54)

As a response to (and an example of) mediation between Africa and Afri-
can America, Wright published his response to Senghor's intervention
("L'esprit de la civilisation ou les lois de la culture négro-africaine" ["The
Spirit of Civilization or the Laws of Negro-African Culture"]) at the Congress as "Tradition and Industrialization: The Plight of the Tragic Elite in
Africa."[33] As Jules-Rosette has shown, "Richard Wright and other American delegates . . . objected to imposing the concept of colonialism on black
Americans and argued that their situation of racial oppression was historically different because it involved an active legal, educational, and political struggle within an established national framework" (Jules-Rosette,
Black Paris, 53). This tenuousness between African and African American
positionalities in 1956 did nothing to diminish the remarkable critical reception of Wright's work in France, which dated back to the publication
in French of *Native Son* (*Un enfant du pays*) in 1947. Yet, as Fabre has
noted, "going to France, when one was *the* foremost black American
writer, was not without implications" (Fabre, *From Harlem to Paris*, 176),
since he was accorded, as Paul Gilroy has shown, the "role of advocate for
the immiserated Negroes whose society he had himself partially escaped."[34] The novel was rewritten for the theater in 1941 by Orson Welles,
and in 1950 the French director Pierre Chenal adapted the novel for the
screen and released the film as *Sangre negra*.[35] Wright was, simply put, the
talk of the town.[36] His work was located at the intersection of some of the
most influential masterpieces of the era, fostering and generating all kinds
of intertextual gestures. In 1953, his own novel *The Outsider* (*Le transfuge*) established a link with Albert Camus's *L'étranger,* much in the same
way as Laye Camara's *L'enfant noir* (*The Dark Child*) would add to this
legacy in 1954.[37] Wright's work and central role in public discourse in
France could not be ignored. Sembene would have been able to read the
translations of Wright's work published in *Les temps modernes* or *Présence africaine,* and even if he did not read those journals, Wright's novels
were widely accessible. On some level, he may not have been looking to
African American writers for validation and inspiration. The interesting
question, though, is what an African writer such as Sembene perceived as
African American versus simply "Black" in his encounters with the translated works of those anglophone writers in the mid-century. Kesteloot has
paid particular attention to the question of literary influences on francophone authors, for whom texts are necessarily imbricated with multiple

literary and political traditions—orality, colonialism, ethnic and national literatures, American, European, and "Negro" literature. Her findings have much to reveal in the context of this analysis.[38]

In her book *Black Writers in French,* Kesteloot surveys more than twenty authors who were active in 1960. Her stated rationale is the following: "It is always interesting, of course, to know the origins of a work and the circumstances surrounding it. Where black authors are concerned, we have found this *indispensable* because their responses differ greatly from those of white Europeans . . . and above all because their works are situated morally and historically in a very specific context" (298–299). Statistics can of course only reveal part of a problematic, but they do add an important component to this investigation. The twenty-one questions she asked of writers include

Question 3:   What, at the time, did you wish to create?
Question 6:   To which writers do you feel closest today and why? To white writers? Which ones? Black writers? Which ones?
Question 16: How do you conceive your role as a writer? [first option:] As an interpreter of Negro problems? (300–301)

My concern here is with extracting as much information as possible about Sembene from this survey. The survey looks at a time very early on in Sembene's career, but of course after the publication of *Black Docker,* which is the focus of my inquiry. Kesteloot underlines that Sembene is somewhat different from his literary counterparts, given that he "alone has only an elementary school education. As a stevedore in Marseilles, he was union-educated and disapproves of Parisian intellectuals, whom he considers 'too bourgeois'" (304). Yet, significantly, "Ousmane Sembene's lower educational level may influence his style but has no clear repercussion on his ideas, which are the same as the other writers'" (304). According to the survey, "Black American novelists were much more widely read by French-speaking writers than black American poets. The elder generation especially liked Claude McKay and Langston Hughes. The young had read Richard Wright and Chester Himes and were not indifferent to their violent realism" (307). The original French version of Kesteloot's study is much more revealing for the purposes of my argument, since it includes information on individual authors that is not available in the English version.[39]

In table 2, "Influences littéraires" ("Literary Influences," Kesteloot, "Situation actuelle," 283), Sembene acknowledges French and Russian influences in the "Influences occidentales" ("Western influences") category and, along with Mongo Béti, Césaire, Damas, Senghor, and Tchicaya U Tam'si, identifies American influences in the "Influences nègres" ("Black influences") category, but not traditional (folktales, proverbs, etc.) or modern African texts. These findings of course contradict Sembene's statements in the interview by Murphy cited earlier. In table 3, "Influences idé-ologiques" ("Ideological Influences," 288) Sembene designates Christian-ity, Marxism-Socialism, Islam, intellectual traditionalism, and concrete traditionalism as factors. In table 4 (293), he underscores as his personal goals and intellectual responsibilities serving as a spokesman for black people, contributing to the liberation of Negro people, expressing himself, and educating the black masses. These concerns are reiterated in table 7 (308), in which Sembene selects questions of accessibility and political engagement as central to his choice of literary genres.

While terms such as "intertextuality," "plagiarism," and "recycling" overlap in various ways, there are important differences between them and we need to be clear about these. Questions of intertextuality are linked to the specific analogies and established linkages between literary products, while "recycling" designates the reincorporation of factors constitutive of the public domain of global blackness. "Plagiarism" in turn introduces a radically different set of meanings, when the transposition of material from one text to another raises doubts about originality and creative agency. The novels of Sembene and Wright are engaged in a complex process of mediation in multiple ways that we shall return to at length, but "intertextuality" might incorporate similarities between the indissociabil-ity of race and criminality in both texts, argumentation in the courtroom, characterization of alleged murderers in newspapers, appeals to justice to restore social homeostasis, and so on, while "recycling" would designate the common systems of referentiality signified by a lexicon including terms such as "segregation," "Harlem," "racism," "Communism," and "slavery."

Henry Louis Gates's book *The Signifying Monkey: A Theory of Afri-can-American Literary Criticism* has proved foundational to any reflec-tion on the question of borrowing and intertextuality.[40] To my earlier com-ments concerning the processes of "abrogation" and "appropriation" in postcolonial literature, Gates adds an important dimension: "Black writ-ers . . . learn to write by reading literature, especially the canonical texts of the Western tradition. Consequently, black texts resemble other, Western texts . . . But black formal repetition always repeats with a difference, a black difference that manifests itself in specific language use" (xxii–xxiii). For Gates, "intertextuality represents a process of repetition and revision" (60), and

> signifyin(g) is the black rhetorical difference that negotiates the language user through several orders of meaning. In formal literature, what we com-monly call figuration corresponds to Signification. Again, the originality of so much of the black tradition emphasizes refiguration, or repetition and difference, or troping, underscoring the foregrounding of the chain of signi-fiers, rather than the mimetic representation of a novel content. (79)

The central question is whether or not Sembene's novel can add itself to a compound chain of signifiers, or must be relegated to the category reserved for works that have engaged in a perceived "excessive amount of 'borrowing'" (Miller, *Blank Darkness*, 218).

As Miller has pointed out, the historical background is crucial in understanding questions of intertextuality: "Texts on Africa were severely limited in number until the nineteenth century and tended to repeat each other in a sort of cannibalistic, plagiarizing intertextuality" (Miller, *Blank Darkness*, 6).[41] His incisive reading of how Yambo Ouologuem's 1968 novel *Le devoir de violence* (*Bound to Violence*) "signified upon" the work of several other writers can help us think through these questions.[42] This gesture is essential if we are to move away from and beyond the reductive and accusatory discourse erected under the label of plagiarism. For Miller, Ouologuem's novel emerges as a "medium of retrieval" (217); it "consciously engages itself in the cross-cultural and interliterary 'zone of interferences' between the two continents and does so not to forge a synthetic response but to exaggerate and undermine the whole tradition we have been reading" (218). The pedagogic branch of the French civilizing mission was concerned with creating French cultural prototypes and disseminating ideology through the colonial schools. In *On the Postcolony*, Achille Mbembe has addressed the justificatory premises for these measures, according to which

> the native as nothing, as thing, and as animal is a creation of the colonizer. It is the colonizer who summons this nothing into existence, creates it as a thing and domesticates it as an animal. This nothing, this thing, and this animal are the creation and object of the colonizer's imagination, the supreme example of the power of his/her arbitrariness.[43]

Intrinsic to this project was the process of memorization, and social advancement was granted to a handful of évolués who demonstrated the capacity to adhere to and regurgitate this discourse. Indeed, Jean de Brunhoff's elephant protagonist Babar is perhaps the most notable example of this process, as we witness young Babar migrating from what Ariel Dorfman has described as a "horizontal nakedness" to verticality (read "évolué status") through exposure to French universal values.[44] The question of African originality is therefore all the more complex given that its potential is partially voided by Africans' recourse to cultural coordinates they do not "own." Issues relating to ownership introduce, of course, a legalistic vocabulary. "To own a copyright," Miller argues, "is to delimit a certain sequence of words, sentences, and paragraphs from other sequences that might infringe on the integrity of the first" (Miller, *Blank Darkness*, 219), and the *Oxford English Dictionary*'s definition of "plagiary" includes the term "a literary thief" (Miller, *Blank Darkness*, 220). This terminology is going to be crucial as I apply it to Sembene's novel. Babar's verticality emerges as a progression toward that ideal of French universality, but the fact nevertheless remains that he does not escape his status as animal; he is indelibly marked as a domesticated subject whose entry into the privileged domain of Frenchness is interrupted by the demands and exigencies of a monolithic cultural and national entity.[45] As we shall see, this example will serve as a symbolic indicator for broader colonial and assimilationist practices. In his seminal work *The Colonizer and the Colonized,* Memmi argues,

> The first ambition of the colonized is to become equal to that splendid model and to resemble him to the point of disappearing in him. By this step, which actually presupposes admiration for the colonizer, one can infer approval of colonization. But by obvious logic, at the very moment when the colonized best adjusts himself to his fate, he rejects himself with most tenacity. That is to say that he rejects, in another way, the colonial situation. (120–121)

This theory can be put into practice by examining *La rue Cases-Nègres* (*Sugarcane Alley*) by the Martinican novelist Joseph Zobel, and *Le gone du Châaba* (*The Kid from the Shantytown*) by the Beur author Azouz Begag.[46] In both novels, the young protagonist is accused of plagiarizing written assignments.

In *La rue Cases-Nègres* (and Euzhan Palcy's film adaptation of the novel), José completes a *rédaction* (written assignment) on the subject "Your most moving childhood memory" (Zobel, 269). José writes about the neighborhood of Petit-Morne and his childhood friend Médouze: "Consumed by inspiration, I wrote my essay in one sitting" (269). Accused of cheating, he claims "I did not copy," to which the teacher responds, "And now you're telling me you didn't copy? Well, it's plagiarized if it's not copied!" (270). This sequence is all the more revealing since the teacher, Mr. Jean-Henri, is not a *métropolitain* (a subject from France) but rather Martinican, and his accusation reveals the degree to which he is blinded by his own assimilation and his mental construct of the Black Martinican subject. Accordingly, he fails to recognize how the text could only be produced—and therefore owned—by the privileged native informer for whom French language literacy provides the paradoxical occasion to disseminate a narrative of oppression for the scrutiny of outsiders and to narrate an experience that would not be recorded elsewhere. The teacher is not yet aware of his own colonization and has not yet learned to embrace his inferiority. His behavior is a dramatic precursor to the consciousness that will follow:

> The candidate for assimilation almost always comes to tire of the exorbitant price which he must pay and which he never finishes owing. He discovers with alarm the full meaning of his attempt. It is a dramatic moment when he realizes that he has assumed all the accusations and condemnations of the colonizer, that he is becoming accustomed to looking at his own people through the eyes of their procurer. (Memmi, *The Colonizer and the Colonized,* 123)

José confirms his narrative authority, stating that "the passages the teacher was accusing me of having 'copied in some book or other' were *precisely* those that were the most personal" (Zobel, 271, emphasis mine). Blinded by his own assimilation, he is only able to see via the prism of his own projections and distortions of self.

When the young protagonist Azouz in Begag's novel *Le gone du Châaba* attends a French school, he effectively enters a contact zone in which sociocultural practices relating to hygiene, inheritance, and so on are addressed. These encounters also reveal the nature of stereotypes that have been assimilated by young children, who function as the spokespersons for broader societal constructs as they employ terms such as *sauvage* (savage) to describe sociocultural variants shared by Azouz and his classmates of North African descent.[47] The young boy's attempts at succeeding and advancing in the French school are hindered by accusations of cheating and plagiarism: "You're a shirker. You have copied Maupassant very poorly" (Begag, *Le gone*, 220), he is told by his teacher. The young boy offers a defense that is at least twofold: "But, ma'am, I didn't copy Maupassant," and then "I didn't know he had written the same story" (220), implying that such texts could not be part of his cultural baggage. This public shaming leads, significantly, to a renunciation of creative originality: "I did all I could to avoid the trappings of originality" (221). Here, the very precondition (namely originality) for distancing himself from previous models and paradigms is voided, as are the potentialities of advancing intertextuality. Paradoxically, those racist assumptions that are made about his creativity provide the opportunity for originality when he is assigned a composition on racism, a domain that he legitimately "owns" and in which he can make claims to authority: "Racism. Now that's what I should write about in my assignment" (222). On this occasion his performance is affirmed and he receives the best grade. Significantly, an earlier passage in the book cannot be ignored, since it underlines the young protagonist's views on cheating. The mother of one of his classmates appeals to his assumed solidarity with Arabs in a scheme that will allow her son Nasser to copy his work. The young Azouz sees this as a "strange request" (78); ultimately, he ignores the request made by the diasporic community in favor of adhering to very specific guidelines: "So you want me to cheat?" (78). The colonial civilizing mission has shifted cultural markers and served to disorient and destabilize colonized subjects. Once protagonists succeed in imitating these new coordinates they are immediately challenged, thereby exposing the colonizer's reluctance to enact the potentiality of an assimilationist potential that would effectively put into question the hierarchy under which they built social order.

Sembene's novel *Black Docker* provides an insightful analysis of the socioeconomic circumstances of minority populations residing in France during the final years of colonial rule. Most significant is the manner in

which the novel decentralizes the topography by focusing on the Mediterranean city of Marseilles rather than on the capital city of Paris.[48] This affords the reader a new perspective while considerably broadening the nature and scope of the inquiry into Africans in France. Marseilles has
played a central role in the complex and complicated history of French-
African relations. An important volume of the journal *Hommes et migrations* was entitled "Marseille: Carrefour de l'Afrique" ("Marseilles: Crossroads of Africa"); more recently, two other studies have been devoted to
the centrality of Marseilles in French history, namely Brigitte Bertoncello's
Colporteurs africains à Marseille: Un siècle d'aventures and Pascal Blanchard and Gilles Boëtsch's *Marseille porte sud: Un siècle d'histoire coloniale et d'immigration.*[49]

The connections with African America are clearly delineated, as the
reader learns that the African quarter is known as "the little Harlem of
Marseilles" (Sembene, *Black Docker,* 41). This neighborhood is extensively described in order to tell the story of Diaw and to provide a historical record of Africans in the city:

> At the beginning of this century, the town of Marseilles counted only a
> dozen or so Africans. Gradually, their number increased. Preferring to live as
> a community, they gathered in groups in the square, place Victor July, in
> what was the old quarter, with its squalid, narrow, dead-end streets. During
> the Second World War, half the old quarter of Marseilles was destroyed.
> Some of the black community left for England, the others went further into
> the town. And when the hostilities drew to an end, their numbers swelled.
> Black people poured in from all sides, drawn by the vicissitudes of seafaring
> and life in general. United by a community spirit and mutual support, they
> formed this village . . . In this little Africa in the south of France, all of the
> countries, all the different ethnic groups were represented. In keeping with
> the customs of their native land, each territory had its own boundaries: the
> cafés. Prejudices and origins were often the subject of argument. (41)

Micronational and microethnic communities are reconfigured, and while
certain rivalries survive and are even exacerbated, the "blacks" are Diaw's
"fellow countrymen" and "brothers." In fact, when Diaw first travels to
Paris to find a publisher for his novel, he represents his community before
the representatives of France d'Outre-mer (France Overseas). Sembene's
novel then proceeds to describe what is required of these modern-day
slaves—workers essentially performing the same kind of work as slaves,
under equally unfavorable conditions. "After years of this work," we learn,
"a man became a wreck, drained inside, nothing but an outer shell. Living
in this hell, each year the docker takes another great stride towards his end
. . . It was the rivalry of bone against steel, a question of which was the
stronger" (70). In this instance, Sembene's own political views gain proximity to those of the narrator, for whom the relationship between machines and human labor is characterized in terms of productive capacity

and organized in a broader framework concerned with the relation between France and Africa, colonial hierarchies, capitalism, labor, and the influence of the French Communist party on anticolonial voices:

> In the new firm where he was employed, both men and machines had the same orders: to double productivity. They carried hundreds of tons on their backs, their arms hurt from the work and their brains throbbed. They all had fits of giddiness and depression from overwork—the infernal pace, the acceleration of the machine . . . The docks certainly deserved their nickname of "man killer." (94–95)

The challenge to racism in France is carefully formulated in Sembene's novel through the accounts the narrator registers of the experiences of various protagonists and their encounters with prejudice. François Sène, for example, who lives in the African quarter, remarks, "The other day, as I was on my way home, there were police saying to the tourists, 'Don't go into the black district.' And yet nobody gets killed there, women don't get attacked. 'Nigger' is synonymous with 'mugger.' But what about them? They are technical barbarians" (102). The term *nègre* has been translated as "nigger" here in order to capture the degree of hostility felt for the African population, and the "district" has become a "no-go" area for outsiders. Once again, while François confronts the tenuous relationship between myth and reality, the fact remains that such popular conceptions are almost impossible to counter. Diaw alludes to these in his response to François:

> I blame your ancestors who crammed your head full of nonsense about our behavior. But if a black person says something sensible, or reasonably sensible, you're surprised. So you have two conflicting pictures, the one inherited from your ancestors and the one you have within your grasp. Sometimes I hear people say, "Oh! He isn't like the rest of them." What strikes them, is that it's a black person saying it, for they didn't expect anything from him. (103–104)

This analysis is of course central to Sembene's text, since the intertextual references are to a long history of writing about Africa; accounts by explorers, ethnographers, travelers continue to be widely disseminated and predetermine the outcome of Diaw's murder trial.

Sembene's text is a historical document on the circumstances of Africans in France after the Second World War that successfully moves beyond the evidentiary mode in order to address broader questions pertaining to African-French relations, racial constructs, and discourses on Africans. It does this through recourse to fiction as an effective device for unpacking a complex historical reality that is engaged predominantly with the experience of sub-Saharan Africans (rather than Maghrebis, for example), as both *ouvriers* (workers) and colonial subjects or *étrangers* (foreigners). *Black Docker* introduces a multiplicity of voices and narratives competing for authority in a framework in which various modes of testimony emerge in order to discuss the fate of the central protagonist, Diaw Falla. The novel is divided into three parts, and we learn in the opening section that Diaw has been imprisoned in France for murdering a French woman novelist. The first part includes four subsections: "La mère" ("The Mother") focuses on the declining health of Diaw's mother following his incarceration and the resulting discussion of his case in the local newspapers and on the streets of her hometown of Yoff; "Cath . . ." presents Diaw's girlfriend in Marseilles as she reviews cuttings from French newspapers concerning the murder; "La coterie" ("The Clique") introduces Diaw's close friends in Marseilles; and finally, the most lengthy subsection of part 1, "Le procès" ("The Trial"), covers legal proceedings and the exchange by the defense and prosecution of "official" narratives concerning the case in question. Part 2, "Le récit" ("The Story"), is juxtaposed with the section on the trial, offering the reader a restored chronology of events. The novel concludes in a third part entitled "La lettre" ("The Letter"), in which Diaw reflects on his life in a letter to his uncle and ventriloquizes his response to a question he had declined to respond to during his trial: "'Has the defendant anything to add?' asked the judge" (37). His testimony therefore takes place outside the legal system, so as to enable Sembene to record a voice otherwise silenced by dominant conventions. In the first part we learn of Diaw's incarceration and await the outcome of his pending trial; the section ends when the jury withdraws to deliberate. The second part resumes chronological linearity by narrating the sequence of events that culminated in his detention and concludes with the verdict, thereby rejoining the fourth subsection of part 1. As we shall see, popular views of Africans become inseparable from the challenge to authorial authority.[50]

The title of the novel, *Black Docker,* grants little room for ambiguity concerning the subject matter under investigation. The racial marker and the class status of the central protagonist are simultaneously foregrounded. Diaw is not only a "docker" but, perhaps more importantly, a "black" one. The term *noir* is employed interchangeably with *nègre* in the original French version; in the English translation a more varied lexicon is used, including "black," "negro," and "nigger," to capture the descriptive categories in question.[51] As a sub-Saharan African living and working in France, Diaw is marked as an outsider by his somatic features, but he is also a partial insider as a colonial subject, albeit one who does not enjoy the privileges of participatory citizenship. Diaw and his fellow African workers are nevertheless precursors of the more contemporary immigrant communities in France, as colonialism increased reciprocal flows in population and capital toward Africa (missionaries, colonial administrators, and commercial interests) and in turn back to the metropole (guest workers and soldiers, such as the *tirailleurs sénégalais*). In this framework Marseilles stands as a privileged site of contact between Africa and France.

In many ways Sembene's novel is less concerned with the legal techni-
calities surrounding Diaw's sentencing and subsequent incarceration than
it is with the centrality and prevalence of a reductive discourse on Africa
and Africans organized around the question of textual ownership. Sembene is concerned with exploring and challenging these constructs, and
fiction provides the opportunity to address these complex issues by introducing a broad range of circumstances and events around which such constructs can be tested, exposed, and ultimately demystified. The novel is
framed around the question of literacy: its dedication is "This book is
dedicated to my mother, although she cannot read." The first section of
the novel introduces Diaw's illiterate mother, Yaye Salimata, who has
learned of her son's arrest and seen his picture on the front pages of local
newspapers. One headline reads, "The trial of the negro Diaw Falla, mur-
derer of the famous novelist, will take place in three days' time at the Seine
Assize court" (2). Diaw is not simply the accused man but also the "negro," an early indication of the importance that will be accorded to this dimension. In fact, as the narrator observes, "the newspapers had cast aside
all their scruples in their bid to outdo each other. Because Diaw was black,
nothing was sacred" (9). These versions of events will in turn be tested
against the story that emerges in the second part of the book, in which actual events are described, thereby revealing inconsistencies but also forcing further reflection on the types of projection evidenced. One passage is
worth quoting at length:

> The negro murderer of the famous novelist has just been arrested. Since his
> atrocious crime, Diaw Falla has been holed up in a hotel room in the rue des
> Petites-Maries, protected by a positive arsenal. He stripped the young
> woman of her possessions, smashed her skull then took refuge in this hotel
> where he was tracked down by the police. This was not an easy task for the
> custodians of public safety who had to use great resourcefulness. As a pre-
> caution there were two busloads of police officers, for the memory of the
> drama which recently cost a police officer his life is still fresh. (9–10)

The correlation between the provisions of the legal system and the needs
of the collectivity are striking, and repeated calls are made for justice to
preserve a status quo that foreigners are perceived to be destabilizing. The
historical subtext is difficult to ignore, since the publication of Sembene's
novel in 1956 coincided with significant reorganization of French territorial control in Indochina, Morocco, and Tunisia, alongside increasing unrest in Algeria. Rising anticolonial opposition and decolonizing imperatives contributed to a growing need to further consolidate and crystallize
such nationalist sentiment. As we learn, there is a disconnect between
news media representations of Diaw's case and the facts: Diaw was not
"protected by a positive arsenal," he did not strip "the young woman of
her possessions" or "smash her skull." These inconsistencies compel the
reader to reflect on Sembene's broader project.

Further newspaper accounts capitalize on social constructs of Africanness and contribute to Diaw's negative image: "Diaw Falla is well known
in the black district, an area inhabited by pimps, thieves and pickpockets.
Local people describe him as a shady, lazy character" (10). As Etienne Balibar has shown,

> a general category of racism is not an abstraction which runs the risk of los-
> ing in historical precision and pertinence what it gains in universality; it is,
> rather, a more concrete notion of taking into account the necessary poly-
> morphism of racism, its overarching function, its connections with the whole
> set of practices of social normalization and exclusion, as we might demon-
> strate by reference to neo-racism whose preferred target is not the "Arab" or
> the "Black," but the "Arab (as) junky" or "delinquent" or "rapist" and so on,
> or equally, rapists and delinquents as "Arabs" and "Blacks."[52]

The deplorable living conditions his community endures remain unquestioned, seemingly justified by the dehumanization of colonial subjects that
reproduces the colonial topography in the metropole, where the privileged
live in the "European quarter" (5) and the *quartiers indigènes* (indigenous
neighborhoods) have been reconfigured as a *quartier noir* in opposition to
"French" neighborhoods. Colonial language is redeployed when the newspaper article shifts to a more descriptive mode to discuss Diaw's uncon-
trollable sexual instincts: "It is easy to imagine how the negro, in a frenzy
of sexual passion, seized poor Ginette Tontisane and raped her, then
banged her head against the edge of the table" (10). The imaginative leap
would not of course be that great for an audience who had already recuperated such a characterization of Africans; the act is "easy to imagine."
"Colonialism, as a relation of power based on violence," as Mbembe has
shown, was "intended to cure Africans of their supposed laziness, protect-
ing them from need whether or not they wanted such protection. Given
the degeneracy and vice that, from the colonial viewpoint, characterized
native life, colonialism found it necessary to rein in the abundant sexuality
of the native" (Mbembe, *On the Postcolony*, 113).[53] In this case, Ginette
Tontisane's accidental death has been reconfigured as a rape by the media,
thereby rendering the attack all the more despicable, but, perhaps more
importantly, the rape functions metaphorically as a violation of the domestic space that is by association inextricably linked to the broader territorial space of the Hexagon itself. Invariably, this results in a mapping
onto Diaw of a behavioral mode that coincides with colonial stereotyping
while functioning as a strategy for mobilizing what effectively amounts to
a collective "class-action suit" aimed at restoring justice and social order.
This response is repeatedly alluded to: "Local shopkeepers are up in arms.
They have circulated a petition in the area, protesting to the city coun-
cilors and demanding the expulsion of negroes and Arabs . . . Given the
evidence, the law should take energetic and radical steps to enable us to
sleep at nights" (11).[54] Diaw is deliberately distinguished from the model

colonial subject, who has both recognized and embraced the value of as-similation: "He bears no resemblance to the big, harmless, naïve 'Sambo,' who is strong, smiling and so dear to the hearts of good Frenchmen" (*Black Docker*, 10); "Il n'a rien du grand 'Mamadou' inoffensif et candide, fort et souriant, cher à nos cœurs de bons français" (*Le docker noir*, 27). This differentiation confirms this reading but is also crucial in building and justifying colonial expansionism.[55]

These mechanisms are of course central to legal proceedings in *Black Docker*. The imperative is thus less justice or the attempt to uncover the truth than it is the reaffirmation of power structures. Diaw's assertions that he is the legitimate author of the published text *The Last Voyage of the Slave Ship Sirius*, and that it has been stolen from him by Ginette Tontisane, become secondary to the social need of prevailing over any counter-narrative offered. In colonial discourse and constructs, Diaw could not have written a prize-winning book (the book earned the Grand Prize for Literature), since such an accomplishment would clearly fall outside of the traditional expectations of African performance. "He still kept to his initial statement in which he claimed to be the real author of the prize-winning novel," we learn from one newspaper account, but ultimately the article concludes that "it seems unlikely" (*Black Docker*, 11). As Murphy has shown, "accepting Diaw Falla's alibi would be tantamount to accepting the notion of the equality of races . . . , thereby relinquishing the exclusive right to speech that Europe had granted itself from its earliest contact with the 'primitive' world," and this would constitute "a violation of France's political and cultural hegemony" (Murphy, "La danse et la parole," 475, 477). Because of this, Diaw becomes the "killer of the novelist" (Sembene, *Black Docker*, 11), collapsing the violent act (killing) with the victim as novelist (profession and no longer individual entity) and dismissing his claim to be the legitimate author. Gbanou maintains that "through the alibi of plagiarism, Sembene sought to register the racial problem whose primary criteria for legitimation is the superiority of the white race" (82). This engenders a renewed appeal by the collective conscience for justice to be restored according to a retributive model that leaves little room for legal maneuvering, requiring the law, as a system, to react responsibly and effectively: "*We hope that for once*, the law will not turn a blind eye" (Sembene, *Black Docker*, 12, emphasis mine). Naturally, we have little evidence to corroborate the popular belief that the "law" has been ineffective in the past ("turned a blind eye"). Rather, the demand reveals a degree and form of social anxiety concerning the pitfalls of a multicultural and pluriethnic society.[56] In this framework, Diaw has little chance of receiving a fair trial and finds himself in many ways guilty not so much of a particular crime (although he is naturally guilty of causing the accidental death of the novelist) but rather of his African origins.

Testifying for the prosecution, the cleaning lady in Ginette Tontisane's building remarks on how she noticed Diaw when he visited, since he was conspicuous in a neighborhood where she claims there were "no Arabs or blacks" (Sembene, *Black Docker,* 21). Asked to speculate on the nature of Diaw's relations with Ginette, she responds, "I can't bring myself to believe they were intimate. Mademoiselle Ginette was honesty itself. If he claims otherwise, it's to give her a bad name" (22). As we learn from Diaw's complete story, Ginette was not, of course, "honesty itself," since she violated Diaw's trust in stealing his manuscript. In further testimony, the publisher of the novel, Claude Martin, quotes Ginette as saying, "Martin, I've done something wrong, I'd like to make amends" (22). However, this crucial piece of evidence is ignored, and in turn speculations concerning Diaw's motivations are brought to the forefront. André Vellin of the Faculty of Medicine is asked to respond to the following question:

> Do you have the impression that he is a sex maniac?
> Among black people, that is natural, and especially when it is a question of a white woman . . . Science has shown that colored men suffer from psychoses when confronted with a white woman. (25–26)

These kinds of beliefs were widely accepted at the time and had been corroborated by numerous scientific reports, all of which, as Mouralis has argued, contributed to "colonial ideology in its goal of objectifying the colonial mission: on the one hand, by blurring the biological with the cultural, and on the other through the affirmation that a hierarchy existed between people at a cultural level" (Mouralis, *Littérature et développement,* 26). This kind of thinking had, of course, been challenged in 1952, shortly before the publication of Sembene's novel, when Fanon published *Peau noire, masques blancs* (*Black Skin, White Masks*).[57] Under oath, Diaw frames the problem of race in different terms:

> Why didn't you go to the police, that's what they are for?
> *They* wouldn't have believed me.
> And why not?
> Because I'm a black!
> There's no segregation here. (26)

While, technically, legal segregation is not practiced, the reality is, of course, quite different. The court expects Diaw to behave and respond rationally in a system that fails to acknowledge the reality of race relations. Diaw emphasizes the nature of the collective "they," stressing that his claim of wrongdoing would most likely have gone unheard. As Memmi demonstrated, "all that the colonized has done to emulate the colonizer has met with disdain from the colonial masters . . . Everything is mobilized so that the colonized cannot cross the doorstep, so that he understands and admits that this path is dead and assimilation is impossible" (Memmi,

The Colonizer and the Colonized, 124–125). In fact, in order to prove the legitimacy of his claim to authorship, Diaw is asked to recite a passage from his book. When he has successfully fulfilled this request, the judge simply asks him, "How long did it take you to learn that?" thereby dismissing his claim to textual ownership. Diaw responds, "I did not learn it in prison. I tell you, I wrote it, wrote it" (Sembene, *Black Docker,* 31). The request made by the court introduces a complex tautology that is ultimately unproductive unless we explore it further.

One must assume that the judge would have a copy of the published text at his disposal in order to allow him to verify the accuracy of Diaw's recitation. Yet one has to ask whether Diaw—or any author, for that matter—could be reasonably expected to provide an accurate rendition of his text on demand. Paradoxically, would this not precisely prove that he must have committed the passage to memory, thereby corroborating the court's expressed skepticism and putting into question his own claim to textual ownership? While the court focuses on Diaw as the impostor, Ginette Tontisane cannot be excluded as the author of the text, since the narration of the voyage of a slave ship is certainly not beyond the imaginative grasp of a skilled writer. However, the logic behind the articulation of the accusation of Diaw is far more complex, and is anchored in a transhistorical context that concerns how French hegemony in the world of letters must first and foremost be restored:

> Diaw Falla's crime holds our institutions up to ridicule. This monster claims to be the author of *The Slave Ship Sirius*! This insult to our literature is also an offence. The French literary world has suffered a terrible loss . . . We must make amends, not only to the victim, but to our literature and to our civilization. (34)

Diaw is subsequently doubly criminalized not just for an act of violence against a woman, but also, and perhaps more importantly, for the offence of posing as the author of a prize-winning text that is assumed to belong to French historiography. As Gbanou has argued, Ginette's theft is premised on her understanding of the workings of race relations and social constructs that allow her to calculate in advance her chance for exculpation: "her behavior is justified by her fame following her previous publications and because she is aware of her victim's social status, thereby ensuring that established favorable French public opinion will be mobilized in her favor" (Gbanou, 85). As Riesz has suggested, the fact that the excerpt read from the novel echoes *négrophile* and antislavery texts popular in the early nineteenth century may partially explain why such a text "could be received with a degree of familiarity by a metropolitan audience" (Riesz, "*Le dernier voyage,*" 185). However, as far as the prosecution is concerned, this imitation is therefore all the more condemnable: "The fact that he submitted himself to the generic stylistic model of négrophile literature makes it seem all the more unlikely to a French audience that he could be the author of the *Last Voyage of the Slave Ship Sirius*" (Gbanou, 87). Ginette Tontisane has understood the sociocultural framework in which she operates, and accordingly Diaw's text "triggers Ginette Tontisane's interest because it corresponds to the expectations of French readers. Reading the manuscript, the novelist recognizes how she might exploit this potential" (Gbanou, 86). Riesz does not subscribe to this reasoning, since he struggles with reconciling the text's African specificity with its reception by the French jury awarding the literary prize (Riesz, "*Le dernier voyage,*" 184). Ultimately, the French reception of the text is not that surprising since Africans were not expected to write, there were numerous thematic precursors to the text itself, and only a specialist would be able to detect, discriminate, and unpack such contradictions.[58]

Citing Hans-Jürgen Lüsebrink's claim that Diaw's text constitutes a "reappropriation of African history (the slave trade in particular),"[59] Riesz objects that this position must be further qualified: "one must then state which European discourse is in question" (Riesz, "*Le dernier voyage,*" 183–184). For Riesz, the question of reappropriation is problematic since he convincingly demonstrates that correlations with Sembene's text are not to be found in nineteenth-century French narratives on slavery but are rather evidenced in another trend, namely that "during the '30s and '40s . . . a large number of books talked about the slave trade and slave merchants" (186), and from which "it becomes possible to establish . . . parallels with adventure stories dealing with the slave trade" (187). For Riesz, "the way in which Ousmane Sembene deals with these elements sets him apart from these French or European 'models'" (188). Ultimately, though, there is an inescapable mediation at work with the nineteenth-century French tradition, since even if Sembene attempts to distance himself from "négrophile" literature as a "necessary step toward forgetting older literary texts about Africa" (193), he cannot escape inscribing it as the norm from which to deviate. For this reason, the reappropriation paradigm emerges as the most convincing and challenges this line of argument. Diaw figures as the rightful "reappropriator" of an African archive, rather than Ginette Tontisane, who is the representative of misguided French interests. "The very desire to break away and negate can lead African discourse back to certain ancient European preoccupations," Miller has argued, and Sembene takes on this problematic, challenging the very reality of what constitutes "the origin and the copy" (Miller, *Blank Darkness,* 218).

The irony and symbolism of the usage of the word *auteur* (author) in the prosecution's summation in both the French and the English versions of Sembene's work cannot be ignored: "The offence is so atrocious, so bestial, that it is truly worthy of its *author,* who has no cause to envy the wild beasts of his native jungle" (Sembene, *Black Docker,* 34, emphasis mine). For Gbanou, "*Black Docker* updates in this sense the reality of Blacks that have emigrated to Europe by integrating this experience into the political and juridical context of the era. The theme of plagiarism functions as an alibi, allowing the narrator to lead the reader behind the scenes of society" (83). My position, however, anchors plagiarism at the very center of the text's concerns. Sembene's *Black Docker* can then be invested with additional authority, since the evidentiary mode provided by the experience of African immigrants living and working in France is a subject over which he occupies a privileged ethnographic authority. As Riesz has argued, "the theme of the slave trade is linked in *Black Docker* with the circumstances of blacks in France or Europe" (Riesz, "*Le dernier voyage*," 191). The connections with Diaw's own work are tantalizing, since *Black Docker* is also about ships, oceans, transatlantic crossings, and the emergence of modern, transcolonial forms of slavery and economic exploitation. For Paul Gilroy, ships emerge as the paradigmatic figure of the transatlantic exchange: "I have settled on the image of ships in motion across the spaces between Europe, America, Africa, and the Caribbean as a central organizing symbol for this enterprise and as my starting point . . . Ships immediately focus attention on . . . the circulation of ideas and activists as well as the movement of key cultural and political artifacts" (Gilroy, *The Black Atlantic,* 4). Somewhat paradoxically, then, one could argue that the rationale informing Ginette Tontisane's act of theft has its origins in what she perceived as the legitimate reappropriation of a text Diaw had stolen from her national literary heritage. Suspecting that Diaw would not therefore come forward to claim a text she could not conceive of as legitimately his, since such a claim would, much as it was perceived in Ouologuem, be construed as "an assault on European assumptions about writing and originality" (Miller, *Blank Darkness,* 219), she allowed herself to publish the text under her own name, thereby adding herself to an established corpus of French texts on the subject.[60] These kinds of formulations are inescapable for African and African American writers at the point of entry into European literacy, since, as Gates has pointed out, "the revising text is written in the language of the tradition, employing its tropes, rhetorical strategies, and its ostensible subject matter" (Gates, 124).

Inadvertently, Falla has been forced into the position of a ghost-writer for Ginette Tontisane (Feuser, "*Native Son,*" 107). Miller has underlined the historical indissociability of the lexicon organized around the term *nègre,* in which *nègre* was synonymous with "slave," and later with "ghost-writer" (Miller, *Blank Darkness,* 225). This is all the more pertinent in Sembene's text, given the slave narrative he recites: "if the plagiarist is the slave of another text, merely repeating it while passing himself off as its master and creator, then the *ghost-writer/nègre* is a master passing himself off as a slave" (Miller, *Blank Darkness,* 225). This also represents a rever-

sal of a longstanding tradition in francophone literature, one that has received renewed attention following the publication of King's controversial
"rereading" of the Guinean author Laye Camara. The trial of Diaw Falla
allows Sembene to further complicate the situation, since he may surely be
suggesting that while these nineteenth-century texts may in fact "belong"
to France, the historical memory of slavery has been appropriated from
the "African experience," much as José and Azouz "owned" their experiences of colonial subjugation and racism at the contact zone with France.
In this framework, as Gates's findings confirm, "the literature of the slave
. . . is the most obvious site to excavate the origins of the Afro-American
literary tradition" (Gates, 127).

For Sembene, the roles of the intellectual and the writer are centered
on the potentialities of political engagement: "You see, a writer must forge
ahead, see things as they are, not be afraid of his ideas" (*Black Docker*,
82). For Nzabatsinda, "Ousmane Sembene thematizes the role of the artist by insisting on social utility as a principle of artistic representations"
(Nzabatsinda, 54). In this framework the writer is compelled to address
the social condition as it presents itself. Diaw Falla wrote about slavery,
while Ginette Tontisane had published two novels, "one on the life of
country folk and the other on the Resistance" (Sembene, *Black Docker*,
11), subjects that are not committed to any particular social or political
agenda or, for that matter, informed by an oppositional politics. Thus one
could argue that a compelling legal case could be made on this issue
alone—namely that the relationship between literature and politics is not
conceptualized by Tontisane according to the same demands and exigencies that are involved in adhering to a particular agenda embraced by Sembene (and by extension Diaw Falla himself).

However, Diaw's defense attorney Riou finds that the task of exculpat-
ing his client proves insurmountable:

> The law does not distinguish between human beings, but our hearts know
> these differences. My client's guilt seems proven simply through the color of
> his skin. He is the beast capable of anything, the savage who drinks the blood
> of his victim. The accusation rests on the hatred stirred up by the press,
> which distorted the facts to make a greater impact on the public. (35–36)

Riou states things unambiguously, attempting to expose the bad faith of
the court and challenging society in general. Responding to the question
"Why did he not turn to the law when he realized he had been duped?"
(36), he emphasizes that "he did not think anyone would believe him because of his double inferiority complex, due to his race and his social position" (36). The demystification process is central to his argument, and
the discourse echoes beliefs about racial constructs in France at the time.
As well as transferring responsibility to the media, the legal system, and
popular racism, Riou also indicts the colonial project as a broader example of the injustices perpetrated against a global blackness: "Alongside our

country, we have created a nation inhabited by black people to whom we have taught our way of life. We have told them that France is a welcoming place, that her inhabitants like them. These words seem derisive when they see what it is really like" (36).

Ginette Tontisane's ownership of the text coincides with the prevailing discourse concerning the impossibility of Diaw's writing a prize-winning text, but also emerges as a metaphorical claim to the broader historical legacy of French ownership of Africa and Africans in the guise of slave labor and territorial dominance under colonial rule.[61] "Society holds my body captive," Diaw claims (113). When Diaw confronts Ginette, he evokes the hardship her actions have caused him, and also by association the legacy of building social and economic capital at the expense of Africans. The term *noir* in the French original is translated here as "nigger," the translator having recourse to a forceful term in order both to better capture the situation and the degree of anger motivating Diaw as an individual and, perhaps more importantly, to express a reverse form of collective rage resulting from centuries of exploitation and revisited here on the perpetrator in the guise of the thieving novelist. "You took me for a 'nigger,'" Diaw exclaims. "For him, 'nigger' meant ignorant, rough, foolish. It was more than a struggle between the robber and the robbed. Two races stood face to face, centuries of hatred confronted each other" (106). Unable to control his rage, "he felt no pleasure in what he was doing, but he had to humiliate her . . . He tried to control his anger. Unable to contain himself, he flew at her. Her head banged against the corner of a piece of furniture, she collapsed" (106). The violent response ends up as a reverse process of humiliation: "To get this book published, I entrusted it to a woman, she stole from me, and then humiliated me . . . Why didn't you try and understand what aroused my anger and prompted this crime which I refuse to recognize? I am black!" (117).

The social discourse on race provides one of the most striking points of commonality between Sembene's novel and the work of African American writers during the 1940s and 1950s, particularly that of Richard Wright. As Feuser has shown, "undeniable parallels reveal Ousmane in the role of apprentice, one who was undoubtedly familiar with the French translation of Wright's novel *Native Son* (Feuser, "*Native Son*," 114). Feuser's essay opens with a caution to the reader concerning "influence studies," insisting on "prudence in the way in which relationships of influence are established" (103).[62] He then outlines the positionality he will adopt:

> It will be for the reader to decide whether the conditions embodied in the above attitudes have been met in the present study which proposes to trace not only the influence of an older black writer on a younger one but also to analyze and compare in some detail theme, structure, characterization and other aspects of the two selected works, whether similar or dissimilar, convergent or divaricate. (103)

Feuser never employs the term "plagiarism," preferring instead to highlight a range of structural and thematic parallels between *Native Son* and
Black Docker. While he performs a close textual analysis of the two novels, he seems concerned, overly conscious of the implications of discussing
some of the more striking parallels, perhaps not having identified the
more compelling links, having been reluctant to engage with them, or simply having decided to silence them. The most important parallels identified
by Feuser can be summarized as follows: (i) "As if murder were not
enough, the yellow press, the role of which in both books is equally bane-
ful, intimates in addition the rape of the white victim" (106); (ii) "The
Black's racial experience in both societies—the American one of Richard
Wright and the French one of Ousmane Sembene—is thus first and foremost the encounter with his own deformed image" (106); (iii) for both
Bigger and Diaw, sexual deviance is essentialized through race; (iv) both
defense lawyers underline "the nexus between blackness and criminality
in prejudiced minds" (107); (v) and both defense lawyers assert a "collective societal responsibility for creating the conditions conducive to the
crimes committed" (108). A few examples of thematic parallels provided
by Feuser and me also extend to more specific textual analogies: (i) "Unless we grasp this problem in the light of this new reality, we cannot do
more than salve our feelings of guilt and rage with more murder when a
man, living under such conditions, commits an act which we call a crime"
(Wright, *Native Son*, 455) and "Alongside our country, we have created a
nation inhabited by black people to whom we have taught our way of life.
We have told them that France is a welcoming place, that her inhabitants
like them. These words seem derisive when they see what it is really like"
(Sembene, *Black Docker*, 36); (ii) "Your Honor, is this boy alone in feeling
deprived and baffled? Is he an exception? Or are there others? There are
others, Your Honor, millions of others, Negro and white, and that is what
makes our future seem a looming image of violence" (Wright, *Native Son*,
468–469) and "If you keep him in chains, his hatred for us will only increase, and with it, the hatred of a whole people. Let us act worthily, of
ourselves, our country and our hearts" (Sembene, *Black Docker*, 37); (iii)
Bigger Thomas's attorney opens his defense with "not only is this man a
criminal, but he is a black criminal" (Wright, *Native Son*, 444) and Diaw's
defense lawyer opens with "My client's guilt seems proven simply through
the color of his skin" (Sembene, *Black Docker*, 35); and (iv) "as an agent
and servant of the law, as a representative of the organized will of the people . . . I urge this for the protection of our society" (Wright, *Native Son*,
474) and "Justice must be done, for the sake of Ginette Tontisane's grief-
stricken family, for the sake of society" (Sembene, *Black Docker*, 34).

My reading of the two texts deviates from Feuser's to the extent that I
think we need to probe the intertextuality a little further. In his novel *Native Son*, Wright addresses the question of race relations in the United

States, and Sembene follows his lead in order to perform a parallel task in France. As Arnold Rampersad has argued in his introduction to Wright's novel, "The long speeches in summation by the state's attorney and the defense lawyer . . . were both pieces of verisimilitude that replicated the activity of a murder trial and, at the same time, indispensable extended statements of rival intellectual positions on the matter of race in America."[63] Feuser makes an important point by claiming that Sembene would have known the French translation of Wright's text; however, the citations he provides in his essay refer only to passages in the original English version.[64] For more revealing examples of textual borrowing, one must look to the French translation of *Native Son* (*Un enfant du pays*) and to the English translation of *Le docker noir* (*Black Docker*). Accordingly, I have juxtaposed the versions in order to call attention to a specific passage in which correlation with "black textual antecedents" (Gates, 120) becomes convincingly transparent:

Ousmane Sembene, *Le docker noir* (Paris: Présence Africaine, 1973), 27. First published by Editions Debresse, 1956.

De taille moyenne, le cou épais, les cheveux lui couvrent presque tout le front, ce qui lui donne l'air obtus; ses bras sont anormalement pendants. Lorsque l'on considère sa démarche, semblable à celle d'un fauve traqué, on peut facilement supposer comment le nègre, sous l'emprise d'une passion sexuelle, a saisi la pauvre Ginette Tontisane pour la violer avant de lui cogner la tête sur le rebord de la table. Surpris au moment du vol, il partit en courant, laissant les billets épars dans le studio . . . Diaw Falla a les épaules arrondies, très musclées. Il semble se replier sur lui-même lorsqu'on lui parle, prêt à bondir, le regard plein de haine et de dédain. On a l'impression de se trouver devant un être n'ayant jamais subi l'influence de la civilisation. Il n'a rien du grand «Mamadou» inoffensif et candide, fort et souriant, cher à nos cœurs de bons Français.

Richard Wright, *Un enfant du pays,* translated by Hélène Bokanowski and Marcel Duhamel (Paris: Gallimard, 1973), 347. First published by Albin Michel, 1947.

Bien que le corps du tueur noir ne paraisse pas spécialement trapu, il donne l'impression d'une force anormale. Il mesure environ un mètre soixante-quinze et sa peau est extrêmement foncée. Sa machoire inférieure est anormalement développée et rappelle celle des animaux de la jungle.

Il a de longs bras qui lui pendent mollement jusqu'aux genoux. Il est facile d'imaginer comment cet homme, sous l'empire d'une obnubilante passion sexuelle, a maîtrisé la pauvre petite Mary Dalton, l'a violée, assassinée, décapitée, puis a fourré son corps dans le calorifère chauffé à blanc pour faire disparaître les traces de son crime.

Il a de formidables épaules, très musclées, et se replie sur lui-même comme s'il s'apprêtait à vous bondir dessus. Il contemple le monde par en dessous avec un étrange et maussade regard, comme s'il voulait défier quiconque d'éprouver pour lui la moindre compassion.

Dans l'ensemble, on a l'impression de se trouver devant un animal, un être n'ayant jamais subi les influences émollientes de la civilisation moderne. Dans son langage comme dans ses attitudes, il n'offre pas le moindre trait commun avec le petit négro du sud, inoffensif, charmant, candide et souriant, si cher au cœur du peuple américain.

Ousmane Sembene, *Black Docker,* translated by Ros Schwartz (London: Heinemann Educational Books, 1986), 10.

Of average height, with a thick-set neck, his forehead is almost entirely concealed by his hair. He appears to be rather obtuse. His arms have an abnormal droop. He has the gait of a hunted animal. It is easy to imagine how the negro, in a frenzy of sexual passion, seized poor Ginette Tontisane and raped her, then banged her head against the edge of the table. Caught red-handed, he ran off, scattering bank notes all over the apartment. Diaw Falla has very round, muscular shoulders. He seems to withdraw into himself when spoken to, ready to spring, his eyes full of hatred and scorn. He is like a creature that has never been exposed to the influence of civilization. He bears no resemblance to the big, harmless, naïve "Sambo," who is strong, smiling and so dear to the hearts of good Frenchmen.

Richard Wright, *Native Son* (New York: Harper Collins, 1993), 322–323. First published by Harper and Brothers, 1940.

Though the Negro killer's body does not seem compactly built, he gives the impression of possessing abnormal physical strength. He is about five feet, nine inches tall and his skin is exceedingly black. His lower jaw protrudes obnoxiously, reminding one of a jungle beast.

His arms are long, hanging in a dangling fashion to his knees. It is easy to imagine how this man, in the grip of a brain-numbing sex passion, overpowered little Mary Dalton, raped her, murdered her, beheaded her, then stuffed her body into a roaring furnace to destroy the evidence of his crime.

His shoulders are huge, muscular, and he keeps them hunched, as if about to spring upon you at any moment. He looks at the world with a strange, sullen, fixed-from-under stare, as though defying all efforts of compassion.

All in all, he seems a beast utterly untouched by the softening influences of modern civilization. In speech and manner he lacks the charm of the average, harmless, genial, grinning southern darky so beloved by the American people.

However, to simply claim without further qualification that Sembene plagiarized Wright confirms very little. My analysis thus far has been aimed precisely at avoiding the pitfalls inherent in such a narrow interpretation of intertextuality. Indeed, as Rosello contended in her discussion of the work of Calixthe Beyala,

> once we notice the echoes between two books, should we automatically conclude that, as readers, we have been "robbed" of something . . . perhaps a point could be made about illegitimate filiations and the ways in which both the novels and the relationship between the two novels thematized and em-

blematized the issues of bastardization and foreignness. The resemblances can be treated as textual events whose social and political significance can be unpacked within the narrative economy of the two stories. (Rosello, *Declining the Stereotype*, 188)

Attentive readers of the writings of Sembene and Wright will notice parallels. Gbanou's essay on *Black Docker* and the Togolese novelist Ekue Akoua provides a formidable example of this, in which Sembene's novel is located as a determining influence on Akoua's *Le crime de la rue des notables*.[65] In fact, "when the reviewers for Nouvelles Editions Africaines established similarities in their report between the manuscript of *Crime de la rue des notables* submitted under the pseudonym Davi Delali and *Black Docker,* Akoua claimed to have never read this novel but that in all likelihood the works of Richard Wright, most notably *Native Son . . .* had left their mark" (Gbanou, 88). This sets up a very complex geometry that I shall endeavor to elucidate. Once similarities between Akoua's work and that of Sembene are established and suspicion raised, Akoua defends herself by dismissing "echoes" of Sembene, whom she claims not to have read. Yet the connection to Wright is assumed and remains unquestioned. The reader of Akoua's manuscript was perfectly correct in identifying echoes of Sembene, and the irony remains that Akoua's intertextuality is exposed because of Sembene's prior borrowing from Wright. Indirectly, then, it was to Wright himself that the resonances should have been attributed, since he was the originary source for both African writers.

I want to return to the question of translation, which requires further scrutiny. As Miller has argued with relation to Ouologuem, "between the identity of the text and the crime of plagiarism, certain observations tend to blur the distinction. The author's rights apply only to form, not content, yet [Ouologuem] was accused of plagiarism *in translation*" (Miller, *Blank Darkness*, 220). Translation functions as the ultimate paradigm of the mediation process and Sembene would have to be accused of plagiarizing *the* translation, since we know he was not linguistically equipped to read the original in English. In this instance, then, multiple violations and copyright infringements would have taken place, including that of Wright as the author of *Native Son*, of Hélène Bokanowsky and Marcel Duhamel as the translators of the text into French, of the original American publisher, Harper and Brothers, and subsequently of the French publisher, Albin Michel. Yet, as Miller maintains,

> translation would normally seem to involve the total transformation of a text, precluding unitary responsibility. Yet the author's rights are recognized as applying to translations, supposing that form is somehow limited not to the actual words but to the sequence of their differences . . . Translation is a *relationship of distance as well as sameness;* like plagiarism, it is understood as the removal of a single object to another place. (Miller, *Blank Darkness,* 220–222, emphasis mine)[66]

This "relationship of distance as well as sameness" interests me here. The most compelling dimensions in the passages cited above, illustrating Sembene's duplication of Wright's text, concern the mapping of physical and behavioral descriptions and characteristics of Wright's central protagonist Bigger, who remains "untouched by the softening touches of modern civilization" ("n'ayant jamais subi les influences émollientes de la civilisation moderne"), onto Diaw himself, who, "n'ayant jamais subi l'influence de la civilisation ("[having] never been exposed to the influence of civilization"), has therefore been transformed from the role-model figure of the "southern darky" ("le petit négro du sud") into "Mamadou" ("Sambo"). Sembene's text establishes transhistorical, transcolonial, and transnational connections between the various original and translated texts. The sociopolitical and cultural analogies between the ways in which racial constructs are conceived, deployed, and disseminated in the African colonial and hexagonal immigrant context and in the African American framework are of course arresting. Rather than conceiving of Sembene's borrowing as a willful act of plagiarism, I prefer instead to think about the manner in which Sembene decentralizes the ownership of the sequence of words Wright used. Sembene is more concerned with underlining how global blackness and the global consciousness of whites have been organized in such a way that analogous phenomena—such as the "southern darky" and "Mamadou"—have emerged in different spaces.[67] The linguistic repetition of Wright in Sembene therefore serves to further emphasize this point—there was little need, beyond the structural imperatives of the narrative in question, to deviate substantially from a concept Wright had expressed articulately. As Gates has shown us, "this form of revision is a process of grounding and has served to create curious formal lines of continuity between the texts that together comprise the shared text of blackness" (Gates, 129). Sembene's novel is about borrowing and stealing; thus Sembene's positionality on these issues can be gauged and a theorization of plagiarism inferred. This is confirmed by the fact that Diaw Falla is less concerned about the actual theft of his manuscript than he is about the wrongful reappropriation by a French author of the memory of slavery; when Diaw confronts Ginette, it is the legacy of racial exploitation that motivates his gestures rather than the simple theft of an unpublished manuscript. There is a radical difference between the actions of Ginette Tontisane and those of Sembene himself, since the former blatantly void authorship and thus deny capital, while the latter do not really violate anything, with the exception of Wright's ownership over the structural organization of a language sequence that includes no neologisms—that is, no vocabulary that he has himself coined or "invented."

Lamine Diakhaté leveled an accusation against Sembene in a different context in a review of *Black Docker* in 1957 in *Présence africaine,* when he accused Sembene of plagiarizing a folktale from Birago Diop's 1947

Les contes d'Amadou Koumba (Riesz, "*Le dernier voyage,*" 182).[68] This is in itself further problematized, of course, by the fact that Diop's text was constituted by a series of transcriptions of exchanges with Amadou Koumba himself.[69] Riesz rejects this allegation, arguing instead that the intertextuality "opens up onto an entirely non-European tradition and field of knowledge" (191), establishing a link between "Senegalese" practitioners outside of European influences. Similarly, the connections with African America are central to Sembene's text, and the imprudence of the Afrocentrist remarks alluded to at the beginning of this chapter must be denounced. Surely, though, Sembene was resisting and dismantling a construct of Africa intrinsic to hegemonic practices, suggesting instead that we consider the various ways in which Africa circulates at a periphery that operates around the potentialities of a minor-to-minor discourse between Africa and African America that in turn bypasses the center in order to arrive at a minor transnationalism.[70]

FOUR

Rhetorical Mediations
of Slavery

> The metaphor of connections allows
> us to demonstrate that contemporary
> globalization is, in fact, contrary to
> the thesis embraced by its adherents,
> far from being new, merely the
> continuation of prior globalizing
> mechanisms.
>
> Jean-Loup Amselle[1]

> Globalisation and universality do
> not go together. Indeed, they might
> be said to be mutually exclusive.
> Globalisation is the globalisation of
> technologies, the market, tourism
> and information. Universality is the
> universality of values, human rights,
> freedoms, culture and democracy.
>
> Jean Baudrillard[2]

Multiple and varied usages have been made of the term "globalization,"
yet it nevertheless provides a useful discursive space for the exploration
of complex cultural, social, and political phenomena. "The current phase
of the world economy is characterized by significant discontinuities with
the preceding periods and radically new arrangements," Saskia Sassen has
observed,[3] while for anthropologist Jean-Loup Amselle, contemporary
globalization constitutes "merely the continuation of prior globalizing
mechanisms" (Amselle, *Branchements,* 7–8). Through a consideration of
a documentary-testimonial work by a Togolese woman, Henriette Akofa,
this chapter proposes to further explore some of these questions. Discourse and research on immigration in France and on so-called postcolo-

nial communities have not sufficiently accounted for the historical context, preferring to focus instead on the contemporaneity of the question.
Yet works such as Ousmane Sembene's *Black Docker* or Bernard Dadié's
An African in Paris, which predate the era of African Independence, always already constituted what are today commonly categorized as immigrant narratives, forcing us to rethink some of these categories and to relocate them in transhistorical frameworks.[4] Ultimately, then, my objective
will be to suggest ways in which a plethora of processes responsible for the
displacement of populations—slavery, colonialism, economic migration,
globalization—transform the nature of transnational exchanges and mediation between cultures.

Akofa's *Une esclave moderne* (*A Modern Slave-Woman*), published in
2000, allows us to explore recent immigration trends in France by relocat-
ing them in a discursive realm indebted to slavery.[5] In Akofa's text, the context has shifted to a postcolonial France and Togo on the brink of the new
millennium. In this analysis, the emphasis on slavery and the accompanying subtext pertaining to its abolition in the nineteenth century becomes
less important than the attempt to identify modern vestiges of it, and ways
it has mutated according to the demands and exigencies of global trade
networks and market forces. Indeed, as Roger Botte has signaled in his essay "Le spectre de l'esclavage" ("The Specter of Slavery"), thinking on the
question of slavery has, for the most part, circumvented the complexity of
the phenomenon by insisting on a binary model that opposes Africa to the
West (slave to master and subsequently colonized to colonizer).[6] According to this approach, responsibility for slavery is placed almost exclusively
on economic and political forces outside Africa. A paradigm that underscores the manner in which transnational economic forces work together
at both the local and global levels would provide a better understanding
of the origins of slavery. This is, of course, contained in "the internal slave-
trading routes" (Botte, "Le spectre de l'esclavage," 160) and Amselle's notion of lateral connections, within a framework that is necessarily imbricated with the broader global forces of the transatlantic slave trade.

In turn, this allows for an understanding of the practice as it survives
today in Africa in a form that is

> quite different from labor migration. They differ in kind but their origins are
> the same: under-development . . . This "new slavery" drives thousands of
> women and children from poor supplier countries toward the continent's
> "rich" countries, "employers" of manpower, where they are subjected to
> forced labor on plantations, domestic servitude, and sexual exploitation.
> (Botte, "Le Spectre de l'esclavage," 162)

It also survives, of course, in population movements toward Asia, Europe,
and the United States. In Akofa's text, the central protagonist, Henriette,
occupies a position of servitude as a domestic worker—a social status that

is unambiguously underlined in the title of the work: *Une esclave moderne*. What we have here is a kind of mediation that is available at the level of intertextuality—that is, between Akofa's text and a long tradition of works by francophone African writers that feature the socioeconomic circumstances of protagonists who travel to Europe—as well as a mediation that emerges from the actual transatlantic "crossing" made by these protagonists who follow in the footsteps of their slave ancestors, who were also transported and transplanted into economic dependence and exploitation outside Africa.

The social condition of women in sub-Saharan Africa continues to receive considerable attention. While many critiques formulated have been sensitive to broader cultural issues, stereotypes concerning the oppression of women are common and have survived into discourses pertaining to the diasporic context. In fact, texts written about African immigration in France have often resorted to a documentary-testimonial format in which a sensationalist rhetoric associated with widespread oppression is evidenced. Accordingly, these texts essentially narrate and record the immigrant experience, and are fictional only in that the names of various protagonists are changed, but otherwise recounting actual events. Akofa's text is described as a "testimony" (Akofa, 9) based on real-life events and written collaboratively with Olivier de Broca (a French writer and translator), thereby further underlining the documentary quality of the work.[7] The author's foreword serves to outline Akofa's intentions in writing her story: "This book recounts my story as faithfully as possible," and "writing has helped me forget about the past" (9). With reference to slave narratives (he has in mind Olaudah Equiano's 1789 *The Interesting Narrative of the Life of Olaudah Equiano*), F. Abiola Irele has argued that "the autobiographical genre affords scope for precisely the kind of introspection inspired by the actualities of experience and the circumstances of these early Africans in Europe . . . Reading is a liberating force in the new dispensation, and writing—as self-expression—is a means of coping with an unprecedented historical experience."[8] Akofa's text appears therefore all the more significant as she adds it to a longstanding tradition of slave narratives—an example perhaps of the "historical past and its narrative present" that Homi Bhabha alluded to[9]—but yet the testimonial dimension is accorded primacy as a mechanism for underscoring the potentialities of the sensationalist component. Accordingly, the central objective is to displace aesthetic concerns and the potential fictitious dimension in favor of an unambiguous message: namely that this is a text about an African woman's struggle (exhibited on the cover of the book in the form of the face of a Black woman on whom the title is superimposed) against slavery in the modern era. As we shall see, this is in fact the account of the real-life experiences of the author, whose legal name is Siwa-Akofa Siliadin.

Akofa's text is prefaced by Robert Badinter (a very well known lawyer and human rights activist), continuing a long tradition of patronage of African texts.[10] As Badinter points out in his opening lines, "the adolescent girl leaves her native Togo for what she believes to be Paris and its lights" (Akofa, 5). Badinter situates his preface within the context of the 1998 celebration of the 150th anniversary of the abolition of slavery in the colonies and evokes the Universal Declaration of the Rights of Man: "Whatever incontestable progress has been made, Henriette's fate is a reminder to all advocates of human rights that the battle is still not over, *even here*" (6, emphasis mine). While Badinter appears to make a necessary move toward recognizing that human rights violations also occur in France, the text is more concerned with African examples of oppressive behavior. Following Badinter's preface (5–7) and an "author's foreword" (9–10), one finds three other sections: the first, entitled simply "Togo" (13–50), is of course set in Togo, while the remaining two sections, "Paris with head held down" (53–196) and "Paris with head held high" (199–212), are set in Paris, and represent three-quarters of the text. Akofa has thus herself relied on a process of mediation in order to formulate her testimonial narrative and introduce a dialogue between the African and French frameworks.

Henriette, the coauthor and protagonist, travels to France to pursue her dream of studying there. In so doing, she joins a long list of African protagonists who engaged in similar travels, as explored in chapter 2—most notably Laye in Laye Camara's novel *L'enfant noir* (1954) and Samba Diallo in Cheikh Hamidou Kane's novel *L'aventure ambiguë* (1961). However, while both of these novels were set in French West Africa during the colonial era at a time when there were no universities in francophone sub-Saharan Africa, Akofa's text is fundamentally different in that Africa can now offer Henriette its own institutions of higher education. Repeated allusions are made to her naïveté and apparent ignorance of the notion of individual rights: Badinter tells us that "Henriette knows that she has been misled, but she is not aware that what she has been subjected to is legally reprehensible. She ignores those inalienable rights that are hers, whatever the borders, family solidarities, and cultural traditions may be" (Akofa, 6–7). On the basis of this statement, one may deduce that specific notions of justice and individual rights are somehow absent or lacking in the African context. Sekai Nzenza-Shand, for example, has argued that "the notion that African women could independently conceptualize equality and construct a system that embodied the principle of equality within specific cultures is not fully understood."[11] Yet, as we shall see in the next chapter, this particular characterization has been contested. Of course, this paradigm rejoins earlier colonial discourses in which the civilizing mission and colonial education claimed they would provide Africans with the tools to be raised to the ranks of the Universal.[12] Henriette's desire to travel to France is also a desire to fulfill an illusory quest. In this framework, Hen-

118 BLACK FRANCE

riette has selectively erased the memory of the terrible injustice of the slave trade and (post)colonial exploitation as a result of earlier European contact with Africa. Instead, an alternative narrative emerges in which Western justice, freedom, and human rights prevail, and are juxtaposed with the abusive structures and obstacles to personal freedom she perceives as located in African culture. This provides a striking example of historical mediation, given that Akofa is unwilling to address the complexity and ambiguous nature of her positionality in articulating her agency and recontextualizing her identitarian concerns only when she distances herself from the African context.

Henriette is employed by several African women to perform domestic labor, thereby creating an interesting dynamic whereby the oppression that is visited upon her always originates in an African perpetrator, namely the succession of African women who occupy the role of benefactress. Thus, while Badinter may conclude that such acts take place "even here," the apparent importance that could be attributed to this statement (through recognition that European feminism has not served to fully emancipate women) is undermined by the fact that outsiders are blamed. At no point are questions of economic exploitation addressed in France, or for that matter issues relating to the erosion of worker's rights, sexism, homophobia, and so forth. In this context, Western women are somehow liberated from the dynamic of domestic violence, exploitation, discrimination, and prejudice that characterizes notions of gender and class relations in the African context. Assumptions are made about the choices African women should make through paradigms indebted to Western feminist discourse in order to achieve a conception of universal, culturally appropriate, and relativistic rights. Badinter's text is written with a sense of mission and a commitment to justice, but the narrative itself betrays more problematic conceptions of freedom. French hypocrisy remains unchallenged and Universalism suspended in the name of some distorted interpretation and reformulation of cultural relativism that will not permit interference with oppressive practices enacted by others upon others.

Henriette's story begins in Togo with a description of her childhood— a time of innocence, in which children play happily outside the home and run around barefoot. This perspective is mediated through the lens of her post-French experience, which has now afforded her the capacity to question and reevaluate through her writing certain Togolese sociocultural practices. The experience in France offers her an alternate perspective, new paradigms for "reading" the African society she was born into. Henriette decides to leave for France when she is presented with an opportunity to study there in exchange for some light housework. Somewhat paradoxically, the "rescue" narrative in this case transforms itself into another survival story. Prior to reaching a decision, Henriette consults her aunt, Bénédicte, who has lived in France: "Apparently you want to leave with this

Simone woman? You know, I heard a story about a girl called Phoebe who spent years with her in Paris. Well, she came back empty-handed, Simone hadn't done anything for her. She claimed Phoebe was a thief. I don't think you should go. So many things happen in France . . ." (Akofa, 45). However, Henriette does not follow her aunt's advice and the unspeakable, unutterable, unarticulated horrors of what awaits her after crossing the ocean are both foreshadowed and contained in the suspension points that conclude the conversation with her aunt. Prior to her departure, her benefactress Simone seduces her with talk of Paris, "City of Lights," recuperating so many of the francocentric images that have lured francophone Africans to travel to the metropole.[13] Henriette seems to have been offered all the security she could expect prior to engaging in such a significant journey. As the reader discovers through her testimony, the departure will turn out to lack the cyclical dimension of its constitutive return.

As the narrative shifts to the second part of the text, "Paris with head held down," Henriette is immediately forced to correct the image she had of Paris: "I went to look at France out the window. In my dreams, I did not see her in this way. I had imagined her with lots of trees and colors. But down there, on the gray boulevard, I could see the same tar and cement as back in Lomé. And what is more, I wasn't used to seeing bars on windows" (Akofa, 56). Imprisoned in Paris, she is rapidly immersed in and consumed by her domestic tasks and responsibilities and reduced to sleeping on the floor beside another African girl, Stéphanie. Simone is hostile toward her, and only the French people she comes into contact with prove to be warm and hospitable (Simone's husband Jo and his mother). The oppressor is Simone, the African woman residing in France but marked as an outsider. She asks to return to Africa, but Simone informs her that this is not an option, manipulates her father during a telephone conversation into instructing his daughter to be more cooperative, and finally forbids her to speak with Stéphanie. Initially, Henriette challenges Simone. She defies the ban on exchanges with Stéphanie, and conversation with her effectively allows her to solicit Stéphanie's testimony. From this account, she discovers that Phoebe, whom her aunt had warned her about, had been her predecessor. "'But why did you stay?' she asks, "No one has the right to make you work like an animal" (Akofa, 77). In order to silence Henriette's growing resistance, Simone emphasizes Henriette's illegitimate status and vulnerability in France as a *sans-papiers* (undocumented resident): "a passport is good for coming in, but it's not enough to stay" (Akofa, 82). Henriette's realization that this is true further contributes to her status as a voiceless victim, but occurs at an important juncture in the text and in Henriette's own psycho-social journey, coinciding with her growing awareness of the oppressive structures that exist around her. However, Henriette does not internalize this lucidity in order to correct the illusory space in which she resides, and continues to have faith that her father will come to France to rescue her. Stéphanie then provides her with her own reality check: "'You must be dreaming. You will never go back to Togo'" (Akofa, 105). Sensing Henriette's increasing unruliness, Simone begins to send her out to help her friend Fabiola. Only the address changes, however, since the abusive treatment starts all over again, strategically transferring the responsibility for the oppression onto another African outsider.

Henriette's journey is, arguably, not one that transports her from innocence to knowledge, since she understands that she has experienced abuse at the hands of Africans. What genuinely complicates the situation is the process of liberating herself from her current circumstances, since this will be conditional upon achieving a clear understanding of parallel structures of oppression evidenced in France: "I was disgusted by the life I was living. When I compared my old dreams to my life today, I told myself that I would have been better off staying at home . . . I was a lost island" (Akofa, 140). This process allows Akofa to expose broader societal complicity in the process of oppressing and subjugating people, yet, beyond this complicity, one cannot help but feel that a justificatory premise for the refusal to act comes from the idea that one cannot interfere with African social customs and traditions. Fabiola's mother-in-law, for example, during Henriette's visit to her home in Normandy, shares some family photographs with her: "You know, I suffered a lot as well during the war. I had to work and take care of the young ones in my family" (Akofa, 142). She draws a parallel between her experiences and Henriette's current circumstances, yet it only serves to explain away her suffering and not to address it. Instead, her suffering is construed as a rite of passage, a kind of initiation into womanhood and society, and not as the exploitation that they all know it is. The complicity extends to a society as a whole that is criminalized (or, perhaps more appropriately, "culpabilized") for its refusal to act. But for Henriette, as indeed for many of the protagonists of the works of other diasporic writers such as Daniel Biyaoula and Alain Mabanckou, the situation is further complicated by the fact that the concept of escape is itself a double illusion (at least), in that simply liberating oneself from oppressive circumstances (namely socioeconomic slavery) constitutes only one victory, since the illusionary quest represented by the voyage to France (and Paris) is both an individual and a collective enterprise:

> I was about to turn eighteen, but the older I got the deeper I plunged into misery, ignorance, and solitude. I had forgotten everything, I was cut off from my family, completely isolated, without a future. Even if I somehow managed one day to return to Togo, everyone back there would mock me: all that time spent in France and you come home empty-handed, without an education, a job, money? I didn't even dare think about going back to Africa. (Akofa, 148)

The notion of return contains simultaneously the idea of returning to a physical space (for Akofa this would be Togo) and the return on an investment. Indeed, this is a common process, available in both colonial (Dadié, Camara, Kane) and postcolonial narratives (Biyaoula, Mabanckou, Diome), in which the impulse to travel or migrate is often located in the pursuit of this dream of educational or material enrichment, each in turn promising to confer cultural and social capital. Henriette's father was partly manipulated and deceived by Simone, but he also refused to believe that the dream could be a fallacy.

Only when a Danish woman living in the apartment building has the initiative to contact the Comité contre l'esclavage moderne (Committee against Modern Slavery) do the police finally come to the apartment and take Henriette away.[14] The fact that it is not a French person who resolves to take action against injustice could of course be purely coincidental, but I am inclined to read a little more into this. Intervention by a Danish woman serves to reinforce the parameters established by Akofa's text whereby the oppression, while taking place "even here," is nevertheless located in another "cultural" domain. Thus, it is a foreigner (albeit a European Union citizen with a legal right to reside in France) who acts and provides Henriette with the opportunity to "tell her story right from the beginning" (Akofa, 194). When Henriette's circumstances are reported to the authorities, their incredulity that this degree of abuse could have taken place in France raises numerous important questions. Akofa's testimony is not necessary in order to recount a narrative that would otherwise have remained unknown, but rather in order to provide a narrative that would otherwise have been silenced because of various complicities. The reader is aware through the testimonial narrative that numerous French individuals have both witnessed and tolerated the injustice, that Henriette's suffering has not been invisible, and the fact remains that she has suffered and remained unassisted on French soil. Yet, as an African woman residing in France, she is marked by her ethnicity as an outsider to whom the universal human rights invoked by Badinter somehow do not apply—after all, her own invisibility in legal terms is a result of her status that locates her, literally, on the "margins of the law."[15] Without legitimate legal status in France, she is only a displaced, identity-less diasporic and immigrant African subject located outside of legal jurisdiction. As we shall see shortly, this situation has been reversed by important juridical decisions.

The mediation of the narrative changes between the beginning of the text and the end, the "head held high" section. At the beginning of the text, Henriette locates oppression only in Africa, but by the end she has broadened her perspectives toward a more global understanding of gender oppression across racial lines. Rather than simply using Africa as a frame of reference, she assumes complete control over her agency as she files an official complaint against Fabiola and starts to attend committee meetings, and this affords her the opportunity of witnessing other narratives and then articulating her own experience: "Words came pouring out, and the more they flowed, the more liberated I felt" (Akofa, 202). Speaking proves to be a liberating, cathartic experience, and her "head held high" becomes a metaphor for her newfound self-reliance, self-esteem, and strength. Having achieved this for herself, she justifies the act of testifying as a necessary gesture of solidarity with other victims of abuse. Henriette blames Africa through her rejection of her parents after her emancipation, and attributes responsibility for her rescue to the Committee against Modern Slavery. In turn, this organization becomes inseparable from the universal human rights that are supposedly understood and adhered to in France, yet that somehow escaped her. Ultimately, certain organizations and mechanisms rescue her once she is removed from the enclave of her successive African "benefactresses"; yet these are only able to partially assist her. While these rescues actually take place in France, there is simultaneously a further kind of invisible mediation established with France's erasure of its own history of slavery, paradoxically abolishing slavery in the contemporary context while forgetting that France once had slaves of its own. This is of course further complicated by the fact that Akofa's text targets a modern form of slavery carried out by Africans while refusing to indict the French for their historical legacy of slavery and existing refusal to adequately consider their part in perpetuating social injustice.

Henriette no longer wants to return to Africa, for France remains a dream-construct for her, a space that is idealized outside the parameters of the oppression she has experienced. Since the Paris of her dreams escaped her until her emancipation, she is somehow able to dispense with the trauma by disassociating it from her hexagonal experience thus far. When Henriette confronts her parents for their failure to hear her appeal for help, she reclaims her autonomy outside of her family structure and attributes this salvation primarily to the Committee against Modern Slavery rather than to her own agency: "I would like to thank those in charge and the volunteers of the Committee against Modern Slavery for their support" (Akofa, 213). These questions are all the more challenging if one considers the archives of the European Court of Human Rights, located in Strasbourg. The court was created by the Council of Europe in 1959 to deal with alleged violations of the 1950 European Convention on Human Rights. I quote its press releases on Siliadin's case at length because the story they tell is crucial to understanding how sovereign French courts are ultimately indicted by the European Court of Human Rights for having failed to adequately protect the real-life defendant Siliadin, whose life is transposed into the narrative of Henriette in *Une esclave moderne*. The case opposed Siliadin and France:

Registrar of the European Court of Human Rights, 3 May 2005:
The European Court of Human Rights is holding a Chamber hearing today Tuesday 3 May 2005 at 2.30 p.m., on the merits in the case of Siliadin v. France (application no. 73316/01).

The applicant

The applicant, Siwa-Akofa Siliadin, is a Togolese national who was born in 1978 and lives in Paris.

Summary of the facts

In January 1994 the applicant, who was then fifteen and a half years old, arrived in France with a French national of Togo origin, Mrs D., who had undertaken to regularise the girl's immigration status and to arrange for her education, while the applicant was to do housework for Mrs D. until she had earned enough to pay her back for her air ticket. The applicant effectively became an unpaid servant to Mr and Mrs D. and her passport was confiscated.

In around October 1994 Mrs D. "lent" the applicant to a couple of friends, Mr and Mrs B., to help them with household chores and to look after their young children. She was supposed to stay for only a few days until Mrs B. gave birth. However, after her child was born, Mrs B. decided to keep the applicant on. She became a "maid of all work" to the couple, who made her work from 7.30 a.m. until 10.30 p.m. every day with no days off, giving her special permission to go to mass on certain Sundays. The applicant slept in the children's bedroom on a mattress on the floor and wore old clothes.

In July 1998 the applicant confided in a neighbor, who informed the Committee against Modern Slavery, which reported the matter to the prosecuting authorities. Criminal proceedings were brought against Mr and Mrs B. for wrongfully obtaining unpaid or insufficiently paid services from a vulnerable or dependent person, an offence under Article 225-13 of the Criminal Code, and for subjecting that person to working or living conditions incompatible with human dignity, an offence under Article 225-14 of the Code.

The defendants were convicted at first instance and sentenced to, among other penalties, twelve months' imprisonment (seven of which were suspended), but were acquitted on appeal. In a judgment of 15 May 2003 the Versailles Court of Appeal, to which the case had subsequently been referred by the Court of Cassation, found Mr and Mrs B. guilty of making the applicant, a vulnerable and dependent person, work unpaid for them but considered that her working and living conditions were not incompatible with human dignity. It accordingly ordered them to pay the applicant the equivalent of 15,245 euros (EUR) in damages.

In October 2003 an employment tribunal awarded the applicant a sum that included EUR 31,238 in salary arrears.

Complaint

Relying on Article 4 (prohibition of forced labour) of the European Convention on Human Rights, the applicant submits that French criminal law did not afford her sufficient and effective protection against the "servitude" in which she was held, or at the very least against the "forced and compulsory" labour she was required to perform, which in practice made her a domestic slave.

Procedure

The application was lodged with the European Court of Human Rights on 17 April 2001 and declared partly admissible on 1 February 2005.[16]

And then on July 26, 2005:

> *Registrar of the European Court of Human Rights, 26 July 2005:*
>
> The European Court of Human Rights has today notified in writing a judgment in the case of Siliadin v. France (application no. 73316/01). The Court held unanimously that there had been a violation of Article 4 (prohibition of servitude) of the European Convention on Human Rights. . . .
>
> *Summary of the judgment*
>
> The Court noted that, in addition to the Convention, numerous international treaties had as their aim the protection of human beings from slavery, servitude and forced or compulsory labour. As the Parliamentary Assembly of the Council of Europe had pointed out, although slavery was officially abolished more than 150 years ago, "domestic slavery" persisted in Europe and concerned thousands of people, the majority of whom were women. In accordance with modern standards and trends in that area, the Court considered that States were under an obligation to penalise and punish any act aimed at maintaining a person in a situation incompatible with Article 4. . . .
>
> . . . the Court considered that Ms Siliadin had, at the least, been subjected to forced labour within the meaning of Article 4 of the Convention. . . .
>
> . . . the Court held that it could not be considered that Ms Siliadin had been in slavery in the traditional sense of that concept.
>
> . . . the Court considered that Ms Siliadin, a minor at the relevant time, had been held in servitude within the meaning of Article 4.
>
> Accordingly it fell to the Court to determine whether French legislation had afforded the applicant sufficient protection in the light of the positive obligations incumbent on France under Article 4. In that connection, it noted that the Parliamentary Assembly had regretted in its Recommendation 1523 (2001) that "none of the Council of Europe member states expressly [made] domestic slavery an offence in their criminal codes." Slavery and servitude were not as such classified as criminal offences in the French criminal-law legislation. . . .
>
> In those circumstances, the Court considered that the criminal-law legislation in force at the material time had not afforded the applicant specific and effective protection against the actions of which she had been a victim. It emphasised that the increasingly high standard being required in the area of the protection of human rights and fundamental liberties correspondingly and inevitably required greater firmness in assessing breaches of the fundamental values of democratic societies.
>
> Consequently, the Court concluded that France had not fulfilled its positive obligations under Article 4.[17]

What is so striking about this case is the fact that only the European Court for Human Rights ultimately recognized that although "slavery and servitude were not as such classified as criminal offences in the French criminal-law legislation," this was inadequate and that accordingly "the criminal-law legislation in force at the material time had not afforded the applicant specific and effective protection against the actions of which she had been a victim." Akofa's text is an important testimonial narrative, and this case shows how the French authorities' attempts to recuperate such narratives as further examples of African "barbarism," at the service of broader culturalist arguments, are ultimately undermined by the European Court for Human Rights' indictment of France's inability to operate according to the most fundamental precepts of a "civilized" society.

Indeed, in this concluding section, I would like to explore the intertextuality and numerous points of contact between Akofa's documentary-testimony and Sembene's short story "La Noire de . . ." ("Black Girl").[18] In many ways, one might argue that Akofa's text ventriloquizes the experience of an early generation documented in Sembene's 1962 text. Sembene's vision and interpretation of colonial practices differs considerably from Akofa's text, in which the myth of France is introduced yet perpetuated through its discursive practices. Significant parallels exist between the two projects—both historical and thematic—as the authors treat, respectively, circumstances in the colonial and postcolonial context. While Akofa's text was published in 2000 and documents the experiences of an African woman in France at the end of the twentieth century, Sembene's short story takes place between Dakar, Senegal, and Antibes, France, in 1958. The central protagonist, Diouana, referred to variously by either her professional status ("maid") or her ethnic/racial identity (*négresse* [Negro girl], "black girl," or *indigène* [native]), accompanies a French family for whom she worked in Dakar when they return to live in the south of France. After several months in France, Diouana commits suicide, and the short story begins with the discovery of her body. The reader is thus made responsible for recovering the narrative and locating the suicidal impulse; one cannot gauge from the French onlookers or informers where these would be located. Sembene's text uses a flashback to establish a chronological linearity. "A long flashback," Mireille Rosello argues, "invites us to take the place of those 'investigators' and of the 'journalists' who did not know how to tell the story . . . the author's text is a deliberate attempt at replacing their interpretation with a different and more complex account."[19] The narrative therefore shifts back to Africa to recover those events that transplant Diouana from colonial Africa to the metropole. As it did to Henriette, a voyage to France represents to Diouana the fulfillment of a lifelong dream: "Though it was a long way, it had no longer seemed so far the past month, ever since Madame had announced she would take her to France. France! Diouana shouted the word in her head. Everything around her had become ugly, the magnificent villas she had often admired seemed shabby" (Sembene, "Black Girl," 45). Having clearly assimilated those representations and constructs of France that were inherent in colonial discourse, Diouana, like so many African migrants across generations, conceives of the voyage to France as a doubly enriching experience, personally and financially:

> Diouana wanted to see France, this country whose beauty, richness, and joy of living everyone praised. She wanted to see it and make a triumphal return. This was where people got rich. Already, without having left African soil, she could see herself on the dock, returning from France, wealthy to the millions, with gifts of clothes for everyone. She dreamed of the freedom to go where she wished without having to work like a beast of burden. (46)

The illusory quality is also foregrounded, and Diouana will only be able to correct it through the migrant experience. Much in the same way as Henriette is warned of the perils that lie ahead, Diouana is also warned prior to her departure, by a man named Tive Correa, that France will not correspond to the idea she has projected upon it. Like Henriette (who refuses to listen to her aunt's narrative concerning Phoebe), she rejects this alternative construct and is unable to think of France outside of the images she has assimilated:

> Diouana would have nothing to do with the drunkard. She didn't listen to Tive Correa's advice. An old sailor, Tive Correa had come home from Europe after twenty years' absence. He had left, rich with youth, full of ambition, and come home a wreck. From having wanted everything, he had returned with nothing but an excessive love for the bottle. For Diouana he predicted nothing but misfortune. (49)

Tive Correa goes so far as to express his concern and opposition to Diouana's departure directly to Monsieur P. "'We haven't forced her to go! She wants to,' Monsieur answered dryly" (49). Effectively, Tive Correa reverses the logic that informs Diouana's migrant impulse (this dimension will be additionally explored in chapters 6 and 7). Instead, the voyage will provide Diouana, as it does many young Africans, with the painful experience that will carry her away from illusion toward reality. Upon arrival in France, Diouana is immediately submerged in domestic tasks, and witnesses nothing of the France she had anticipated:

> The third month began. Diouana was no longer the joyous girl with the ready laugh, full of life. Her eyes were beginning to look hollow, her glance was less alert, she no longer noticed details. She had a lot more work to do here than in Africa. Of France, la Belle France, she had only a vague idea, a fleeting vision. (50)

Ignored by the family, exhibited to their friends and neighbors, essentialized by the discursive authority of her employers on the subject of a "'native' psychology" (53), Diouana begins to internalize these negative images. Subsequently tormented by the children, whose games and role-playing activities are indebted to the racist constructs they have learned from observing their parents—for example, they take turns at playing "explorer" while Diouana unwittingly performs the role of the "savage" subjected to their ethnographic scrutiny—Diouana begins to manifest the physical and psycho-emotional signs of abuse:

Perpetually harassed, Diouana began to waste away. In Dakar she had never had to think about the color of her skin. With the youngsters teasing, she began to question it. She understood that here she was alone. There was nothing that connected her with the others. And it aggravated her, poisoned her life, the very air she breathed . . . Where was France? The beautiful cities she had seen in movies in Dakar, the rare foods, the interesting crowds? . . . Little by little she was drowning. (51)

Faced with radically different social structures in France, and outside of the oppressive colonial economy of labor, Madame P. is unable to find domestic workers willing to work the hours and complete the tasks she expects of them. She therefore resorts to importing Diouana from Africa, since "in Africa, Madame had acquired bad habits when it came to servants. In France when she hired a maid not only was the salary higher but the maid demanded a day off to boot" (46). As Rosello has shown, "if she insists so much on having Diouana with her in Antibes, it is because she has had a chance to discover that even a difference in social class does not give her any power over other women as soon as she is no longer protected by the colonial system" (Rosello, *Postcolonial Hospitality,* 131). In the contemporary context of immigration in which a reversed colonization can be evidenced, these former colonial labor practices have now become common. Fatou Diome, in her collection of short stories entitled *La préférence nationale,* has underscored this transition: "As for the sound of a vacuum cleaner, well, it just about always signals the presence of an African, Portuguese, or Asian woman."[20] Like Simone in Akofa's work, Madame P. takes it upon herself to secure Diouana's commitment to travel to France: "Madame sang the praises of France. For three thousand francs a month, any young African girl would have followed her to the end of the earth" (Sembene, "Black Girl," 46). Through the invocation of the island of Gorée, Sembene offers the reader an ominous metaphor that foreshadows Diouana's experience in France, but also engages in the sort of mediation I alluded to earlier as a mechanism for establishing a transhistorical connection to the question of slavery:

Leaning out of the wide window overlooking the sea, transported, Diouana watched the birds flying high above in the immense expanse of blue. In the distance she could barely make out the Island of Gorée. She was holding her identity card, turning it over and over, examining it and smiling quietly to herself. The picture was a gloomy one. She wasn't pleased with the pose or with the exposure. "What does it matter? I'm leaving!" she thought. (Sembene, "Black Girl," 47)

Diouana has secured the "legal" documents necessary to make the crossing—undertaken by sea rather than air, thus duplicating the mode of transportation of her slave ancestors. The Island of Gorée served as a transition point for slave-holders, and thus remains indissociable from the symbolic crossing that will bring Sembene's protagonist to the shores of southern France. While the slave crossing is of course forced, Diouana's is not entirely "voluntary," given economic imperatives and the power of the lure toward France that has resulted from colonial indoctrination and that is recuperated and embraced by colonial subjects. Furthermore, Diouana's capacity to arrive at a carefully formulated decision is voided by the illusionary nature of her representation of France. Here, it serves as an indictment of the colonizer's powers of deception and as a testimony to Diouana's repression and denial with regard to the myth of France. Interestingly enough, it is within the African context that Diouana locates the harsh demands associated with work (of course, this is her only point of reference at this juncture in her biography), while France promises to offer her the necessary prerequisites for freedom upon her return. While in the African context Diouana's status as a colonized subject was essentially unquestioned in the rigorous separation enacted by the colonial hierarchy, she becomes increasingly conscious in France of her ethnic identity and of the multiple levels on which she is exploited. Gradually, she establishes a link between the various points of intersection of her oppression, and begins to recontextualize her status as analogous to that of her slave ancestors: "'Sold, sold. Bought, bought,' she repeated to herself . . . They lured me, tied me to them, and I'm stuck here like a slave" (Sembene, "Black Girl," 53–54). However, clearly unable to assume the type of autonomy or agency that would have emancipated her (or, perhaps more appropriately, offered her the opportunity for enfranchisement), Diouana sees suicide as the only viable escape (a decision also reached by many captured slaves). "Diouana, who slashes her throat," Rosello suggests, "paradoxically reoccupies the place of the subject by claiming her right to die. Like the Hegelian slave whose only freedom is to reappropriate his own body by destroying it, Diouana reestablishes borders between the house and herself, between her identity and that of her employers" (Rosello, *Postcolonial Hospitality*, 129).

Sembene's short story allows for a mediation with the postcolonial diasporic context in which these ideologies and constructs have survived. This framework also ignores the prevalence of oppressive societal structures outside of the African matrix, and how "the servile aspects of hospitality can be delegated, because another woman, the colonized woman, will take over, [enacting a] redistribution of roles" (Rosello, *Postcolonial Hospitality*, 133). The originality of Rosello's analysis resides in the identification of oppressive mechanisms as foundational to Western social organization, "for servants obviously do not disappear when nations become independent . . . Europe continues to function as a crucible in which gender tests the category of race while racially marked subjects point to the limits of Western feminism" (135). The projection onto the other is a convenient gesture, but as Sembene shows, Madame is able to transplant her colonial behavior to France much in the same way as Henriette's "benefactresses" are accommodated. While in a more general context Sembene would recognize African complicity in the slave trade, in this context the fundamental difference between the texts emerges in the shift in the treatment of slavery from the tolerated practice of "domestic slavery" in the 1960s to a more hidden form by the end of the twentieth century. Significantly, while the texts approach slavery differently, both essentially consider the manner in which important social issues struggle to be introduced through *fait divers* (namely those news items relating the suicide of a young African woman and the existence of slavery in modern France) as stories or narratives prior to achieving a historical status. The points of commonality between Sembene's and Akofa's texts are striking, yet each author in turn deals with the subject in different ways—in Sembene's work, the African is constructed as the victim of French colonial ideology, while in Akofa's, the victim is subject to oppressive structures in both postcolonial Africa and the Diaspora in France.

A further intertextual parallel emerges from a juxtaposition of the respective projects of explorers, missionaries, and colonial administrators who went to Africa and the experiences of Diouana and Henriette—as transnational exchanges and examples of mediation between cultures available in hegemonic imperialist adventures. "From an emphasis on the sovereignty of the people of a nation and the right to self-determination, we see a shift in emphasis to the rights of individuals regardless of identity" (Sassen, *Globalization,* 96). Colonialism corresponded to the explicit incorporation of Africa into the global capitalist economy, and Diouana and Henriette serve as symbolic markers of that transition. From the decolonizing imperative of the late 1950s to the circumstances of France's contemporary postcolonial communities, the "African experience" in both works reveals how stereotypes and reductive projections that were intrinsic components of the colonial project need to be confronted in order to demystify official French discourse and expose current racist and prejudicial reformulations of these earlier processes.

Sembene's short story criminalizes colonial discourse and practices and represents a powerful case study of oppressive practices; while Akofa's text may not sufficiently fault the French authorities for their silent complicity in oppression by refusing to recognize the category of slavery, the "paratext" offered by the European Court of Human Rights ends up fulfilling this potential discursive space. The existence of an organization such as the Committee against Modern Slavery, evoked by Akofa, implies that Diouana's story might, today at least, have been radically different—but perhaps more important in this instance is the fact that the outcome of Akofa's terrible experience has not, thankfully, been the same as that of Diouana's. Naturally it would be anachronistic to assume that such opportunities as the Committee provided were available to Diouana at that historical juncture, and to profoundly underestimate the degree to which she was dependent on her colonial masters; of course, while Akofa's story ends differently, modern forms of slavery and servitude remain central components of the constantly mutating landscapes of globalization. The globalized process of slavery needs to be understood within a transnational and transhistorical framework, and although almost forty years separate these two texts, important connections can be made if the postcolonial critic elects to underscore the historical significance and contributions of various narratives of complicity.

FIVE

Afro-Parisianism and African Feminisms

I thought I'd found another way of
making a bridge between here-and-
there, between my two othernesses,
my double unbelonging.

Salman Rushdie[1]

As I embark upon this chapter, in which I propose to deal with complex feminist issues in writings by selected African women, but more specifically with the controversial issue of female excision, I am further reminded of the importance of Adrienne Rich's 1984 essay "Notes toward a Politics of Location."[2] As a European critic working in the United States, I have always been acutely aware of my so-called "location" and have never allowed myself—or, for that matter, been allowed—to take it for granted. I addressed this issue in the introduction to my book *Nation-Building, Propaganda, and Literature in Francophone Africa*: "it is my sincere hope that the book's commitment to incorporate a more inclusive range of narratives through the treatment of a multiplicity of voices will yield a more accurate version of the history of decolonization, which even if ventriloquized through the words of a European scholar will nevertheless constitute a step in the right direction."[3] The focus shifts in the next chapter to the phenomenon of *La sape*; this provides us with the occasion to explore a different facet of gender given its masculinist quality. However, as we shall see, both the underexplored homosocial and homoerotic components of the practice and the broader sociocultural context of shifting colonial and postcolonial gender relations provide the opportunity to reconsider its (counter-)hegemonic dimension while also further underscoring what we have to learn from examining multiple aspects of gender relations in the African and diasporic context, and accordingly in the bilateral flows of external and internal critiques that are, as Obioma Nnaemeka and Joy Ngozi Ezeilo have argued, "complex and rife with obstacles."[4]

In this chapter, though, my argument has less to do with one's positionality with regard to excision—I for one am opposed to all forms of oppression and both embrace and insist upon, in my teaching and scholarly practices, the importance of an ethical humanities. External demands requiring one to situate oneself in one of the various "camps"—universalist, relativist, oppositionalist—to my mind oversimplify and obfuscate the problematic components of an ethnocentrist history and the responses it has generated. Instead, what I am endeavoring to do here is to document and analyze the emergence of what I consider to be both valid and important testimonial narratives by African women who have experienced discrimination both in Africa and in the French Diaspora, while also highlighting another dimension of the disturbing practice I discussed in the previous chapter, namely the fostering of "sensationalist" discourse by the French authorities in the service of a recuperative culturalist agenda that further relegates African immigrants to the margins of French society. These texts share numerous points of commonality with those explored by Alec G. Hargreaves in his essay "Testimony, Co-authorship, and Dispossession among the Maghrebi Minority in France," in which he demonstrates how the textual coauthorship of several recent Maghrebi texts has served to reascribe a paternalistic role to France while simultaneously "reaffirming their unassimilability," as exemplified in such titles as *Mariée de force* (*A Forced Bride*), *La Fatiha: Née en France, mariée de force en Algérie* (*Promised: Born in France, Married by Force in Algeria*), *Dans l'enfer des tournantes* (*Inside the Hell of Gang Rape*), and *Brûlée vive* (*Burnt Alive*).[5]

Some scholars have adopted the label "Francophone Studies" in order to designate the study of those literatures and cultures outside of France or within France's postcolonial communities that share French-language usage, and this designation has been practical in rethinking French Studies and fostering interdisciplinarity. The adversarial component of the term concerns the role of France itself in this category, since many have argued that Francophonie itself, as a governmental and institutional phenomenon, transfers and relocates France's colonial centrality in the era of decolonization and postcoloniality. Acknowledging the polemics of this debate and in turn expressing my own positionality alongside those who have questioned Francophonie's hegemonic potential, I want to take the opportunity to return and consider how globalization is not exclusively "homogenizing/hegemonic" or "heterogenetic/interpenetrating," but rather a process in which individuals and groups are "transformed by diasporas and intercommunication."[6] Indeed, as the editor of a recent special issue of *Afrique contemporaine* on excision has argued, it is only through an inclusive framework (incorporating African countries and countries with high African immigration) that we can begin to comprehend this question.[7] To this end, the implicit mediation that takes place between Africa and diasporic Africans with regard to women and feminist practices is particularly striking; this chapter then does not aim (or for that matter claim) to provide a conclusive account or overview of African feminisms,[8] but merely to explore how the most compelling and sophisticated theorizations of "third-world" feminism might help us elucidate and think through the problematical image of African women available in Fatou Keïta's 1998 novel *Rebelle (Rebel)*.[9] As Nnaemeka has stated in *Female Circumcision and the Politics of Knowledge: African Women in Imperialist Discourses*, "we seek to engage the discourse on female circumcision and in the process (re)trace, expose, and map a long lineage of imperialist and colonial discourses."[10] Keïta's novel provides the opportunity to illuminate a new facet of this discourse.

One of the principal areas of inquiry, in which such an approach seems particularly pertinent, is francophone African writings that have adopted diasporic and transnational frameworks in order to address questions relating to African women. In this area, Roland Robertson's term "glocalization" (used to better designate the interaction and interpenetration of the local and the global) becomes useful in recontextualizing the relationship between Africa and the diasporic communities residing in the Hexagon,[11] as does French anthropologist Jean-Loup Amselle's recent emphasis on the synonymous links he identifies between the "global" and the "universal" in constructing globalization as another universalism.[12] The interconnection of populations is also central to Amselle's notion of *branchements* (connections), given his insistence on the transhistorical manner in which all populations are necessarily imbricated. Both transnational and transcolonial approaches, but also multisited ethnographies, have much to offer us in this process. If the imperative is to "deterritorialize" (Amselle, *Branchements*, 15) Africa, then perhaps the circumstances of African women could serve as the paradigmatic deterritorialized signifier, containing simultaneously the opportunity to contextualize and recontextualize a multitude of identities around a common, global defining characteristic. Indeed, Nnaemeka has underscored the importance of such a framework:

> In this day and age of globalization with massive population and cultural flows that are increasingly blurring the line between the inside and the outside, African women do not have the luxury of contending with a distinct outside and grappling with a clear-cut inside. The internal and the external are ever evolving, always contaminated and contested, mutually creating and recreating each other. The complex nexus of transformations and shifts makes the balancing act more difficult and precarious. (Nnaemeka, "Mapping African Feminisms," 31)

A number of recent texts by African writers have reflected a disturbing pattern, effectively displacing and shifting the responsibility for the plight

of African women in the Diaspora away from the West in order to reat-
tribute it to Africa, highlighting some of the more problematic dimensions
of discourse on human rights, universalism, and hegemony. In these instances, African women are consistently represented as the victims of a
system of African values and customs from which salvation and emancipation are to be obtained in proximity to Western "universalist" principles; "in effect," as Nnaemeka has shown in a brilliant deconstruction of
the para-discourse of female excision or circumcision, "African women
are doubly victimized: first from within (their culture) and second from
without (their 'saviors')." Because of this, "the language of development,"
Nnaemeka argues, "is the language of necessity and desirability (the so-
called Third World needs and must have 'development') and, by implication, the language of the indispensability and relevance of those who believe it is their prerogative to make development happen."[13] This is a key
example of transcolonial discourse as we witness the shift from the "humanistic" justificatory component of the colonial project toward the development discourse that has informed the politics of postcoloniality. African protagonists therefore travel or escape to France in order to gain
cognizance of their status as alienated, disenfranchised, and oppressed
subjects, realizations attributed to ignorance about or the absence of local
notions of individual rights. Keïta's text emerges as the repository of intersecting discourses, blurring the line between insiders and outsiders,
Africans in Africa, and Africans in France.

The location of the African woman is often overlooked, and African examples of activism and feminism for the most part ignored. Sekai
Nzenza-Shand has shown how these internal systems and external forces
operate in a constitutive framework, although external components are
usually privileged. The effort here is to redress this imbalance: "Western
interpretations of human rights are automatically seen as superior to the
African conception of human rights."[14] Two films by the Senegalese filmmaker Ousmane Sembene partially reverse this situation by indicating
forms of local agency; in *Faat-Kine,* whose central protagonist is an autonomous and resourceful woman, and in *Molaade,* a confrontation of female circumcision and a powerful statement of support for local agency
and initiatives. This goes to the heart of the tenuous relationship between
internal and external voices and the interpenetrative dimension and potential of diasporic voices that might partially redress the problem discussed by Nzenza-Shand: "while the impact of Western feminism has been
beneficial to African women, its positive effects have constantly been diminished by the role of Western activists who insist on speaking on behalf
of African women and thus silence them . . . By eroding the concept of
Western ownership of human rights, we may increase the possibility of
real dialogue across cultures. With contribution from non-Western societies, human rights dialogue can lose the stigma of having the West as the

authoritative interpreter of human rights" (Nzenza-Shand, 68–77).[15] Keïta is an interlocutor in this exchange, but part of the difficulty in establishing what function her text performs comes from the fact that it exhibits a polyvocal dimension that exceeds simple classification. Part of the challenge of this chapter comes precisely from the need to consider the question of audience and reception, and in turn to identify what is at stake in identifying the various constituencies and locations that inform this work.

While not negating or denying the relevance and potential importance of works that deal with women in France's postcolonial communities, I insist on recognizing how these works are marked and altered upon entry into the public domain by an official discourse that has the potential of undermining the positive dimension by distorting and recuperating content, and thereby further marginalizing women. As Eloïse Brière has argued,

> The American tendency to focus exclusively on one corner of Africa or one aspect of African culture corresponds to an imperialistic totalizing strategy wherein a chosen element stands as a metaphor for the whole. As a result, the information on excision tends to exoticize African women by decontextualizing their circumstances and constituting them as the West's "other." Exoticism effaces contexts and hard facts and lends itself to *sensationalism*. (emphasis mine)[16]

This connects with my argument in the introduction, in which I underlined the crucial importance of embracing Etienne Balibar's insistence on the racial dimension in discussing postcolonial immigrant politics: "a racism of the era of 'decolonization' . . . whose dominant theme is not biological heredity but the insurmountability of cultural differences, a racism which, at first sight, does not postulate the superiority of certain groups or peoples in relation to others but 'only' the harmfulness of abolishing frontiers, the incompatibility of life-styles and traditions."[17]

The 1998 novel *Rebelle*, by the writer Fatou Keïta from the Ivory Coast, explores the particular sociocultural circumstances of African women in francophone sub-Saharan Africa and in the francophone African Diaspora. While examining questions pertaining to women's rights, Keïta's work reconfigures and articulates a broad range of projections concerning African women. The text focuses on a young woman named Malimouna who escapes her rural village when, after an arranged marriage, her new husband discovers that she has not been excised. Homeless, on the run, she finds a position as a nanny in the urban capital and ends up moving with a French family to the Hexagon, the catalyst that allows the topography to shift away from Africa to France, and into the Black diasporic community. Prompted by her own experiences in France and her observations of the treatment of African women in the diasporic context, she decides to help other immigrant women. Malimouna's interventions provide the novel with the occasion to address several dimensions of the question of excision—through diverse individual and collective experiences—and thereby engage with the intense debate that took place in France during the 1980s and 1990s.[18] As Lionnet has explained, "the debate opposes two apparently conflicting versions of human rights, one based on the Enlightenment notion of the sovereign individual subject, and the other on a notion of collective identity grounded in cultural solidarity."[19]

One such narrative concerns a young woman from Mali, named Fanta, who has been sent by her family to France to live with the husband that was chosen for her. Malimouna and Fanta immediately develop a friendship. However, while Fanta may feel confused by her new environment when she first arrives in France, she does not question the sociocultural codes her husband embraces and which she shares—the "local" value system has here been reproduced in the diasporic context. The distance between the private values of the diasporic home and the standards of the public space soon become evident. In fact, as Laurence Porgès has shown, "maintaining the practice of excision allows immigrants to avoid marginalization, and therefore rupture with the society of origin, but perhaps more importantly to build ties with the African community residing in France" (Porgès, 61). The rift between Malimouna and Fanta grows wider when Fanta comes to her in order to solicit assistance with a growing domestic problem, namely her daughter's refusal to undergo her own scheduled excision. The visit provides Malimouna with the opportunity to reflect on the situation, to question the logic that informs the practice, and to confront a complex ideological challenge. Her attempts at dissuading Fanta prove futile, since Fanta is committed to adhering to cultural codes whose validity is not diminished in the immigrant context. Somewhat paradoxically, as Lionnet has argued,

> the refusal to allow the excision of the daughter could endanger the mother's opportunity to engage in the slow process of liberation that now allows African women living in France to oppose polygamy . . . *so long as* they are not perceived by the immigrant community to be imposing these "new" values on their own daughters.[20]

The situation is further complicated by the fact that Malimouna is confused by the context in which she is acting and the seemingly irreconcilable nature of the binary discourses with which she is faced; while opposed to the practice of excision, she also has difficulty accepting the consistent French legal characterization of the practice as a "barbarous mutilation."[21] For Chima Korieh, "the inscription in the female circumcision polemics of nineteenth-century anthropological terms—'savage,' 'primitive,' and 'barbaric' used to describe non-Western societies—raises questions about the insensitivity inherent in Western representations of other peoples."[22] Clearly, the signifiers such terminology registers bring us to the heart of what Sondra Hale has so admirably captured in her essay "Colonial Discourse and Ethnographic Residuals: The 'Female Circumcision' Debate and the Politics of Knowledge," in seeking to find a postcolonial location in which "ethnically, racially, and culturally diverse feminists and womanists" could "be allies of each other" given that "there are people both 'inside' and 'outside' (and those 'inside' who are 'outsiders,' that is, marginalized by their own society, those in exile, and the like) of the cultures where we find the practices that hold these views."[23] Before exploring this questions further, I want to contrast Keïta's position with the activist, literary, and media work of France's most famous "minority" writer, Calixthe Beyala.

In two works of nonfiction that have received relatively little attention in scholarship on Beyala, *Lettre d'une Africaine à ses sœurs occidentales* (*Letter from an African Woman to her Western Sisters*, 1995) and *Lettre d'une Afro-française à ses compatriotes* (*Letter from an Afro-French Woman to her Compatriots*, 2000), Beyala adopts a global framework with which to address the circumstances of African women.[24] The titles of these texts deserve additional commentary. In the former, Beyala situates herself as an African woman, and it is from that perspective that she establishes a connection and solidarity with her Western sisters. However, in the latter, her positionality has shifted to that of an "Afro-French woman" and her audience—her compatriots—are rendered as ambiguous as the hyphenated identity marker from which she speaks. The compatriots she has in mind are specifically the French women she is surrounded by in the territory she has adopted and into which she attempts to integrate. Yet an alternative reading might allow us to suggest that she simultaneously engages both the African diasporic populations living in the Hexagon and her Cameroonian compatriots who might benefit from the text's forthright assessment of race relations in France. As Jacques Chevrier has argued with reference to her novel *C'est le soleil qui m'a brûlée* (1987), "not only is her text a declaration of war against traditional patriarchal society, but it is also accompanied by a genuine program aimed at restoring women's most fundamental rights . . . passage from Africa to Europe results in a widening identitarian gap between men and women, for the most part to the benefit of the latter."[25] In the *Lettre d'une Africaine à ses sœurs occidentales,* Beyala deals with gender questions (excision, polygamy, and patriarchy) in the African context, while in the *Lettre d'une Afro-française à ses compatriotes,* the emphasis has shifted to racism, xenophobia, and minority populations in the Hexagon itself.

Beyala has adopted the role of a public intellectual in France. It might be worth noting that she has her own website, *http://calixthe.beyala.free.fr/,* on which her multiple public activities are announced and recorded. She serves as president of the organization Collectif égalité (Collective for Equality), which has advocated for minority and women's rights alongside other national groups such as Ni putes, ni soumises (NPNS; Neither Whores Nor Doormats), and in particular for the greater visibility of "la population noire" (the Black population) on French television. In 1998, Collectif égalité published an "open letter to the prime minister" announcing a new "movement for an immigrant citizenship." In "Calixthe Beyala: Black Face(s) on French TV," Nicki Hitchcott has indicated that "what Beyala's media career reveals is a woman struggling to position herself between these poles, sometimes as assimilated, sometimes as a rebel, sometimes as neither, sometimes as both. Unfortunately, as a media icon of black femininity, Calixthe Beyala, like her Collectif égalité, has so far failed to produce any real change in the negative status quo."[26] Collectif égalité is motivated by what could be described as a dual agenda that is concerned with the representation of minorities on television as both a qualitative and a quantitative issue. As Hitchcott shows, the Conseil supérieur de l'audiovisuel (CSA), which regulates French television, commissioned two studies "of French television's representation of ethnic minorities" (Hitchcott, "Black Face(s)," 474), the first entitled "Présence et représentation de l'immigration et des minorités ethniques à la télévision française" and the second "Présence et représentation des 'minorités visibles' à la télévision française."[27]

Bennetta Jules-Rosette has shown how, in *Lettre d'une Africaine à ses sœurs occidentales,* Beyala "elaborates on identity construction as an African woman . . . Nostalgically, she looks back upon French feminism of the 1950s, but also claims that the era of mass movements is over. Each woman must create her own identity and her own destiny." This allows her to deploy a new concept, namely that of "feminitude," that is anchored in "the egalitarian difference between men and women."[28] This adherence to Western feminism naturally engages with the polemic surrounding the dangers of reproducing imperial discourses given their transcolonial nature. Nnaemeka has highlighted the risks associated with a "mindset that emanates from a specific location (Western)" and that can "mimic the imperial arrogance of white explorers, imperialists, and colonizers," whereby "the West is arguing with itself for/against women used as tools to affirm or perpetuate a long history of political, imperialist, and racist positions anchored in moralizing (but morally bankrupt) assertions of superiority" (Nnaemeka, "The Challenges of Border-Crossing," 5, 8).[29]

Nevertheless, situating these texts in dialogue with one another enables us to highlight multiple sites of oppression, and thereby potentially circumvent the reductive implications of a universalist agenda. The kind of mediation that is contained in Beyala's multidirectional discourse—from *Africaine* (African woman) to *Afro-française* (Afro-French woman) and from *sœurs occidentales* (Western sisters) to *compatriotes* (women compatriots)—shares some contextual points of commonality with Nnaemeka's theorization of "nego-feminism," namely the feminism of negotiation . . . In the foundation of shared values in many African cultures are the principles of negotiation, give and take, compromise, balance. Here, negotiation has the double meaning of "give and take/ exchange" and "cope with successfully/go around." African feminism . . . challenges through negotiations and compromise.[30]

Keïta's text is thus indicative of the kind of dilemma that the French authorities and courts have introduced by refusing to conceive of the question of excision beyond reductive paradigms in which the potential of "negotiation" is a priori voided. Keïta endeavors to go beyond this framework by trying to find a language that other immigrant women may be able to adopt and adapt in turn, and that would replace the primary focus of Western feminists, who "have brought to the fore intense debates about the conception of good, social justice, and moral responsibility from which, unfortunately, the humanity of those to be rescued is relegated to the background" (Nnaemeka, "Nego-feminism," 371). Practices of negotiation, while intrinsic to the postcolonial framework Nnaemeka addresses, were always already present in the "complementary" nature of gender relations during the colonial era described by Niara Sudarkasa in "'The Status of Women' in Indigenous African Societies,"[31] or for that matter in any structure that aims to move beyond the kind of gendered oppositionality against which Chandra Talpade Mohanty has so eloquently argued: "such simplistic formulations are both historically reductive; they are also ineffectual in designating strategies to combat oppressions. All they do is reinforce binary divisions between men and women."[32]

Malimouna's own ambiguity with regard to what she perceives as internal and external conceptions of sociocultural practices echo in turn those of the novelist Keïta in her attempt to articulate a carefully conceived position. Somewhat paradoxically, resistance to Western feminism both in Africa and in the diasporic context arises because it is perceived as interfering in sociocultural practices, when in fact "the resistance from Africans is not necessarily against the termination of the practice; rather it is against the strategies and methods (particularly the imperialistic underpinnings) used to bring about this desirable goal . . . the resistance of African women is not against the campaign to end the practice, but against their dehumanization and the lack of respect and dignity shown to them in this process." The "backlash" against these women has also led to their being "labeled, indicted and dismissed as defenders of female circumcision" (Nnaemeka, "If Female Circumcision Did Not Exist," 172–173, 177). Naturally, criticism from the "outside" is also complicated by several factors; firstly the assumption that "insiders" act in a homogeneous manner and are likely to be incapable of achieving consciousness or awareness of the dangers of normative behavior models, and secondly through the implication that "outsiders" are automatically at the service of postcolonial development discourse. These are the pitfalls of the kind of bilateral symbiotic discourse Mohanty summarizes:

> a comparison between western feminist self-presentation and western feminist representation of women in the third world yields significant results. Universal images of "the third-world woman" (the veiled woman, chaste virgin, etc.), images construct[ed] from adding the "third-world difference" to "sexual difference," are predicated on (and hence obviously bring into sharper focus) assumptions about western women as secular, liberated and having control over their own lives . . . For without the overdetermined discourse that creates the *third* world, there would be no (singular and privileged) first world. Without the "third-world woman," the particular self-representation of western women mentioned above would be problematical. I am suggesting, in effect, that the one enables and sustains the other. (Mohanty, "Under Western Eyes," 69)[33]

How might one begin to move beyond this problem? How can Keïta's project not in turn find itself reconstructed as a sensational rhetorics that appeals to an official French audience whose prejudices can only be further confirmed by the authenticity of a narrative delivered by an African "native" informer? Nnaemeka's notion of "negotiation" shares points of commonality with the process of mediation I have argued for throughout this book: "Seeing feminist theorizing through the eyes of the 'other,' from the 'other' place, through the 'other' worldview," as Nnaemeka has illustrated, "has the capacity to defamiliarize feminist theory as we know it and assist not only in interrogating, understanding, and explaining the unfamiliar but also in defamiliarizing and refamiliarizing the familiar in more productive and enriching ways" (Nnaemeka, "Nego-feminism," 381).

In her *Lettre d'une Africaine à ses sœurs occidentales,* Beyala acknowledges her own indebtedness to European feminist models elaborated from the 1950s onward and their importance for African women, and even calls for the support of Western women in scrutinizing cultural, political, and social practices. Beyala simultaneously underscores the mutually constitutive component of this "sisterhood," signaling through a globalizing transcolonial and transnational framework what women have to learn from each other's struggles (Beyala, *Lettre d'une Africaine,* 103). In this context, Western feminism does not stand alone. This allows Beyala to in effect dismiss the potentially unilateral nature of Western feminist discourse, substituting in its place an approach that replicates her personal and intellectual trajectories. Beyala's own in-betweenness (perhaps even her own form of the "double unbelonging" alluded to in the epigraph to this chapter) affords her a privileged perspective from which to comment on these questions.[34] Rejecting the marginalizing impact of the hyphenated identitarian status that is implied by the term "franco," utilized in France to describe minority populations (Franco-Algerian, Franco-African)—"always this franco something that situates the other within spheres of difference, distancing them from the national community and creating within itself subnational communities" (Beyala, *Lettre d'une Afro-française*, 40)—Beyala replaces the negative quality of this label with the affirmative qualities of a multicultural, multiethnic, and multinational signifier.

Invariably, one's position with regard to the practice of excision is secondary to the broader implications of this discourse. "To condemn excision as a violation of human rights," Lionnet has argued, "is to arbitrarily presume that such a practice is the only culturally sanctioned form of violence that deserves to be denounced, whereas we know that many other forms of violence are not repressed by law in the Western context, and that some of our own practices are objectionable and shocking to Africans" (Lionnet, "Feminisms and Universalisms," 373). Rather, what is at stake is the implications both for the African and the diasporic immigrant context in determining whether feminist engagement is merely designed to maintain French assimilationist and recuperative hegemony through the dissemination of negative discourses pertaining to African sociocultural practices. Indeed, that is what Beyala has argued. If that is the case, then such discourse will continue to impede and limit the dynamism associated with the heterogeneous nature of transformations in the immigrant context. However, questioning and challenging this mechanism provides the opportunity to displace responsibility and allow African women to become agents of change. This is an important step toward the type of argument advocated by Lionnet, in which "this form of universalism does not objectify the other and subsume her into my own world view; what it does is create a relational space where intersubjectivity and reciprocity become possible," and that in turn makes it "pointless to claim that the issue opposes communitarian values to universal ones; the actual conflict hinges on the opposing claims of two different communities, one of which would like to believe that its culture is a 'universal' one" (Lionnet, *Postcolonial Representations*, 153, 166). For Beyala, the question of validating cultural difference contains its own boundaries: "let us not confuse things: the respect of cultural differences does not mean accepting any kind of insanity, any kind of barbarism with which certain societies—notably African society—shower us with" (Beyala, *Lettre d'une Africaine*, 99). This statement by Beyala serves to underline what I have described as the polyvocal nature of the issue and also the question of location; clearly, different processes are at work when Beyala evokes "barbarism" than when the French courts do, for example.

Beyond any kind of relativistic discourse, the fact remains that this is a debate that needs to take place both in Africa and beyond the continent, and this can be effected by infusing the debate with a deterritorialized notion of Africa that would allow for dialogue and mediation with African Diasporas in global contexts; this rejoins the "interpenetrative" dimension of globalization studied by Ashcroft (Ashcroft, *Post-colonial Transforma-tions*, 214). "The development process, as it is engineered from outside and 'above,'" Nnaemeka argues, "has dragged Africans along while leaving behind African ideals of humanity, responsibility, compromise, and true partnership at the heart of democratic values that would have smoothed the rough edges of the so-called development in theory and practice" (Nnaemeka, "Nego-feminism," 375). Such gestures have failed to eliminate the potential shortcomings associated with a conception of universalism that ignores an incorporative paradigm of ethical conduct constructed outside of the principles and coordinates of Western codes and standards. Keïta's text is more concerned with exploring the complicated locations from which arguments are formulated than it is with aesthetic factors such as literariness; this work embraces a more popular usage of literature in the service of social causes. What complicates the dialogue is that the advocacy and appeal for individual rights take place initially in France, where such notions have themselves been rejected by the universalizing exigencies of Frenchness in addressing the potentialities of a multicultural society.

I propose to examine some of the ways in which these questions surface in *Rebelle*. The particular sociocultural circumstances of African women both in francophone sub-Saharan Africa and in the African Diaspora in France are explored. Rather than heralding the emergence of a model of feminist contestation and oppositionality, Keïta's novel shares proximity with Western emancipatory structures pertaining to women's rights, gender equity, and sexual oppression. France continues to control the publication and distribution of texts produced by francophone African cultural practitioners, and the fact that the readership is for the most part located outside of Africa raises important questions, of course. For many uninformed readers, *Rebelle* corresponds quite closely to popularly received notions of African gender relations. The text begins with the central protagonist's abduction by her first husband's brothers, who forcibly bring her from the village where she was born and from which she had fled after an arranged marriage over twenty years before. During the journey, Malimouna "saw her life go by" (Keïta, 5). This flashback sequence provides the author with the opportunity to recount Malimouna's story. While there is no indication that the novel itself constitutes an autobiographical narrative, the format is clearly indebted to a documentary-testimonial mode from which Malimouna's story gains a certain authenticity.

Every effort is made to emphasize the traditionalism of the rural setting into which Malimouna is born. As a young girl she enjoys the visits of her friend Sanita, who lives in the urban capital. These young girls are constructed as binary oppositions and serve to highlight the various contributions the cultural training of each can bring the other. On the one hand, Malimouna begins to learn French from her exposure to Sanita, who speaks almost exclusively the language associated with the urban center, while Sanita's parents are eager for their daughter to make regular visits to the village so that she can gain familiarity with her "culture and language of origin" (Keïta, 6). These representations and distinctions between rural and urban spaces have a tendency to offer stereotypical constructs of what are usually far more complicated sociocultural spaces, particularly in the contemporary era in which Keïta's novel is set. These images were more commonly associated with francophone sub-Saharan African novels during the 1950s—most notably Laye Camara's *The Dark Child* and Cheikh Hamidou Kane's *Ambiguous Adventure*—in which such representations of Africa were employed in order to describe an uncontaminated African culture predating colonial contact.[35]

A dramatic transition occurs for Malimouna when she happens upon the respected village exciser, Dimikèla, in the throes of passion with a young man named Seynou. She observes them from the branch of a tree, and the lovers only become aware that they have been discovered when Malimouna falls from the branch and injures herself. Terrified of Dimikèla, Malimouna realizes that she has, unwittingly, become privy to a secret that will have serious repercussions for her. Afraid that Malimouna will reveal her transgressive liaison with Seynou, and aware of Malimouna's objections to her own excision, Dimikèla later simulates the effects of an excision during Malimouna's official excision ceremony by cutting her inner thigh instead. This self-serving act establishes a silent pact between the two women, one that will come back to haunt them.

The introduction of Malimouna's excision ceremony (when the protagonist reaches her eighth birthday) allows the narrator to articulate a number of questions concerning this ritual and rite of passage. As preparations for the ceremony get underway, we learn that these young women "were about to become worthy of respect, and for that they had to summon up all their courage and dignity . . . The entire village would then admire them and they would have become real women" (Keïta, 13). In this instance, courage and dignity are delineated as prerequisites for the acquisition of respect, and as a precondition for access to the status of woman (womanhood). Subsequently, the narrator asks, "Were they not born women?" (13). This question intertextually rejoins Simone de Beauvoir's famous statement "One is not born a women, one becomes a woman" in her pathbreaking book *Le deuxième sexe* (*The Second Sex*), in which she argued that womanhood was defined not as an essential status, but rather as one that could only be achieved through conscious emancipation and the assumption of personal responsibility.[36] Thus, while Keïta's question raises a similar problematic, the objective is displaced away from the meaning de Beauvoir accords the idea, to the extent that for Keïta birth as a woman serves as a sufficient identitarian marker outside of the exigencies of *becoming* associated with and required by sociocultural conventions.

Indeed, it is precisely because of the injury Malimouna sustains during her fall that she is able to delay her own excision. During this time period, she begins to state her objections to the ritual to her mother. The latter immediately locates this resistance in the proximity her daughter has gained, through her friendship with Sanita, to what she perceives as the values of the urban capital: "Frequenting these people could not be without consequence since Malimouna would surely be tempted to imitate them" (Keïta, 17). Having in fact assimilated and embraced these values, which her mother feels threaten her traditional sociocultural training, and which she associates with those Western worldviews that have emerged from colonialist assimilationist ideologies, she states that "this cursed little city girl who acted like a Toubab [a white person, usually in a position of authority] had become her daughter's friend, and must have given her all these bad ideas" (15). Recognizing the powerful lure these values represent, she redoubles her efforts to fulfill her role and responsibility as a mother, which consists in preparing her daughter for the successful transition to womanhood. As Lionnet has explained, "This rite of passage is meant to mark entrance into adulthood and is normally accompanied by extensive psychological preparation in the form of religious teachings and ritualized observances" (Lionnet, *Postcolonial Representations,* 155). A powerful contrast is provided between her perspective and that of Sanita's parents, who choose to protect their daughter from the practice:

> Her parents, who boasted about their pride in their traditions, preferred, for whatever reason, to shield their daughter from this crucial rite of passage in the life of a woman. Motou, though, was determined, no matter what it took, to save her daughter from this disaster and to prevent her from finding herself banished from society. She would make sure of this. (Keïta, 18)

Having "escaped" the ritual, Malimouna is able to protect her secret for another six years until, when she is fourteen, her father takes an interest in marrying her to his friend Sando. The prospect of this arranged marriage generates tremendous anxiety for Malimouna, who lives in fear of her incomplete excision being exposed. In fact, her reluctance to engage in this relationship and her terror of consummating her marital union is dramatized by her first sexual encounter with her husband, which is narrated as a rape scene. In the description of this encounter, the focus remains exclusively on male pleasure:

> She would have yelled out in pain had he not gagged her with his large hand. She felt crushed under the full weight of his body. It felt as if it lasted for several hours. And then, intoxicated with ecstasy, he had wanted to start all over again. Holding her legs spread, he had straightened himself so as to better admire the spectacle of her young body, and it was at that point that his focus had lingered on her vulva. (39)

The violence contained in this sequence is epitomized by the placing of a white sheet on the conjugal bed in order to ascertain that Malimouna is in fact a virgin, while her husband enjoys a reputation as an "old romantic" (38). However, upon realizing that she has not been excised, Sando attempts to leave the room to announce his discovery. Malimouna responds immediately and knocks her husband unconscious with a fertility statue to gain time to escape—perhaps further underlining the inextricable link the author establishes between violence and reproductive sexuality. The implication is of course that this escape serves as a metonym for a more general escape—from tradition, from patriarchy, and from subjugation: "Just like her friend Sanita, she had always wanted to discover new horizons; never did she think she would run away from home like a criminal" (50). Malimouna thus leaves her village and makes her way to the capital.

Upon her arrival in the capital, Malimouna witnesses a hit-and-run accident in which a white woman is knocked over by a car. As the victim lies injured, Malimouna tends to the woman's child, and ends up accompanying her to the hospital. She continues to take care of the child while the mother receives medical attention. When the father shows up at the hospital, he is impressed with the attention she gives the infant and her obvious competence in matters of child care, and he offers her a position as their nanny. Homeless, on the run, she willingly accepts their proposition. In fact, he is so touched by the image of this stranger nurturing his child that it brings tears to his eyes: "Malimouna was intrigued as she stared at him. A man never would have cried like this in her home over so little, and especially not in front of a woman" (52). Through Malimouna's observations, the narrator provides us with some indication of the rigorous codes of masculinity the protagonist has experienced. Furthermore, while Malimouna is literally rescued by this French couple living in Africa, she processes and filters her new environment through the education she received in her native village. For example, she observes gender roles in this household: "It was pleasant being a woman in this household. Michèle was a princess whom her husband Gérard took care of as if he revered her. She did virtually nothing. Looking at her, Malimouna thought of her mother. Matou's day began at four in the morning with prayer" (55). These rationalizations and interpretations inaugurate a more problematic process in which the French are associated with a more enlightened interpretation of gender relations, a dimension I shall return to later.

Malimouna's stay in this French family comes to an abrupt end when Michèle begins to sense her husband's growing attraction to Malimouna. She quickly finds her a new position with a French family that is about to return to France for an extended vacation. And so, rapidly, the topography shifts from Africa to France, where Malimouna finds herself increasingly isolated and alienated, her existence literally engulfed by domestic responsibilities analogous to those of so many other young African protagonists, from Diouana in Sembene's "Black Girl" to Henriette in Akofa's *Une esclave moderne:* "She felt weary and depressed. A profound feeling of solitude overcame her . . . She could not wait to be back on African soil. She felt too much of an outsider here, too ignored" (66–67). Once again, her stay with this French family ends when the husband, Monsieur Bineau, makes inappropriate sexual advances: "This time she was not running away. She was leaving" (69). With this departure, Malimouna gradually begins her discovery of the African Diaspora. Following a brief stay with a pastor and his wife who extend hospitality to her, she finally opts to leave for Paris, and finds refuge in an African shelter: "In this shelter, she had found Africa again, so far behind her at this stage. Here, several nationalities from that continent came together, but the overwhelming mood was one of depression, unhappiness. A real African popular quarter in the very heart of Paris" (77). Malimouna is able to earn a living, but, now aged twenty-two, she aspires to enroll in the Institute for Social Studies. She is prompted to pursue this objective by her own experiences in France and her observations of the treatment of African women in the diasporic context: "She wanted to be of assistance to African women in France" (83).

In this way, Malimouna meets Fanta from Mali, who has been sent by her family to France to live with the husband they chose for her. Malimouna and Fanta immediately develop a friendship, and Malimouna takes it upon herself to "guide her around and show her how to live in France" (91). However, while Fanta may feel confused by her new environment when she first arrives in France, she does not question the sociocultural codes her husband embraces and which she shares. Thus, when she becomes repeatedly pregnant, she is subjected to Malimouna's disapproval and anger: "But how are you going to get by with all these babies . . . And you who spoke of educating yourself like me!" (92). Malimouna suggests that Fanta start taking birth control pills: "Fanta had in fact discussed this with her husband that very evening . . . He had slapped her, telling her that it was contrary to their religion and that only fickle women needed that kind of protection . . . In any case, he was the one that provided for them, not her. The discussion was over" (92–91). After the birth of Fanta's fourth child, she and Malimouna arrange for her to secretly start taking birth control, but this strategy is soon uncovered by her husband, who proceeds to beat her and reassert his authority. Malimouna finds herself caught in a dilemma between her instinct to protect Fanta and the realization that reporting this violence to the French authorities would undermine the solidarity of the African diasporic community: "Her husband was all she had in this foreign city. And in any case, how could she, Malimouna, a black woman, make problems for another black person in a country in which the color of one's skin caused so much hardship? No one would forgive her for that back at the shelter" (95).

Malimouna is forced to remain silent. However, she further resolves to devote her life to improving the circumstances of women in the African Diaspora: "she would struggle to help her sisters" (95). Having completed a three-year program of study as preparation for a career in social work and become literate in French, Malimouna has gained a more solid grasp of gender relations in France as well:

> She smiled to herself when she thought back to the idea she had of women in Europe from watching Michèle, her boss in Salouma who was treated like a queen by her husband. How wrong she had been in thinking that white women were better off than those in her country! . . . Things were different back home, the customs and mores were not the same, but a woman was still a woman. (99–100)

However, this is an important step toward the type of positionality Lionnet has described, in which

> what does appear to be "universal" when we carefully examine the whole cultural contexts within which the debate is situated is the way in which *different* cultures, for better or for worse, impose *similar* constraints on the bodies of their members, especially when those bodies are already marked by the sign of the feminine. (Lionnet, *Postcolonial Representations,* 166)[37]

Later, she starts to work in an organization that is primarily designed to assist immigrant women:

> Malimouna would have her own office space and would endeavor to solve, as best she could, the problems of impoverished women, women who had often been beaten and who were prisoners of the feminine condition. The first goal she would set for herself—and she knew just how difficult this would be—was to make her protégées understand that the key to their problems resided in instruction. (Keïta, 105)

Her activism coincides with the early days of her intimate relationship with her former academic advisor and the awakening of her sexuality. However, they do not live in a vacuum, and their relationship subjects them to the scrutiny of others: "He was well aware that their relationship troubled and would be troubling to people both in his milieu and in hers. But should one give in when faced with what he saw as stupidity?" (118). When Fanta shows up at the guidance center where Malimouna works, Malimouna is aware that her friend and the African community frown on her exogamous relationship:

> Malimouna knew that Fanta would not understand how she could love a white man. In African circles, men could date white women and even marry them without too much condemnation. But as soon as a black woman so much as dared follow through with what was considered taboo, namely falling in love with a white man, well then she was immediately pilloried and subjected to the worst of calamities. (122)

In French Maghrebi communities and other French African communities, it is often the case that relationships between French men and African women are less acceptable than those between French women and African men.[38]

The purpose of Fanta's visit provides further indication of the distance between Malimouna's value system and her friend's. Fanta has come to her in order to solicit assistance with a growing domestic problem, namely her daughter's refusal to undergo her scheduled excision:

> She is eleven right now, and must be excised tomorrow, and wants to hear nothing of it! Our children who grow up in France no longer understand anything to do with our traditions and their importance. My husband will kill me if she is not excised tomorrow! . . . My husband has threatened to repudiate both of us . . . He's accusing me of putting ideas in her head. (123–124)

Fanta is unaware of her friend's own biography and act of rebellion. The visit provides Malimouna with the opportunity to reflect on the situation and to question the logic that informs the practice of excision: "Tell me, Fanta, you were excised, right? Have you forgotten how painful it was? Is that what you want for your daughter? Is that how you want to show her your love?" (124). This rejoins some of the central issues discussed at the beginning of the chapter concerning questions of location:

> Malimouna was well aware that these hollow and superficial discourses were those she had herself heard so often from Westerners. These people who usually see everything from the outside and nevertheless feel they have the right to hurl sterile and unjust condemnations at everyone else. (125)

Malimouna recognizes that argumentation will prove futile, since her friend conceives of her maternal role in terms of a responsibility to perpetuate tradition that represents "HER truth, HER reality" (125). Malimouna's opposition to the practice and unwillingness to assist Fanta in her predicament effectively constitute an invalidation of Fanta's choices, and Fanta can only respond by identifying Malimouna as the enemy. She also attributes Malimouna's ideological position to her relationship with a white French man. This encounter serves to highlight the discrepancy between the values the parents adhere to and impose in the private space, and those to which their children are exposed in the public space that is constituted by the school, youth culture, television, radio, and so forth. As a result of medical complications resulting from her excision, Fanta's daughter dies, and her story enters the public domain, thereby echoing the various *fait divers* explored in "Black Girl" and *Une esclave moderne* in the previous chapter: "The news had reached all the papers. They had all repeated the story, most notably the tabloid press, which was particularly partial to this kind of information. Little Noura had hemorrhaged to death and suffered terribly" (126). While Malimouna is opposed to the practice of excision, she questions whether imprisonment of its practitioners is in fact the most useful solution. Indeed, as Lionnet has pointed out,

> By criminalizing the practice of excision and sending the parents to jail, the French courts have judged individuals guilty of an act of violence, when in fact they had no intention of committing violence; their behavior was in accord with deeply held sociocultural and religious beliefs about the nature of femininity and the function of sexuality in their respective collectivities. Anthropologists and social critics have argued that legal sanctions will have little if any positive impact, since families may continue to have excisions performed either clandestinely in France (and with greater risk to the girls' life and health) or back in Africa during school vacations. (Lionnet, *Postcolonial Representations*, 156)

Furthermore, Malimouna struggles with the court's verdict and her partner's statement concerning the barbarous nature of the practice: "There is nothing to understand—mutilation is mutilation, and it is a barbarous act" (Keïta, 127). Malimouna rejects his universalist principles, which she sees as betraying a simplistic logic: "What do you know about barbarism?" she yelled, incensed. "It's all too easy to judge when you're outside of all this!" (127). In so doing, she demonstrates the degree to which she is confused by her attempts at expressing her opposition to the practice without simultaneously adopting a universalist stance. She emphasizes that Alain, her French partner, cannot fully understand or access the specificity of the African context. "Didn't he understood that things weren't that simple? For these people, there was nothing barbarous or cruel about them. They loved their children and were convinced that it was for their good that they acted in this way" (127). At this stage in Keïta's text, Malimouna is unable to reconcile the two positions, and to this extent the programmatic dimension must be found elsewhere. Nevertheless, the most significant and revealing point to emerge from this section concerns the author's implied awareness of the risks associated with the novel she has written. The "tabloid press" is "partial" to stories about excision, readily exploiting their inflammatory potential. Of significance here is the fact that these newspapers are known in France as the *presse à sensation*—that is, "sensationalist" newspapers eager to fuel the official culturalist argument as it pertains to the unassimilability of immigrants and to defend France's paternalism. In this treatment of public discourse, Keïta's text therefore anticipates the recuperative potential of the novel, *Rebelle*, she has written.

Shortly after the trial of Noura's parents, Malimouna returns to Africa, accompanied by Alain. Residing in a neighborhood that is primarily inhabited by Europeans, she feels alienated from other Africans in her own country. Eventually, after a miscarriage, she and Alain separate, and she meets an African man named Karim. As their relationship develops, she begins to trust him enough to share her testimony; Karim even travels to her village and helps reunite her with her mother. Marriage soon follows,

then a successful pregnancy. During her early years as a mother she continues to work part-time for an association devoted to the welfare of
women. However, as time passes, her husband becomes increasingly distant, starts having an affair, and even expresses disapproval of her involvement with the association. For all intents and purposes, Malimouna
is abandoned by her husband. As her children grow older, she becomes
more active with the association, confronting problems of education, public awareness, and women's rights. One of the main obstacles she attempts
to overcome is the resistance she encounters from other African women
who do not share her perception and interpretation of the gender inequities in the sociocultural environment in which they reside:

> Those that were disparaging of her efforts went around saying that women
> had never been slaves to men, and that all these beliefs were recuperations of
> Western conceptions aimed at perpetuating the negative image of men, and
> black men in particular . . . Africa, they insisted, had enough difficulties to
> overcome as it was without needing to go and look for others in another
> world, another milieu. (182–183)

In fact, the argument most commonly made by supporters of traditional
patriarchal structures and critics of universalist standards originates in repeated accusations that African opponents are merely adopting "Western
attitudes" (181). Malimouna is faced here with the community's attempt
to preserve the social homeostasis and its rejection of the interpenetrative
potential of both alternative internal and external positions. Ange-Marie
Hancock has discussed this divisive concept, wherein "insiders" are accused of being "outsiders": "Many women in various African nations face
charges of Western cooptation when asserting their rights as women to
attack patriarchy . . . African males have resorted to portrayals of mid-
dle-class women as 'too Westernized to be true African women.'"[39] Malimouna, aware of her own status as a victim of abuse, ignores her detrac-
tors and becomes an increasingly active and recognized campaigner for
women's causes:

> She relentlessly denounced violence against women. Violence that started
> with excision, she argued, moved on to the forced marriage of young girls,
> their subsequent suffocation in the home, and often the accompanying do-
> mestic brutalities. Additionally, she underscored, this violence also mani-
> fested itself in the refusal to women of the right to education. (189)

When Malimouna initiates an important meeting on the subject of excision, an occasion that will "feature a number of testimonies . . . Testimonies that would be of capital importance. For the first time, women
would dare to speak out in public" (194–196), the novel's more programmatic component emerges as an innovative option is provided through education and a deconstruction of the rationale that had served to justify the
practice:

As mothers, by allowing and at times even encouraging this custom, they had made mistakes, albeit because of ignorance, but often sharing in the responsibility. Today, women could no longer ignore not only the uselessness of this practice—this ritual without religious foundation—but also and in particular its harmful character. (197)

Additionally, she attempts to reverse the logic of some of the arguments that have been invoked, stating for example that

the object, it was said, was to remove from the woman's body that which resembled the penis, the ultimate symbol of masculinity. But what about breasts, weren't they the supreme symbols of femininity? If so, hadn't anyone ever thought of removing this feminine attribute from men? (197)

Keïta ends up confronting broader gender problems as they pertain to the postcolonial space in general. In Sony Labou Tansi's novels, for example, corporal disfigurement and dismemberment, along with violent sexualities, serve to articulate a commentary on the nature of the social body itself, and analogous constructs have provided the subject matter of numerous powerful works by francophone sub-Saharan African women authors such as Calixthe Beyala and Ken Bugul.

However, there are serious consequences of "speaking out." Malimouna's husband comes under increasing pressure from other men concerning his wife's activities, and his own masculinity is put into question—he is now tauntingly called "Mister Malimouna" (198). To restore order, he accuses her of having traded her allegiance to tradition for "Western" standards: "Stop playing at being a Toubab, we have our realities . . . You are my wife, go home, that's it!" (209). In a desperate attempt at reclaiming his authority and reinstating his social status as it is defined by specific masculinist codes to which he adheres, he proceeds to rape his wife. However, silence is no longer an option for her; *not* speaking is more problematic for her than the threat of violence itself: "She had won a battle, but not yet the war" (217). Through testimony, Keïta demonstrates how African women can achieve solidarity and sisterhood:

These women were in raptures upon discovering solidarity and hope. They were genuinely becoming conscious of an injustice they had never considered as such, conditioned and resigned as they were to a fate they could not really escape. What they had lived was considered the norm, but they were coming to realize that it was up to them to revise and correct this norm, so that this domination that had been exerted on their bodies and minds would progressively soften. (219–220)

After giving her speech to her captive audience, Malimouna begins the final leg of her journey when she is kidnapped by her first husband's brothers and taken back to her native village. A village council meets to decide her fate, and Malimouna is subjected to customary law concerning her first marriage. However, in a final gesture of solidarity, a large contingent of women from the association have traveled to the village to rescue her: "furious, Malimouna's friends shouted at the villagers, calling them savages" (231). Use of the term "savage" will surely not promote the kind of respectful dialogue likely to engender change, but the implications of this expression of solidarity for both the African and the diasporic immigrant context are evident. Examining some of the more constructive reflections on transnational discourse may help to connect with the programmatic dimension of Keïta's project.

In her book *The Claims of Culture: Equality and Diversity in the Global Era*, Seyla Benhabib has highlighted the dangers intrinsic to such questioning, in which

> multicultural institutional arrangements and legal compromises very often work to the detriment of women. Either they imprison them in arcane arrangements of dependency upon their husbands and male relatives . . . or they render them vulnerable to oppression by withdrawing legal protection to which they would be entitled were they not considered members of cultural minorities.[40]

Benhabib's notion of "democratic equality," which insists on establishing "impartial institutions in the public sphere and civil society where this struggle for the recognition of cultural differences and the contestation for cultural narratives can take place without domination" (Benhabib, *Claims of Culture*, 8), accordingly generates a form of "interactive universalism" that allows one to "become aware of the *otherness of others,* of those aspects of their identity that make them concrete others to me, only through their own narratives" (14). However, Benhabib's model has limitations when applied to the African framework (and surely others as well), since it underestimates the power of those social forces that determine cultural and social practices. For example, as Vicki Kirby shows, "what is 'other' for the West must thereby forfeit its own internal contradictions and diversities in this homogenizing identification of alterity."[41] There are crucial differences among and between—and within—national spaces and Diasporas. The organizing principles of Benhabib's "universalist deliberative democracy" are "egalitarian reciprocity," "voluntary self-ascription," and "freedom of exit and association": the right of the "individual to exit the ascriptive group must be unrestricted, although exit may be accompanied by the loss of certain kinds of formal and informal privileges" (Benhabib, *Claims of Culture*, 19). Tested against the case of excision, these principles cannot function, because the practice is "a cultural rite of passage derived from ancient customs [that] produces gendered identity and the religious and social integration of women [and functions as a] means of affirming gender and inscribing sexual identity on the body,"[42] *and* it is a rite of passage required as a precondition for access to the community. Similarly, Benhabib's insistence on the "voluntary" nature of human agency emphasizes the foundational importance of "choice." "The question of choice," Lionnet insists, "thus remains problematic when one focuses not just on individual rights, but on the way such rights may be in conflict with the broader social, religious or communitarian values to which an individual woman has to subscribe if she is to remain a respected member of her community, as opposed to being a 'free' agent in our increasingly atomized capitalist culture" (Lionnet, "Feminisms and Universalisms," 374). As Porgès has shown, "in cases where women refuse excision, they would be subjected to public recrimination and if necessary operated on by force or forced to submit themselves to common law" (Porgès, 53).

Keïta's work faithfully introduces into literature the kind of social transformation that is evidenced in Africa today and whose recognition Hancock emphasizes: "What has been commonly overlooked by development professionals and Western feminist activists are those resources already possessed by African women" (Hancock, 249). A solution may be available in what she has described as an "egalitarian multicultural coalition politics" (246) and by further consideration of important contributions made by African feminists such as Molara Ogundipe-Leslie and Philomena Okeke, who have written about these complex debates, requiring that our analyses go "beyond the single issue of anti-FGM activism to a global analysis of power relations" (253).[43]

French colonial policy "tolerated" excision in the colonies, whereas postcolonial legal argumentation structures excision as a violation of "fundamental human principles" (Lionnet, *Postcolonial Representations*, 165)—surely this must lead us to interrogate the moment at which France's "internal" position, its policy of noninterference, is interrupted and ceases to be applicable at the limits of the Hexagon, and therefore to ask how a consideration of the transcolonial framework reveals contradictions that point to the problematic component of the "clash of civilizations" culturalist argument recuperated from colonial discourse and remapped on the landscape of post-1980 immigrant politics in order to foster the "absolute noncommensurability of the two cultural systems" (164).[44]

"Culture," as Nnaemeka reminds us, "as an arena of political and ideological struggle, needs constant and close scrutiny to separate reality from invention or trace invention's transformation into reality. Culture is dynamic in the sense that it derives its meanings, evolution, and reformulation from people's encounter with and negotiations in the context of historical imperatives" (Nnaemeka, "Nego-feminism," 374). Immigration policies and the socioeconomic circumstances of African immigrants in France should be subjected to the kind of concerted attention and scrutiny that so-called incompatible cultural practices receive in the service of conserving and preserving a monolithic conception of French society. As Mali's former minister of culture, Aminata Traoré, has argued in her forceful critique of the negative impact of economic globalization on Africa, the possibility of working with "women's organizations in the Northern hemisphere that believe, as indeed we do, in the possibility of a new Africa and that work toward this objective, in collaboration at times with African organizations" (Traoré, *Le viol de l'imaginaire,* 148), should be embraced as a further mediation between Africa and the African Diaspora, as an alternative mechanism for "nego-tiating" African feminisms with multiple coordinates.

SIX

Fashion Matters: *La sape* and Vestimentary Codes in Transnational Contexts and Urban Diasporas

What young African doesn't dream of going
to France? Unfortunately, they confuse living
in France with being a servant in France. I
come from the village next to Diouana's, in
Casamance. There, we don't say the way you
do that it is the light that attracts the moth,
but the other way round. In my country,
Casamance, we say that the darkness
pursues the moth.

Ousmane Sembene[1]

In the postcolony, magnificence and the desire
to shine are not the prerogative only of those
who command. The people also want to be
"honored," to "shine," and to take part in
celebrations . . . in their desire for a certain
majesty, the masses join in the madness and
clothe themselves in cheap imitations of
power to reproduce its epistemology.

Achille Mbembe[2]

A product manufactured by the colonizer
is accepted with confidence. His habits,
clothing, food, architecture are closely
copied, even if inappropriate.

Albert Memmi[3]

When one thinks of various colonial centers and their respective architectural and geo-political spaces that constituted the peripheries of empire, associations with France remain indissociable from its capital city, Paris.

The focus of this chapter is provided by a discussion of the symbiotic relationship between Paris as a narrative construct in the minds of its former colonial subjects and the complex manner in which urban spaces and narrative productions are simultaneously reconfigured according to the cultural, political, and sociological agendas of cultural practitioners; while in chapter 2 the acquisition of cultural capital was addressed with regard to colonial education, the focus here shifts to the acquisition of social capital in the form of a secular quest or pilgrimage to France (as opposed to Mecca).[4] Throughout I argue for the necessity of analyzing the complex and complicated dynamic that is contained in the process of demystifying various narrative mechanisms associated with thinking about the particularities of the diasporic experience in the Hexagon. These fundamental questions are explored through specific reference to Alain Mabanckou's novel *Bleu-Blanc-Rouge* (1998) and Daniel Biyaoula's novels *L'impasse* (1996) and *Agonies* (1998), while extending the argument to issues of immigration and transnationalism and establishing points of commonality with similar phenomena in other sociocultural contexts, in Africa and elsewhere.[5] This chapter will also further extend the discussion of gender that informed the analysis of Fatou Keïta's work in the preceding chapter, but from a very different perspective. As an intrinsically masculinist practice, centered on European aesthetic codes and value systems, *La sape* has much to reveal, especially because its masculinism has been relatively ignored.[6] As Barbara Burman and Carole Turbin have argued, "gender issues are interwoven into this emerging field of dress and textile history."[7]

Recent critical approaches in the social sciences have provided useful paradigms and contextual frameworks for exploring these occurrences. Jean-Loup Amselle's book *Branchements: Anthropologie de l'universalité des cultures* allows us to adequately assess the complex manner in which populations and histories have become imbricated. The implications of this recontextualization are tremendously helpful in delineating and illustrating how this theoretical apparatus could be put into practice in order to understand the dynamics of colonialism, immigration, and transnationalism. Amselle's objective is to break with "traditional anthropological approaches that privilege the local over the global";[8] in a similar fashion, this chapter in turn explores the various ways in which all actors—the colonized and the colonizer, immigrants and receiving countries—are transformed by and in diasporic, multicultural, and transnational spaces. For Amselle, "Africa therefore represents a construct, a concept whose operational laws obey a semantic logic that is totally independent of any territorial attachment. The Africa-concept belongs to all those who want to get hold of it, connect to it" (Amselle, *Branchements*, 15).

In this instance, the movement known as *La sape* provides a striking example of a sociocultural phenomenon to which a transnational matrix can be applied. The word *sape* originated as an acronym for the Société des ambianceurs et des personnes élégantes (Society of *Ambianceurs* and Persons of Elegance), whose members were and are primarily young men from Brazzaville (Republic of the Congo) and Kinshasa (Democratic Republic of the Congo). The *sapeurs* travel to France in order to acquire designer clothes as part of a broader identitarian agenda associated with the shifting cultural, political, and social coordinates of the colony and postcolony as determined by hegemonic and counter-hegemonic practices. However, there are important differences between the objectives of the *sapeurs* and those of other migrants, given that the motivating factor—the migrant impulse—of the former is inextricably linked to the anticipated return to Africa as an integral component of the transcontinental adventure and a prerequisite for the enhanced social status conferred on them as a result of the successful completion of the circular mission.[9]

Explored by anthropologists and sociologists, and more recently in the work of Congolese novelists Daniel Biyaoula and Alain Mabanckou, *La sape*, as Janet MacGaffey and Rémy Bazenguissa-Ganga have demonstrated in their book *Congo-Paris: Transnational Traders on the Margins of the Law*, offers "a new perspective on a little known and altogether different facet of relations between the local and the global, one focused on individuals and their counter-hegemonic activities rather than on nation states and large companies."[10] The relationship between these national spaces—the Republic of the Congo, the Democratic Republic of the Congo, and France—is symbiotic to the extent that *La sape*, as Justin-Daniel Gandoulou has shown in his study *Au cœur de la sape: Mœurs et aventures de Congolais à Paris*, essentially does not exist outside of these spaces.[11] MacGaffey and Bazenguissa-Ganga call for an approach that allows for "multisited ethnographies," thereby rejoining the structure Amselle has advocated through *branchements* (connections). Their focus is on "the ways in which these traders organize their trade, the cultural factors on which it depends, and the part the commodities of the trade play in structuring identity among West Central African migrants in Europe . . . how it is able to function in the absence of a supportive legal system, and how opportunities can be found to avoid oppressive constraints by operating outside state laws" (MacGaffey and Bazenguissa-Ganga, 3–4).

Any thinking on the concept of *La sape* inevitably compels us to consider the broader framework represented by the formation of African diasporic communities in general, and, more specifically, that of the Congolese Diaspora. This contextual framework serves to further underline the singularity of the *sapeurs'* experience, while also providing insights into migrant itineraries from Africa toward Europe. Indeed, this framework establishes links with a plethora of social issues that have to do with immigration legislation, reforms of citizenship criteria, and the increasing reluctance of European nation-states to provide hospitable environments for migrant communities. Elie Goldschmidt has investigated these trends in "Migrants congolais en route vers l'Europe" ("Congolese Migrants on the Route to Europe") through a focus on Congolese migration from Brazzaville and Kinshasa to Morocco after 1997 as preparation for passage into the European Union.[12] While migratory patterns have created multiple Congolese diasporic communities across Africa, one of Goldschmidt's central arguments is that we must avoid a reductive homogeneous categorization of migrants within some kind of imaginary unified diasporic community. As we shall see in our consideration of Mabanckou's novel, the objectives of migrants are multifarious and serve to enact a tenuous relationship among them. In fact, the *sapeurs* make a concerted effort to distance themselves from associations with economic migrants, and thus strategically avoid being incorporated in an African diasporic community in the Hexagon, thereby further underlining the tangential nature of their respective goals in the complex process of identity formation.

One cannot attempt to discuss the phenomenon of *La sape* without considering the particular role that Paris (as the Hexagon's capital) played in the minds of colonized African subjects, and has continued to play since decolonization. Indeed, the significance of Paris has been central to the work of a number of Africanists: F. Abiola Irele, in *The African Imagination: Literature in Africa and the Black Diaspora;* Christopher L. Miller, in *Nationalists and Nomads: Essays on Francophone African Literature and Culture;* and Manthia Diawara, in *In Search of Africa.*[13] As Lydie Moudileno has observed in her reading of contemporary African writing, "Since the beginning of the 1990s, then, young authors who have come out of an African immigrant experience have been recentering France in their fiction."[14] In addition to these contributions, studies of Paris have also been foundational to a broadening of the field of African American studies in the United States, as exemplified by Tyler Stovall's *Paris Noir: African Americans in the City of Light* and Bennetta Jules-Rosette's *Black Paris: The African Writers' Landscape.*[15] Gandoulou's findings in his book *Dandies à Bacongo: Le culte de l'élégance dans la société congolaise contemporaine* seem to echo this argument, since for him, "it would seem that for a significant number of Congolese men, reaction to the Western myth constitutes one of the positive motivating factors of emigration."[16] Parallels can of course be established with other francophone areas of Africa; Eric de Rosny, for example, has introduced the notion of an "emigration virus" in his case study of youth in Cameroon.[17] In this instance, Rosny argues that exposure to cable and satellite broadcasting and the Internet has exponentially increased the desire to migrate: "the phenomenal impact of new media has fueled the desire of dissatisfied youth to emigrate" (626). France, and Paris in particular, continue to occupy the mythic status they were invested with when they stood at the central point of France's colonial empire. This image had been widely disseminated through colonial ideology as a component of the civilizing mission and, of course, delivered through the pedagogic arm of the imperial machinery in colonial schools. It has in turn survived in the postcolonial context, where, as Didier Gondola has shown, "it remains above all a response, a way for this 'sacrificed' youth to adjust to changing realities over which they have virtually no control. Through this voyage into the *sape* we witness the death of reality and its reincarnation in dreams."[18]

At this juncture, I would like to take up Ackbar Abbas's usage of the term "fascination" in order to further explicate the migrant impulse: "We are reminded time and time again that in the allure of fascination lies a lure."[19] Abbas's analysis of Walter Benjamin's objective of locating the "unconscious of modernity . . . when the shock of modernity overwhelms and smothers the individual, threatening to reduce private life in the big city to inconsequentiality" (Abbas, 54), may in fact find parallels with the colonial experience and the introduction of Africa into Western modernity and capitalism. For Benjamin, this moment provides examples of an "unconscious form of resistance . . . this makes it difficult to place and hence to control them" (Abbas, 55). In this framework, "even the dandy, whom the very notion of protest would strike as inelegant and hence alien, shows traces of resistance," since, according to Benjamin, "the dandies . . . developed the ingenuous training that was necessary to overcome these conflicts. They combined an extremely quick reaction with a relaxed, even slack demeanor and facial expression" (Abbas, 55).[20] Clearly, as we shall see, *La sape* shares interesting points of contact with the activities of the dandies at the encounter with modernity. For Ngũgĩ wa Thiong'o, a tenuousness can be located between the project of "decolonizing the mind" and the countering of the fascination/myth/lure equation, since, in the words of Gayatri Chakravorty Spivak, "I think decolonization also involves a re-fashioning of the structures that we inherit from colonial days . . . Of course it does also require a change of mind."[21] If indeed such a gesture is enacted, then Irele's mechanism that entails the "deconstruction of the Western image of the native" (Irele, *The African Imagination,* 72) may be enacted, yielding the potentiality for a rethinking and demystification of the origins of the metropolitan fascination. With the French context in mind, Tahar Ben Jelloun has addressed similar issues in his book *Hospitalité française: Racisme et immigration maghrébine;* his call to decolonize the imaginary ("décoloniser l'imaginaire")[22] further complicates these circumstances by highlighting the elaborate manner in which the other imagines the other—how Africans look at the French and the French look at Africans—and how these processes are also interconnected. Indeed, as we shall see, just as Ferdinand Oyono's novel *Une vie de boy* (*Houseboy*) undertook the task of demystifying the colonial myth, so too does Mabanckou's novel set out to demystify the immigrant context.[23]

There is some disagreement concerning the historical origins of *La sape* and the corresponding movement that emerged from this phenomenon. Nevertheless, few would disagree that the emergence of the organized movement of *La sape* as it manifests itself today can be associated with similar cultural and vestimentary trends going back as early as the thirties. Indeed, as Gondola has argued, "contemporary *sapeurs* represent at least the third generation of Congolese dandyism" (Gondola, "Dream and Drama," 27). Its adherents were primarily working- or lower-middle-class youth and high school drop-outs, although membership grew considerably among increasingly disenfranchised youth under Marxism-Leninism in the Republic of the Congo (1969–1991) and Mobutu's rule in the Republic of Zaire (from 1970 onward). According to MacGaffey and Bazenguissa-Ganga,

> The movement of *la Sape* emerged among unemployed youth in Brazzaville in the 1970s. They competed for status by acquiring French designer clothing and wearing it as part of an ostentatious lifestyle. This movement brought young people into trade in the 1970s, as they sought the means to go to Paris and buy expensive clothing that identifies them. The cult of appearance soon spread to the youth of Kinshasa and has become part of the popular culture in both Central African countries. Through their trade and other activities, the traders protest and struggle against exclusion. (MacGaffey and Bazenguissa-Ganga, 3)

Clearly, colonial influences are inextricably linked to transitions in vestimentary codes. However, it remains of paramount importance to note that imported codes were not adhered to in any kind of homogeneous manner, that clothes were systematically employed as a way of establishing markers of autonomous differentiation, and that examples of similar phenomena existed in precolonial Africa, thereby making it inaccurate to ascribe such influences only to the colonizer. The most comprehensive analyses of these transformations are available in Jean Comaroff's book *Body of Power, Spirit of Resistance,* through the examination of "the reciprocal interplay of human practice,"[24] and in Phyllis M. Martin's highly original study of Brazzaville, *Leisure and Society in Colonial Brazzaville:* "The presentation of self in outward display was an important aspect of pre-colonial society and it was a tradition transferred and transformed in the urban area."[25] However, colonial influences cannot be underestimated, not only for their transformative powers, but also for the counter-hegemonic practices they generated. Indeed, "interaction with Europeans also influenced tastes in clothes. According to informants, their fathers and grandfathers wanted to dress as much like Europeans as possible, for this was the mark of an *évolué*" (Martin, "Dressing Well," 158–159). Given the process of othering that is intrinsic to colonial discourse and the accompanying recognition of otherness that coincides with the realization of the impossibility of assimilation, this generated conscious attempts at achieving difference. Clothing provides the occasion for the subversion of established modes and the rejection of the dictates of accepted norms. The attempt at controlling the colonized body through a standardization of clothing was challenged by the refusal to partially assume the external appearance of the other.[26] The adoption of alternative aesthetic codes presents itself as a symbolic gesture aimed at reclaiming power. This is what Pierre Bourdieu has described as diverse "strategies of self-presentation," "signs of distinction," and the ways in which "fashion offers one of the most favorable terrains and which is the motor of cultural life as a perpetual movement of overtaking and outflanking."[27]

The parallels between the colonial and postcolonial eras are striking. For example, when individuals were allowed to select their own clothing during the colonial era, evidence suggests that "on these occasions clothing and ornamentation not only conveyed the moment in time but also personal taste, resources and status," and that, significantly, "European dress was more and more adopted as the preferred attire of townsmen . . . newly arrived workers were looked down on, as European styles, refashioned in line with local tastes, became the norm" (Martin, "Dressing Well," 154, 165). A similar dynamic is evidenced between the *sapeurs* and the economic migrants they encounter in France, who, through their categorization as *paysans* (peasants), are relegated to an inferior status that recuperates prior colonial hierarchies of rural and urban communities and the various associations and encodings associated with popular perceptions and constructs. The *sapeurs* endeavor to circulate outside of those matrices, and this distantiation is intended to avoid stereotypes and projections traditionally attributed to colonized subjects and that survive today in France in characterizations of African immigrants.[28] These colonial patterns had not yet come to constitute the type of "counter-culture" available in the sixties and seventies, "when fashion became a statement against economic deprivation and attempts at political dominance by the party youth organization"; nevertheless, "the young men of the colonial period blended their fascination for clothes with the formation of mutual-aid associations . . . Through their 'cult of elegance' young men sought to define their social distinctiveness, while at the same time deriving a great deal of personal pleasure from wearing stylish clothes, admiring each others' dress and, hopefully, attracting girls" (Martin, "Dressing Well," 171). The pertinence and applicability of the historical framework to the contemporary circumstances of postcoloniality are unquestionable, and serve as indicators and precursors to more recent developments: "In their appreciation of the powerful symbolism of clothes and the significance of dress in mediating social relations, modern-day Brazzavillois are celebrating a tradition that stretches back into the pre-colonial past but which town life has only strengthened" (172).

The discourse on clothing as a symbol of assimilation has perhaps been most powerfully exemplified in the transformation of Jean de Brunhoff's eponymous hero Babar, in *Le roi Babar.*[29] The connections between Brunhoff's stories and broader social discourses and colonial ideologies are now widely accepted, and have perhaps been most articulately and persuasively addressed by Ariel Dorfman in *The Empire's Old Clothes*. In this text, Dorfman demonstrated that "no sooner has he [Babar] lost his horizontal nakedness and seen his clothed twin in a mirror, than he becomes aware of his stature, his skin, his clothes."[30] Indeed, having himself successfully assimilated—the adoption of and adherence to Western-style clothing serves as the explicit symbolic marker of this—Babar disseminates this code: "Babar holds true to his promise: he handed each and every elephant a gift and also solid clothes to work in, along with superb costumes for parties" (18). Homi Bhabha's work on mimicry provides a useful paradigm for further exploring this dimension. In his "Of Mimicry and Man: The Ambivalence of Colonial Discourse," Bhabha illustrates how "mimicry emerges as the representation of a difference that is itself a process of disavowal . . . mimicry is at once resemblance and menace." What is more, "the *menace* of mimicry is its *double* vision which in disclosing the ambivalence of colonial discourse also disrupts its authority . . . The question of the representation of difference is therefore always also a problem of authority."[31] Further insights into these important questions are provided by Leslie W. Rabine in her book *The Global Circulation of African Fashion,* in which she adopts a transnational framework (Kenya, Senegal, and the United States) in order to explore African fashion in the global economy.[32]

I would like to take up Rabine's structural framework, according to which "studies of globalization usually focus on dominant, high-tech networks—of the mass media, the Internet, or mass-marketed consumer culture—produced and disseminated by corporate capitalism. But this does not tell the whole story of transnationally disseminated culture" (Rabine, 2). Rabine's objective of correcting this paradigm is crucial in underlining the manner in which certain global networks function outside of readily identifiable trade lines—thereby echoing MacGaffey and Bazenguissa-Ganga's agenda in their book *Congo-Paris*—but also in avoiding reductive discourses on globalization that fail to take into account the multifarious ways in which sociocultural processes are deployed. According to Paul Gilroy, "chaotic cultural dissemination in more and more elaborate circuits itself enjoys a complicated relationship to the technologies that have conquered distance, compressed time, and solicited novel forms of identification between the creators of cultural forms, moods, and styles and various groups of users who may dwell far from the location in which an object or event was initially conceived."[33] *La sape* as a concept shares many points of commonality with the theoretical implications of Rabine's project, but also distinguishes itself from them. For Rabine, "whatever value the overused terms 'subversion' or 'resistance' may have for studies of mass-market consumer culture, they and the logic they connote do not apply here" (Rabine, 5). *La sape* is a different example of transnational-ism, since it not only locates itself outside of the other forms of "transna-tional disseminated culture" underscored by Rabine (2), but also situates itself on the peripheries, through its existence outside of economic migra-tion. Fashion, as evidenced in *La sape,* introduces the vocabulary and ac-companying signifiers that are "hegemony," "assimilation," "subversion," and "resistance"—effectively rejoining Bhabha's evocation of the "prob-lem of authority" (Bhabha, 89). "In the postcolony," Mbembe observes, "magnificence and the desire to shine are not the prerogative only of those who command. The people also want to be 'honored, to 'shine,' and to take part in celebrations . . . in their desire for a certain majesty, the masses join in the madness and clothe themselves in cheap imitations of power to reproduce its epistemology" (Mbembe, *On the Postcolony,* 131–133). The phenomenon engages discursively and semiotically with dominant, hege-monic norms and standards, thereby inaugurating the space for a counter-hegemonic semiology—perhaps gaining proximity to what Rachel Lee has referred to as "dissenting literacy," which "acknowledges that in every act of access to power (further incorporation into modernity, further dissemi-nation in a wider expanse) there is also discoordination with language/ modes/forms of modernity that make, for instance, minority cultures avail-able to translation and that teach them, as well, a literacy in those lan-guages/modes/forms."[34] "Dissenting literacy," then, might be recontextual-ized as a way of deciphering various codes as they pertain to the colonial context—the country and city, the rural and the urban—or the postcolo-nial era—urban elites and Diasporas and minority populations. All evi-dence indicates that parallel discourses survive in both discursive and so-ciological spaces.

The ostentatious dimension functions similarly for political power and *La sape.* Indeed, the mere possession of power in the postcolony was in-sufficient: "state power organizes for dramatizing its own magnificence" (Mbembe, *On the Postcolony,* 104). Postcolonial African fiction has pro-vided a multiplicity of examples of such practices, from leaders obsessed with villas, cars, wine, and women in Sony Labou Tansi's novel *La vie et demie,* the concerns of Nkem Nwankwo's novel *My Mercedes is Bigger than Yours,* and Ousmane Sembene's film and novel *Xala,* in which the transfer of power from colonial to autonomous rule takes place in a strik-ing scene in which traditional African clothes are abandoned in favor of the Western-style *costard* (suit) as a symbolic marker of power.[35] Likewise in the diasporic context, such questions have been addressed in, for exam-ple, novels such as Simon Njami's *African Gigolo.*[36] Similarly, the *sapeurs* require opportunities to wear, display, and exhibit their clothes. "The *sape,*" Gondola observes, "is there to conceal his social failure and to transform it into apparent victory" (Gondola, "Dream and Drama," 31). Indeed, *La sape* generated considerable societal conflict in the People's

Republic of the Congo, because the ostentatious performances associated with the activities of the *sapeurs* challenged official Party ideology.

The act of embracing French fashion, the semiology of the *accoutre-ment,* constituted for the government authorities a gesture of assimilation and identification with bourgeois ideology, aesthetic codes, and values that had nothing to do with the stated parameters of government ideology. With this embrace, the *sapeurs* create a "particular form of resistance through the creation of an oppositional, counter-hegemonic culture. With-in this culture, they assert their identity and compete for status according to their own system of values. In this process, they exclude those who are part of the system that has excluded them" (MacGaffey and Bazenguissa-Ganga, 137). Not unexpectedly, this tenuous relationship with the author-ities was itself full of contradictions. Denis Sassou-Nguesso—president from 1979 to 1991—was himself called a "Cardin-Communist" as a way of underlining his fondness for Pierre Cardin clothes. The context is even more fascinating when one looks at variations across the Congo river in Mobutu's Zaire. Shortly after his election in 1970, Mobutu outlined his project of "zaïrianisation," effectively deploying a campaign of "authentic-ity" whose guidelines were provided by a conscious distancing from Euro-pean influences. Among these newly delineated standards was the required "abacost," the "male attire favored by Mobutu and promoted as part of the authenticity campaign, consisting of a short-sleeved suit worn without a tie. The word *abacost* is derived from the French *à bas le costume,* or 'down with the suit.'"[37] This style was immediately adopted by members of the established political party. The internationally acclaimed "world mu-sic" artist Papa Wemba is widely perceived as one of the most powerful advocates of *La sape,* and for him it constitutes "a form of rebellion against poverty and the blues, but *La sape* is also a way of fighting against the dic-tatorship of the *abacost,* a local form of the three-piece suit and also the quasi-official uniform of men under Mobutu's regime."[38] Likewise, Chéri Samba, the famous painter from the Democratic Republic of the Congo, has both featured *sapeurs* in his work and also been a *sapeur* himself.[39] In this context, *La sape* is clearly reformulated as a counter-hegemonic prac-tice that operates symbiotically with the dictates of political authority that serve as a catalyst for its dynamism. Nevertheless, as we shall see, the broader problematic of adapting and adopting European aesthetic codes to subvert local practices raises a number of issues, particularly since Afri-can women have been harshly criticized when they have adhered to femi-nist discourses located in the West. This question receives additional at-tention later in the chapter through a consideration of the gendering of *La sape.*

The question of power is central to Jean Allman's edited volume *Fash-ioning Africa: Power and the Politics of Dress,* which seeks to highlight "the ways in which power is represented, constituted, articulated, and contested through dress. It seeks to understand bodily praxis as political praxis, fashion as political language."[40] Likewise, clothing plays an integral role in the construction of identity, and *La sape* has much to reveal about a broad range of gender-related issues in not only the Congolese context but also the African context more generally, especially since this dimension has not received significant critical attention.[41] Rigid social categories of differentiation and prescriptive modes of behavior are often only to be found in official discourses; however, these are always open to explicit or implicit challenge and redefinition.

The figure of the "dandy" warrants additional focus and provides an interesting point of entry to a consideration of the homosocial and homoerotic dimension of *La sape* as a masculinist practice. In her discussion of the American context, Ruth P. Rubinstein has pointed out that "older, venerated patriarchs such as Thomas Jefferson were chided as 'dandified' and accused of having what were identified as female characteristics."[42] The construction of image as a relative, juxtapository phenomenon is revealed in the deliberate attempt by heterosexual men to distance themselves from gay male culture, in a process through which they "began defining themselves in opposition to all that was soft and womanlike" (Rubinstein, 125). In many ways, the economic and social emasculation of Congolese youth partially explains how alternative expressions of masculinity could have played a role in structuring a hyper-adherence to masculinist codes (clothes, fashion, sexual exploits). As Joanne Entwistle has shown in her book *The Fashioned Body: Fashion, Dress, and Modern Social Theory,* the dandy was "a figure who made it his occupation to be a man of leisure, who prided himself on his aesthetic superiority, seeking distinction through the exercise of his exquisite taste . . . Frequently without occupation, with no regular source of income and generally no wife or family, the dandy lived by his wits."[43] One cannot help but draw an analogy to the concept of *débrouillardise* or the *système D* (resourcefulness, fending for oneself) that is associated with Congolese society and explored in Mweze Ngangura's film *La vie est belle* (*Life is Rosy,* 1987). All of these characterizations apply to the *sapeurs,* for whom the ostentatious nature of the practice is a defining component. Interestingly enough, the practice itself is not unrelated to other Western examples of identity construction. Maurizia Boscagli's book *Eye on the Flesh: Fashions of Masculinity in the Early Twentieth Century* is all the more interesting in this context since part of its analysis focuses on Michel Leiris's autobiography *Manhood* (1946) and D. H. Lawrence's novel *The Plumed Serpent* (1926). For Boscagli, these works reveal

> how the "native" as represented by the early twentieth century discourses of aesthetic and ethnographic primitivism was deployed by a heterogeneous strand of modernist writing in the years following the First World War to resexualize western versions of masculinity and to covertly display the

male body as an object of homoerotic desire . . . For the western male subject under threat and seeking to recover phallic plenitude, the encounter
with the primitive promised to be both rewarding and dangerous: His im-
mersion in tribal culture and his identification with the native could produce a further dissolution of his rational subjectivity, and with it, of his
masculinity.[44]

Naturally, the work of Eve Kosofsky Sedgwick has been foundational in
further elucidating homosocial desire. In *Between Men: English Literature and Male Homosocial Desire,* Sedgwick shows us how "male homosocial desire" operates as an essentially oxymoronic construct that
contains both "discriminations and paradoxes," since the term "homosocial" "is a neologism, obviously formed by analogy with 'homosexual,'
and just as obviously meant to be distinguished from 'homosexual.'" Yet,
"in a society where men and women differ in their access to power, there
will be important gender differences, as well, in the structure and constitution of sexuality . . . society could not cease to be homophobic and have
its economic and political structures remain unchanged."[45] This is the
component that interests me here in relation to the African context I am
exploring, particularly if one considers the ways in which sexual power relations and patriarchal order have been articulated and contested in the
works of postcolonial francophone sub-Saharan African authors such
as Calixthe Beyala and Sony Labou Tansi. As Ange-Marie Hancock has
insisted, "any study of African women should situate them in a context
of social relations in which they are both instruments and agents of
power."[46]

Gondola's essay "Popular Music, Urban Society, and Changing Gender Relations in Kinshasa, Zaire (1950–1990)" provides an insightful account of these issues, showing "the extent to which the triptych gender,
colonization, and urbanization functioned in Léopoldville (now Kinshasa), and how in its origins Congolese popular music appeared as an
eminently male culture . . . From the colonial perspective, the African city
. . . was a male bastion from which women had to be excluded."[47] Colonial
practices are shown to have consciously structured the urban environment, and thus to have much to reveal concerning the development of cultural practices within these spaces: "Congolese music culture owed much
to various musical currents that were also characterized by male initiative
. . . Fashion, for instance, was one of the elements that manifested this
[gender] gap and fostered the invisibility of women and, by contrast, the
visibility of men." Not surprisingly, the social environment is characterized by its homosocial nature: "Heavy smoking, drinking, obscene sexual
jokes, and sexual talk were the favorite pastime for male customers" (Gondola, "Popular Music," 70).

Important reformulations of gender relations could be witnessed during the final years of colonial rule, when women began to alter urban de-

mographics. Several developments are worth noting. Firstly, the "appearance of the *associations féminines d'élégances,* women's social clubs whose main purpose was mutual assistance . . . explains how women became influential through music" (Gondola, "Popular Music," 72). Secondly, "the fashions adopted by these clubs suggest resistance to European values. Unlike African men, who rapidly borrowed the European suit, African women avoided wearing European dresses and skirts" (74). And finally, in what is arguably the most striking component of these transitions, we find the emergence of "gigolos," "a social phenomenon that has become much more visible since the 1980s, facilitated by the convergence of two other phenomena: the new economic power attained by middle-aged women traders and the upsurge in the number of unemployed male high-school, and even college, graduates" (78). The popular song entitled "Mario" addresses this development, and is all the more important given that "Mario's behavior and attitudes make us wonder if he is really a 'man'" (81). Masculinist codes are invoked here to preserve the status quo and patriarchal authority that are further threatened by this behavior and social marginalization.[48]

The homosocial aspect of *La sape* that privileges, rewards, or at the very least condones modes of behavior (alcohol consumption, promiscuity) deemed unacceptable for women may hardly seem surprising or new in sociopolitical environments traditionally dominated by men. What do seem worthy of further inquiry, however, are the homoerotic aspects of *La sape.* In their study entitled *African Ceremonies,* Carol Beckwith and Angela Fisher devote a section to the preparations for a circumcision ceremony in Benin:

> During the eight months preceding circumcision, the initiates are looked after by guardians called Kumpara. The Kumpara also act as entertainers on market days to announce the forthcoming rituals. They constantly devise new ways to amuse their audiences. Acting as lewd clowns, they lampoon the crowd and engage in exaggerated sexual horseplay, providing light relief from ritual solemnity. Goaded on by spectators, they bring out large wooden phalluses known as "father spirits of the penises," and imitate every imaginable sexual position with exaggerated mannerisms . . . that drive the audience wild.[49]

The fact that the entry into masculinity in this context, in which circumcision serves to demarcate boyhood from adulthood and bestow upon the young man the responsibilities and enhanced social status that come with maturation, features social interaction in the form of the transgression of taboos linked to homosexuality as they pertain to codes and rules of masculine behavior is of course intriguing. Certainly, the *sapeurs* would never entertain the slightest insinuation that the practice is in any way marked by homoerotic desire. Yet the concern with recovering an identity that has been partially reduced by economic and social exclusion and

marginalization generates an overcompensation for stereotypical masculinist behavior in its crudest homosocial manifestation, in turn partially
undermined in the tenuous link between this social emasculation and the
kind of constitutive associations alluded to in Sedgwick's work between
this imposed positionality and the threat of being labeled homosexual.
As Tim Edwards has argued in his book *Men in the Mirror: Men's Fashion, Masculinity, and Consumer Society,* "the problematic relationship of
homosexuality to masculinity and the part myth/part reality of effeminacy,
although mixed up and undermined in various ways throughout the centuries, has never quite been severed."[50] His analysis of an analogous phenomenon that emerged at a similar historical time, albeit in a radically different sociocultural context, might help further elucidate the context of
the *sapeurs:*

> The Vogue Movement referred to an underground network of posing and
> impressionist dancers taking place in New York and some other major cities
> where young, gay and often black men would don the costumes and appear-
> ances of many cult icons, including Hollywood idols and some, more con-
> temporary, hegemonic images of femininity and masculinity. These were
> then paraded in front of audiences on the street or in bars and nightclubs, as
> if in a fashion show, and often set to music as part of a particular contest or
> competition. The men were otherwise deeply oppressed as outsiders racially,
> sexually or simply in terms of their effeminacy and poverty, and the practice
> of voguing partly parodied and partly affirmed the aspirational dreams of
> the famous magazine and, in particular, the desire for the front cover. (T. Ed-
> wards, 109)

Prior to applying these concepts and findings to Mabanckou's novel, I suggest we engage in a further detour and consider parallels between *La sape*
and similar occurrences in other cultural contexts. These have much to reveal concerning the African context and *La sape* itself, given that points of
intersection can be identified between Africa, African diasporic cultures in
France, African American culture, and Chicano/a frameworks.

   In "Crimes of Fashion: The Pachua and Chicana Style Politics," Catherine Ramírez demonstrates how "style politics" can be constructed as "an
expression of difference via style."[51] Considering the example of the zoot
suit, Ramírez is able to identify the role of "zoot subculture of the early
1940s" as definitional "in the politicization of Mexican Americans and in
the creation of an oppositional, rather than assimilationist, Chicano cultural identity . . . the zoot suit functioned as a sign of defiance and difference" (Ramírez, 1–2). Obvious parallels with the African context emerge
from this analysis, in that "to wartime working-class youths, especially recent transplants from rural areas to urban centers, the zoot suit may have
functioned as a status symbol because its wearers were working-class and
urban, rather than poor and *del rancho*" (7). Entry into urban centers
clearly implements divisions between social groups, much in the same way

as migration from rural areas functioned in colonial Africa, and subsequently in the way the *sapeurs* condescendingly demarcate themselves from the economic migrants they classify as peasants.

The area that is of particular interest here is the manner in which aesthetic codes are defined and identities in turn structured with regard to fashion. Who, one might ask, determines what comes to constitute fashionable apparel? In the context Ramírez explores, the zoot suit "became a signifier of both conspicuous leisure and conspicuous consumption during World War II" for young men, and provided "the impression that they did not (or did not have to) work" (Ramírez, 6), which was accorded paramount importance. Indeed, zoot suit wearers' conspicuousness and their concern with being visible was central to their achieving an authentic positionality, enabling them to "claim a public space for themselves" (7). Yet, significantly, "to 'people of taste'—in particular, middle- and upper-class Anglo Americans and Mexican Americans—the zoot suit may have appeared 'loud' (i.e., excessive) and pretentious precisely because many of its wearers were working-class and 'ghetto'" (7).[52] Integration through the assertion of a Chicano identity remained central to the enterprise, and although it is primarily the return that counts for the *sapeurs,* the identitarian posture remains crucial, definitional. In the same way that the relationship between "people of taste" and those people located at the social margins is a tenuous one, so too is the dynamic between dominant norms and the manner in which they are recuperated, combined and recombined through the complex process of self-affirmation and the inscription of alternative signifiers for communication. This connects inevitably with the question of literacy—accepted codes and signifiers—but also of course with Lee's notion of "dissenting literacies." Once again, the relationship is a symbiotic one, since neither part can function without the other.

As Martin was able to show, colonial employees often chose to wear their shirts outside their pants rather than tucking them in. The *sapeurs* made a concerted effort to distance themselves from African immigrants but simultaneously from dominant fashion norms. Hildi Hendrickson has addressed these questions:

> The body surface has been a powerful arena in which colonial relations have been enacted and contested. While colonial projects may entail the rigorous separation of social and economic interaction between colonizer and colonized, colonial domination ultimately is grounded in the face-to-face relations between local coresidents . . . Under these conditions the body is a signifier that is shared cross-culturally yet assigned contrasting, simultaneous meanings. Especially in the absence of shared spoken language, colonial encounters can be seen as a particular kind of semiotic event in which a visual language of bodily forms is especially critical . . . Possibilities for resistance lie in the fact that this semiotic process can never be fully controlled, even by a dominating colonial power.[53]

Jean Baudrillard certainly made considerable inroads in the theorization he provided in *Simulacra and Simulation,* arguing that "everything is metamorphosed into its opposite to perpetuate itself in its expurgated form."[54] The *sapeurs'* fashion choices render them immediately recognizable, but in adhering to codes they have delineated for themselves they create a space outside of the standard Parisian matrix, thereby reclaiming their own form of Parisianism according to autonomous aesthetic codes. In fact, "the world of *haute couture* has provided another space where [African Americans] have been able to enjoy a successful life in Paris," particularly at a time when American society effectively practiced a politics of exclusion (Stovall, *Paris Noir,* 316–317). It is precisely his "look" that renders the famous Congolese recording artist Koffi Olomide recognizable and confers status upon him: "He takes special pride in his appearance and in selecting his clothes. His suits are usually close to red in color. These colors stand out on stage and for the cameras when his movie clips are being shot. Like most Congolese artists, Koffi Olomide is an amateur of fine clothes. He is a 'Sapeur.'"[55] Furthermore, as Roland Barthes showed us in *Système de la mode* (*The Fashion System*), the "vestimentary code" reveals various principles through which practices are coded, and of course the *sapeurs* have their own conventions and message.[56]

Initially, the *sapeurs* gathered in clubs and groups for the purposes of showing off their outfits:

> The display of these clothes conforms to specific practices, including the "dance of designer labels" and the issuing of "challenges." The first entails showing off the labels of the clothes one is wearing by means of gestures. The second occurs when an argument arises between two *sapeurs* and their friends put an end to it by proposing that the two protagonists present themselves the next day at an appointed place, superbly dressed. These friends (also well dressed) make up the jury, which passes judgment on which of the two is better turned out, pronouncing on the merit of his clothes, according to price, quality, etc. and deciding whose are the best . . . The challenge is thus taken up in a symbolic conflict in which the weapons are clothes. (MacGaffey and Bazenguissa-Ganga, 140)

Obvious parallels emerge here between these conventions and "bling bling" in America, in which "jewelry, material showoff, glitter of diamonds" are evidenced.[57] The *sapeurs,* appropriating clothes made by a plethora of international designers such as J.-M. Weston, Valentino, Gianni-Versace, and Yves Saint-Laurent,[58] initiate the "dance of designer labels," which "consists in allowing the protagonists to dance and show off their clothes and designer labels" (Gandoulou, *Au cœur de la sape,* 209). "The clothes were worn in dancing halls and dance moves were especially choreographed by music groups to allow the dancers to exhibit their shoes or European designer labels on their clothes" (Goldschmidt, 222). This exhibition takes on the form of a "ritual," a "challenge," or even "a declared battle" (Gandoulou, *Dandies à Bacongo,* 106, 122). This is very similar to "battling," the "war between or among rappers, dancers, DJs, or emcees for prizes or bragging rights and to see who is best. The winner is judged by crowd applause or originality. When lyrics are involved it's what's said and how it is delivered—the cadence and complexity of the lyrics; if music is used, the originality and quality of production also are judged" (Westbrook, 8).[59] The *sapeur* who emerges victorious will take the title of "Grand" (big man) and be considered an "accomplished sapeur" (Gandoulou, *Dandies à Bacongo,* 67). This status is the result of completing a carefully coded process. Filled with "an irrepressible desire to obtain an honorable social status in the eyes of their peers" (Rosny, 624), and "motivated by great curiosity and encouraged by the perspective and desire for self-realization" (Goldschmidt, 239), they cannot imagine failure and the accompanying shame: "Most of them don't even entertain this eventuality since they know they would risk being shamed for returning after failing" (Goldschmidt, 239).

Young people are motivated by the desire to engage in a transcontinental adventure ("to take off on an adventure") to Paris in order to acquire designer clothes. A successfully completed adventure and subsequent descent to the country of departure results in the title of "Parisian" being conferred upon the traveler (this is an interesting transcolonial reappropriation of the attributes deployed by Dadié in his novel *An African in Paris,* explored in chapter 2). Furthermore, as Mabanckou illustrates, once back from Paris, now a Parisian, "he obtains as much consideration as a civil servant or important member of society" (Mabanckou, *Bleu-Blanc-Rouge,* 93). The migrant impulse is, however, structured around a number of foundational principles: the dream/fascination component I alluded to earlier, the search for recognition, and finally a very important dimension, namely the anticipated benefit and prestige the sapeur will bestow upon his family and community in Africa: "Very few young people . . . leave with the idea of expatriating themselves for good. This desire to return explains why families do nothing to discourage departures. On the contrary, a trip abroad contains the promise of enrichment for the group as a whole" (Rosny, 628).

The trials and tribulations the *sapeur* may encounter in France are ignored, and the extremely dangerous and perilous nature of the quest is perhaps indicative of the degree of fascination. In this light, Mabanckou's work gains additional importance in the process of demystifying and countering the colonial project and the ongoing appeal of the idea of the metropole. "In fact, the dream, the social imaginary of the sapeur has two components: the initiatory Parisian voyage, conditioned by the acquisition of a whole range of clothing gear, and then the descent, the moment of apotheosis and consecration" (Gandoulou, *Dandies à Bacongo,* 73).[60] Given the sociopolitical circumstances in the postcolony, dreaming and the imagination emerge as necessary mechanisms, for the confrontation of reality and fiction accordingly provides the opportunity to humanize experience. "We were allowed to dream. It cost us nothing. It did not require an exit visa, a passport, an airline ticket," explains Massala-Massala, the central protagonist of Mabanckou's *Bleu-Blanc-Rouge* (36). The desire to reach Paris provides the migrant impulse, but this quest goes beyond the simple physical journey that transports the individual from one geographic space to another. The dimension of displacement locates the transportation of the individual in what is a quest for self, for the exploration of the individual—and this is where the journey's impulse is actually enacted. As MacGaffey and Bazenguissa-Ganga have shown, "Symbolically, France is simultaneously the home of these migrants and yet not their home. In the minds of these young people, France and Congo are two aspects of the same world, of which France represents the center . . . Thus the departure for France, besides the fact of actually making a journey, also signifies a journey into the interior of the self" (MacGaffey and Bazenguissa-Ganga, 62). The transposition of this question into fiction has the capacity to reach a different audience and to offer an alternative position—much as Akofa's and Keïta's works in chapters 4 and 5 brought to our attention different facets of global interaction.

I propose to respect the structural framework of Biyaoula's novel *L'impasse* in order to explore its contribution to the discourse on *La sape*. The novel is divided into three sections: the "first constriction" (11–141), that comprises the departure of the central protagonist, Joseph Gakatuka, from France for Brazzaville; the "second constriction" (143–241), including his return to Paris; and finally, the third section, entitled "transformation" (243–327). Somewhat significantly, the novel begins in the ultimate space of transnationalism, namely Paris's largest airport, Roissy-Charles-de-Gaulle, as Joseph prepares to board a flight for Brazzaville. For Joseph, this journey symbolizes a return to his native land, from which he has been away fifteen years. As Joseph deplanes and is reunited with his family and friends, he comes to realize that there is a significant discrepancy between the image he offers and that which his people expect of him: "It doesn't take me long to figure out that they expected something of me, that I didn't bring it from France, that I do not embody an ideal, that I am shattering people's dreams" (30). This discrepancy is in part due to his fifteen-year absence, to the significant societal changes the Congo had undergone during Marxist-Leninist rule, and to the experience of exile, but more specifically to his failure to correspond to the image that is expected of young men returning from exile in Paris.

When these young men leave the Congo for Paris, they are welcomed by a network of compatriots who provide them with housing, working papers, and so forth, thus enabling then to rapidly adjust to the demands of exile. Although the socioeconomic circumstances of residing in France are extremely challenging and have little to do with the mythic constructs they had assimilated of life there, young immigrants, referred to as adventurers, draw upon their tremendous resourcefulness in order to achieve their primary objective of eventually undertaking a glorious descent on either the capital, Brazzaville, or the main town on the west coast, Pointe Noire. The adventure is often a lengthy process, one that begins at a young age in the Congo, and that is sustained over the years through a transnational dialogue with young men who have already undertaken the quest. In fact, these young men are so well prepared when they arrive in Paris that they are already acquainted with the city's topography, métro, monuments, and so forth.

Joseph has established residence in France for the purpose of employment, and does not partake in the sociocultural practice that is *La sape*. However, he chooses to ignore it at his own peril, since when he returns to the Congo he effectively fails to fulfill his family's expectations, and his brother Samuel informs him of his shortcoming:

> He cleared his throat and then told me that there were rules to follow, that I might not like wearing suits, but that I was a Parisian, that a Parisian has an image to uphold, and that the members of my family would be permanently disgraced if there were a Parisian among them who did not resemble one. (39)

The transnational experience, the hybridity of the subject, and the belonging and nonbelonging to each respective space become increasingly problematic. Indeed, Joseph's relationships with his people at "home" are characterized through terms such as "separation," "distance," and "barriers." While his national status as a citizen of the Republic of the Congo has not changed, he is constructed as an outsider: "Listen, Joseph, you must understand that you're almost a foreigner here in Brazza" (81). Yet there is no room for his French life in his Congolese one. For example, his relationship with Sabine, a white French woman, is unacceptable (in his second novel, *Agonies,* Biyaoula explores the problematic nature of exogamous unions, particularly when they take place between an African woman and a French man). Furthermore, he is informed that his newly acquired values have no currency in the Congo: "forget about how things take place in France" (93). He soon learns that the identity he claims for himself is irrelevant, and that he must accept, instead, that identity which is constructed for him, as a Parisian, and act accordingly. Furthermore, his own nostalgic image of Africa and constructions of homeland from exile have no correlation with the reality on the ground, thus further displacing him: "When I'm in Poury . . . I dream of Brazza, of the warmth in which one lives here. But once I'm back there, I realize that things aren't any better" (96). By the time Joseph finally returns to Paris, he has compromised his identity, relinquished his autonomy, and capitulated to the exigencies of his family and friends.

Whether through the images available in literature, in popular discourse, on television, or in the music of Congo-Zaire's most celebrated performer, Papa Wemba, Paris remains a mythic construct. For Joseph, however, displacement to France is initially conceived as a quest to solve the following mathematical equation: "x + African man + African woman + cosmetic products = skin discoloration + hair straightening" (86). He is finally able to solve the equation by recognizing that the enigmatic "x" in fact refers to the constructed superiority of whites over Blacks. However, the process through which Joseph reaches this conclusion has much to reveal about France itself and about the situatedness of the African immigrant there, and ultimately contributes to the complex process of uncovering the mythic constructs that have everything to do with the continued positive representation of Paris (and of course France) in the African imagination. This was Mabanckou's project in *Bleu-Blanc-Rouge* in charting the itinerary of Moki, the central protagonist. As Pierrette Herzberger-Fofana has shown, "Throughout the novel, he will be the victim of the Blue-White-Red dream. He will be the one who will inform his compatriots at home, the one who will remain trapped in the mirage. But he will have pursued his goal to the end."[61] Moki's proximity to France and French culture allows him to distinguish between illusion and reality, to expose the delusionary qualities of the imaginary construct and challenge the assimilationist dream that is contained in the invocation of the blue, white, and red of the French flag.

The cover of the novel, created in 1998 by Saliou Démanguy Diouf (who also produced the cover of Biyaoula's *Agonies*), combines a multitude of ethnic features and colors (blue, white, red, black, orange), in what cannot but remind one of what Françoise Lionnet has described in her analysis of antiracist posters in France as the "indeterminate, inclusionary identity" in which "the other and the self clearly share a space and an intersubjective realm in which hair, eye and skin color are secondary to the ability to engage in another form of identification: that which is mediated by the geographical space of France."[62] Joseph is of course an outsider in France, and unambiguously made to feel that way through his repeated encounters with racist practices. Some of the more striking instances occur during a dinner he has been invited to at the home of his girlfriend's parents. Sabine's father provides an appropriate example of the type of ignorance and prejudicial constructs to which Joseph is constantly exposed. For example, Mr. Rosa takes it upon himself to discuss Joseph's housing, when the latter politely comments upon the nice home in which his family lives:

> You have a nice apartment, I said.
> Things aren't that bad here, are they! responded Mr. Rosa. You live in public housing, right?
> Yes, that's right, Mr. Rosa.

Of course, you can't really compare the two . . . It can't be much fun living over there?

To tell you the truth, it's not that pleasant!

For you it must be a nice change from home! Apparently it's even worse there!

It's not quite the same thing.

Yes, because Alain told us that people in your countries live in appalling, inhumane conditions. He was overwhelmed, very shocked . . . It must be quite something for you to live in a civilized country even if you're in public housing! . . . Please forgive me if I seem nosy. I hope I haven't offended you? . . . And how do you see yourself? Because after all this time, you can't feel much like a real African any longer! (154–155)[63]

The articulation of these comments, accompanied by the statement "I hope I have not offended you?" void the legitimacy of a response and force Joseph to remain silent, to decline the invitation to respond for fear of offending the host who has extended hospitality to him in the form of an invitation to dinner.[64] Furthermore, the conclusion to Mr. Rosa's statement underlines the inescapability of Joseph's African origins, since, through their invocation, they are simultaneously reconfirmed, thus emphasizing the impossibility of the assimilationist or integrational ideal.

Institutionalized racism simply reiterates the preconceived notions and prejudicial representations he has himself assimilated. While opposition to racism in France may be widespread among certain groups, the manner in which immigrants continue to be imagined remains problematic. While these images prevail, the discourse will remain self-defeating, as will society's efforts at eradicating racism. Racial injustice is intellectualized, rationalized, in order to objectify immigrant subjects and deny them their humanity, while society focuses instead on the emotional appeal of housing projects, crime, the shortcomings of single parenthood, drug habits, and poverty, for which there are somehow always explanations. There is evidence that claims, assertions, and articulations of the injustice of racism are being formulated, but these are being underpinned by the semiology in its emphasis on stereotyping immigrants.

Joseph's relationship with Sabine becomes increasingly problematic, as racial tension contributes to the gradual disintegration of their union—or at least as Joseph experiences more and more pressure from his immigrant circumstances (unemployment, social alienation, racism, and so forth), in addition to other pressures concerning their exogamous union, in particular from other Africans who see his union as a betrayal, a refusal to accept other Africans. Somewhat paradoxically, when Sabine tells him that his mistake lies in seeing himself through what others think of him (166), she actually anticipates in many ways the manner in which Joseph will attempt to recover his self-esteem. However, her comment also underlines her faith in the ability of their relationship to survive outside of and beyond societal constructs. Joseph, however, is unable to live in a vacuum, because

he experiences social pressures every day. While Sabine may overcome social prejudice in her pursuit of a relationship with Joseph, the pressures on
her are, arguably, radically different in nature. Indeed, Joseph begins to
manifest physical symptoms in the form of severe headaches caused by
stress, generating additional anxiety and culminating in acute depression,
from which a subsequent mental breakdown provides the necessary escape. The point of no return occurs when his friend Dieudonné is murdered, and marks, symbolically, the end of his union with Sabine and the
end of the second constriction.

The final section of the novel, contained under the heading "the transformation" (*la mue*), a term which in French can also signify molting,
sloughing, shedding, and metamorphosis, explores Joseph's attempts at
recovery. This is an important notion because it underlines the reciprocal
nature of transnational influences, not only in terms of the transforma-
tional imperative that is incumbent upon the immigrant subject as a precondition for assimilation or integration, but also in the implied cultural
and social changes that the immigrant's entrance (or, as anti-immigrant
rhetoric would characterize the dynamic, the immigrants' contaminating
influence) will enact upon the receiving territory. In Joseph's particular
case, these transitions are mediated through a number of factors, which include fashion, race, and broader identitarian concerns. Indeed, as Edouard
Glissant has observed in his book *Caribbean Discourse,*

> There is a difference between the transplanting (by exile or dispersion) of a
> people who continue to survive elsewhere and the transfer (by the slave
> trade) of a population to another place where they change into something
> different, into a new set of possibilities. It is in this metamorphosis that we
> must try to detect one of the best kept secrets of creolization. Through it one
> can see that the mingling of experiences is at work, there for us to know and
> producing the process of being. We abandon the idea of fixed being.[65]

A number of expressions in French are pertinent to this investigation.
One, "changer de peau" ("shed one's skin"), takes on particular significance here given the ethnic/racial identity of the narrator: to shed one's
skin means to become a different person. Someone can also be described
as being "mal dans sa peau" ("uncomfortable in one's skin," ill at ease),
and one can even attempt to "se mettre dans la peau de quelqu'un" ("put
oneself in another's skin," or, in the English idiom, in another's place or
shoes), which is of course the assimilationist ideal. Joseph relinquishes his
struggle with racial identity and finds salvation through the assistance of
Dr. Malfoi, a psychotherapist, leading to the recovery of his self-esteem
through the acquisition of the status of adventurer and *sapeur:* "I've got to
conform completely to the image I present to others, to the image they've
come to expect" (268). His psychotherapist also finds him a job, and thus
effectively allows Joseph to plan a successful descent on Brazzaville: "And
since I have an income, I plan to take a trip home two years from now"

(267–268). Joseph gradually begins to command the respect of his immigrant peers and to attend social gatherings. However, as it did for Mabanckou's protagonist Moki, "this duplicity and this ambivalence lead to a personality change" (Mabanckou, "A l'écoute"), and this newfound socialization is not without its own shortcomings as a consequence of the superficial human relationships that are generated, and the role models they yield for a new generation of disenfranchised African youth. (The irony is hinted at in Malfoi's name, which connects easily with the French *mauvaise foi,* bad faith.) In a chance encounter with Sabine, several months after their separation, he discovers that she has a child, and although he refuses to entertain the possibility that the child is his, the most significant component of this moment is contained in the fact that he relinquishes parenthood and the possible reconciliation that this cross-cultural model of hybridity could offer. While this could be read as a commentary on the impossibility of interracial métissage in the current political climate in France, perhaps a more significant issue is raised here. Joseph is so consumed by the masculinist exigencies of *La sape* that he neglects his parental responsibilities—a behavior that has received much criticism in works by francophone sub-Saharan women, such as Mariama Bâ and Calixthe Beyala.

A symbolic meeting at a party with a young man named Justin, nicknamed "le Goudron" (Tar), plays an important part in Joseph's itinerary. Later that evening Justin dies in a car accident. Joseph establishes similarities between the fate of this young man and his current predicament: his own childhood name Kala (Coal) shares points of commonality with Justin's, as does, indeed, his account of exile and immigration. The circularity of experience motivates him to engage in further psychotherapy and eventually to acknowledge that his identity as a *sapeur* has no solid foundation. In turn, Biyaoula's novel contains a counter-narrative that—much as Justin's death "saves" Joseph—might serve to warn potential adventurers, whose origins may become clearer and their journey less painful. In many ways, the notion of descent, as it is employed by Biyaoula, functions as a symbol for transnationalism, one that is not fully encompassed by the notion of "return" that I discussed earlier, or contained in Glissant's use of the term "detour" in his discussion of "diversion" and "reversion" in *Caribbean Discourse.*[66] Instead, it attempts to incorporate the multitude of communities and populations that undergo transformation through the complex mechanisms and manipulations that are generated in the organization of transnational communities outside of the homeland, foremost among which are the community of origin, the receiving territory, and of course those individuals whose identities as immigrants are transformed through the experience of transplantation or displacement. As we shall see, the work of Mabanckou offers interesting variations in his treatment of *La sape.*

Mabanckou was born in the Republic of the Congo in 1966, and moved to France in the 1980s.[67] He has achieved considerable critical acclaim, especially for his superb novel *Verre cassé* (2005), published by the prestigious Editions du Seuil, which has received the Ouest-France/Etonnants Voyageurs prize, the Cinq Continents de la Francophonie prize, and the Radio France Outre-mer prize.[68] The publication of *Bleu-Blanc-Rouge* marked Mabanckou's entry on the literary scene as a novelist (culminating in the award of the Grand prix littéraire de l'Afrique noire), and inaugurated a new direction for this author, who had until then restricted his productions to the field of poetry (editing five volumes between 1993 and 1997). In many ways, Mabanckou's novel explores themes that have long informed the narratives of those francophone sub-Saharan authors for whom the experiences of displacement—exile, travel, nomadism, return— have been central markers.[69] However, notions of departure and return are invested with additional symbolism in the context in which Mabanckou locates these transitions, although of course they continue to share some important parallels with the motives and objectives of prior generations. Furthermore, his narrative offers a similar framework with which to formulate social commentary and explore alienating practices and mechanisms, while also outlining various expectations on the individual, collective, and immigrant level.

In Mabanckou's novel *Bleu-Blanc-Rouge,* the narrative and topography shift accordingly between Africa and France, between the point of origin, the destination, and eventually the space to which one returns. This structure is important in delineating the spaces in which the narrative takes place, and has much to reveal with regard to the issues Mabanckou has chosen to explore. The preface to the text (9–27) informs the reader of the aborted illusory quest of the central protagonist, Massala-Massala a.k.a. Marcel Bonaventure, reiterating his commitment to exploring the chronology of events and the various processes that culminated in his downfall or failure: "I wish everything could return to some kind of chronological order. That each link in the broken chain could return to its place. Each fact and gesture be accurately repeated. That my thoughts could become clear again" (13–14).

The first part of the book, "The country" (29–118), takes place in Pointe Noire, on the west coast of the Republic of the Congo, after which the topography shifts to Paris's 14th and 18th arrondissements (119– 209).[70] The epigraph to the African section of the novel is taken from Marcel Proust's *A la recherche du temps perdu* and underlines the hallucinatory dimension of the voyage: "Better to dream one's life than to live it, if only living it were not to dream it over again" (31). The epigraph that introduces the second part of the book serves as a premonition of the problematic voyage that lies ahead for Proust's namesake Marcel; it both underlines the mythic dimension that France promises to offer and forewarns us that this quest may in fact be a fallacy: "Apparently, the gates of hell are next to those of heaven / The great carpenter made them out of the same crude materials" (121). These words are taken from the Moroccan poet Abdellatif Lâabi's book *Le spleen de Casablanca* (enacting an obvious intertextual gesture toward Baudelaire's famous text *Le spleen de Paris*), and the fact that the "hexagonal" section of the novel begins with an epigraph from a francophone author while the "African" section opened with an epigraph from Proust (subverting and questioning canonical traditions) serves to further underline the symbolic and symbiotic associations between French and African spaces.

The final section of the novel, entitled "Closure" (211–222), offers Massala-Massala a sense of psychological closure, to the extent that the recounting of his story provides him with the opportunity to reflect on and process his choices. Furthermore, this final section rejoins the opening one, thus effectively completing the cyclical narrative, but also duplicating the experience of the adventurer for whom the journey away from and then back to the Congo is also complete—this is what Moudileno has described as the "fundamental circularity" (Moudileno, "La fiction de la migration," 183). The novel opens with the narrator's incarceration in France, so that the reader finds out immediately that the outcome of the journey to Paris has not been that which was projected. The text is thus less about the outcome (although our curiosity drives us to explore this dimension and accord the narrative some kind of linearity) than it is about the manner in which France (here, primarily Paris) continues to represent a mythic space for the African subject in the era of postcoloniality.

The novel begins with the narrator's commitment to authenticity as a precondition for emancipating himself from the anxiety that this experience has afforded him: "What counts at this stage is to better understand things. To look at everything without abbreviating or falsifying the facts. I would not want to relive the illusion that started me out on this journey . . . This reminiscence will begin with a close and inescapable internal exam that will rid me of the remorse that clogs my thoughts" (Mabanckou, *Bleu-Blanc-Rouge*, 27). His anxiety is inextricably associated with his failure to live up to expectations and to fulfill his people's dreams, hopes, and aspirations. The first part of the book engages in an exploration of those mechanisms and events that served as a catalyst for the departure, of the inner and physical journey that transports him from Pointe Noire to Paris and back again. One of the most significant indicators is located in the manner in which France is represented as a mythic, imaginary construct:

> It was that distant country, inaccessible in spite of the fireworks that scintillated in the least of my daydreams and left me, upon awakening, with the sweet taste of honey in my mouth . . . Who, of my generation, had not visited France *through the mouth*, as one said back home? Just one word, *Paris*, was

sufficient for us to find ourselves almost like magic before the Eiffel Tower, the Arc de Triomphe, or the Avenue des Champs Elysées. (36)

The paradigm for Massala-Massala, as indeed for other would-be adventurers, is provided by fellow Congolese who have successfully completed the departure-descent-return components of the equation. The paradigmatic figure whom Massala-Massala will endeavor to emulate is exemplified by Moki, a character who serves as a double or mirror image of the identity he will attempt to migrate into: "I was Moki's shadow. He molded me" (39). Furthermore, Moki's multiple returns or descents on the homeland do not go unnoticed—as we shall see, the purpose of such trips is precisely to exhibit the newly acquired markers of the transplanted migrant's identity. However, Moki's name has a particular significance. "The expression *milikiste*," as Gondola has shown, "designates the young Congolese who live in Europe and, to a lesser extent, in North America . . . *Miliki* in Lingala is the plural for *mokili,* the 'world,' and has become synonymous for Europe. When the French suffix is added, the word identifies the young who made it to Europe" (Gondola, "Dream and Drama," 28).[71] Moki's status as a Parisian also bestows tremendous prestige on the family, and while his father has never been to France himself, he has nevertheless succeeded in establishing a strong sense of French history. From this information, one can deduce that these representations of France contributed to the myth that young Moki would later explore. The repeated references by Moki's father to General de Gaulle's famous visit to Brazzaville in 1948 serve to further underline historical links between the metropole and the Congo. Something of a storyteller, Moki's father is able to captivate his audience with his descriptions of France, much in the same way that Moki uses this inherited skill to narrate compelling stories during his descent on the Congo.

When his son Moki comes back to Pointe Noire, he makes every effort to reproduce the imagined French environment. In a symbolic reversal of the performative dimension of the Colonial Exposition held in Paris in 1931, the returning native informer is now on exhibit so that his fellow Africans may observe his Frenchness: "A small table made of liana was set up under the mango tree, right in the middle of the courtyard. That's where the Parisian would have his meals . . . In reality, this was so that everyone could either see him or know about him having his meals outside" (51). The transformed native subject, who has deliberately altered his complexion through the application of skin-lightening substances, gained considerable weight, and changed his hair color and even his way of speaking—after all, "there is a world of difference between speaking *in* French and speaking *the* [i.e., proper] French" (63)—has now mutated into an object of ethnographic scrutiny, whose every gesture and item of clothing stands to be emulated by those privy to the encounter. Significantly, he now refuses to eat manioc and foufou, symbolically rejecting the

African component of his personality by no longer ingesting the African part of his diet. MacGaffey and Bazenguissa-Ganga have commented on the importance of manioc as a key marker of cultural symbolism: "Manioc holds a special place . . . For members of the Diaspora from both banks of the Zaire river, it marks both national and family identity" (MacGaffey and Bazenguissa-Ganga, 61–62).

The narrator plays a significant role in that his observations provide the reader with information on Moki's life in Paris, while simultaneously subverting Moki's ethnographic authority to the extent that he is transformed, through the narrator's gaze, into an archival object. The narrator observes and records—for us, the readers—those actions performed by Moki in the spectacle he delivers before the adulating crowd of onlookers:

> As soon as he was out of the car, making sure that everyone was looking at him, he set about a demonstration that was close to a fashion show, much to the pleasure of his fans who had besieged the bar. He unbuttoned his jacket and handed it over to one of his brothers following closely behind him. Beneath his transparent shirt, one could see his light, almost pale skin, with none of the blemishes or other allergies local imitations caused. This metamorphosis stupefied the crowd. The Parisian adjusted his pants up to his belly button. The gesture was measured, controlled, and studied, with the aim of highlighting his socks that perfectly matched his tie. (70)

Using a photograph album that he carries with him, Moki narrates a representation of Paris that he has constructed for his audience and to which they willingly subscribe, unquestioningly and without doubting his authority—he has assumed the position of insider with regard to the France in which he resides. The text offers a specific idea of a space in which his actual status as an immigrant outsider restricts him to the peripheries, which he is able to exceed only as a Parisian in the homeland. In the next chapter, a similar master narrative is presented through the migrant experience of "l'homme de Barbès" (the man from Barbès).

Onlookers are mesmerized and seduced by this narrative, and intent on finding out how they too can engage in this secular quest and become Parisians. Moki reiterates that "clothes are our passport. Our religion. France is the country of fashion because it's the only place on earth where you can still judge people by appearances" (78). This obsession with appearance underlines the need to articulate a specific, authentic narrative, in order to avert the possibility of a crisis of legitimacy that a challenge to the *sapeurs'* narrative authority would engender. Anticipating the possibility of alternative discourses on France and Paris—that is, of narratives that would destabilize the hegemonic discourse they have created and on which the myth of Paris and the experience of the adventurers is constructed—Moki proceeds to denigrate the type of person he describes as a peasant: "He lacks elegance. He has no idea what elegance is . . . He complains about how difficult life is in France. Liar! Always telling lies . . . Luckily the Parisian is there to tell us the contrary. To bring us light. To speak to us about the City of Lights. Of the Paris we love" (89–91). The *sapeurs* thus delegitimize the alternative narrative offered by other migrants in order to legitimize their own and sustain the myth/dream/illusion to which they subscribe. "The peasant represents a threat to the fiction of emigration"—for this reason, Moki carefully reformulates "his own personal epic, and the odyssey of migration imposes itself as a new foundational narrative" (Moudileno, "La fiction de la migration," 186, 185). Massala-Massala takes up the challenge that is contained in Moki's concluding words: "There is no other country that resembles France in my imagination . . . To go there is to accept to henceforth never live without her again" (Mabanckou, *Bleu-Blanc-Rouge*, 86). In this statement, Proust's words from the epigraph to the novel are rejoined, underlining Massala-Massala's conflictedness as he pursues this illusory quest. The lack of hope at home motivates him to leave, or at least provides the logical framework for leaving, for entertaining that the illusion—and perhaps even the delusion that is implied in Proust's statement—that elsewhere will be better. As his father says to him, "I always knew that one day you would leave. Go far, far away from here. Far from all this misery" (94). These words echo those of Laye's father in a prior generation of francophone sub-Saharan African literature, namely Laye Camara's 1954 novel, *The Dark Child,* as Laye prepared to leave for France in order to pursue further education: "I knew quite well that eventually you would leave us" (*The Dark Child,* 181).

However, Massala-Massala's immediate identitarian shift, symbolized in the abandonment of his previous identity when he adopts the name Marcel Bonaventure for the adventure, is an indicator of how the act of relinquishing the foundations of his identity constitutes the first of many steps toward the crisis of legitimacy he experiences. This decision to change his name is linked to his desire to cast aside his prior experiences in order to focus on the task at hand. This process culminates in a profound identitarian crisis, as he gradually distances himself both physically from Africa and psychologically from the identity he has carried up to this point. Rather than duplicating the form letters fellow migrants send home—letters that operate as revisionist narratives of the migrant experience—Moki initially writes letters (which he refrains from mailing) that are anchored in nostalgia and homesickness for the homeland. These constitute more emotionally grounded accounts of the mental responses to transplantation. However, Moki's response to Marcel's narrative reveals the problematic component of this experience, and forces him to confront the dynamic he has instituted between homeland and migration, in terms of how expectations have been placed upon him. "They won't believe you back home," Moki tells him. "These people have never changed, and the tears you have shed won't earn you any compassion. They love to dream. Do you hear me, to dream" (Mabanckou, *Bleu-Blanc-Rouge,* 131–132). The point of transition for him can therefore be located at that moment when he becomes aware of the necessary delusion that accompanies the adventure, and how his contribution to perpetuating the myth—constructed and sustained in the homeland—is grounded in subscribing to an official "form letter" (132), a self-reproducing prototypical narrative offering a positive image of transculturalism, exile, and migration—itself a "foundational text in the imaginary of migration" (Moudileno, "La fiction de la migration," 187). From this arises the symbiotic dimension of the experience, and the inextricable link to the homeland underlines the adventure, in order to maintain the status of the myth.

Once in France, Massala-Massala's/Marcel's primary concern shifts to obtaining documents that will enable him to prolong his stay, to legalize his status in order to avoid the risk of expulsion: "I too had to play cat and mouse with the authorities" (Mabanckou, *Bleu-Blanc-Rouge,* 141). In order to conform to the legal requirements and conditions of residency in France, Marcel Bonaventure obtains a fake birth certificate, a measure that allows him to file a lost identity card report and thus to secure the documents he needs to live, ironically, within the parameters of the law. This further removes Marcel from his identity upon leaving the Congo, and allows the narrator to expose immigration bureaucracy. While pursuing the objectives outlined for an adventurer to become a Parisian, the narrator occupies and moves within the diasporic space that is constituted by the 14th and 18th arrondissements of Paris. The *sapeurs* generally avoid other Africans in Paris, but there are times when exposure to the African diasporic community provides an element of relief. These spaces also allow Marcel to come into contact with many other adventurers, enabling the narrator to describe their respective experiences of migration and the wide range of mostly illicit activities they have engaged in in order to survive and attain their goals, including provision of illegal documents, lists of unoccupied properties, and stolen goods.

Marcel's first assignment, which he has to complete in order to repay the assistance he has been given in securing documents and settling down in Paris, is referred to as a baptism. It consists of buying monthly métro passes with a stolen checkbook. However, while he successfully purchases the passes, he is arrested for selling them. Incarceration provides him with the opportunity to reflect on his adventure, to focus on the homeland, and to reexperience those feelings of nostalgia he had repressed: "In the darkness, I rediscovered the shadows, the faces, and the images of my home country, the only true loves that gave any joy in life, in the hope that I would one day get over this cold wall. Beyond this cell, I dreamed of a space where an honest and sober happiness could be found. The country was there" (203).

After eighteen months in prison, he is expelled from France. The adventure has ended in failure and disillusionment. This he resolves to come to terms with, but the more challenging task that lies ahead is to confront the disappointment of those he left behind. The originality of the novel resides in this concluding sequence, since it is Mabanckou's novel that assumes the responsibility for demystifying the migrant experience. Moudileno argues that, "by imagining a narrative that provides us with perspectives on and the reality of the failure of migration, Mabanckou . . . undertakes to tell us 'everything': to tell the truth about social conditions, to reveal formulas, to repudiate predecessors, and to reestablish a few truths" (Moudileno, "La fiction de la migration," 188).[72] *Bleu-Blanc-Rouge* exhibits a complex structure in which several narratives challenge one another in a constitutive framework, one that juxtaposes the experiences of the *sapeurs* and economic migrants (peasants) who circulate between urban spaces in Africa and France with the process of unveiling that is intrinsic to Mabanckou's project. "Expulsion from French territory, however, is the most damaging possible punishment, because it signals failure in the process of 'becoming somebody'" (MacGaffey and Bazenguissa-Ganga, 56–57). The protagonist thus finds himself located somewhere between Africa and France, between the postcolony and the former colonial center, having reconfigured his own narrative through the reformulation and demystification of the previous transnational urban myth and narrative of Paris and having failed to acquire the necessary designer clothes for a successful descent. In fact, an earlier African text, examined in chapter 4, had provided a parallel narrative and warning, namely Sembene's 1962 short story "Black Girl," in which a migrant worker cautioned young Diouana prior to her departure for France:

> What young African doesn't dream of going to France? Unfortunately, they confuse living in France with being a servant in France. I come from the village next to Diouana's, in Casamance. There, we don't say the way you do that it is the light that attracts the moth, but the other way round. In my country, Casamance, we say that the darkness pursues the moth. ("Black Girl," 49)

SEVEN

African Youth in the Global Economy

And my non-enclosure island, its clear
boldness standing at the back of this
Polynesia, before it, Guadeloupe split
in two along its backbone and sharing
our misery, Haiti where negritude
stood up for the first time and said
it believed in its humanity and the
comic little tail of Florida where the
strangulation of a nigger is about to
be completed and Africa gigantically
caterpillaring as far as the Hispanic
foot of Europe, its nakedness where
Death swings its scythe widely.

Aimé Césaire, *Notebook of a
Return to My Native Land*[1]

Migration to the French metropole has been a constant feature of francophone sub-Saharan African literature from colonial times to the contemporary moment of postcoloniality. Naturally, this phenomenon can be
located in a much broader transhistorical economic and political framework in which the displacement of populations has been a common de-
nominator over several centuries. These factors have much to reveal about
the dynamic between the symbiotically related spaces that are sub-Saharan
Africa and France. Indeed, explorations of colonial history have helped us
to better contextualize recent trends in population movements between
Africa and France and France and Africa, and have convincingly demonstrated the complex connections evidenced in the mythic construct of
France evoked by colonial and postcolonial subjects. The Senegalese
writer Fatou Diome, who resides in the city of Strasbourg in northeastern
France, explores the bilateralism of French-African relations in her novel

Le ventre de l'Atlantique, thereby inscribing herself in a long intertextual genealogy of African writers to whose writings this mediation has been foundational.[2]

The question of migration has of course been a central factor in connecting colonialism and postcolonialism, although the term has taken on even greater significance as African nation-states have been confronted by the economic and social realities of globalization and the accompanying challenge to sovereignty.[3] Indeed, as Saskia Sassen has argued,

> The specific forms of the internationalization of capital over the past twenty years have contributed to mobilizing people into migration streams. They have done so principally through the implantation of Western development strategies . . . At the same time the administrative, commercial, and development networks of the former European empires and the newer forms these networks assumed under the Pax Americana (international direct foreign investment, export-processing zones, wars for "democracy") have not only created bridges for the flow of capital, information, and high-level personnel from the center to the periphery but . . . also for the flow of migrants from the periphery to the center.[4]

A rather unusual set of circumstances inform the African context, particularly if one takes into consideration regional and national particularities, such as a broad range of colonial and decolonizing experiments, recent experiences of national sovereignty, vast discrepancies in natural resources, uneven border control, and population mobility, as well as complex regional trade networks. Naturally, "through these apparently novel forms of integration into the international system," as Achille Mbembe writes, "and the concomitant modes of economic exploitation, equally novel technologies of domination are taking shape over almost the entire continent."[5]

For Arjun Appadurai, "the greatest of these apparently stable objects is the nation-state, which is today frequently characterized by floating populations, transnational politics within national borders, and mobile configurations of technology and expertise."[6] As we shall see, this tenuous relationship between the imperatives of national sovereignty and those of globalization (considered as a transnational phenomenon that works toward the eradication of national borders) is contained in the conclusion to Diome's novel. Given the bilateralism of African-French relations intrinsic to Diome's work, she would surely concur with Fredric Jameson, who signaled that the result of globalizing processes would inevitably be "the forced integration of countries all over the globe into precisely that new division of labor."[7]

Whereas writers during the colonial era such as Ousmane Socé, Cheikh Hamidou Kane, and Bernard Dadié (all of whom Diome alludes to in her novel) were concerned with the "ambiguous" nature of the cultural encounter with France—initially in colonial schools through the exigencies of the civilizing mission, and subsequently through travel to the metropole—Diome extends and updates the implications and parameters of her work in order to situate her observations and critique within the contextual framework of a reflection on globalization and its impact on Africa. Xavier Garnier has convincingly illustrated how Diome's work foregrounds "bilateral relations" between France and Senegal in order to address the "interstitial space" that connects the realities of "dictatorship in Africa" and "the broader mythic construct of Europe itself."[8] This myth has emerged as a factor in "relieving the weight of reality," but has shifted Africa's "center of gravity" outside of the continent (Garnier, "L'exil lettré," 31–32). Accordingly, the "ambivalence" of this positionality structures the coordinates of "local-global" links that inform her text (35), and Garnier highlights not only how Diome has signaled the transcoloniality of this phenomenon through multiple references to colonial novels in which this question was central, but also how these early literary myths and mirages, available in texts and oral narratives, have now been accelerated and intensified by new communication technologies and literacies that provide for the rapid delivery and dissemination of images.

The striking pertinence of her work as a text engaged with the broader concerns of globalization becomes all the more evident if one applies the criteria outlined by Philippe Hugon in his essay "L'Afrique dans la mondialisation" ("Africa in Globalization"), according to which globalization "corresponds to the interdependence of five processes: financial globalization, worldwide organization of production, free circulation of goods, migrations and movements of population, and the instantaneous nature of information."[9] Accordingly, rather than addressing the limits and potentialities of the assimilation of young African protagonists, Diome considers the socioeconomic realities confronting individual and collective migrants upon entry into the sociopolitical zones of both France and of course the European Union as well. The experiences of these migrants are now informed by the difficulties associated with the new lexicon of migration, namely border control, travel and residency documents, refugee status, and the risks of clandestinity. "In 1993," Mireille Rosello shows, "the so-called Pasqua laws became the most obvious manifestation of the French government's anti-immigration attitude. They reflected an increasingly repressive and restrictive philosophy, turning the 'clandestin' (illegal/undocumented immigrant) into an enemy of the state."[10] In turn, Etienne Balibar has highlighted the impact on human rights:

> There is another aspect that has been forced on our attention by the problems relative to the treatment of asylum seekers and the modalities of control of so-called clandestine immigrants in Western Europe, which pose serious problems of the protection and institution of human rights: the system of identity verifications (generally occurring within the territory) allowing a triage of travelers admitted to and rejected from a given national territory.[11]

Ultimately, though, while Diome's novel explicitly acknowledges the trans-colonial nature of African-French relations, the author emerges as a new voice in the category that has become known in France as "literature of immigration." Rather than restricting her narrative to the provision of a reductive account of some of the complex mechanisms connected with immigration to Europe (incarceration, exploitation, repatriation), Diome endeavors to contribute to the process of demystifying the centrality of France as a construct for African youth circulating at the global periphery, but also goes a step further in incorporating a programmatic component that consists in proposing a solution to what Eric de Rosny has character-ized as an "emigration virus."[12]

Diome's first published work was a collection of short stories entitled *La préférence nationale* (*National Preference*), published by Présence Africaine in 2001, that explored the question of immigration and integra-tion in contemporary France.[13] Many of those issues are also addressed in her first novel, *Le ventre de l'Atlantique,* which was published in 2003. The central protagonist, Salie, has, like the author herself, taken up resi-dence in Strasbourg. The experience of exile affords her the opportunity to reflect on her encounter with the economic and social realities of being a sub-Saharan African residing in France and the quotidian experience of racism, in order to offer an image of France that contests the imagined idea her younger half-brother Madické, living in Senegal, adheres to. (We later discover that Madické's full name is, in fact, Samba Madické. Samba is a common name, of course, but it is hard to avoid seeing a link with the earlier Samba Diallo of Kane's *Ambiguous Adventure.*) For her, much in the same way as for other African women writers of an earlier generation (such as Mariama Bâ), writing provides the space to explore the ambiguity of her displacement and the opportunity to reflect on the circumstances of migration as they pertain to Senegal in general and her native island of Niodior more specifically.[14] Of course, her observations are pertinent in many ways to analogous situations in other African countries in which population movements are now well documented. This framework also allows her to consider her own choices and trajectory, while simultane-ously exploring her marginalized status in France. From this positionality, she juxtaposes her narrative with the projections and expectations of those "back home" in Senegal, by whom she is perceived as residing in a veritable "paradise" (Diome, *Le ventre,* 21) across the Atlantic.

The relationship between the socioeconomic realities in France and the distorted projections of them from Africa provides the central discon-nect that Diome proposes to analyze. After marrying a Frenchman and moving to France, Salie is confronted with the inescapability of her posi-tion once her relationship comes to an end: "determined not to return home with my head held down after a failure that many had happily pre-dicted, I stubbornly persisted with my studies" (51). She relies on work as a cleaning lady in order to subsidize her studies and living costs, but no one at "home" can conceive of the living conditions of Africans in France, since they are blinded by their own domestic circumstances: "The Third World cannot see Europe's wounds since it is blinded by its own; it cannot hear its cries, its own are so deafening" (51). Indeed, as Joseph Stiglitz has argued in his book *Globalization and Its Discontents,* "To many in the developing world, globalization has not brought the promised economic benefits. A growing divide between the haves and have-nots has left increasing numbers in the Third World in dire poverty."[15] There are of course numerous reasons why populations are displaced, and Michel Samuel has explored many of these in his book *Le prolétariat africain en France.*[16] The text is structured around a series of interviews conducted with young sub-Saharan Africans. Each account underlines the lack of local opportunities as the primary motivating factor for departure, particularly for the uneducated illiterate proletariat, thereby creating the conditions for a permanent migration. "Young people are right to go to France," we hear from one interviewee, because "here, at home in Mauritania, even educated people have no place; so it makes even more sense for those who are illiterate . . . they can make money in France, feed themselves and their old parents. In the years to come, I plan on continuing to work in France. When I make money, I prefer leaving during the holidays, coming home, chatting a little with my folks, and then returning, going to work there again" (Samuel, *Le prolétariat africain,* 173).[17] These kinds of comments, along with both real and imagined socioeconomic disparities between Africa and France, might help us to better grasp how Salie's position as a domestic worker in France could be the target of great envy in Senegal. Naturally, this envy is more than just ironic; it serves as an indicator of the ideological structure deployed by global capitalism and simultaneously further underlines the power such relativistic constructs are accorded at the service of dominant hegemonic structures of oppression. Appadurai's research corroborates this finding:

> Globalization (understood as a particular, contemporary configuration in the relationship between capital and the nation-state) is demonstrably creating increased inequalities both within and across societies, spiraling processes of ecological degradation and crisis, and unviable relations between finance and manufacturing capital, as well as between goods and the wealth required to purchase them. (Appadurai, "Grassroots Globalization," 17)

While struggling herself to confront the "solitude of exile," Salie is thought of as living in a "European Eden" (Diome, *Le ventre,* 51) by those still in Senegal. However, "having chosen a path completely foreign to my people, I was determined to prove its validity to them. I had to 'succeed' at all costs so as to assume the role assigned to every child in my country: to serve as a safety net for our loved ones. This obligation of assistance is the greatest burden carried by those who emigrate" (51–52). Aware of the unreasonable expectations placed on her by her family and community,

faced with her own "ambiguous adventure" (74) (an obvious allusion to
Kane's critically acclaimed novel by that title), she is determined to counter the narrative offered by a man referred to as "the man from Barbès," a
figure who has emerged as a prototype in recent immigration narratives.
The man from Barbès regularly travels to Senegal with his material acquisitions, tangible evidence of the possibility for success by those "that have
come from France" (70). As Diome argues, "After the historical recognition of colonialism, a new form of mental colonization reigns: young soccer players venerated and continue to venerate France. In their eyes, all
that is enviable comes from France" (60). My objective in chapter 2 was to
show how this mental colonization was intrinsic to the colonial era, as indicated by the lure of francocentrism and the acquisition of cultural capital. The fact that Diome's novel alludes to these earlier texts further in-
scribes the transcolonial dimension of these questions, and we shall return
to these shortly.

Diome quotes the refrain of a popular American song circulating in
Africa: "Anything you want, you've got it!"; in French, it is "Quand on
veut, on peut" (Diome, Le ventre, 29). The meaning of this song plays a
very important role in the novel, since it indicates Diome's positionality
on migration, emphasizing her faith in what she perceives as the benefit of
remaining in Africa rather than leaving the continent. The translation underscores the notion of potentiality contained in the lyrics, and is recuperated in economic terms as a component of the migratory project. However, there is also a second interpretation available in the ambiguity of the
English sentence structure; one could foreground the dimension of finality
and closure as evidenced by "you've got it," in which case the suggested
migration becomes redundant, since the local is adequate. In many ways,
as will become evident, these words anticipate the concluding message
Diome is elaborating in her text. Accordingly, the mediation of Salie's perceived privilege must of course be framed in the context of circumstances
in Senegal. For example, only one television is available to local youth and
its presence is thanks to the man from Barbès, who transported it back
from France. Given the opportunity to recount his experiences in France
to an audience that is both attentive and full of admiration, "the man
from Barbès . . . never ran out of marvelous stories about his odyssey"
(93). Young people are eager to learn more about the mythic city: "So uncle, how was it over there in Paris?" (95).[18] They relish the occasion, and
the setting echoes the format of the traditional communal palabre:

> It was such that you will never be able to imagine it. Just like on TV, but bet-
> ter because you see it all for real. If I tell you what it was like you won't be-
> lieve me. Having said that, it was magnificent, and the word doesn't do it jus-
> tice . . . I landed in Paris at night; you'd have thought the good Lord gave
> those people billions of red, blue, and yellow stars to light things up; the city
> was lit up everywhere . . . I lived in this immense city of Paris. Their airport

is bigger than our village. Before going there, I never thought it possible that such a beautiful city could exist. But I saw it, right there, with my own eyes. The Eiffel Tower and the Obelisk, they look like they reach the sky. And there are so many luxury boutiques lining the Champs-Elysées, all of them overflowing with extraordinary merchandise you cannot stop yourself from admiring, so much so that you need at least a whole day to walk the length of the avenue. And there are beautiful historical monuments, such as the Arc de Triomphe, because, you should know, the French are proud; and since they are rich, they erect a monument for the slightest of their exploits. That allows them also to remember the great men in their history. (95–96)

There are of course remarkable parallels between this performance and those given by the *sapeurs* in the novels of Daniel Biyaoula and Alain Mabanckou. In this instance, the narrative is organized around what Pierre Nora has described as "memory sites," places and monuments that are linked to the record of history and national consciousness, establishing common denominators in a shared memory of the nation. Well-known topographic sites—streets, commemorative monuments, burial grounds— are organized into readily identifiable repositories of collective memory, themselves broadly disseminated through colonial education in the former French empire:

The young listeners never tired of his digressions. They wanted to hear stories about over there; there where the dead slept in palaces, the living must surely dance in heaven. And so they urged on their narrator, who wanted nothing more than to be spurred on by their curiosity. Assessing the growing interest in his story, the man from Barbès sipped away at a cup of tea, offered up a big toothy smile, and started up again with an even more lively voice. (97)

Yet these memory sites call for further interpretation, since they are also the markers of France's Republican ideals and a celebration of military and colonial glory. "This uprooting of memory, its eradication by the conquering force of history," Nora argues, "has had the effect of a revelation, as if an ancient bond of identity had been broken, calling into question something once taken for granted: the close fit between history and memory."[19] Because of this, the various monuments alluded to in the master narrative offered by the man from Barbès serve to highlight the degree of conditioning that has taken place; since he is seemingly unaware of the very irony of his commentary (unlike his predecessor Tanhoe Bertin in Dadié's novel *An African in Paris*), he cannot therefore be relied upon to correct the illusory nature of his formulations. "Like all old capitals, moreover," Maurice Agulhon shows us, "Paris is dotted with important commemorative sites invested with more or less clearly understood political or ideological significance."[20] The Obelisk functions as a symbol of the domination and invasion of Africa, the Arc de Triomphe as a metonym for various military accomplishments, and the Champs-Elysées as a mythic, enchanted construct. The Eiffel Tower is of course inextricably linked to the Universal Exposition of 1889 and the celebration of technological progress, imperial expansion, and the centennial of the Republic. As Henri Loyrette has demonstrated, France "erected [the Eiffel Tower as] a proud monument as proof of its technological prowess and symbol of its role as a beacon among nations."[21] Beyond the historicity of these sites, one also has to consider how a process of amnesia and revisionism has generated redefinitions of the symbolic nature of these sites. Indeed, Agulhon has addressed these developments, in which "the logic of spatial requirements preceded the logic of local preference," and this is particularly relevant to the manner in which the man from Barbès conceives of these memory-relations (Agulhon, 545).

His return to Africa is granted significant attention. "Every two years," we are informed, "their son came back for a whole month during the summer. He handed out a few banknotes and poor-quality goods [*pacotille*] made in France that no one would have traded for a block of emeralds. Here, secondhand goods from Barbès gave you an air of importance and that, that was priceless" (Diome, *Le ventre,* 35). The central objective remains an exhibitionary one, located in his material identity: "Upon his arrival, people were contentedly admiring his purchasing power" (37). With each visit, the symbols of his success in France become more tangible: "On his third leave, he started to build an imposing home . . . That home would guarantee him forever the respect and admiration of the villagers . . . [It was] the emblem of his successful emigration" (38). For local youth, this kind of economic success supports the powerful narrative that Diome and other writers are concerned with countering and undermining. In fact, rejoining the aforementioned reference to the material acquisitions "made" in France, Agulhon's essay "Paris: A Traversal from East to West" has much to reveal: "There is of course a whole commerce of tourism. The relative permanence of souvenir items both shapes and reflects public opinion. The Eiffel Tower, the Arc de Triomphe, Notre Dame, and Sacré-Cœur all but monopolize the market for *trinkets,* for great monuments reduced to the size of paperweights" (Agulhon, 524, emphasis mine). In this way, the man from Barbès ultimately ends up according importance to the very antithesis of the monuments and sites he had evoked, erecting himself new monuments in the guise of commodities and raw materials that may very well not be made in France, and that are the contemporary products of labor forces located in Africa, other former colonies, and so-called Third World countries around the world feeding these Western markets. In actuality—and this further contributes to the remarkable irony and even pathos of the situation—this network of relations is also contained in the very presence of Africans in France who also serve the dominant order within mechanisms (such as sweatshops, underpaid jobs, and undeclared operations) that are now inseparable from the functioning and operations of global cities. The authoritative account provided by the man from Barbès is invested with the legitimacy of experience, and he claims that the French are "very rich," that they live in "luxurious apartments" with electricity and running water, and that they also have cars, televisions, refrigerators, freezers, washing machines and dishwashers, vacuum cleaners, and supermarkets (Diome, *Le ventre*, 97–98). The narrative is of course self-serving and would not stand up to concerted scrutiny, but it nevertheless safeguards the legitimacy of his position.

The Paris neighborhood of Barbès itself has become inextricably associated with the African Diaspora in France and enjoys a mixed reputation (along with such analogous areas as Belleville) as simultaneously the nucleus of a vibrant multiculturalism and the focal point of negative characterizations of the immigrant underclass; because of this, deconstruction of the term "Barbès" reveals a multiplicity of signifiers pertinent to the bi-directionality of projections in Diome's work organized around the simultaneously "exotic" (in the African imaginary) and "pejorative" (in French stereotypes) site of Barbès. For example, the title itself, "from Barbès," unambiguously becomes an honor in the African context, and the prestige accorded to the "man from Barbès" as a result of this enhanced social status following his multiple returns to Niodior (he has the status of "village dignitary" [Diome, *Le ventre*, 60]) resembles the descent of the *sapeurs*, who are themselves invested as Parisians once they have completed a similar circular trajectory.[22] The label "Barbès" is a variation on the traditional title of "Parisian" that confers social capital on those that have completed the secular pilgrimage of travel to Paris. With the Congolese context in mind, Justin-Daniel Gandoulou has observed that "the Occidental myth constitutes one of the positive motivating factors for emigration," and Didier Gondola has shown that "it remains above all a response, a way for this 'sacrificed' youth to adjust to changing realities over which they have virtually no control. Through this voyage into the *sape* we witness the death of reality and its reincarnation in dreams."[23] In both cases, one could argue that the *avenir* (the promise of enhanced social status in the future) lies in the *revenir* (the anticipated constitutive return that is both a physical journey but also of course a symbol of economic advancement). Because of this, the man from Barbès emerges as an emblem of opportunity and therefore of power, but in reality, contextualized within global capitalism, he stands paradoxically as an instrument of continued oppression since his master narrative both relegates him to a position of perpetual subjugation and triggers successive migrations that perpetuate a myth that ultimately serves the capitalist interests of European markets that control the economy and further marginalize Africa.

Diome provides two further intertextual references to earlier francophone sub-Saharan African novels that had explored migration to France from French colonies, namely Bernard Dadié's *An African in Paris* and Ousmane Socé's *Mirage of Paris*.

Biting his cheek, the man from Barbès threw himself down on his bed, re-
lieved at having yet again preserved, better even, consolidated his rank. He
had been *An African in Paris* and had set out, upon his return, to keep alive
the *mirages* that crowned him with prestige. Relying on orality to combat all
those who had written about this city, he had become France's best ambas-
sador. (Diome, *Le ventre*, 101)

A linearity from the colonial era to contemporary globalization emerges
in terms of the economics of human mobility. While the man from Barbès
must take full responsibility for his deception, for what he selectively si-
lences, he both perpetuates a myth and partially responds to the local need
for a such a narrative about France. To this end, the newly arrived griot
serves the desired purpose by delivering a well-received performance, and
the absence of veracity remains a matter for his conscience. In fact, he
even justifies his lie: "what harm was there in him being selective about his
memories, in methodically choosing those that could be told and leaving
the others buried beneath the trap door of oblivion? Not once did his tor-
rential stories ever let slip anything about the wretched life he had led in
France" (101–102).[24] Nevertheless, the fact remains that he sustains a
myth, an illusion, and erects a fiction that renders him complicit in a
process that will culminate in further migration and disillusionment.
These issues were at the very heart of what Dadié, Kane, and Socé were
exploring, and while Diome's work deviates in numerous ways from this
intertextual historiography, these parallels are paradigmatic of the kind of
approach I have insisted upon throughout *Black France*. In Kane's novel,
recourse to philosophical discourse provided the framework with which
to explore the myth of occidental superiority, and to examine the colo-
nizer/colonized relationship that is so crucial to our understanding of the
migration myth. To this end, the works of Dadié and Socé provide unique
examples of the ways in which the myth of French cultural superiority operates as a strategic device for imposing colonial rule, and how in turn it
can be unpacked and demystified by an attentive observer of these elaborate dynamics. If the novels of Kane and Socé (among others, of course)
foregrounded displacement as the mode through which greater consciousness was achieved in order to decondition and question colonialism, then
Dadié's novel exhibits a key difference by distancing itself from this
process in order to provide an unprecedented concentration on the foundations of the ideological project as a way of demystifying the fantasy of
Occidental superiority.

The tremendous appeal of migration for African youth naturally warrants further consideration. As Stiglitz has explained, "Fundamentally,
[globalization] is the closer integration of the countries and peoples of the
world which has been brought about by the enormous reduction of costs
of transportation and communication, and the breaking down of artificial
barriers to the flows of goods, services, capital, knowledge, and (to a lesser

extent) people across borders. Globalization has been accompanied by the creation of new institutions that have joined with existing ones to work across borders" (Stiglitz, 9). Economic disparities between geographic and continental zones provide, of course, the central determining indicator, but one cannot underestimate the fundamental centrality of France with regard to the African periphery—a phenomenon that has survived beyond colonial propagandist mechanisms into the postcolonial imagination. Both economic and cultural factors were intrinsic to colonial relations between Africa and Europe, and these factors continue to inform the bilateralism of relations in the form of transnational capital and labor as constitutive markers of globalization. Furthermore, while Diome's novel is very much anchored in a contemporary context, the text itself calls for precisely this kind of transhistorical contextualization in its repeated allusions to the colonial texts I mentioned. These links are not arbitrary, but rather serve to underscore the fact that while African-French relations may have changed from colonial to postcolonial times, African interests are still not well served. Central to this phenomenon are more complex circumstances pertaining to the desperation of African youth, who are able to express their disillusionment with the local economy by engaging in transnational migration as part of an externalization process that involves identification with the perceived potentialities and possibilities of enhanced economic mobility in global cities such as Brussels, London, Los Angeles, New York, Paris, and Rome.[25] As Sassen rightly concludes, "The worldwide evidence shows rather clearly that there is considerable patterning in the geography of migrations, and that the major receiving countries tend to get immigrants from their zones of influence" (*Globalization*, 8).[26] Thus, Diome proposes a counter-narrative to that of individuals such as the man from Barbès, aligning herself with a long list of African authors who have engaged in similar oppositional practices from the colonial period to the present day.

Diome's novel is set in the popular context of world soccer, and it is within this framework that the analysis of globalization and its impact on African youth is mapped out. The opening section takes us to the 2000 European championship. Significantly, Salie's half-brother—quite unlike his local friends—is obsessed with the Italian sensation Paolo Maldini (in fact, he has gone so far as to adopt Maldini's name as his own nickname). This might be partly explained by the fact that Italy remains a privileged destination for Senegalese migrants,[27] but his process of identification with global "commodities" is indicative of the degree to which Africa is of course influenced by a highly complex network of global cultural influences outside of former colonial ties.[28] Because of the striking inequities of global communications systems and the disproportionate cost of making calls relative to local income and GDP, Madické relies on his sister's phone calls to a call center to receive regular score updates and match summaries. Madické, of course, cannot even entertain the thought that these exchanges might represent a financial burden on his sister, since he perceives the position she occupies as a resident in France as privileged. This affords Salie the opportunity to engage with this imaginary projection in order to further reflect on the disconnect between myth and reality:

> How many miles, days of hard work, and sleepless nights still separate me from what remains a hypothetical success, yet a success that has been a given for my loved ones ever since I announced my departure for France? So I move on, my steps heavy with their dreams, my thoughts filled by my loved ones. I move on without knowing my destination. I'm not sure on which flagpole they will raise the flag to my victory, and I also have no idea which fountains will be capable of washing away the affront of failure. (Diome, *Le ventre*, 15)

The challenge facing Salie (and therefore by association Diome's literary project) is to correct the illusion by describing the socioeconomic conditions of immigration in France. At the heart of her analysis is the realization that the man from Barbès has caught himself in a lie from which it gets more difficult to extricate himself each time he recounts his story: "Scepter in hand, how could he have admitted that he had started out by haunting métro exits, been forced to pilfer to appease his hunger, begged, survived the winter thanks to the Salvation Army, before finding a squat to share with companions in misfortune?" (102). Compelled to conceal the reality of his experiences in France for the dual purpose of enhancing his social capital and fulfilling the needs and expectations of his community, he has become only too aware that "his body was his only capital" (102). The immigrant's body and the slavery topos are common features of Diome's text as she establishes further transhistorical links pertaining to the relations between Africa and France and the ongoing problem of exploitation in competitive labor markets. Arguably, though, while both the slave and the migrant worker are reduced to bodily labor, a distinction can be drawn given that the slave's body does not function as capital, precisely because slavery is unpaid labor. Colonial ideology is central to this construct given that it indicates how raw materials and labor served the interests of European market economies in which Africans functioned as physical laborers, a topos that is recuperated transcolonially as the immigrant's body is now also a disposable commodity. Indeed, these questions are central to Rebecca's Saunders's discussion of the figure of the "global foreigner."[29] As Saunders has indicated, "the transnationalization of labor has not only dramatically increased global migration, but solidified the association of the foreigner with poverty, and with particular ethnic groups" (Saunders, 89). In many cases, governments and international organizations rely on GDP as the indicator of progress, and these evaluative mechanisms have proved grossly inconclusive in measuring the economic, social, and political stability and growth of various countries.[30]

One must consider the rationale for deploying such mechanisms. A widely held misconception that informs immigration policy has led organizations and governments "to promote economic growth in the migrant-sending countries by encouraging direct foreign investment and export-oriented international development assistance, in the belief that raising economic opportunities in the developing world will deter emigration" (Sassen, *Globalization,* 32). However, Sassen has successfully illustrated how the "very measures commonly thought to deter immigration—foreign investment and the promotion of export-oriented growth in developing countries—seem to have had precisely the opposite effect" (34). In fact, such conceptualizations of economic inequities provided the logic behind the introduction of Structural Adjustment Programs (SAP), and pressures from the International Monetary Fund (IMF) and the World Bank to enact economic liberalism and development politics.[31] As S. M. Ravi Kanbur has explained, the objective is to "attain stabilization through demand-side measures, increase production tradeables, liberalize the domestic and international sectors . . . and reduce the scope of the public sector."[32] However, "the IMF's allegedly liberatory practices," Saunders continues, "are customarily effected through the mechanism of Structural Adjustment Programs—and the term *adjustment* (to settle, put in order, regulate, make fit for use, alter slightly) merits its own analysis—which insists on privatization of health services, water supplies, education, public housing and transport, safety, sanitation, and other public services. These services, that is, are transferred into the hands of transnational corporations to be operated as profit-generating businesses, which will, in turn, produce revenue to service the debt" (Saunders, 94). With the American context in mind, Sassen underscores that governments have failed "to appreciate the political and economic forces that give rise to immigration in the first place" and that

> international migrations are partly embedded in conditions produced by economic internationalization both in sending and in receiving areas. While a national state may have the power to write the text of an immigration policy, it is likely to be dealing with a complex, deeply embedded and transnational process that it can only partly address and regulate through immigration policy as conventionally understood. (Sassen, *Globalization,* 31, 13)

These findings are corroborated by Rosello's analysis of the contradictory nature of "postcolonial hospitality."

Both scholars and groups such as Africa Trade Bill Alert and the Africa Faith and Justice Network have been critical of the African Growth and Opportunity Act, whose objective since 2000 has been to encourage African countries to develop free markets; they see it as serving the interests of multinational corporations. Makhtar Diouf, in his book *L'Afrique dans la mondialisation,* has insisted on the importance of adopting a transcolonial framework in order to adequately assess the place of Africa in global economic relations and structural adjustment measures since 1990.[33] While the World Bank assessed the Senegalese public works and employment agency AGETIP as a "development success,"[34] the International Labor Organization has reached radically different conclusions:

> Structural adjustment programmes in many developing countries and some industrialized countries have also caused hardship, especially to the lower income strata of the population. These programmes advocate liberalization in economic affairs, thus providing a golden opportunity for the rich and the educated—and sometimes also the unscrupulous and powerful—to profit at the expense of the weaker sections of society . . . While these problems affect all countries, there is a general consensus that the situation of most developing countries—particularly of Africa—is critical and requires special attention and action.[35]

Now, the man from Barbès is at least aware of his marginalized status in France. Indeed, Diome explores his predicament:

> The solitary hunter is alone in knowing the cost of his game. If he comes home smiling, the village is happy to praise his skill and bravery. Having survived, the lion conceals his scars beneath his glossy coat. The man from Barbès did just the same, and he was quite sure his veneer ran no risk of being scratched. The grown-ups envied him too much to try and make trouble for him, and as for the young, well, their claws weren't solid enough yet to worry him. Small pelicans thirsting after new horizons, they needed his beakfuls of color to paint the sky. As they said their goodbyes after an evening spent in his company, they were always thankful and respectful. (Diome, *Le ventre*, 104)

Anyone who attempts to counter these fables faces a daunting task. However, the village schoolteacher is determined to avoid the further disillusionment of young African men and shares with them the story of the failed migration of a young man named Moussa.[36] "The schoolteacher was the only one who knew the complete version of the story. Upon his return, the young man had made him his confidant" (109), and he is therefore invested with a particular rhetorical agency. Moussa was recruited to join a soccer training camp in France, and all kinds of promises were made to him. Gradually, however, he discovered that he had entered into a sinister "pro-slavery process" (112). The slavery topos reemerges with his realization that he has become a commodity because he has mortgaged his future for the funds he needed to travel to France. His own travels across the Atlantic effectively lead him into slavery, since when he fails to progress to the next level and obtain a remunerated contract, his clandestine status in France renders him vulnerable to exploitation and deportation:

> A buddy of mine has a boat. We'll go and see him and I'll get him to take you on over there. We won't ask for too much, and that'll help him keep things quiet. He'll pay your wages to me, and when you're done reimbursing

me you'll be able to save enough to go and live it up back home. You're a
solid guy, you'll take care of things. But don't forget, sh! Don't forget you're
an illegal. (117)

The link with slavery is explicit once again as Moussa labors alongside his
fellow "galley workers" (123). His predicament is further complicated by
additional pressure from his family back in Africa, who insist on the importance of his success: "Spare us any shame from our people. You must
work, save, and return to the country" (119), and then by his arrest in
Marseilles. Following in the footsteps of another sub-Saharan African
protagonist, namely Diaw Falla in Ousmane Sembene's *Black Docker,* he
ventures out into the city of Marseilles, where he is immediately subjected
to the equivalent of racial profiling.[37] The assumptions by the police concerning his clandestine status are confirmed in this particular case, but
have less to do with efficient policing than they do with a complex network of stereotypes and projections. His visit to France ends with deportation and further engagement with the brutal realities of contemporary
immigration. In this instance the African body as a commodity is declared
undesirable in France now that it is marked as clandestine.

Deportation is only the first of his concerns, since he must now also
disappoint his family. Festivities have been arranged to celebrate his return, but ultimately he opts to share with them the official story: "No
longer able to let his loved ones go into more debt to honor him, he gave
them a summary of his experience in France. The explosion of truth cov-
ered him in cinders. He ceased to shine from European light and became
less interesting than the most sedentary islander. Just about everyone de-
spised him" (126). He is blamed for his failure and the marginalization he
experienced in France is now reproduced on the other side of the Atlantic.
In this, he joins the long list of disillusioned Africans who have either traveled to the metropole or returned to Africa, and for whom suicide provides the only escape. In this instance, Ndétare retells Moussa's biography
as an attempt to preempt further migrations: "France is not paradise.
Don't let yourselves get ensnared in the nets of emigration" (132).[38] The
fact that such narratives have existed since the colonial period and survived into the contemporary era is an indicator of the magnitude of the
task of reconditioning with which they are confronted. Returning to the
central problem confronting African youth addressed earlier—namely the
lack of economic and social opportunities on a continent that continues to
be relegated to the margins of the global economy—we note that several
factors have exacerbated local conditions. Manthia Diawara, for example,
has assessed the dramatic impact of the devaluation of the CFA franc on
January 10, 1994. Prior to this event, globalization was already viewed
with a pronounced skepticism: "Some people perceived it as the new colonialism of cultural forms of life in Africa by transnational corporations in
complicity with Western governments and corrupt African leaders. Others

viewed it as an opportunity for African artists and entrepreneurs to leave the periphery and join the metropolitan centers in Europe and America."[39] The solution Diawara proposes to the hegemonic impulses of globalization, based on extensive analysis of local and regional economies and transnational cultural, economic, and social networks, is located in African market economies: "West African markets, traditionally the centers of international consumption and cross-cultural fertilization, provide a serious challenge to the scheme of globalization and structural adjustment fostered by the World Bank and other multinational corporations that are vying to recolonize Africa" (Diawara, "Toward a Regional Imaginary," 114). Diawara's support of regionalism coincides with Diome's faith in the local, yet it remains crucial to emphasize that while such positions may well be recuperated in order to justify the kinds of adjustment politics described earlier, this is certainly not their intention. It is one thing to underscore the need to develop local socioeconomic structures that are capable of engaging with the transnational economy, and quite another to address the reality of the disparities in place that foster exploitative structures. "This role of the market," Diawara insists,

> is often overlooked by African political scientists who, in their desire to become advisers to the World Bank, ignore the role of European governments and international institutions in the corruption of the state and blame African traditions for failing to embrace modernization because of their innate predisposition to debauchery. (123)

All of these measures share points of commonality with the efforts of new organizations, such as the Union nationale des commerçants et industriels du Sénégal (National Union of Senegalese Retail Merchants and Industrialists, UNACOIS), that, as Momar-Coumba Diop has shown, comprise factors "that explain the need to carefully understand the protocol that attempts to shift sources of national influence to the local level by allowing for the creation and development of underexploited complex strategies at the heart of communities."[40] Ultimately, none of these enterprises will be productive unless a specific set of cautions provided by Mbembe in his essay "On Private Indirect Government" are taken seriously:

> it is impossible to approach these issues without first placing three major historical processes at the very center of our analysis: first, the de-linking of Africa from formal international markets; second, the forms of its integration into the circuits of the parallel international economy; and third, the fragmentation of public authority and emergence of multiple forms of *private indirect government* accompanying these two processes.[41]

Our consideration of these issues should not overlook the fact that Salie left Senegal under different circumstances than Moussa did. However, this factor cannot obfuscate the fact that her experience of return to Africa is characterized by sentiments similar to his, since in addition to her marginal status in France, she is also identified as an outsider in the local context: "Yet returning has become the same as departing for me. I go home as one goes abroad, because I have become the *other* for those I continue to call my loved ones" (Diome, *Le ventre,* 190). Her idea of home has been displaced by exile and she no longer fully belongs to Africa. The teacher implores her to tell them her "truth," to share the parameters of the immigrant context in order to arrive at an alternative topography anchored outside of and reversing the sites of memory evoked in the mythic construct. At this point, Diome begins to delineate some of the links she indicated at the beginning of the novel between international soccer and the politics of migration. The question of sport is central to the broader discourse on immigration in France.[42] As Salie states to her brother and his friends about the French authorities,

> Well, as for their policy of integration, at the very best it applies to their national soccer team. *Blacks, Blancs, Beurs,*[43] that's just a slogan as a showcase for the world . . . Foreigners are accepted, loved, and even claimed as their own only when they are among the best in their field. *Blacks, Blancs, Beurs:* if that were a given, you wouldn't need a slogan for it. (204–205)

Indeed, the tremendous visibility of the French national soccer team during the 1998 World Cup, which was held in France, generated considerable discussion of the question of multiculturalism, since the team's multiethnic make-up was capitalized upon by the authorities and certain media outlets as a kind of example of France's progressive politics of integration. Perhaps the most compelling moment occurred when the image of the French captain Zinadine Zidane (the child of North African immigrants) was beamed onto the Arc de Triomphe. France's national team does of course reflect a long and complicated history of African-French relations, but the alignment of players of multiple ethnic origins under the aegis of the "bleu-blanc-rouge" (blue, white, and red, the colors of the French flag) had very little to do with broader social policy and the circumstances of minority populations in France. Diome challenges this official discourse on successful integration, highlighting the shortcomings of these integrational objectives. Indeed, this approach connects with her position in her first book, *La préférence nationale,* in which she suggested that mobility in French society centers on epidermal factors contained in an "epidermic preference" (Diome, *La préférence nationale,* 202). Gradually, Diome frames these questions in the broader context of globalization and the position of Africa in the economically disenfranchised zones of the South, where the cultural, political, and social problems of under-development (poverty, issues of women's rights, polygamy, and reproductive concerns) are immediate symptoms: "The worst of the twentieth century's indecencies," as Salie argues, "is the image of an obese West juxtaposed with a Third World suffering from rickets" (Diome, *Le ventre,* 192). For Salie, exile is characterized by loss and displacement, as she is positioned in the transnational space characterized by the kind of cultural and social "double-unbelonging" alluded to by Salman Rushdie,[44] whereby she is no longer completely African and not quite French: "With roots everywhere, permanently exiled, I am at home at that point where Africa and Europe lose their pride and are content with becoming one" (210). The central point of intertextuality between colonial and postcolonial texts is located in the shared concern with assessing, documenting, and recording the genealogy of economic and social struggle, the disintegration of the social fabric, and the impact of that disintegration on African youth. The multi-generational component is highlighted in disturbing militaristic terminology through the evocation of "economic bazookas aimed at us from the West" (214). Diome's work serves to further substantiate Mongo Beti's denunciations, in his *Main basse sur le Cameroun: Autopsie d'une décolonisation* and *La France contre l'Afrique: Retour au Cameroun,* of the uneven and exploitative nature of France's treatment of Africa from colonial to postcolonial times, and to underscore the growing disparities between the two regions.[45]

Juxtaposed with Salie's own "solitary life in Europe" (Diome, *Le ventre,* 220) is the equally negative experience of being back in Senegal. Rather than staying only with her family, she decides to travel and visit her own country. At first, hotel receptionists assume she is a prostitute, but once they realize she is in fact on vacation "from" France, she is labeled as an outsider by the term "Francenabé" (228). "A foreigner in France," she points out, "I was welcomed as such in my own country: as illegitimate with a resident's permit as with my identity card" (228). Her entry into France had been mediated through a series of formalities that forced her to select between passenger lines in the arrivals terminal according to the categories of "European passports" and "foreign passports" (234) and then to navigate and negotiate her way by the customs officer, who has become a "caretaker for the nation" (235); the notion of a "passport" and the implied crossing through ports—from "pass" to "port"—has a particular resonance in this context. While she makes it past these obstacles, she witnesses a couple being taken away to the transnational zones reserved for the clandestine.[46] Further connections with slavery are established here when Diome delineates parallel conventions related to the medical status of the displaced slave and the immigrant required to undergo medical evaluation prior to the issuance of residency documents: "at a time when one went about selling negroes, ebony, and spices, no one would buy a sick slave" (248). Salie decries and deplores these new formalities: "Passports, a certificate of domicile, visas / And all the other things they don't tell you about / Have become the *new chains of slavery*" (250, emphasis mine). Writing offers an escape mechanism with which to process her anxiety—"Nostalgia is my open wound and I cannot stop myself from sticking my pen into it" (259)—thereby enabling her to reconcile the duality of her transnationality, "two selves: the *I* from here, and the *I* from there" ("double soi: *moi* d'ici, *moi* de là-bas," 259).

This context leads us to a consideration of the significance of Senegal's May 31 victory over France in the 2002 soccer World Cup. Immediately after the event, bumper stickers were widely available for sale in the Senegalese capital of Dakar: "France 0 Senegal 1 / Nous n'oublierons JAMAIS" ("We will *never* forget").[47] Diome's novel is framed around this victory, and it provides an initial step toward the rethinking of the myth of French superiority and an occasion to celebrate a newfound pride in the autonomous nation-state of Senegal, now accorded visibility on the global stage. Celebrations adopt a transnational quality: "Even those who are afraid to go back home with their bags filled with failure, humiliation, and deception came out of their projects in the Hexagon to yell out the new pride they had discovered" (Diome, *Le ventre,* 278–279). This challenge by the "Senegalese in Paris" (also referred to as the "Senegauls" [*Sénégaulois,* 281]) leads to a rethinking of the hegemonic paradigm that has become inseparable from the French Republican ideal of assimilation. Once again, the metaphor of slavery is evidenced as Diome's text evokes "the slave trade in soccer players" ("la traite du footeux," 282). Indeed, the circulation of athletes is a fascinating dimension of global labor markets, and one should note that some twenty-one out of the twenty-three players selected for the Senegalese national squad actually trained and played in France at the time. Ironically, some even characterized the victory as a betrayal of France's codes of hospitality, as a symbolic affront by an ungrateful guest!

One might have expected the accolades bestowed on Senegalese players (the majority of whom enjoy lucrative contracts in European clubs) after their victory to have made the myth of migration even more complex to counter. Significantly, Salie's brother does not call her after the World Cup, as he had previously after every match. With the funds he has received from his sister, he decides to start a small business. In fact, he even begins to pressure her to come home, but her circumstances are more complex: "Hybrid being that I am, Africa and Europe are asking themselves which part of me belongs to them" (294). After going to live in France, she now confronts her "fragmented identity" (295). However, with her brother's change of heart, Diome is able to articulate the broader message I discussed earlier concerning her faith in local solutions. There are no simple solutions to these new twenty-first-century challenges—adjustment policies have not been beneficial to Africa, nor has the migration myth been entirely countered. Mbembe has addressed this challenge in the following terms:

> To conceptualize globalization adequately, the classical distinction between spatiality and temporality has to be made more relative. Interpreted from what is wrongly considered to be the margins of the world, globalization

sanctions the entry into an order where space and time, far from being opposed to one another, tend to form a single configuration. The domestica-
tion of global time proceeds by way of the material deconstruction of existing territorial frameworks, the excision of conventional boundaries, and the
simultaneous creation of mobile spaces and spaces of enclosure intended to
limit the mobility of populations judged to be superfluous.[48]

Madické now finds himself carefully negotiating a space for himself outside of the context of migration, preferring instead to remain in Senegal.
The Senegalese victory has provided one of the only examples in the novel
of a local indicator of success and pride, as opposed to the multiple indicators available concerning Africans in France—the marriage of former president Léopold Sédar Senghor to a white French woman, the Senegalese
athletes training in France, and so on. The objective is not to condone a return to antiquated models of development politics, but rather to address
and reconsider the inequality of bilateral relations between France and Africa and the disproportionate circulation of economic and human capital.
To this end, the very transcoloniality of these phenomena also needs to be
addressed, whereby, as Obioma Nnaemeka has argued, "colonialism's focus on natural resources, institutions, and frameworks is matched by development's focus on economics, institutions, and processes," and "development discourse and practice stand to gain from the development of the
particular. Until development assumes an individual, human face instead
of the anonymity of the collective (the poor, the needy), it will remain an
unrealizable goal in the 'third world.' The goal will be accomplished
through an honest effort to humanize development processes and not assume that economic growth guarantees development."[49] In this case, we
witness Madické's recovery of self as a result of a gesture of partial demystification of France through its trenchant defeat in the World Cup. The victory is naturally only a symbolic one since, much as France's 1998 victory
did nothing to change race relations in France, Senegal's victory has not ultimately transformed or realigned French-Senegalese relations. Nevertheless, the victory operates in such a way as to allow Madické to confirm his
newfound interest in the potential of the local. To a certain extent, this
conclusion coincides with political transitions in Senegal itself since 2000,
when Abdoulaye Wade's Front pour l'alternance (FAL) replaced Abdou
Diouf in power, triggering various socioeconomic restructuring initiatives.[50]

Whereas for Salie writing offers a way to process the legacy of migration in which exile represents a "geographic suicide" (Diome, Le ventre,
263), Madické ultimately relinquishes solutions that would take him away
from Africa. In so doing, he distances himself from the portrait gallery of
dislocated sub-Saharan African protagonists who constituted the earlier
demographics of migration, and effectively maps out the new coordinates
of a transnational geometry in which the periphery is repositioned as an-

other center, even if this new center is to be found in "le ventre de l'Atlantique," the belly of the Atlantic. "The future of the Senegalese state," Donal Cruise O'Brien has argued, "will surely depend more on decisions made by the Senegalese than on international initiatives."[51] These new coordinates align themselves with a similar position adopted by Ousmane Sembene when he rejected the implication that African film required mediation through Western critical reception: "Europeans don't care whether or not Africa is represented. It's not their navel. Much in the same way that they are not our center. Europe is our periphery."[52]

Conclusion

Black is not a color, it's an experience.
Black de France[1]

Black France has underlined the importance of the racial signifier as a way of validating ethnicity as a category of inquiry and in order to counter and negate the French authorities' historical inclination to address immigration issues in the Hexagon through an undifferentiated paradigm. Accordingly, the framework adopted in *Black France* has insisted on the importance of a transcolonial approach in order to better access the connections between colonial Occidentalist concepts of superiority and their inherited reformulations in contemporary postcolonial France at the service of culturalist arguments linked to the consolidation of antiquated and mythic notions of French identity. The centrality of Paris as former center of the metropole and French capital city is acknowledged and its continued importance accentuated; but the site is also partially decentered by shifting the focus of the analysis to provincial sites while also suggesting how Paris operated, and continues to operate, as a broader iconic symbol for the metropole and the Hexagon as mutable territorial concepts circulating in the imaginations of migrants and writers. Finally, *Black France* demonstrates that both francophone colonial and postcolonial sub-Saharan African literatures have always been symbiotically linked to French historiography, and the constitutive nature of literary production that emerges from this demonstration complicates French and European debates on identity and singularity. As a whole, these factors have aimed to provide a better contextualization of the bilateral histories of African-French relations, and in so doing to account for blackness in its multiple expressive forms in France as a lived experience, particularly since these questions have, until recently, been ignored in France. Richard Senghor, in an essay in the journal *Esprit,* outlined the parameters of a rising Black consciousness in France (expressed through the formation of Black activist groups, claims for civil rights, debates on communitarianism and positive discrimination), and traced the roots of this emerging consciousness back to the 1998 commemorations of the 150th anniversary of the abolition of slavery.[2]

A consideration of political discourse in France is indicative of the confused and conflicted approach to minority populations. The most negative components have to do with an apparent consolidation of extreme right-wing positions that have coincided with increasing border control throughout "fortress Europe" and revitalized discussions of the parameters of a European identity. These developments have been accompanied by the deployment of a new official lexicon with which to classify and designate asylum seekers, foreigners, immigrants, and refugees. In *We, the People of Europe: Reflections on Transnational Citizenship*, French philosopher Etienne Balibar was one of the first to signal this phenomenon and to expose its broader implications. Additionally, a number of "affairs" and crises have been at the forefront of public debate and have received extensive media coverage. For example, on August 23, 1996, several hundred sub-Saharan Africans were removed from the Eglise Saint-Bernard in Paris in what has come to be known as the "affaire des sans-papiers" ("the undocumented immigrant affair"), and in 2004, some fifteen years after the initial "affaire du foulard" ("headscarf affair") and subsequent "affaire du voile" ("veil affair"), Bernard Stasi published his report, commissioned by the French government, on the state of secularism in France. (That state was aptly characterized by Emmanuel Terray as "Headscarf Hysteria!"[3]) Perhaps one of the most disturbing expressions of these tensions is contained in street graffiti observed in Paris in 1997 by Catherine Raissiguier, namely "Islam = SIDA" (Islam = AIDS); "'Islam' is used here to represent a whole set of undesirable immigrants who will not/cannot be integrated into French society."[4] Indeed, if these questions focus on Africa in France, another dimension has also received concerted attention, namely the continuing presence of France in Africa. To this end, the history of French "contact" with Africa has been addressed in the writings of Mongo Beti, such as *Main basse sur le Cameroun: Autopsie d'une décolonisation* (1972) and *France contre l'Afrique: Retour au Cameroun* (1993). France's foreign policy on Africa has been the object of much criticism, particularly through the term *françafrique,* which combines the French words for France and Africa to reflect the underhanded quality of economic and political relations that are perceived—often rightly so, if one examines the evidence—to function at the expense of African populations and to hinder their ability to compete in the global economy.[5]

Naturally, though, these elements do not constitute the full picture, and the contradictory nature of the French government's actions is confirmed by many alternative examples that offer a glimpse of hope. For example, while legislation was being debated in the French National Assembly that would encourage the positive reevaluation of the colonial project, plans were moving ahead to open a museum of the history of immigration, the Cité nationale de l'histoire de l'immigration—while I (along with many others) have underscored some of the ways in which the encouraging aspects of this commemorative project are undermined by the accompanying semiology, I nevertheless do not want to seem disparaging of what may very well turn out to be a step in the right direction. At the very least, public debate on this issue might very well lead to a rearticulation of some of the initial premises that informed the initiative in its embryonic stages. The French "no" vote in 2005 against the latest draft of the European Union constitution triggered government reform and the promotion of Dominique de Villepin to the post of prime minister. No sooner had he taken up office than he appointed the critically acclaimed Beur writer and sociologist Azouz Begag (born in France to Algerian parents) as the first-ever minister of equal opportunity. Since ethnicity is not officially recognized by the French Republic, Begag will face a real challenge in meeting his responsibility to identify, label, and document concrete instances of inequality, and then to rectify them, particularly since these inequities became all the more apparent during the civil unrest of October and November 2005. As Patrick Weil has lucidly argued, "In France, the need for equality is all the more crucial given that the very principle has, since the Revolution, been inscribed at the very heart of Republican values."[6]

Having said this, a work of nonfiction, *Je suis noir et je n'aime pas le manioc (I'm Black but I Don't Care for Manioc)*, which was published in 2003 by Gaston Kelman (who is himself Black) and became a best-seller, effectively ventriloquizes the kind of recuperative discourse fostered by the French authorities in favor of a color-blind policy of assimilation.[7] Kelman self-identifies as a *bourguignon* (a man from the Burgundy region of France), and although he recognizes that race is a problem in France, he insists that ethnic specificity should be relinquished in the name of dominant norms, and even denounces what he perceives as the "victimary" discourse advocated by figures in the Black community, such as Calixthe Beyala.[8] "All that is asked of each inhabitant is to live as we live in France and not how one lives in the country of one's distant origins . . . To be French is to be assimilated, to dissolve into the local milieu" (Kelman, 166). In what might well be described as the "affaire des incendies," namely the apartment-building fires that occurred in Paris during the summer of 2005 and that took the lives of several low-income sub-Saharan African immigrants, profound social inequities were brought to public attention.[9] The right-wing National Front may draw upon racist principles as a way of enlisting support, but these exclusive agendas are being passionately combated by such organizations as SOS-Racisme, Collectif égalité, and the Mouvement contre le racisme et pour l'amitié entre les peuples, which are successfully mobilizing supporters. As Beyala has argued, "by refusing to deal in a concerted manner with the problem of the integration of visible minorities, they [French authorities] are contributing to the existence of an ossified system, ill-adapted to the multiracial and multicultural realities of France."[10]

Culture and politics are inextricably linked in the French context, as Danielle Marx-Scouras's cultural history of one of France's most successful "multiethnic" groups, Zebda, illustrates.[11] In *La France de Zebda, 1981–2004: Faire de la musique un acte politique*, Marx-Scouras locates Zebda's contributions in a broader discourse that concerns both immigration policies and the French state's pro-active role in controlling urban culture. In some cases, these have helped bring greater visibility to France's multicultural expressive cultures. For example, 2006 was devoted to the Festival francophone en France (see http://*www.francofffonies.fr*), which included numerous conferences, symposia, and cultural events throughout France, in addition to the already well established Festival international des Francophonies in Limoges, the Etonnants voyageurs meeting in Saint-Malo, and Festafrica in Lille. In many ways, this government involvement and interference in the cultural domain has simply served to provide official recognition of vibrant cultural practices that have been in evidence in every artistic domain in the Hexagon as cumulative historical processes. A cursory glance at African influences in and on the Hexagon yields a substantial list: a number of African-themed films have been produced, from Paulin S. Vieyra's *Afrique sur Seine* (1957), Mamadou Kone's *Un village africain à Paris* (1980), and Ben D. Beye's *Les princes noirs de Saint-Germain-des-Prés* (1975) to Cheik Doukouré's more recent *Paris selon Moussa* (2003);[12] magazines and journals that either sometimes feature Africa-related events or are entirely devoted to them, such as *Cité black, Jeune Afrique, Bingo, Présence africaine, Le nouvel observateur, Libération, Le monde, Le figaro*, and *Politique africaine*, are widely available at newsstands and bookstores throughout France; soccer icons such as Thierry Henri have attained global name recognition; restaurants such as *Le petit Dakar* in the Marais are now familiar sights; African detective fiction now jumps back and forth between Kinshasa and Château-Rouge; art galleries display Africa-related art; the works of playwrights such as Sony Labou Tansi, Tchicaya U Tam'si, Kossi Efoui, and Koffi Kwahulé have been performed in France (Marie N'Diaye has even been staged at the Comédie française!);[13] French television has been compelled to rethink "the multicultural reality that is contemporary France and its homogeneously white representation on national TV";[14] new voices and approaches to the exigencies of bicultural experiences are to be found each year, most notably with Abdourahman A. Waberi, Sami Tchak, Bilguissa Diallo, and Sayouba Traoré,[15] and in turn these authors are finding new outlets for their works as the publishing industry has come to recognize the broad constituencies to whom they speak;[16] and musical influences have had a dramatic impact on radio broadcasting structures (MC Solaar, IAM, NTM, Zebda). While this list cannot claim to be exhaustive, it nevertheless reflects the diversity of influences that have tangibly affected the cultural landscape. A conclusive indicator of this was the brilliant exhibit held at the Centre Georges Pompidou in Paris during the summer of 2005, Africa Remix, of which the African writer Simon Njami served as chief curator.[17] As Njami wrote, "An opposition thus appeared between a collective memory that sealed [Africans'] sense of belonging and laid down roots, and a personal memory where a jumbled combination of sexuality, politics, feminism, race and origins all confronted each other."[18]

Invariably, these questions have taken on a very different dimension today, and in many ways have everything to do with current debates on the future cultural, economic, political, and social coordinates of the European Union.[19] Boniface Mongo-Mboussa has even suggested (drawing on a concept evoked by Achille Ngoye) that a writer such as Sami Tchak "might just be announcing (indirectly) the emergence of a black or euroblack literature."[20] Productive links may thus be found in further exploring the ways in which writers such as Azouz Begag, Farida Belghoul, Alain Mabanckou, and Sami Tchak intersect with and diverge from writers across the Channel in Britain, such as Diran Abedayo, Monica Ali, Biyi Bandele-Thomas, Hanif Kureishi, and Zadie Smith, in their respective investigations into the challenges of building coalitions and fostering harmonious coexistence across complex (post)colonial divides. The question, of course, as Balibar has signaled, concerns the reconfiguration of membership as contained under the "We" to which he alludes in the title to his book on Europe. There lies the challenge.

Proposed solutions to the imminent dangers of failing to achieve a more incorporative model of citizenry in Europe have been numerous, and have ranged from Balibar's notion of *civilité* (civility), "that would allow individuals and groups the means to identify and disidentify themselves, to travel in identity. To claim at the same time the right to difference and equality, solidarity and community,"[21] to Achille Mbembe's "cosmopolitanism," for which the prerequisite would be the "idea of a *common world, of a common humanity*, of a shared history and future" that would in turn negate the inclination of official discourse to seek "refuge behind the purely ahistoric mask of universalism in order to claim more assertively its move beyond 'race.'"[22] The most compelling have come from the Association pour la connaissance de l'histoire de l'Afrique contemporaine (ACHAC) under the leadership of Pascal Blanchard, who, along with the associates of the collective, remains committed to not only simultaneously documenting and recording the Asian, Maghrebi, and sub-Saharan immigrant experience through such works as *Le Paris noir, Le Paris arabe: Deux siècles de présence des Orientaux et des Maghrébins, 1830–2003,* and *Le Paris Asie: Du rêve d'Asie à Chinatown, 1854–2004,* but also to underscoring the transcoloniality of current issues in *La fracture coloniale: La société française au prisme de l'héritage colonial* so as to bridge the gap between the revisionist imperative and social activism.[23]

Black France builds on the pathbreaking work of many other scholars in disciplines too numerous to enumerate again at this juncture. What this points to is the growing interdisciplinary potential of recontextualizing history through a focus on the various mediations of global blackness and the multiple ways in which people circulate. I am reminded of a poster at the James S. Coleman African Studies Center at my home institution of UCLA: "When you study Africa, you study the world." Salman Rushdie has used the phrase "new empire within Britain" to describe the various ways in which racial fissures in Britain mirror imperial practices,[24] and Mbembe has evoked how decolonization has generated a kind of reversed colonization: "The colony was 'elsewhere,'" but at this time "the colony has moved and has planted its tent here" (Mbembe, "La République et l'impensé de la 'race,'" 140). Africa and France are forever imbricated, and I have endeavored through a historical framework anchored across colonial divides to emphasize how the African presence in France—while of course having altered demographic and cultural identities—should by no means be understood as a threat to "Frenchness" but should rather, alongside other immigrant experiences, emerge as constitutive of hexagonal and European identity. The responsibility and methodological imperative in which we all share will consist in monitoring Europe's ability to let go of reductive and misinformed monolithic and unilinear historical narratives. In a recent series of interviews with Françoise Vergès, Martinican poet, playwright, and politician Aimé Césaire further underscored the importance of the term "Black" in order to designate an incorporative and inclusive understanding of Africa's "transcontinental history."[25] If France is able to successfully navigate its way across this terrain, to acknowledge that traces of the past have forever impregnated the shared trajectories of the future, then Africa and France as mutually constitutive categories may permit "blackness" in France to be less of a "color" and more of an "experience."

Notes

1. INTRODUCTION

1. Jean Genet, *The Blacks* (New York: Grove Press, 1960).

2. Léopold Sédar Senghor, "Poème liminaire," in *Œuvre poétique* (Paris: Seuil, 1990), 7.

3. Frantz Fanon, *Black Skin, White Masks,* trans. Charles Lam Markmann (New York: Grove Press, 1967).

4. I find Obioma Nnaemeka's distinction between the French and English terms useful: "*La mondialisation,* derived from *le monde* with its double meaning of the physical world (materiality) and people (humanity), captures both the materiality and humanity of globalization. The humanity that is at best minimized and at worst ignored in the discourse and practice of globalization in general takes center stage in discourses and practices that I see evolving in Africa." Obioma Nnaemeka, "Nego-Feminism: Theorizing, Practicing, and Pruning Africa's Way," *Signs: Journal of Women in Culture and Society* 29, no. 2 (Winter 2004): 371.

5. Benjamin Barber, *Jihad versus McWorld: How Globalism and Tribalism Are Reshaping the World* (New York: Crown, 1995); Samuel Huntington, *The Clash of Civilizations* (New York: Simon and Schuster, 1996); Michael Hardt and Antonio Negri, *Empire* (Cambridge, Mass.: Harvard University Press, 2001), xii, and *Multitude* (New York: Penguin, 2004); and Jean-François Bayart, *Le gouvernement du monde* (Paris: Fayart, 2004). Bayart's faith in the nation-state is somewhat at odds with most conclusions and findings concerning practices of globalization, as exemplified by Alain Joxe, for example, who characterizes these trends in the following terms: "These organisms [states and governments] have now been stripped of almost all their former political power to shape local society through the transnationalization of capital and multinational conglomerates." Alain Joxe, *Empire of Disorder* (New York: Semiotext(e), 2002), 104–105. However, I do think that an unusual set of circumstances inform the African context, particularly if one takes into consideration regional and national particularities. Some of these might include (i) a broad range of colonial and decolonizing experiences; (ii) relatively recent, historically speaking, experiences of national sovereignty; (iii) vast discrepancies in natural resources (such as oil and diamonds); (iv) uneven border control and examples of population mobility; and (v) complex regional trade networks.

6. Lawrence Kritzman, "Identity Crises: France, Culture, and the Idea of the Nation," *SubStance* 76–77 (1995), 13; and Pierre Nora, ed., *Les lieux de mémoire,* 7 vols. (Paris: Gallimard, 1984–1992). Such debates have proved to be of great general interest and have received extensive newspaper coverage, and more recently informed the diplomatic tension between America and France.

7. Of course, these debates are not unique to the French context. See for example the Turkish novelist Orhan Pamuk's treatment of this question in *Snow* (New York: Alfred A. Knopf, 2004).

8. Dominic Thomas, *Nation-Building, Propaganda, and Literature in Francophone Africa* (Bloomington: Indiana University Press, 2002).

9. Saskia Sassen, *Globalization and Its Discontents: Essays on the New Mobility of People and Money* (New York: New Press, 1998), 96.

10. Jean-Marc Moura has been at the forefront of literary debates in France, arguing "the necessity of a transnational literary history, distinct from a literary history centered on the national canon," in "Des études postcoloniales dans l'espace littéraire francophone," in *Exotisme et lettres francophones* (Paris: Presses Universitaires de France, 2003), 200. See also his *Littératures francophones et théorie postcoloniale* (Paris: Presses Universitaires de France, 1999); Jacqueline Bardolph, *Etudes postcoloniales et littérature* (Paris: Champion, 2001); and Michel Beniamino, *La francophonie littéraire: Essai pour une théorie* (Paris: L'Harmattan, 1999).

11. Arjun Appadurai, "Grassroots Globalization and the Research Imagination," in *Globalization,* ed. Arjun Appadurai (Durham, N.C.: Duke University Press, 2001), 5.

12. Nancy L. Green, *Repenser les migrations* (Paris: Presses Universitaires de France, 2002), 1. See also Maxime Tandonnet, *Migrations: La nouvelle vague* (Paris: L'Harmattan, 2003).

13. Manthia Diawara, *In Search of Africa* (Cambridge, Mass.: Harvard University Press, 2000); F. Abiola Irele, *The African Imagination: Literature in Africa and the Black Diaspora* (Oxford: Oxford University Press, 2001); Mireille Rosello, *Postcolonial Hospitality: The Immigrant as Guest* (Stanford, Calif.: Stanford University Press, 2001); and Jean-Loup Amselle, *Branchements: Anthropologie de l'universalité des cultures* (Paris: Flammarion, 2001).

14. Henri Lopes, *Ma grand-mère bantoue et mes ancêtres les Gaulois* (Paris: Gallimard, 2003).

15. Yambo Ouologuem, *Lettre à la France nègre* (Paris: Le Serpent à Plumes, 2003); and Mongo Beti, *La France contre l'Afrique: Retour au Cameroun* (Paris: La Découverte, 1992).

16. Bernard Dadié, *An African in Paris,* trans. Karen C. Hatch (Urbana: University of Illinois Press, 1994), 3.

17. Pius Ngandu Nkashama, *Vie et mœurs d'un primitif en Essone quatre-vingt-onze* (Paris: L'Harmattan, 1987); Blaise N'Djehoya, *Nègre de Potemkine* (Paris: Lieu Commun, 1988); Simon Njami, *African gigolo* (Paris: Seghers, 1989); Léandre-Alain Baker, *Ici s'arrête le voyage* (Paris: L'Harmattan, 1989); V. Y. Mudimbe, *Entre les eaux* (Paris: Présence Africaine, 1973); Denis Oussou-Essui, *La souche calcinée* (Paris: L'Harmattan, 2004; first pub. 1973); Sally N'Dongo, *Exil, connais pas* (Paris: Editions du Cerf, 1976); Gaston-Paul Effa, *Tout ce bleu* (Paris: Grasset, 1996); Monique Ilboudo, *Le mal de peau* (Paris: Gallimard, 2001); Saïdou Boukoum, *Chaîne* (Paris: Denoël, 1974); Sayouba Traoré, *Loin de mon village, c'est la brousse* (La Roque d'Anthéron, France: Editions Vents d'Ailleurs, 2005); Bilguissa Diallo, *Diasporama* (Paris: Editions Anibwe, 2005); Lauren Ekué, *Icône urbaine* (Paris: Editions Anibwe, 2005); Léonora Miano, *L'intérieur de la nuit* (Paris: Plon, 2005); Aleth-Felix Tchicaya, *Lumière de femme* (Paris: Hatier, 2003); and Gaston-Paul Effa, *Voici le dernier jour du monde* (Monaco: Editions du Rocher, 2005).

18. Saskia Sassen, "Spatialities and Temporalities of the Global: Elements for a Theorization," *Public Culture* 12, no. 1 (Winter 2000): 221; and Romuald Fonkoua, "Diasporas littéraires: Quels statuts? Ecrire après les dictatures," *Notre librairie,* nos. 155–156 (July–December 2004): 22. See also Yves Chemla, "Dire l'ailleurs," *Notre librairie,* nos. 155–156 (July–December 2004): 48–53; and Papa Samba Diop, "Le pays d'origine comme espace de création littéraire," *Notre librairie,* nos. 155–156 (July–December 2004): 54–61.

19. Emmanuel Dongala, "From Negritude to Migritude: The African Writer in Exile," speech delivered at UCLA, October 14, 2005, as part of the conference "Experiencing Exile in Literature and the Arts."

20. Jacques Chevrier, "Afrique(s)-sur-Seine: Autour de la notion de 'migritude,'" *Notre librairie,* nos. 155–156 (July–December 2004): 96.

21. Albert Memmi, *Portrait du décolonisé arabo-musulman et de quelques autres* (Paris: Gallimard, 2004).

22. Adele King, *Rereading Camara Laye* (Lincoln: University of Nebraska Press, 2002), 5. See for example André Gide, *Voyage au Congo* (Paris: Gallimard, 1927), and *Retour du Tchad* (Paris: Gallimard, 1928); and also Michel Leiris, *L'Afrique fantôme* (Paris: Gallimard, 1934).

23. Eileen Julien, *African Novels and the Question of Orality* (Bloomington: Indiana University Press, 1992), 8.

24. Elisabeth Mudimbe-Boyi, "Travel Representation and Difference, or How Can One Be a Parisian?" *Research in African Literature* 23, no. 3 (Fall 1992): 34.

25. See for example Xavier Garnier, "L'exil lettré de Fatou Diome," *Notre librairie,* nos. 155–156 (July–December 2004): 30–35.

26. Achille Mbembe, *On the Postcolony* (Berkeley and Los Angeles: University of California Press, 2001), 242.

27. According to Stéphane Dufoix, the notion of an African Diaspora first appeared in print in F. Abiola Irele, "Négritude or Black Cultural Nationalism," *Journal of Modern African Studies* 3, no. 3 (October 1965): 321–348, and "Négritude—Literature and Ideology," *Journal of Modern African Studies* 3, no. 4 (December 1965): 499–526. See Stéphane Dufoix, *Les diasporas* (Paris: Presses Universitaires de France, 2003), 15.

28. See Brigitte Bertoncello and Sylvie Bredeloup, "Marseille, carrefour d'Afrique," *Hommes et migrations,* no. 1224 (March–April 2000).

29. Emmanuel Todd, *Le destin des immigrés: Assimilation et ségrégation dans les démocraties occidentales* (Paris: Seuil, 1994), 406–407. See also Allen F. Roberts and Mary Nooter-Roberts, eds., *Passport to Paradise: The Senegalese Mourides* (Los Angeles: UCLA, Fowler Museum of Cultural History, 2003); François Manchuelle, *Les diasporas des travailleurs soninké (1848–1960): Migrants volontaires* (Paris: Karthala, 2004); Mahamet Timera, *Les Soninkés en France: D'une histoire à l'autre* (Paris: Karthala, 1996); and B. Granotier, *Les travailleurs immigrés en France* (Paris: Maspéro, 1971).

30. For the Caribbean context of blackness and Diaspora, and the mediation between the Caribbean and France, see Philippe Dewitte, ed. "Diasporas caribéennes," special issue of *Hommes et migrations,* no. 1237 (May–June 2002).

31. There have even been shifts in methodological approaches that have yielded renewed critical options. See Ali Behdad, "Postcolonial Theory and the Predicament of 'Minor Literature,'" in *Minor Transnationalism,* ed. Françoise Lionnet and Shu-mei Shih (Durham, N.C.: Duke University Press, 2005), 223–236.

32. Hafid Gafaiti, "Nationalism, Colonialism, and Ethnic Discourse in the Construction of French Identity," in *French Civilization and Its Discontents: Nationalism, Colonialism, Race,* ed. Tyler Stovall and Georges Van Den Abbeele (Lanham, Md.: Lexington Books: 2003), 193; and Christopher L. Miller, *The French Atlantic Triangle: Literature and Culture of the Slave Trade.* (Durham, N.C.: Duke University Press, forthcoming).

33. William B. Cohen, *The French Encounter with Africans: White Response to Blacks, 1530–1880* (Bloomington: Indiana University Press, 1980); and Patrick

Manning, *Francophone Sub-Saharan Africa, 1880–1985* (Cambridge: Cambridge University Press, 1998).

34. See Alice L. Conklin, *A Mission to Civilize: The Republican Ideal of Empire in France and West Africa, 1895–1930* (Stanford, Calif.: Stanford University Press, 1997).

35. For French discourse on Africa, see Christopher L. Miller, *Blank Darkness: Africanist Discourse in French* (Chicago: University of Chicago Press, 1985); and Cohen, *The French Encounter with Africans*.

36. As a member of the UCLA-based Multicampus Group on Transcolonial and Transnational Studies, I have benefited enormously from conversations with other members engaged in contemporary theorizations of the humanities and social sciences.

37. Françoise Lionnet, "Transnationalism, Postcolonialism, or Transcolonialism? Reflections on Los Angeles, Geography, and the Uses of Theory," *Emergences: Journal for the Study of Media and Composite Cultures* 10, no. 1 (May 2000): 28–29. Stovall has also applied a transcolonial model to illustrate how "the interweaving of colonialism and postcolonialism, like that of race and class, constitutes an important characteristic of French identity in the twentieth century as a whole," in "From Red Belt to Black Belt: Race, Class, and Urban Marginality in Twentieth-Century Paris," in *The Color of Liberty: Histories of Race in France*, ed. Susan Peabody and Tyler Stovall (Durham, N.C.: Duke University Press, 2003), 363.

38. Françoise Lionnet and Shu-mei Shih, "Thinking through the Mirror, Transnationally," in Lionnet and Shih, *Minor Transnationalism*, 11, 8.

39. See Pierre-André Taguieff, "The Doctrine of the National Front in France (1972–1989): A 'Revolutionary' Programme?" *New Political Science*, nos. 16–17 (Fall–Winter 1989): 29–70, and "Le Front national: Du désert à l'enracinement," in *Face au racisme*, vol. 2, *Analyses, hypothèses, perspectives*, ed. Pierre-André Taguieff (Paris: La Découverte, 1991), 83–104; and also Sennen Andriamirado, "Le Pen, quel dangers pour les Africains?" *Jeune Afrique*, no. 1426 (May 4, 1998): 13–15.

40. See Michèle Tribalat, *De l'immigration à l'assimilation: Enquête sur les populations d'origine étrangère en France* (Paris: La Découverte, 1996).

41. Tyler Stovall, *Paris Noir: African Americans in the City of Light* (New York: Houghton Mifflin, 1996); Michel Fabre, *La rive noire: Les écrivains noirs américains à Paris, 1830–1995* (Marseille: André Dimanche, 1999), published in English as *From Harlem to Paris: Black American Writers in France, 1840–1980* (Urbana: University of Illinois Press, 1991); Bennetta Jules-Rosette, *Black Paris: The African Writers' Landscape* (Urbana: University of Illinois Press, 1998); and Pascal Blanchard, Eric Deroo, and Gilles Manceron, *Le Paris noir* (Paris: Editions Hazan, 2001). See also Boniface Mongo-Mboussa's declaration in a *Figaro littéraire* interview conducted by Bertrand Galimard Flavigny on January 6, 2005, that "Paris is Africa's cultural capital."

42. Pascale Casanova, *The World Republic of Letters*, trans. M. B. DeBevoise (Cambridge, Mass.: Harvard University Press, 2004).

43. On the legacy of Senghor, see for example F. Abiola Irele, ed., "Léopold Sédar Senghor," special issue of *Research in African Literatures* 33, no. 4 (Winter 2002); and André-Patient Bokiba, ed., *Le siècle Senghor* (Paris: L'Harmattan, 2001).

44. Edmund White, *The Flâneur: A Stroll through the Paradoxes of Paris* (London: Bloomsbury, 2001), 66.

45. Brent Hayes Edwards, *The Practice of Diaspora: Literature, Translation, and the Rise of Black Internationalism* (Cambridge, Mass.: Harvard University Press, 2003), 13–14. Edwards is citing Stuart Hall's use of concepts such as "articulation," in "Race, Articulation, and Societies Structured in Dominance" (1980), reprinted in *Black British Cultural Studies: A Reader*, ed. Houston A. Baker, Manthia Diawara, and Ruth H. Lindeborg (Chicago: University of Chicago Press, 1996), 16–60.

46. See Bennetta Jules-Rosette, "Conjugating Cultural Realities: *Présence Africaine*," in *The Surreptitious Speech: Présence Africaine and the Politics of Otherness, 1947–1987*, ed. V. Y. Mudimbe (Chicago: University of Chicago Press, 1992), 14–44.

47. See also William A. Shack, *Harlem in Montmartre: A Paris Jazz Story between the Great Wars* (Berkeley and Los Angeles: University of California Press, 2001).

48. See Phyllis Rose, *Jazz Cleopatra: Josephine Baker in Her Time* (New York: Vintage Press, 1989); Tyler Stovall, "Bringing the Jazz Age to Paris," in *Paris Noir*, 25–81; and David Murphy, "La danse et la parole: L'exil et l'identité chez les Noirs de Marseille dans *Banjo* de Claude McKay et *Le docker noir* d'Ousmane Sembene," *Canadian Review of Comparative Literature* 27, no. 3 (September 2000): 462–479.

49. Paul Gilroy, *The Black Atlantic: Modernity and Double Consciousness* (Cambridge, Mass.: Harvard University Press, 1993), 3, and *There Ain't No Black in the Union Jack: The Cultural Politics of Race and Nation* (Chicago: University of Chicago Press, 1987).

50. Lisa Lowe, *Immigrant Acts: On Asian American Cultural Politics* (Durham, N.C.: Duke University Press, 1996), 67.

51. Blanchard, Deroo, and Manceron, *Le Paris noir*, 8; and Cohen, *The French Encounter with Africans*, 132.

52. Valérie Zerguine, "Fier d'être noir," *De l'air: Reportages d'un monde à l'autre* 11 (June–July 2002): 8.

53. Didier Gondola, "'But I Ain't African, I'm American!': Black American Exiles and the Construction of Racial Identities in Twentieth-Century France," in *Blackening Europe: The African American Presence*, ed. Heike Raphael-Hernandez (New York: Routledge, 2004), 212.

54. Homi K. Bhabha, *The Location of Culture* (London: Routledge, 1994), 38.

55. See Salman Rushdie, *East, West* (London: Jonathan Cape, 1994), 141.

56. Mireille Rosello, "The 'Beur Nation': Toward a Theory of 'Departenance,'" trans. Richard Bjornson, *Research in African Literatures* 24, no. 3 (Fall 1993): 13.

57. May Joseph, "New Hybrid Identities and Performance," in *Performing Hybridity*, ed. May Joseph and Jennifer Natalya Fink (Minneapolis: University of Minnesota Press, 1999), 2.

58. Bonnie Honig, *Democracy and the Foreigner* (Princeton, N.J.: Princeton University Press, 2001), 8.

59. James Clifford, *Routes: Travel and Translation in the Late Twentieth Century* (Cambridge, Mass.: Harvard University Press, 1997), 255, 251–252.

60. Jean-Loup Amselle and Elikia M'Bokolo, eds., *Au cœur de l'ethnie: Ethnies, tribalisme et état en Afrique* (Paris: La Découverte, 1985); and Jean-Loup Amselle, *Logiques métisses: Anthropologie de l'identité en Afrique et ailleurs* (Paris: Payot, 1990). Lionnet's work has made the most significant contributions to

demonstrating how métissage can be used as a critical framework for the comparative investigation of a wide range of sociocultural mechanisms. See for example *Postcolonial Representations: Women, Literature, Identity* (Ithaca, N.Y.: Cornell University Press, 1995).

61. See William Safran, "Diasporas in Modern Societies: Myths of Homeland and Return," *Diaspora* 1 (1991): 83–99.

62. See Paul Gilroy, *Postcolonial Melancholia* (New York: Columbia University Press, 2005).

63. Bill Ashcroft, *Post-colonial Transformation* (London: Routledge, 2001), 214.

64. On these theoretical paradigms, see Edouard Glissant, *Le discours antillais* (Paris: Seuil, 1981); and Jean Bernabé, Patrick Chamoiseau, and Raphaël Confiant, *Eloge de la créolité* (Paris: Gallimard, 1989), respectively.

65. Nurrudin Farah, *Yesterday, Tomorrow: Voices from the Somali Diaspora* (New York: Cassell, 2000).

66. René Maran was of course the first black man to win the prestigious Prix Goncourt in 1921 for his novel *Batouala, véritable roman nègre*.

67. Françoise Lionnet, "*Logiques métisses:* Cultural Appropriation and Postcolonial Representations," in *Postcolonial Subjects: Francophone Women Writers,* ed. Mary Jean Green, Karen Gould, Micheline Rice-Maximin, Keith L. Walker and Jack A. Yaeger (Minneapolis: University of Minnesota, 1996), 339.

68. Calixthe Beyala, *Les honneurs perdus* (Paris: Albin Michel, 1996).

69. See Graham Huggan, *The Post-colonial Exotic: Marketing the Margins* (London: Routledge, 2001).

70. See for example Graziella Parati's work on immigrant literatures in Italy, in particular her edited volume *Mediterranean Crossroads: Migration Literature in Italy* (Madison, N.J.: Farleigh Dickinson University Press, 1999) and her *Migration Italy: The Art of Talking Back in a Destination Culture* (Toronto: University of Toronto Press, 2005). In Théo Ananissoh's novel *Lisahohé* (Paris: Gallimard, 2005), the central character moves between Germany and the Central African Republic.

71. Salman Rushdie, "The New Empire within Britain," in *Imaginary Homelands: Essays and Criticism, 1981–1991* (London: Granta, 1991), 132. See also Tirthandar Chanda, "Les écrivains noirs d'Angleterre: Naissance d'une tradition," *Notre librairie,* nos. 155–156 (July–December 2004): 88–95.

72. See for example Ian Baucom, *Out of Place: Englishness, Empire, and the Locations of Identity* (Princeton, N.J.: Princeton University Press, 1999). Jean-Yves Loude treats similar questions in Portugal in *Lisbonne dans la ville noire* (Paris: Actes Sud, 2003).

73. Mark Stein, *Black British Literature: Novels of Transformation* (Columbus: Ohio State University Press, 2004), xv, 8. Among works by writers either born in Nigeria, of Nigerian descent, or of partial Nigerian heritage currently living in Britain whose works are concerned with issues analogous to those treated by their francophone counterparts, Stein includes Diran Adebayo, *Some Kind of Black* (London: Virago, 1996), and *My Once Upon a Time* (London: Abacus, 2000); Biyi Bandele, *The Street* (London, Picador, 1999); and Bernardine Evaristo, *Lara* (Kent: Angela Royal, 1997), and *The Emperor's Babe* (London: Penguin, 2001); in addition of course to the more established and better known authors, such as Buchi Emecheta and Ben Okri. See also Courttia Newland and Kadija Sesay, eds., *IC3: The Penguin Book of New Black Writing in Britain* (London: Hamish Ham-

ilton, 2000); and James Procter, ed., *Writing Black Britain: An Interdisciplinary Anthology* (Manchester: Manchester University Press, 2000).

74. See Jean-Pierre Dozon, *Frères et sujets: La France et l'Afrique en perspective* (Paris: Flammarion, 2003).

75. Susan Peabody and Tyler Stovall, "Race, France, Histories," in Peabody and Stovall, *The Color of Liberty*, 4–5. See also Pierre-André Taguieff, *La couleur et le sang: Doctrines racistes à la française* (Paris: Fayard, 2002).

76. Achille Mbembe, "At the Edge of the World: Boundaries, Territoriality, and Sovereignty in Africa," trans. Steven Rendall, in Appadurai, *Globalization*, 24.

77. See Jules-Rosette, *Black Paris*. Michel Laronde has argued that these labels are often more indebted to attempts by cultural critics to categorize authors than they are to sociocultural realities. Rather than underlining how a writer like Calixthe Beyala can be classified as both an African and an Afro-French writer, I prefer to foreground the bilateralism and transversality of her work as it relates—in each and every text—to Africa (as continent) and France (as hexagonal space) in a transcolonial framework. See Michel Laronde, "Les littératures des immigrations en France: Question de nomenclature et directions de recherche," *Le Maghreb littéraire* 1, no. 2 (1997): 25–44.

78. The primary focus is provided by Yodi Karone, *Nègre de paille* (Paris: Karthala, 1982), and *A la recherche du cannibale amour* (Paris: Nathan, 1988); and Njami, *African gigolo*.

79. More recently, Odile Cazenave has contributed to the further elaboration of this problematic concept. See Odile Cazenave, *Afrique sur Seine: Une nouvelle génération de romanciers africains à Paris* (Paris: L'Harmattan, 2003).

80. Boniface Mongo-Mboussa, "Grammaire de l'immigration," in *L'indocilité: Supplément au Désir d'Afrique* (Paris: Gallimard, 2005), 103.

81. Alec G. Hargreaves, *Voices from the North African Immigrant Community in France: Immigration and Identity in Beur Fiction* (London: Berg, 1991), 1.

82. For Laronde, "the term *beur* must be understood in its ethnic dimension (novels written by the Beurs) and also expanded toward a dialectic meaning (works that address the circumstances of young maghrebis in contemporary French society)." Michel Laronde, *Autour du roman beur: Immigration et identité* (Paris: L'Harmattan, 1993), 6.

83. Odile Cazenave, *Afrique sur Seine: A New Generation of African Writers in Paris* (Lanham, Md.: Lexington Books, 2005), first published as *Une nouvelle génération de romanciers africains à Paris* (Paris: L'Harmattan, 2003).

84. The journal *Notre librairie* devoted an issue to this question. See "Nouvelle génération," *Notre librairie*, no. 146 (October–December 2001).

85. Bernard Magnier, "Beurs noirs à Black Babel," *Notre librairie*, no. 103 (October–December 1990): 102, 106, 103.

86. Abdourahman A. Waberi, "Les enfants de la postcolonie: Esquisse d'une nouvelle génération d'écrivains francophones d'Afrique noire," *Notre librairie*, no. 135 (September–December 1998): 11, 8.

87. Lydie Moudileno, "Littérature et postcolonie," *Africultures*, no. 26 (March 2000): 11.

88. Thomas, *Nation-Building*, 7. The main focus is provided by a consideration of Guy Ossito Midiohouan's revised historiography and challenge to Lilyan Kesteloot's insistence on "engagement" as a category in *L'idéologie dans la littérature négro-africaine d'expression française* (Paris: L'Harmattan, 1986), and also questions Jacques Chevrier's criteria for classifying African writers in *Anthologie*

africaine d'expression française, vol. 1, *Le roman et la nouvelle* (Paris: Hatier, 1981).

89. Furthermore, I should add, the importance accorded to the aesthetic component of the literary project is certainly not a new feature of African literature. See for example Bernard Geniès' article on Sony Labou Tansi, "Africain d'accord, écrivain d'abord," *Le nouvel observateur,* August 19–25, 1988, 58–61.

90. As Boniface Mongo-Mboussa has argued, "This passage from memory to history is not unique to writers addressing the colonial problematic, it can also be found in the 'novel of emigration.'" "Les méandres de la mémoire dans la littérature africaine," *Hommes et migrations,* no. 1228 (November–December 2000): 76.

91. The 1997 edition of his book *Voices from the North African Immigrant Community in France,* for example, includes a new chapter devoted to developments during the 1990s, and he has continued to redefine the parameters of that identity, theorizing both its usefulness and its limitations. Laronde's own book on the Beurs underlined this problem and this was implicit in its title, *Autour du roman beur (Around the Beur Novel).*

92. Mamadou Diouf, "Africain, citoyen du monde du XXIe siècle," in *Etudiants africains en France, 1951–2001,* ed. Michel Sot (Paris: Karthala, 2002), 173.

93. Etienne Balibar, "De la préférence nationale à l'invention de la politique," in *Droit de cité* (Paris: Presses Universitaires de France, 2002), 98–99; and Fatou Diome, *La préférence nationale* (Paris: Présence Africaine, 2001).

94. "In fact," as Gérard Noiriel has argued, "history shows that by altering the criteria employed to define immigration from the juridical domain to the 'cultural' or 'ethnic' domain, one arrives upon a fundamental problem that has profoundly affected French political life since the nineteenth century." *Le creuset français: Histoire de l'immigration, XIXe–XXe siècles* (Paris: Seuil, 1988), 9–10. See also Diane Béranger, "Les chiffres de l'immigration en France," *Regards sur l'actualité,* no. 299 (March 2004): 6–9; Michèle Tribalat, ed., *Cent ans d'immigration: Etrangers d'hier, Français d'aujourd'hui* (Paris: Presses Universitaires de France, 1991), and *De l'immigration à l'assimilation;* and Patrick Weil, *La France et ses étrangers: L'aventure d'une politique de l'immigration, 1938–1991* (Paris: Calmann-Lévy, 1991).

95. Michel Wieviorka, "Culture, société et démocratie," in *Une société fragmentée? Le multiculturalisme en débat,* ed. Michel Wieviorka (Paris: La Découverte and Syros, 1996), 15–16, *L'espace du racisme* (Paris: Seuil, 1991), and *Le racisme, une introduction* (Paris: La Découverte et Syros, 1998).

96. Rey Chow, *The Protestant Ethnic and the Spirit of Capitalism* (New York: Columbia University Press, 2002), 127. See also Maxim Silverman's distinction between *indigènes* and nationals in *Deconstructing the Nation: Immigration, Racism, and Citizenship in Modern France* (London: Routledge, 1992), 30.

97. Haut conseil à l'intégration, "La connaissance de l'immigration et de l'intégration" (Paris: La Documentation Française, 1992), 14.

98. André Lebon, *Immigration et présence étrangère en France en 1999: Premiers enseignements du recencement* (Paris: La Documentation Française, 2001), 9.

99. In *L'immigration* (Paris: La Découverte, 1990), 94, Ezzedine Mestiri cited a poll conducted in France in 1990, in which 30 percent of respondents said there were "too many" Blacks in France, and 16 percent said there were "far too many." The corresponding numbers for Arabs were 35 percent ("too many") and 41 per-

cent ("far too many"), and for Muslims, 34 percent ("too many") and 37 percent ("far too many").

100. Todd's figures are slightly higher. Of significance are the figures he provides for Tunisians, who he says numbered 206,336 by 1990. *Le destin des immigrés,* 338.

101. Alec G. Hargreaves, *Immigration, "Race," and Ethnicity in Contemporary France* (London: Routledge, 1995), 8. See also the Haut conseil à l'intégration's report to the prime minister, "La connaissance de l'immigration" (Paris: La Documentation Française, 1992), 20.

102. Philippe Dewitte, *Les mouvements nègres en France, 1919–1939* (Paris: L'Harmattan, 1985), 25.

103. Michelle Guillon, "La mosaïque des migrations africaines," Vues d'Afrique, *Esprit,* no. 317 (August–September 2005): 174.

104. The number of Asians from former French colonies (Vietnam, Laos, and Cambodia) rose from 11,368 in 1968 to 112,915 in 1990. Todd, *Le destin des immigrés,* 406.

105. Hargreaves, *Immigration, "Race," and Ethnicity,* 1–2. *Jus sanguinis* was privileged initially over *jus solis.* "The 1993 reform," Hargreaves explains, "which ended the automatic acquisition of French nationality by the children of immigrants at the age of majority, was the first under a republican regime to move in an exclusionary direction" (161). See in particular Alec G. Hargreaves, "National Identity, Nationality, and Citizenship," in *Immigration, "Race," and Ethnicity,* 149–176; and Patrick Weil, *Qu'est-ce qu'un Français? Histoire de la nationalité française depuis la Révolution* (Paris: Grasset, 2002).

106. Lorenzo Prencipe, "Médias et immigration: Un rapport difficile," *Migrations société* 14, nos. 81–82 (May–August 2002): 140.

107. Etienne Balibar, "Racism and Crisis," in *Race, Nation, Class: Ambiguous Identities,* ed. Etienne Balibar and Immanuel Wallerstein (London: Verso, 1991), 220.

108. See Alyssa Goldstein Sepinwall, "Eliminating Race, Eliminating Difference: Blacks, Jews, and the Abbé Grégoire," in Peabody and Stovall, *The Color of Liberty,* 28–41; Roger Little, "Seeds of Postcolonialism: Black Slavery and Cultural Difference to 1800," in *Francophone Postcolonial Studies: A Critical Introduction,* ed. Charles Forsdick and David Murphy (London: Arnold, 2003), 17–26; and Annette Smith, *Gobineau et l'histoire naturelle* (Geneva: Droz, 1984).

109. Pascal Blanchard, Nicolas Bancel, and Sandrine Lemaire, eds., *La fracture coloniale: La société française au prisme de l'héritage colonial* (Paris: La Découverte, 2005).

110. Pascal Blanchard and Nicolas Bancel, "Les origines républicaines de la fracture coloniale," in Blanchard, Bancel, and Lemaire, *La fracture coloniale,* 38, 37.

111. See Pierre-André Taguieff, *La République enlisée: Pluralisme, communautarisme et citoyenneté* (Paris: Editions des Syrtes, 2005). To designate what he sees as a limitless pluralism that ends up being self-defeating since it eliminates or voids tolerance of difference, Taguieff uses the terms "hyperpluralism" (23) and "multicommunitarianism" (24). See also Michel Wieviorka, "Un débat nécéssaire," in Wieviorka, *Une société fragmentée?* 5.

112. Etienne Balibar, "Racism and Nationalism," in Balibar and Wallerstein, *Race, Nation, Class,* 43.

113. Etienne Balibar, "Is There a 'Neo-Racism'?" in Balibar and Wallerstein, *Race, Nation, Class,* 21.

114. For further discussion of these questions, see Mireille Rosello, "Tactical Universalism and New Multiculturalist Claims in Postcolonial France," in Forsdick and Murphy, *Francophone Postcolonial Studies*, 135–143.

115. David Blatt, "Immigrant Politics in a Republican Nation," in *Post-colonial Cultures in France*, ed. Alec G. Hargreaves and Mark McKinney (London: Routledge, 1997), 40–41.

116. Most notably, one might mention the 1980–1981 Rock against the Police; the 1983 Marche pour l'égalité et contre le racisme (March for Equality and against Racism), also known as La marche des Beurs (The March of the Beurs); Convergence 84; and the launching of SOS Racisme's yellow-hand symbol expressing solidarity: "Touche pas à mon pote" ("Hands off my buddy"). See Harlem Désir, "Pour l'intégration: Conditions et instruments," in Taguieff, *Face au racisme* (Paris: La Découverte, 1991), 1:106–119. Africans make contributions in all realms of French society, including ethnic solidarity, music (including world music, rap, and hip-hop, by such artists as NTM, IAM, MC Solaar, Khaled, Cheb Mami, Zebda, Salif Keita, Alpha Blondy, Papa Wemba, and Angélique Kidjo, among others), tagging, and of course sport, while simultaneously intersecting with urban housing policies. See "La prison pour NTM: L'insulte faite aux jeunes," *L'événement du Jeudi*, no. 629 (November 21–27, 1996); "Les chanteurs de NTM condamnés à la prison ferme pour outrage à la police," *Le monde*, November 16, 1996; Chris Warne, "The Impact of World Music in France," in Hargreaves and McKinney, *Post-colonial Cultures in France*, 133–149; Steve Cannon, "Paname City Rapping: B-Boys in the Banlieues and Beyond," in Hargreaves and McKinney, *Post-colonial Cultures in France*, 150–166; and Christian Mousset, "La musique africaine et la France," in Sot, *Etudiants africains en France*, 163–167. On housing policy, from the *bidonvilles* (shantytowns), *cité de transit* (temporary housing), and *habitation à loyer modéré* (rent-controlled housing, H.L.M.) to the housing projects of La Courneuve, Nanterre, and Sartrouville (to the north and west of Paris), Vaulx-en-Velin and Vénissieux (in Lyon), and *les quartiers du nord* (in Marseilles), and Clignancourt, la Goutte-d'Or, and Château-Rouge in Paris itself, see for example Alec G. Hargreaves, "Socio-economic Structures," in *Immigration, "Race," and Ethnicity*, 38–84. See also Loïc Wacquant, "Banlieues françaises et ghetto noir américain: De l'amalgame à la comparaison," *French Politics and Society* 10, no. 4 (Autumn 1992): 81–103.

117. Christopher L. Miller, *Nationalists and Nomads: Essays on Francophone African Literature and Culture* (Chicago: Chicago University Press, 1998), 54.

118. Pascal Blanchard and Eric Deroo, "Contrôler: Paris, capitale coloniale," in *Culture impériale: Les colonies au cœur de la République, 1931–1961*, ed. Pascal Blanchard and Sandrine Lemaire (Paris: Editions Autrement, 2004), 120.

119. See for example Pascal Blanchard and Eric Deroo, *Le Paris Asie: Du rêve d'Asie à Chinatown, 1854–2004* (Paris: La Découverte, 2004); and Pascal Blanchard, Eric Deroo, Driis El-Yazami, Pierre Fournié, and Gilles Manceron, *Le Paris arabe: Deux siècles de présence des Orientaux et des Maghrébins, 1830–2003* (Paris: La Découverte, 2003).

120. On these newspapers, see Miller, *Nationalists and Nomads*, 28–48. See also Jean-Claude Michel, *The Black Surrealists* (New York: Peter Lang, 2000), on *Légitime Défense*. According to Midiohouan, "the distribution of all these newspapers was regularly interrupted by government decrees." Midiohouan, *L'idéologie*, 36.

121. See Dewitte, *Les mouvements nègres en France*, 126–170.

122. Philippe Dewitte, *Deux siècles d'immigration en France* (Paris: La Documentation Française, 2003), 29. See also John Horne, "Immigrant Workers in France during World War I," *French Historical Studies* 14 (1985): 57–88; Tyler Stovall, "Colour-blind France? Colonial Workers during the First World War," *Race and Class* 35, no. 2 (October–December 1993): 35–55; and Marc Michel, *Les Africains et la Grande Guerre: L'appel à l'Afrique, 1914–1918* (Paris: Karthala, 2003).

123. Midiohouan has talked of 211,000 *tirailleurs* in Africa in 1918. *L'idéologie*, 68.

124. See Bernard Mouralis, *République et colonies: Entre histoire et mémoire; La République française et l'Afrique* (Paris: Présence Africaine, 1999), 33. On the *tirailleurs sénégalais*, see Myron Echenberg, *Colonial Conscripts: The* Tirailleurs Sénégalais *in French West Africa, 1857–1960* (Portsmouth, N.H.: Heinemann, 1991); Ousmane Sembene's 1987 film *Camp de Thiaroye;* János Riesz, "The *Tirailleur sénégalais* Who Did Not Want to Be a 'Grand Enfant': Bakary Diallo's *Force-Bonté* (1926) Reconsidered," *Research in African Literatures* 27, no. 4 (Winter 1996): 157–179; János Riesz, "La folie des tirailleurs sénégalais: Fait historique et thème littéraire de la littérature coloniale à la littérature africaine de langue française," in *Black Accents: Writing in French from Africa, Mauritius, and the Caribbean,* ed. J. P. Little and Roger Little (London: Grant and Cutler, 1997), 139–156; Charles Onama, *La France et ses tirailleurs: Enquête sur les combattants de la République* (Paris: Duboiris, 2003); Mar Fall, *Des Africains noirs en France: Des tirailleurs sénégalais aux Blacks* (Paris: L'Harmattan, 1986); and János Riesz and Joachim Schultz, eds., *Tirailleurs sénégalais* (Frankfurt-am-Main: Peter Lang Verlag, 1989).

125. The votes were 471,000 for Yes and 1,120,000 for No. See Marc Ferro, *Histoire des colonisations des conquêtes aux indépendances, XIIIème–XXème siècle* (Paris: Seuil, 1994), 478.

126. David E. Gardinier, "Historical Origins of Francophone Africa," in *Political Reform in Francophone Africa,* ed. John F. Clark and David E. Gardinier (Boulder, Colo.: Westview Press, 1997), 13. See also Catherine Coquery-Vidrovitch, "Colonisation, coopération, partenariat: Les différentes étapes (1950–2000)," in Sot, *Etudiants africains en France,* 29–48.

127. Fabienne Guimont, *Les étudiants africains en France, 1950–1965* (Paris: L'Harmattan, 1997), 13.

128. Abdoulaye Gueye, *Les intellectuels africains en France* (Paris: L'Harmattan, 2001), 49.

129. See also Hélène d'Almeida-Topor, "Le nombre d'étudiants africains en France (1951–2000)," in Sot, *Etudiants africains en France,* 109–115. A number of factors account for the drop in African students in France: development of African universities, reduction in bursaries for international education, and stricter guidelines for issuing student visas. D'Almeida-Topor, "Le nombre d'étudiants," 110–111.

130. Mamadou Diouf, "Postface," in Gueye, *Les intellectuels africains en France,* 246.

131. See Sekou Traoré, *La Fédération des étudiants d'Afrique noire en France* (Paris: L'Harmattan, 1985); and Guimont, *Les étudiants africains,* 107–124.

132. J.-P. N'Diaye, *Enquête sur les étudiants noirs en France* (Paris: Editions Réalités Africaines, 1962), 83, 84, 285. See also Achille Mbembe, *Les jeunes et l'ordre politique en Afrique noire* (Paris: L'Harmattan, 1985).

133. As Gueye points out, this is partly corroborated by Manthia Diawara's experience as recounted in his book *In Search of Africa*. See also Gueye's new research findings, in "Les chercheurs africains en demande d'Occident," Vues d'Afrique, *Esprit*, no. 317 (August–September 2005): 219–227.

134. See Irele, "Négritude or Black Cultural Nationalism."

135. Jacques Chevrier, "La littérature francophone et ses héros," Vues d'Afrique, *Esprit*, no. 317 (August–September 2005): 83.

136. Saskia Sassen, *Guests and Aliens* (New York: New Press, 1999), 63. See also Gilles Manceron, "La République et son passé coloniale," in *Marianne et les colonies: Une introduction à l'histoire coloniale de la France* (Paris: La Découverte, 2003), 7–23.

137. Nicolas Bancel, Pascal Blanchard, and Françoise Vergès, *La République coloniale: Essai sur une utopie* (Paris: Albin Michel, 2003), 41.

138. Jean-Loup Amselle, *Affirmative Exclusion: Cultural Pluralism and the Rule of Custom in France,* trans. Jean Marie Todd (Ithaca, N.Y.: Cornell University Press, 2003), first published as *Vers un multiculturalisme français: L'empire de la coutume* (Paris: Flammarion, 2001); and F. Gaspard and F. Khosrokhavar, *Le foulard et la République* (Paris: La Découverte, 1995).

139. Adrian Favell, *Philosophies of Integration: Immigration and the Idea of Citizenship in France and Britain* (Basingstoke: Palgrave, 1998), 2. See in particular "France: The Republican Philosophy of *Intégration;* Ideas and Politics in the 1980s," 40–93.

140. Alec G. Hargreaves, "Multiculturalism," in *Political Ideologies in Contemporary France,* ed. Christopher Flood and Laurence Bell (London: Cassell, 1997), 198.

141. These practices received considerable public attention, and racism itself was explicitly the subject of two books by the Moroccan author Tahar Ben Jelloun, winner of the Goncourt Prize, namely *L'hospitalité française* (Paris: Seuil, 1984) and *Le racisme expliqué à ma fille* (Paris: Seuil, 1990), published in English as *Racism Explained to My Daughter,* trans. Carol Volk (New York: New Press, 1999).

142. Jean-Paul Sartre, "Présence noire," *Présence africaine,* no. 1 (November–December 1947): 28.

143. These questions were of course central to Tvetan Todorov's discourse on the Other in *The Conquest of America: The Question of the Other,* trans. Richard Howard (New York: Harper and Row, 1984), and to his *Nous et les autres* (Paris: Seuil, 1989). See also Arnauld Le Brusq, "De 'notre' mémoire à 'leur' histoire: Les métamorphoses du Palais des colonies," in Blanchard, Bancel, and Lemaire, *La fracture coloniale,* 255–262. In this essay, Le Brusq explores the architectural layerings upon which the CNHI will rest: the former Palais des colonies, the Musée permanent des colonies, the Musée de la France d'Outre Mer, and finally the Musée des arts africains et océaniens.

144. See for example Pascal Blanchard and Sandrine Lemaire, "Les colonies au cœur de la République," in Blanchard and Lemaire, *Culture impériale,* 5–32.

145. Jacques Toubon, *Mission de préfiguration du Centre de ressources et de mémoire de l'immigration* (Paris: La Documentation Française, 2004).

146. Ali Behdad, *A Forgetful Nation: On Immigration and Cultural Identity in the United States* (Durham, N.C.: Duke University Press, 2005), 3–4.

147. Marc Augé, *Oblivion,* trans. Marjolijn de Jager (Minneapolis: University of Minnesota Press, 2004), 3. See also Sarah Frohning Deleporte, "Trois musées,

une question, une République," in Blanchard, Bancel, and Lemaire, *La fracture coloniale,* 105–111. Noiriel has highlighted the central dilemma that confronts the project, whose objective is to "strengthen national cohesion" by emphasizing "the national 'we' ("le 'nous' national") and "honoring the French who have come from elsewhere" ("venus d'ailleurs"), in "Histoire, mémoire, engagement civique," *Hommes et migrations,* no. 1247 (January–February 2004): 22. See also Gilles Manceron, "De la débauche de propagande au 'trou de mémoire' colonial," in *Marianne et les colonies,* 267–282.

148. Benjamin Stora anticipated this response in many ways in his book *La gangrène et l'oubli* (Paris: La Découverte, 1991).

149. See Françoise Lionnet, "The Mirror and the Tomb: Africa, Museums, and Representation," *African Arts* 34, no. 3 (Fall 2001): 50–59.

150. Michel Wieviorka, *La différence: Identités culturelles; Enjeux, débats et politiques* (Paris: Editions de l'Aube, 2005), 180; and Patrick Weil, *La République et sa diversité: Immigration, intégration, discriminations* (Paris: Seuil, 2005), 108. As Wieviorka signals, these distinctions have of course been central to the work of Paul Ricœur, *La mémoire, l'histoire, l'oubli* (Paris: Seuil, 2000); Tvetan Todorov, *Les abus de la mémoire* (Paris: Arléa, 1995); and Pierre Nora, ed., *Les lieux de mémoire* (Paris: Gallimard, 1984).

151. Pascal Blanchard, Nicolas Bancel, and Sandrine Lemaire, "La fracture coloniale: une crise française," in Blanchard, Bancel, and Lemaire, *La fracture coloniale,* 30.

152. See Bruno Etienne, *La France et l'Islam* (Paris: Hachette, 1989); and Gilles Kepel, *Les banlieues de l'Islam* (Paris: Seuil, 1987).

153. The bilateral process of corruption is widely known as "la françafrique." See François-Xavier Verschave and Philippe Hauser, *Au mépris des peuples: Le néocolonialisme franco-africain* (Paris: La Fabrique Editions, 2004); François-Xavier Verschave, *La françafrique: Le plus long scandale de la République* (Paris: Stock, 1998); and Jean-Paul Gourévitch, *L'Afrique, le fric, la France: L'aide, la dette, l'immigration, l'avenir; Vérités et mesonges* (Paris: Le Pré aux Clercs, 1997). Jean-François Bayart emphasizes "internal" responsibility as well. See his "The 'Social Capital' of the Felonious State," in *The Criminalization of the State in Africa,* ed. Jean-François Bayart, Stephen Ellis, and Béatrice Hibou (Oxford: James Currey; Bloomington: Indiana University Press, 1999), 32–48. Usage of the term "social capital" in this context differs of course from my invocation of the acquisition of cultural and social capital through travel to France, and in this instance denotes "the ensemble of configurations and the texture of relationships which are the outcome of sub-Saharan Africa's long historical trajectory, or rather of the cluster of historical trajectories, distinct but acting upon one another over long periods, of an entire sub-continent." Bayart, "The 'Social Capital,'" 32.

154. Pascal Blanchard and Nicolas Bancel, *De l'indigène à l'immigré* (Paris: Gallimard, 1998), 90–91. Cilas Kemedjio has also drawn on the analysis formulated by Blanchard and Bancel in order to demonstrate how "forgetting or reconstructing colonial history has consequences for the perception of the peoples of the postcolonial era, or the peoples coming from former colonies . . . The spread of an imagination that is essentially negative and misery-laden over Africa opens the road to a celebration of the colonial epic that should never have been interrupted by the instigators of independence." Cilas Kemedjio, "The Western Anticolonialist of the Postcolonial Age: The Reformist Syndrome and the Memory of Decolonization in (Post-)Imperial French Thought," in *Remembering Africa,* ed. Elisabeth

Mudimbe (Portsmouth, N.H.: Heinemann, 2002), 48. See also Susan Sontag, *Regarding the Pain of Others* (New York: Penguin, 2003); and Jean-Pierre Chrétien, "L'Afrique face aux défis du monde," *Esprit,* no. 317 (August–September 2005): 8–16.

155. Seyla Benhabib, *The Claims of Culture: Equality and Diversity in the Global Era* (Princeton, N.J.: Princeton University Press, 2002), 8.

156. Ousmane Socé, *Mirages de Paris* (Paris: Nouvelles Editions Latines, 1937); Laye Camara, *L'enfant noir* (Paris: Plon, 1954); Bernard Dadié, *Un nègre à Paris* (Paris: Présence Africaine, 1959); Ferdinand Oyono, *Chemin d'Europe* (Paris: Julliard, 1960); and Cheikh Hamidou Kane, *L'aventure ambiguë* (Paris: Julliard, 1961). See also Bernard Dadié, *Patron de New York* (Paris: Présence Africaine, 1969), *One Way: Bernard Dadié Observes America,* trans. Jo Patterson (Urbana: University of Illinois Press, 1994), and *La ville où nul ne meurt* (Paris: Présence Africaine, 1968), published in English as *The City Where No One Dies,* trans. Janis A. Mayes (Washington, D.C.: Three Continents Press, 1986).

157. Ousmane Sembene, *Le docker noir* (Paris: Présence Africaine, 1973; first pub. 1956); Richard Wright, *Native Son* (New York: Harper Collins, 1993; first pub. 1940).

158. Ousmane Sembene, "La Noire de . . ." in *Voltaïque* (Paris: Présence Africaine, 1962), 149–174; and Henriette Akofa, with Olivier de Broca, *Une esclave moderne* (Paris: Michel Lafon, 2000).

159. Fatou Keïta, *Rebelle* (Paris: Présence Africaine, 1998); and Calixthe Beyala, *Lettre d'une Africaine à ses sœurs occidentales* (Paris: Spengler, 1995), and *Lettre d'une Afro-française à ses compatriotes* (Paris: Editions Mango, 2000).

160. The question of polygamy is also related to these questions. See C. Poiret, "Le phénomène polygamique en France," *Migrants-formation,* no. 91 (December 1992): 24–42; Gérard Petitjean, "Polygamie: Les femmes d'à côté," *Le nouvel observateur,* no. 1389 (June 2–26, 1991): 52–53; and Rabia Abdelkrim-Chikh, "Les femmes exogames: Entre la loi de Dieu et les droits de l'homme," in *L'Islam en France: Islam, état et société,* ed. Bruno Etienne (Paris: CNRS, 1991) , 235–254.

161. Alain Mabanckou, *Bleu-Blanc-Rouge* (Paris: Présence Africaine, 1998); and Daniel Biyaoula, *L'impasse* (Paris: Présence Africaine, 1996), and *Agonies* (Paris: Présence Africaine, 1998).

162. Fatou Diome, *Le ventre de l'Atlantique* (Paris: Editions Anne Carrière, 2003).

2. FRANCOCENTRISM AND THE ACQUISITION OF CULTURAL CAPITAL

1. Ferdinand Oyono, *Chemin d'Europe* (Paris: Julliard, 1960), 45.

2. Jean-Paul Sartre, preface to *The Wretched of the Earth,* by Frantz Fanon (London: Penguin, 1971), 7.

3. Nicolas Bancel, Pascal Blanchard, and Françoise Vergès, *La République coloniale: Essai sur une utopie* (Paris: Albin Michel, 2003), 142.

4. I am borrowing the term "francocentrism" from Christopher L. Miller, *Nationalists and Nomads: Essays on Francophone African Literature and Culture* (Chicago: University of Chicago Press, 1998), 62.

5. Pascale Casanova, *The World Republic of Letters,* trans. M. B. DeBevoise (Cambridge, Mass.: Harvard University Press, 2004), 25.

6. Laye Camara, *L'enfant noir* (Paris: Plon, 1954), published in English as *The Dark Child,* trans. James Kirkup (London: Collins, 1955) and *The African Child,* trans. James Kirkup and Ernest Jones (New York: Noonday Press, 1954); Cheikh Hamidou Kane, *L'aventure ambiguë* (Paris: Julliard, 1961), published in English as *Ambiguous Adventure,* trans. Katherine Woods (London: Heinemann, 1972; first translated in 1969); Ousmane Socé, *Mirages de Paris* (Paris: Nouvelles Editions Latines, 1937); and Bernard Dadié, *Un nègre à Paris* (Paris: Présence Africaine, 1959), published in English as *An African in Paris,* trans. Karen C. Hatch (Chicago: University of Illinois Press, 1994).

7. Cameroonian novelists Mongo Beti and Ferdinand Oyono would figure as the most important authors of this period. For Beti, see for example *Ville cruelle* (Paris: Editions Africaines, 1954) as Eza Boto, *Le pauvre Christ de Bomba* (Paris: Laffont, 1956), *Mission terminée* (Paris: Buchet-Chastel, 1957), and *Le roi miraculé* (Paris: Buchet-Chastel, 1958). His works are powerful critiques of a dimension that remains relatively unexplored in this chapter, namely the role of missionaries in assisting the colonial project. For Oyono, see *Une vie de boy* (Paris: Julliard, 1956), *Le vieux nègre et la médaille* (Paris: Julliard, 1956), and *Chemin d'Europe.* On these questions, see V. Y. Mudimbe, "The Power of Speech," in *The Invention of Africa: Gnosis, Philosophy, and the Order of Knowledge* (Bloomington: Indiana University Press, 1988); Richard Bjornson, *The African Quest for Freedom and Identity: Cameroonian Writing and the National Experience* (Bloomington: Indiana University Press, 1991); and Eloise A. Brière, *Le roman camerounais et ses discours* (Ivry: Editions Nouvelles du Sud, 1993).

8. It might be worth noting that while African writers were focusing on France, a number of French writers were looking to Africa for inspiration. Most notably, see André Gide, *Voyage au Congo* (Paris: Gallimard, 1927), and *Retour du Tchad* (Paris: Gallimard, 1928); and of course Michel Leiris, *L'Afrique fantôme* (Paris: Gallimard, 1934).

9. Ch.-André Julien, *Les techniciens de la colonisation (XIXe–XXe siècles),* Colonies et empires, 1. sér., Etudes coloniales 1 (Paris: Presses Universitaires de France, 1947); and Robert Delavignette, "Faidherbe," in *Les politiques d'expansion impérialiste,* Colonies et empires, 1. sér., Etudes coloniales 5 (Paris: Presses Universitaires de France, 1949), 83. See also Sandrine Lemaire, "Promouvoir: Fabriquer du colonial," in *Culture impériale: Les colonies au cœur de la République, 1931–1961,* ed. Pascal Blanchard and Sandrine Lemaire (Paris: Editions Autrement, 2004), 45–60; and János Riesz, "Regards critiques sur la société coloniale, à partir de deux romans de Robert Randau et de Robert Delavignette," in *Regards sur les littératures coloniales: Afrique francophone; Approfondissements,* ed. Jean-François Durand (Paris: L'Harmattan, 1999), 51–77.

10. Bernard Mouralis, *République et colonies: Entre histoire et mémoire; La République française et l'Afrique* (Paris: Présence Africaine, 1999), 88.

11. See Barthélémy Kotchy, "Critique des institutions coloniales," in *La critique sociale dans l'œuvre théâtrale de Bernard Dadié* (Paris: L'Harmattan, 1984), 94–123.

12. See William B. Cohen, *The French Encounter with Africans: White Response to Blacks, 1530–1880* (Bloomington: Indiana University Press, 1980); and Patrick Manning, *Francophone sub-Saharan Africa, 1880–1985* (Cambridge: Cambridge University Press, 1998).

13. See for example Henri Brunschwig, *Mythes et réalités de l'impérialisme colonial français, 1871–1914* (Paris: Armand Colin, 1960), and *L'avènement de*

l'Afrique noire du XIXe siècle à nos jours (Paris: Armand Colin, 1963); Jean Suret-Canale, "Le système administratif," in *Afrique noire: L'ère coloniale, 1900–1945* (Paris: Editions Sociales, 1964), 93–121; and Catherine Coquery-Vidrovitch, *L'Afrique et les Africains au XIXe siècle* (Paris: Armand Collin, 1999).

14. Bernard Mouralis, *Littérature et développement: Essai sur le statut, la fonction et la représentation de la littérature négro-africaine d'expression française* (Paris: Silex, 1984), 22, 30. See also Marc Ferro, *Histoire des colonisations, des conquêtes aux indépendances, XIIIe–XXe siècle* (Paris: Seuil, 1994).

15. See Guy Ossito Midiohouan, *L'idéologie dans la littérature négro-africaine d'expression française* (Paris: L'Harmattan, 1986), 44–51.

16. Alice L. Conklin, *A Mission to Civilize: The Republican Ideal of Empire in France and West Africa, 1895–1930* (Stanford, Calif.: Stanford University Press, 1997), 1.

17. Hans-Jürgen Lüsebrink, "Acculturation coloniale et pédagogie interculturelle: L'œuvre de Georges Hardy," in *Sénégal-Forum: Littérature et Histoire,* ed. Papa Samba Diop (Frankfurt: IKO Verlag, 1995), 114.

18. Georges Hardy, *Une conquête morale: L'enseignement en A.O.F.* (Paris, Armand Colin, 1917); see also his *L'enseignement au Sénégal de 1817 à 1857* (Paris: Larose, 1920) and *Histoire sociale de la colonisation française* (Paris: Larose, 1953); J.-P. Makouta-Mboukou, *Le français en Afrique noire: Histoire et méthodes de l'enseignement du français en Afrique noire* (Paris: Bordas, 1973); and Bernard Mouralis, "L'écriture, le réel et l'action: Le cas de Georges Hardy dans Egarste ou la vocation coloniale," in Durand, *Regards sur les littératures coloniales,* 63–84.

19. Philippe Dewitte, "Un centre de l'histoire de l'immigration: Pourquoi et comment?" *Hommes et migrations,* no. 1247 (January–February 2004): 9; and indeed the whole of that issue is relevant to the discussion here.

20. See http://www.assembleenationale.fr/12/propositions/pion0667.asp and http://www.admi.net/jo/20050224/DEFX0300218L.html, respectively. The latter was sponsored by Jean-Louis Debré and is collectively referred to as the Loi Debré.

21. Sandrine Lemaire, "Colonisation et immigration: Des 'points aveugles' de l'histoire à l'école?" in *La fracture coloniale: La société française au prisme de l'héritage colonial,* ed. Pascal Blanchard, Nicolas Bancel, and Sandrine Lemaire (Paris: La Découverte, 2005), 95–96. See also a chapter and two appendixes in *La fracture coloniale* concerning the study conducted in Toulouse on colonial memory by Bancel, Blanchard, and Lemaire: "Les enseignements de l'étude conduite à Toulouse sur la mémoire coloniale," 247–254; "Méthodologie de l'étude 'Mémoire coloniale, mémoire de l'immigration, mémoire urbaine' menées à Toulouse en 2003," 263–267; and "Synthèse des principaux résultats de l'étude de Toulouse," 269–300.

22. Mohamadou Kane, *Roman africain et tradition* (Dakar: Les Nouvelles Editions Africaines, 1982), 39–40.

23. See Thomas G. August, *The Selling of the Empire: British and French Imperialist Propaganda, 1890–1940* (Westport, Conn.: Greenwood Press, 1985); and Catherine Hall, *Civilising Subjects: Metropole and Colony in the English Imagination, 1830–1867* (Chicago: Chicago University Press, 2002).

24. Guy Ossito Midiohouan, *Ecrire en pays colonisé: Plaidoyer pour une nouvelle approche des rapports entre la littérature négro-africaine d'expression française et le pouvoir colonial* (Paris: L'Harmattan, 2002), 28–29.

25. Sayouba Traoré, "Un Burkinabé dans la brousse," interview by Eloïse Brezault, *Notre librairie*, no. 158 (April–June 2005): 48.

26. See Raoul Girardet, *L'idée coloniale en France de 1871 à 1962* (Paris: Editions de la Table Ronde, 1962).

27. Albert Memmi, *The Colonizer and the Colonized*, trans. Howard Greenfield (Boston: Beacon Press, 1991; first pub. 1957), 79.

28. The main critical works that have focused on what is traditionally understood as "colonial literature" are, chronologically, by Roland Lebel, *L'Afrique occidentale dans la littérature française* (Paris: Larose, 1925), and *Etudes de littérature coloniale en France* (Paris: Larose, 1931); Léon Fanoudh-Siefer, *Le mythe du nègre et de l'Afrique noire dans la littérature française, de 1800 à la 2e guerre mondiale* (Paris: Klincksieck, 1968); Martine Astier Loufti, *Littérature et colonialisme: L'expansion coloniale vue dans la littérature romanesque française* (Paris: Mouton, 1971); and Léon-François Hoffman, *Le nègre romantique: Personnage littéraire et obsession collective* (Paris: Payot, 1973).

29. Dominic Thomas, *Nation-Building, Propaganda, and Literature in Francophone Africa* (Bloomington: Indiana University Press, 2002), 5.

30. Ahmadou Mapaté Diagne, *Les trois volontés de Malic* (Paris: Larose, 1920); Bakary Diallo, *Force-Bonté* (Paris: Rieder, 1926); and Lamine Senghor, *La violation d'un pays* (Paris: Bureau d'Editions, de Diffusion et de Publicité, 1927).

31. These findings are corroborated by Philippe Dewitte, *Les mouvements nègres en France, 1919–1939* (Paris: L'Harmattan, 1985), 50–51.

32. Most notably, prefaces were written to Paul Hazoumé's *Doguicimi* (Paris: Larose, 1938) by Georges Hardy, and to Ousmane Socé's *Karim: Roman sénégalais* (Paris: Nouvelles Editions Latines, 1935) by Robert Delavignette. On the importance of these paratextual devices, see Richard Watts, *Packaging Post/Coloniality: The Manufacture of Literary Identity in the Francophone World* (Lanham, Md.: Lexington Books, 2005).

33. See Yves Bénot, *Les parlementaires africains à Paris, 1914–1958* (Paris: Editions Chaka, 1989); and Jacques Frémeaux, "L'union française: Le rêve d'une France unie," in Blanchard and Lemaire, *Culture impériale*, 163–174.

34. See Bernard Dadié, interview by Bennetta Jules-Rosette, in *Black Paris: The African Writers' Landscape*, by Bennetta Jules-Rosette (Urbana: University of Illinois Press, 1998), 140–146.

35. Christopher L. Miller, "*L'enfant noir*, Totemism, and Suspended Animism," in *Theories of Africans: Francophone Literature and Anthropology in Africa* (Chicago: University of Chicago Press, 1990), 159.

36. Charles Nokan, *Le soleil noir point* (Paris: Présence Africaine, 1962), 22.

37. Yambo Ouologuem, *Le devoir de violence* (Paris: Seuil, 1968), published in English as *Bound to Violence*, trans. Ralph Manheim (London: Heinemann, 1971).

38. For examples in the Maghrebi community in France, see Azouz Begag, *Le gone du Châaba* (Paris: Seuil, 1986), and *Béni ou le paradis privé* (Paris: Seuil, 1986).

39. In the study of *La sape* in chapter 6, I return to the question of fashion and cultural capital.

40. The Congolese novelist and playwright Sony Labou Tansi talked about an analogous practice "in which his colonial teachers daubed him with human feces as a punishment for his early grammatical solecisms." Quoted in Kwame Anthony

Appiah, *In My Father's House: Africa in the Philosophy of Culture* (New York: Oxford University Press, 1992), 52. As Emily Apter has argued, "these concerns are of particular significance in places with a history of colonial or neocolonial rule in which standard languages have been imposed and native tongues are over-managed, banned, or reduced to the status of endangered species." Emily Apter, "On Translation in a Global Market," in "Translation," ed. Emily Apter, special issue of *Public Culture* 13, no. 1 (Winter 2001): 6.

41. F. Abiola Irele, "In Praise of Alienation," in *The Surreptitious Speech: Présence Africaine and the Politics of Otherness, 1947–1987,* ed. V. Y. Mudimbe (Chicago: Chicago University Press, 1992), 202.

42. Achille Mbembe, *On the Postcolony* (Berkeley and Los Angeles: University of California Press, 2001), 104.

43. Later, in *Dramouss* (Paris: Plon, 1966), published in English as *A Dream of Africa,* trans. James Kirkup (Glasgow: William Collins Sons, 1968), Camara would introduce a protagonist named Fotoman who initially evoked the seductive qualities of Paris: "the Eiffel Tower with its multicolored lights that sweep the sky and the Invalides, with a dome shaped like a balloon" (62–63). Later, when his scholarship (bursary) is taken away from him, he comes into contact with a different France as he joins the ranks of the numerous other Africans, "the young disinherited men of the Latin Quarter" (81). Eventually he finds a position at the Simca automobile factory, where, "right at 6 a.m., the metallic forest started to hum" (98), and immigrant workers daily confront harsh socioeconomic realities. Eventually, compelled to confront the failure of his migration to the North, he returns to his native Guinea. Indeed, in *Kocumba, l'étudiant noir* (Paris: Flammarion, 1960), the novelist Aké Loba, from the Ivory Coast, also explores the trials and tribulations of study in France, the appalling living and working conditions of immigrants, but unlike other African protagonists of his generation, the protagonist of *Kocumba* successfully returns and reintegrates into African society. Some years later Kanaan Niane, the central protagonist of Saïdou Boukoum's novel *Chaîne* (Paris: Denöel, 1974), abandons his legal studies in France and ends up wandering through the streets of Paris.

44. Mildred Mortimer, *Journeys through the French African Novel* (Portsmouth, N.H.: Heinemann, 1990), 55.

45. See Jean-Loup Amselle and Elikia M'Bokolo, eds., *Au cœur de l'ethnie: Ethnies, tribalisme et état en Afrique* (Paris: La Découverte, 1985).

46. As Appiah has shown, V. Y. Mudimbe's novel *Entre les eaux* "provided a powerful critique of this binarism: we can read it as arguing that if you postulate an either-or choice between Africa and the West, there is no place for you in the real world of politics, and your home must be the otherworldly, the monastic retreat." Kwame Anthony Appiah, *In My Father's House: Africa in the Philosophy of Culture* (New York: Oxford University Press, 1992), 155.

47. Léopold Sédar Senghor, *Liberté I: Négritude et humanisme* (Paris: Seuil, 1964), and *Liberté II: Nation et voie africaine du socialisme* (Paris: Seuil, 1971); and Cheikh Anta Diop, *Nations nègres et culture: De l'antiquité négro-égyptienne aux problèmes culturels de l'Afrique noire aujourd'hui* (Paris: Présence africaine, 1954), *L'Afrique noire précoloniale: Etude comparée des systèmes politiques et sociaux de l'Europe et de l'Afrique noire, de l'antiquité à la formation des états modernes* (Paris: Présence Africaine, 1960), *L'unité culturelle de l'Afrique noire* (Paris: Présence Africaine, 1960), and *Antériorité des civilisations nègres: Mythe ou vérité historique?* (Paris: Présence Africaine, 1967).

48. Frantz Fanon, *Peau noire, masques blancs* (Paris: Seuil, 1995), published in English as *Black Skin, White Masks*, trans. Charles Lam Markmann (New York: Grove Press, 1967); Aimé Césaire, *Discours sur le colonialisme* (Paris: Présence Africaine, 1955); Edouard Glissant, *Le discours antillais* (Paris: Seuil, 1981), published in English as *Caribbean Discourse: Selected Essays*, trans. J. Michael Dash (Charlottesville: University of Virginia Press, 1989); and Jean Bernabé, Patrick Chamoiseau, and Raphaël Confiant, *Eloge de la créolité* (Paris: Gallimard, 1989).

49. The centrality of literacy is evoked here. For other examples, see Begag, *Le gone*; and Joseph Zobel, *La rue Cases-Nègres* (Paris: Présence Africaine, 1974).

50. As a special issue of the journal *Notre librairie* illustrates, these images have been around for some time. See "Images du noir dans la littérature occidentale: Du Moyen-Age à la conquête coloniale," *Notre librairie*, no. 90 (October–December 1987).

51. Edwin Hill, "Imagining *Métissage:* The Politics and Practice of *Métissage* in the French Colonial Exposition and Ousmane Socé's *Mirages de Paris,*" *Social Identities* 8, no. 4 (2002): 634.

52. See also Nicolas Bancel, Pascal Blanchard, Gilles Boëtsch, Eric Deroo, and Sandrine Lemaire, *Zoos humains: De la Vénus hottentote aux* reality shows (Paris: La Découverte, 2002); and Pascal Blanchard and Sandrine Lemaire, "Les colonies au cœur de la République," in Blanchard and Lemaire, *Culture impériale,* 5–32. See also Jean-Michel Bergougniou, Rémi Clignet, and Philippe David, *"Villages noirs" et visiteurs africains et malgaches en France et en Europe, 1870–1940* (Paris: Karthala, 2001).

53. Subsequently, some of the structures from the Colonial Exposition came to form the Musée des colonies, then the Musée de la France d'Outre-Mer, and finally the Musée des arts africains et océaniens. This museum closed on January 31, 2003, and the site will be used for the new Musée de l'histoire et des cultures de l'immigration en France. See Jacques Toubon, *Mission de préfiguration du Centre de ressources et de mémoire de l'immigration* (Paris: La Documentation Française, 2004); and Philippe Dewitte, ed., "Vers un lieu de mémoire de l'immigration," *Hommes et migrations,* no. 1247 (January–February 2004). On museums in France, see Herman Lebovics, "The Dance of the Museums," in *Bringing the Empire Back Home: France in the Global Age* (Durham, N.C.: Duke University Press, 2004), 143–177.

54. Fanon addressed this kind of exchange in *Black Skin, White Masks*.

55. Pierre Nora, ed., *Les lieux de mémoire,* 7 vols. (Paris: Gallimard, 1984–1992). Of particular interest in this context would be Charles-Robert Ageron, "L'exposition coloniale de 1931: Mythe républicain ou mythe impérial," in *La République*, vol. 1 of Nora, *Les lieux de mémoire,* 493–515.

56. See also Lynn E. Palermo, "Identity under Construction: Representing the Colonies at the Paris *Exposition Universelle* of 1889," in *The Color of Liberty: Histories of Race in France*, ed. Sue Peabody and Tyler Stovall (Durham, N.C.: Duke University Press, 2003), 285–301.

57. See also Hans-Jürgen Lüsebrink, "Les expositions coloniales: Lieux d'exhibition et de débats identitaires," in *La conquête de l'espace public colonial: Prises de parole et formes de participation d'écrivains et d'intellectuels africains dans la presse à l'époque coloniale* (Frankfurt: IKO Verlag für Interkulturelle Kommunikation, 2003), 175. Miller writes, "The continuing prosperity—and later (after the onset of the depression in France in 1931), the economic recovery of France—depended on the colonies. In order for the French public to support this

vital colonial endeavor, they needed to be seduced, they needed to be made to dream of the colonies." *Nationalists and Nomads,* 74.

58. Emmanuel Dongala, *Jazz et vin de palme* (Paris: Le Serpent à Plumes, 1982).

59. Hans-Jürgen Lüsebrink, "Métissage et société coloniale," in *La conquête de l'espace public colonial,* 215.

60. Alice Conklin, "Redefining 'Frenchness': Citizenship, Race Regeneration, and Imperial Motherhood in France and West Africa, 1914–40," in *Domesticating the Empire: Race, Gender, and Family Life in French and Dutch Colonialism,* ed. Julia Clancy-Smith and Frances Gourda (Charlottesville: University Press of Virginia, 1998), 76–77.

61. Tyler Stovall, "Love, Labor, and Race: Colonial Men and White Women in France during the Great War," in *French Civilization and Its Discontents: Nationalism, Colonialism, Race,* ed. Tyler Stovall and Georges Van Den Abbeele (Lanham, Md.: Lexington Books: 2003), 297.

62. See for example Philippe Farine, ed., "Colonisations, immigration: Le complexe impérial," special issue of *Migrations société* 14, nos. 81–82 (May–August 1982).

63. Failed métissage is common in postcolonial novels set in France. See for example Daniel Biyaoula, *Agonies* (Paris: Présence Africaine, 1998). Mireille Rosello has also shown how mixed couples raise complex questions in Calixthe Beyala's novel *Le petit prince de Belleville* (Paris: Albin Michel, 1992). In *Declining the Stereotype: Ethnicity and Representation in French Cultures* (Hanover, N.H.: University Press of New England, 1998), she writes, "The text makes it clear, however, that the presence of an interracial couple, or even their friendship, should not be equated with a simple solution. In fact, it is always difficult to ascertain whether Beyala's novels celebrate such possibilities or mock those who imagine that there is an adequate response to institutionalized racism" (146).

64. Bernard Dadié, *Climbié* (Paris: Seghers, 1956), published in English as *Climbié,* trans. Karen C. Chapman (London: Heinemann, 1971).

65. Elisabeth Mudimbe-Boyi, "Travel Representation and Difference, or How Can One Be a Parisian?" *Research in African Literatures* 23, no. 3 (Fall 1992): 27, 35. See also Aedín Ní Loingsigh, "Immigration, Tourism, and Postcolonial Reinventions of Travel," in *Francophone Postcolonial Studies: A Critical Introduction,* ed. Charles Forsdick and David Murphy (London: Arnold, 2003), 156–165.

66. Ali Behdad, *Belated Travelers: Orientalism in the Age of Colonial Dissolution* (Durham, N.C.: Duke University Press, 1994). See also Jean-Marc Moura, "Littérature coloniale et exotisme: Examen d'une opposition de la théorie littéraire coloniale," in Durand, *Regards sur les littératures coloniales,* 21–39.

67. On epistolarity and *Un nègre à Paris,* see Mwamba Cabaculu, "L'épistolarité dans l'œuvre de Bernard B. Dadié: Le cas de *Un nègre à Paris,*" in *Bernard Bilin Dadié: Conscience critique de son temps,* ed. Valy Sidibé and Bruno Gnaoulé-Oupoh (Abidjan, Ivory Coast: Centre d'Edition et de Diffusion Africaines, 1999), 185–190.

68. Pierre Bourdieu, *La distinction: Critique sociale du jugement* (Paris: Editions de Minuit, 1979).

69. This translation is my own, since the line is omitted from the English version: "j'en arrive à dire qu'on connaît mal un peuple en ne le connaissant que par les ouvrages qu'on écrit sur lui" (*Un nègre à Paris,* 140).

70. Jean-Loup Amselle, *Mestizo Logics: Anthropology of Identity in Africa and Elsewhere*, trans. Claudia Royal (Stanford, Calif.: Stanford University Press, 1998), originally published as *Logiques métisses: Anthropologie de l'identité en Afrique et ailleurs* (Paris: Payot, 1990); Miller, *Theories of Africans;* V. Y. Mudimbe, *The Idea of Africa* (Bloomington: Indiana University Press, 1994); and Françoise Lionnet, "*Logiques métisses:* Cultural Appropriation and Postcolonial Representation," in *Postcolonial Representations: Women, Literature, Identity* (Ithaca, N.Y.: Cornell University Press, 1995), 1–21.

71. See Pierre Halen, "Pour en finir avec une phraséologie encombrante: La question de l'Autre et de l'exotisme dans l'approche critique des littératures coloniales et post-coloniales," in Durand, *Regards sur les littératures coloniales,* 41–62.

72. In the context of postcolonial France and the perceived threat to Republican ideals posed by "headscarves" and "veils," Emmanuel Terray has characterized early twenty-first-century responses to these questions in terms of "hysteria." See his "Headscarf Hysteria," *New Left Review* 26 (March–April 2004): 118–127.

73. André-Patient Bokiba, *Ecriture et identité dans la littérature africaine* (Paris: L'Harmattan, 1998), 172, 155.

74. Jean-Pierre Makouta-Mboukou, *Introduction à l'étude du roman négro-africain de langue française: Problèmes culturels et littéraires* (Abidjan, Ivory Coast: Les Nouvelles Editions Africaines, 1980), 247.

75. Edward Said, *Orientalism* (New York: Pantheon, 1978).

76. Jean Derive, "*Un nègre à Paris:* Contexte littéraire et idéologique," in *Bernard Dadié: Hommages et études* (Ivry-sur-Seine: Nouvelles du Sud, 1992), 190. See also Jacques Chevrier, "Lecture d'un Nègre à Paris: Où il est prouvé qu'on peut être Parisien et raisonner comme un Agni," *L'Afrique littéraire et artistique* 85 (1989): 42–50.

77. F. Abiola Irele, *The African Imagination: Literature in Africa and the Black Diaspora* (Oxford: Oxford University Press, 2001), 70.

3. TEXTUAL OWNERSHIP AND THE GLOBAL MEDIATION OF BLACKNESS

1. Ousmane Sembene, "Interview with Ousmane Sembene at Filmi Doomireew, Dakar, 30 November 1995," interview by David Murphy, in *Sembene: Imagining Alternatives in Film and Fiction,* by David Murphy (Oxford: James Currey, 2000), 227–228.

2. Albert Memmi, *The Colonizer and the Colonized* (Boston: Beacon Press, 1991; first pub. 1957), 120.

3. FBI file on Richard Nathaniel Wright, file number 100–157464, part 1b, page 20, http://foia.fbi.gov/foiaindex/rnwright.htm. The FBI's introductory web page says, "This famous writer was investigated by the FBI for being a member of the Communist Party between 1932 and 1942. He left the party in 1942 because of ideological disputes." The Public Information Act has also forced the FBI to make available the files of Josephine Baker, James Baldwin, W. E. B. Du Bois, and Langston Hughes.

4. Bill Ashcroft, Gareth Griffiths, and Helen Tiffin, *The Empire Writes Back: Theory and Practice in Post-colonial Literatures* (London: Routledge, 1989), 38,

39. Frantz Fanon addressed this important question in "The Negro and Language," in _Black Skin, White Masks,_ trans. Charles Lam Markmann (New York: Grove Press, 1967), 17–40.

5. A broadening of this perspective, as suggested by Kwame Anthony Appiah, might also be important: "If there is a lesson in the broad shape of this circulation of cultures, it is surely that we are all already contaminated by each other." Kwame Anthony Appiah, _In My Father's House: Africa in the Philosophy of Culture_ (New York: Oxford University Press, 1992), 155.

6. Jacques Chevrier, _Littérature nègre_ (Paris: Armand Colin, 1984), 118.

7. See Christopher L. Miller, _Theories of Africans: Francophone Literature and Anthropology in Africa_ (Chicago: University of Chicago Press, 1990); F. Abiola Irele, _The African Experience in Literature and Ideology_ (London, Heinemann, 1981); Richard Bjornson, _The African Quest for Freedom and Identity: Cameroonian Writing and the National Experience_ (Bloomington: Indiana University Press, 1991); Adrien Huannou, _La question des littératures nationales en Afrique noire_ (Abidjan, Ivory Coast: CEDA, 1989); Guy Ossito Midiohouan, _L'idéologie dans la littérature négro-africaine d'expression française_ (Paris: L'Harmattan, 1986); and Dominic Thomas, _Nation-Building, Propaganda, and Literature in Francophone Africa_ (Bloomington: Indiana University Press, 2002).

8. Jean-Paul Sartre, "Orphée noir," in _Les temps modernes,_ no. 37 (October 1948): 590.

9. "Sony Labou Tansi," _Equateur,_ no. 1 (October–November 1986): 30.

10. Christopher L. Miller, "Dis-figuring Narrative: Plagiarism and Dismemberment in Yambo Ouologuem's _Le devoir de violence,_" in _Blank Darkness: Africanist Discourse in French_ (Chicago: University of Chicago Press, 1985), 216–245; Nicki Hitchcott, "Calixthe Beyala and the Post-colonial Woman," in _Post-colonial Cultures in France,_ ed. Alec G. Hargreaves and Mark McKinney (London: Routledge, 1997), 211–225; Nicki Hitchcott, "Calixthe Beyala: Prizes, Plagiarism, and 'Authenticity,'" in "Textual Ownership in Francophone African Writing," ed. Alec G. Hargreaves, Nicki Hitchcott, and Dominic Thomas, special issue of _Research in African Literatures_ 37, no. 1 (Spring 2006): 100–109; Adele King, _Rereading Camara Laye_ (Lincoln: University of Nebraska Press, 2002); and Jean Derive, "_Un nègre à Paris:_ Intertexte et contexte," _Komparatistische Hefte_ 15–16 (1987): 177–195.

11. On the theorization of intertextuality, see Mikhail Bakhtin, _Dialogism,_ trans. Caryl Emerson and Michael Holquist (Austin: University of Texas Press, 1981); and of course Julia Kristeva, "Bakhtine, le mot, le dialogue et le roman," _Critique,_ no. 239 (April 1967): 438–465, and _Le texte du roman_ (La Haye: Mouton, 1970); and Roland Barthes, _Le plaisir du texte_ (Paris: Seuil, 1973).

12. Ousmane Sembene, _Le docker noir_ (Paris: Editions Debresse, 1956). Quotations in French are from the 1973 Présence Africaine edition, and quotations in English from the translation by Ros Schwartz, _Black Docker_ (London: Heinemann, 1987).

13. Lilyan Kesteloot, _Black Writers in French: A Literary History of Negritude,_ trans. Ellen Conroy Kennedy (Philadelphia: Temple University Press, 1974); Dorothy S. Blair, _African Literature in French_ (Cambridge: Cambridge University Press, 1976); Chevrier, _Littérature nègre;_ Bernard Mouralis, _Littérature et développement: Essai sur le statut, la fonction et la représentation de la littérature négro-africaine d'expression française_ (Paris: Silex, 1984); Wilfried F. Feuser, "_Na-_

tive Son and Ousmane Sembene's *Le docker noir,*" *Konparatistische Hefte* 14 (1986): 103–116, also published as "Richard Wright's *Native Son* and Sembene Ousmane's *Le docker noir,*" in *Essays in Comparative African Literature,* ed. Wilfried F. Feuser and I. N. C. Aniebo (Lagos, Nigeria: Centre for Black and African Arts and Civilization, 2001), 252–267 (quotations are from the 1986 publication); János Riesz, "*Le dernier voyage du Négrier Sirius:* Le roman dans le roman," in *Sénégal-Forum: Littérature et histoire,* ed. Papa Samba Diop (Frankfurt, Germany: IKO Verlag, 1995), 178–196; Anthère Nzabatsinda, "La figure de l'artiste dans le récit d'Ousmane Sembene," *Etudes françaises* 31, no. 1 (Summer 1995): 51–60; Sélom Komlan Gbanou, "Textes, contextes et intertextes dans les romans *Le docker noir* de Sembene Ousmane et *Le crime de la rue des notables* de Ekue Akoua T.," *Palabres: Revue culturelle africaine* 1, nos. 3–4 (1997): 81–93; and David Murphy, "La danse et la parole: L'exil et l'identité chez les Noirs de Marseille dans *Banjo* de Claude McKay et *Le docker noir* d'Ousmane Sembene," *Canadian Review of Comparative Literature* 27, no. 3 (September 2000): 462–479. Two additional studies of *Le docker noir* are forthcoming: Christopher L. Miller, "African 'Silence,'" in *The French Atlantic Triangle: Literature and Culture of the Slave Trade;* and Francis Higginson, "*Le docker noir* or Race, Revolution and the Novel," in "Blood and the Canon: The Advent of Francophone African Crime Fiction."

14. Richard Wright, *Native Son* (New York: Harper Collins, 1993; first pub. 1940 by Harper and Brothers, New York), published in French as *Un enfant du pays,* trans. Hélène Bokanowsky and Marcel Duhamel (Paris: Albin Michel, 1947). *Native Son* was also translated into Russian in 1945 and was popularly acclaimed. See Kate A. Baldwin, *Beyond the Color Line and the Iron Curtain: Reading Encounters between Black and Red, 1922–1963* (Durham, N.C.: Duke University Press, 2002).

15. Ousmane Sembene, "Sembene présente *Molaade* à Cannes: Une présence africaine plus importante est possible," interview by Walfadjiri, http://www.africatime.com/togo/nouv_pana.asp?no_nouvelle=119602&no_categorie=.

16. Michel Fabre, *From Harlem to Paris: Black American Writers in France, 1840–1980* (Urbana: University of Illinois Press, 1991), 92. The importance of this dialogue and mediation between Africa and African America has been exploited in postcolonial works. See for example Emmanuel Dongala's collection of short stories, *Jazz et vin de palme* (Paris: Le Serpent à Plumes, 1982), in which he writes about John Coltrane and America during the 1960s.

17. Claude McKay, *Banjo: A Story without a Plot* (New York: Harper and Brothers, 1929), published in French as *Banjo,* trans. Ida Treat and Paul-Vaillant Couturier (Paris: Rieder, 1931). Citations are to the original English edition.

18. Manthia Diawara, *In Search of Africa* (Cambridge, Mass.: Harvard University Press, 1998), 63. See in particular the chapter "Richard Wright and Modern Africa," 59–76. These issues receive further attention in his *We Won't Budge: An African Exile in the World* (New York: Basic Civitas Books, 2003).

19. Our attention should also be drawn to Tyler Stovall's foundational study of African Americans in Paris, *Paris Noir: African Americans in the City of Light* (New York: Houghton Mifflin, 1996), in which he corroborates these positions, arguing that Wright "also exercises a strong influence on the younger generation of negritude writers, notably Ousmane Sembene, whose novel *The Black Docker* owed much to both *Native Son* and Claude McKay's *Banjo*" (197).

20. The work of Kristin Ross is one example of this. See *Fast Cars, Clean Bodies: Decolonization and the Reordering of French Culture* (Cambridge, Mass.: MIT Press, 1995).

21. See for example Pascal Blanchard and Nicolas Bancel, *De l'indigène à l'immigré* (Paris: Gallimard, 1998); Bernard Mouralis, "Le colonisé est-il un étranger?" in *République et colonies: Entre histoire et mémoire; La République française et l'Afrique* (Paris: Présence Africaine, 1999), 34–39; and Elizabeth Ezra, *The Colonial Unconscious: Race and Culture in Interwar France* (Ithaca, N.Y.: Cornell University Press, 2000).

22. Brent Hayes Edwards, *The Practice of Diaspora: Literature, Translation, and the Rise of Black Internationalism* (Cambridge, Mass.: Harvard University Press, 2003), 4, 7.

23. For more specific information on the long history of African Americans in France, see Michel Fabre, *La rive noire: Les écrivains noirs américains à Paris, 1830–1995* (Marseille: André Dimanche, 1999), 21–41.

24. Christopher L. Miller, *Nationalists and Nomads: Essays on Francophone African Literature and Culture* (Chicago: University of Chicago Press, 1998), 22. See also Wayne F. Cooper, *Claude McKay: Rebel Sojourner in the Harlem Renaissance; A Biography* (Baton Rouge: Louisiana State University, 1987); and Tyrone Tillery, *Claude McKay: A Black Poet's Struggle for Identity* (Amherst: University of Massachusetts Press, 1992).

25. In critical readings of McKay's work, such conclusions have become common. See Fabre, "Claude McKay, visiteur averti," in *La rive noire,* 95–107; and Sandra L. West, "Paris," in *Encyclopedia of the Harlem Renaissance,* ed. Aberjhani and Sandra L. West (New York: Checkmark Books, 2003), 253–256. West notes that McKay "never forgot, however, and never feared to discuss, the hard-to-accept, little acknowledged fact (by African Americans) of the exploitation of Africans by the French" (255).

26. Richard Wright, "Le feu dans la nuée," parts 1 and 2, trans. Marcel Duhamel, *Les temps modernes,* no. 1 (October 1, 1945): 22–47; no. 2 (November 1, 1945): 291–319.

27. Richard Wright, "Littérature noire américaine," trans. René Guyonnet, *Les temps modernes,* no. 35 (August 1948): 193–221, and "J'ai essayé d'être communiste," trans. René Guyonnet, *Les temps modernes,* no. 45 (July 1949): 1–45.

28. Edouard Glissant, "Terre à terre," *Les temps modernes,* no. 36 (September 1948): 429–438; Sartre, "Orphée noir"; and Michel Leiris, "Martinique, Guadeloupe, Haïti," *Les temps modernes,* no. 52 (February 1950): 1345–1368, and "Poèmes," *Les temps modernes,* no. 37 (October 1948): 607–625.

29. See Lilyan Kesteloot, "In Paris: Founding *Présence Africaine*" and "The Nature and Influence of *Présence Africaine*" in *Black Writers in French,* 279–287, 288–297; Bennetta Jules-Rosette, "Conjugating Cultural Realities: *Présence Africaine,*" in *The Surreptitious Speech: Présence Africaine and the Politics of Otherness, 1947–1987,* ed. V. Y. Mudimbe (Chicago: Chicago University Press, 1992), 14–44; Mildred A. Hill-Lubin, "*Présence Africaine*: A Voice in the Wilderness, a Record of Black Kinship," in Mudimbe, *The Surreptitious Speech,* 157–173; and Elisabeth Mudimbe-Boyi, "Harlem Renaissance and Africa: An Ambiguous Adventure," in Mudimbe, *The Surreptitious Speech,* 174–184.

30. Richard Wright, "Claire étoile du matin," trans. Boris Vian, *Présence africaine,* no. 1 (November–December 1947): 120–135.

31. Madeleine Gautier, "Un romancier de la race noire: Richard Wright," *Présence africaine*, no. 1 (November–December 1947): 163–165. Subsequent volumes also featured Wright's work. See Claudine Chonez, "De *L'enfant noir* à la libération de l'homme," *Présence africaine*, no. 3 (1948): 515–518; and R. J. Rougerie, "Les enfants de l'oncle Tom par Richard Wright," *Présence africaine*, no. 3 (1948): 518–519.

32. Detailed analysis of the Congress can be found in Bennetta Jules-Rosette, "Antithetical Africa: The Conferences and Festivals of *Présence Africaine*, 1956–73," in *Black Paris: The African Writers' Landscape* (Urbana: University of Illinois Press, 1998), 48–78.

33. Richard Wright, "Tradition and Industrialization: The Plight of the Tragic Elite in Africa," special issue of *Présence africaine*, nos. 8–10 (June–November 1956): 347–360.

34. Paul Gilroy, *The Black Atlantic: Modernity and Double Consciousness* (Cambridge, Mass.: Harvard University Press, 1993), 152. Additional concerns raised by Gilroy are extremely pertinent in the context of this chapter: "Analysis of Wright's legacy has been impoverished as a result of his being overidentified with the same narrow definitions of racialized cultural expression that he tried to overturn . . . What would it mean to read Wright intertextually with Genet, Beauvoir, Sartre, and the other Parisians with whom he was in dialogue? Examining his route from the particular to the general, from America to Europe and Africa, would certainly get us out of a position where we have to choose between the unsatisfactory alternatives of Eurocentrism and black nationalism" (186).

35. See Schofield Coryell, "Itinéraire d'un écrivain engagé: Richard Wright le subversif," *Le monde diplomatique*, August 2003.

36. See for example James Campbell, *Exiled in Paris: Richard Wright, James Baldwin, Samuel Beckett, and Others on the Left Bank* (Berkeley and Los Angeles: University of California Press, 2003); and Hazel Rowley, *Richard Wright: The Life and Times* (New York: Henry Holt, 2003).

37. Richard Wright, *The Outsider* (New York: Harper and Brothers, 1953), and *Le transfuge* (Paris: Gallimard, 1953); Albert Camus, *L'étranger* (Paris: Gallimard, 1942); and Laye Camara, *L'enfant noir* (Paris: Plon, 1954). The two English-language versions of Camara's novel avoid the direct translation of the title into English—"Black Boy" or "The Black Child"—that would have inscribed further proximity to Wright's title; it was published instead as *The Dark Child*, trans. James Kirkup (London: Collins, 1955) and *The African Child*, trans. James Kirkup and Ernest Jones (New York: Noonday Press, 1954).

38. In fact, when one considers the multiple points of referentiality to which francophone writers have been exposed, from specifically "indigenous" cultural influences, through the colonial pedagogical project that provided for new ancestors ("nos ancêtres les Gaulois"), to the Caribbean and African America, among others, I am inclined to expand the "triangular" framework proposed by Roger Little in his "Reflections on a Triangular Trade in Borrowing and Stealing: Textual Exploitation in a Selection of African, Caribbean and European Writers in French," in "Textual Ownership in Francophone African Writing," ed. Alec G. Hargreaves, Nicki Hitchcott, and Dominic Thomas, special issue of *Research in African Literatures* 37, no. 1 (Spring 2006): 16–27.

39. References henceforth will be to Lilyan Kesteloot, "Situation actuelle des écrivains noirs," in *Les écrivains noirs de langue française: Naissance d'une lit-*

térature (Brussels: Institut de sociologie de l'Université libre de Bruxelles, 1963), 273–315.

40. Henry Louis Gates, *The Signifying Monkey: A Theory of African-American Literary Criticism* (New York: Oxford University Press, 1988).

41. The question of "literary cannibalism" has received considerable critical attention in recent years. In 2003, for example, the Guadeloupean author Maryse Condé offered a seminar entitled "Literary Cannibalism in the Antillean Novel" at the School of Criticism and Theory at Cornell University that considered the question in a transnational framework. See also Françoise Lionnet, "Transcolonialismes: Echoes et dissonances de Jane Austen à Marie-Thérèse Humbert et d'Emily Brontë à Maryse Condé," in *Ecrire en langue étrangère et de cultures dans le monde francophone,* ed. Robert Dion, Hans-Jürgen Lüsebrink, and János Riesz (Quebec City: Editions Nota Bene, 2002), 227–243; and Caryn James, "Stop! Thief! An Author's Mind Is Being Stolen!" *New York Times,* June 25, 2004.

42. Yambo Ouologuem, *Le devoir de violence* (Paris: Seuil, 1968), published in English as *Bound to Violence,* trans. Ralph Manheim (London: Heinemann, 1971). See also Seth I. Wolitz, "L'art du plagiat, ou une brève défense de Ouologuem," *Research in African Literatures* 4, no. 1 (Spring 1973): 130–134.

43. Achille Mbembe, *On the Postcolony* (Berkeley and Los Angeles: University of California Press, 2001), 188.

44. Ariel Dorfman, *The Empire's Old Clothes* (New York: Penguin, 1996; first pub. 1983), 18. See Jean de Brunhoff, *Le roi Babar* (Paris: Hachette, 1988; first pub. 1939).

45. See for example how this process has operated in relation to Arabs in France, in Thomas Deltombe and Mathieu Rigouste, "L'ennemi intérieur: La construction médiatique de la figure de l'"Arabe,'" in *La fracture coloniale: La société française au prisme de l'héritage colonial,* ed. Pascal Blanchard, Nicolas Bancel, and Sandrine Lemaire (Paris: La Découverte, 2005), 191–198.

46. Joseph Zobel, *La rue Cases-Nègres* (Paris: Présence Africaine, 1974); and Azouz Begag, *Le gone du Châaba* (Paris: Seuil, 1986).

47. See Alec G. Hargreaves, *Voices from the North African Community in France: Immigration and Identity in Beur Fiction* (London: Berg, 1991), 123.

48. Marseilles also provides the site for Sembene's short story "Letters from France," in *Tribal Scars* (London: Heinemann, 1974). In "Letters from France," Nafi mails a series of letters to Africa describing her living conditions: "My dear, you can't possibly imagine my disillusionment . . . I'm not in France, at least not the France that came into our dreams and fed our ambitions. I'm in a different world, a gloomy, depressing world which weighs me down, is slowly killing me off, day by day" (56). See also Yaël Simpson Fletcher, "Catholics, Communists, and Colonial Subjects: Working-Class Militancy and Racial Difference in Postwar Marseille," in *The Color of Liberty: Histories of Race in France,* ed. Sue Peabody and Tyler Stovall (Durham, N.C.: Duke University Press, 2003), 338–350.

49. Brigitte Bertoncello and Sylvie Bredeloup, eds., "Marseille, carrefour d'Afrique," *Hommes et migrations,* no. 1224 (March–April 2000), in particular the editors' article "Commerce africain, réseaux transnationaux et société locale," 5–21; Brigitte Bertoncello, *Colporteurs africains à Marseille: Un siècle d'aventures* (Paris: Autrement, 2004); and Pascal Blanchard and Gilles Boëtsch, *Marseille porte sud: Un siècle d'histoire coloniale et d'immigration* (Paris: La Découverte, 2005).

50. On the question of writing in *Le docker noir,* see Nzabatsinda, "La figure de l'artiste," 51–60.

51. On usage of the term *nègre,* see Miller, *Nationalists and Nomads,* 30–43; Edwards, "Translating the Word *Nègre,*" in *The Practice of Diaspora,* 25–38; and on usage of the term "negro" and its broader associations in colonial discursive constructs, see Mbembe, *On the Postcolony,* 180–181.

52. Etienne Balibar, "Racism and Nationalism," in *Race, Nation, Class: Ambiguous Identities,* ed. Etienne Balibar and Immanuel Wallerstein (London: Verso, 1991), 49. Balibar's notion of "neo-racism" applies to the postcolonial context, but clearly Sembene's text emphasizes the transcolonial nature of the concept.

53. See also Ann Laura Stoler's brilliant study of colonial "intimacies," *Carnal Knowledge and Imperial Power: Race and the Intimate in Colonial Rule* (Berkeley and Los Angeles: University of California Press, 2002); T. Sharpley-Whiting, *Black Venus: Sexualized Savages, Primal Fears, and Primitive Narratives in French* (Durham, N.C.: Duke University Press, 1999); and Nacira Guénif-Souilamas, "La réduction à son corps de l'indigène de la République," in Blanchard, Bancel, and Lemaire, *La fracture coloniale,* 199–208.

54. Some years later, Sartre's exploration of racism in the American South in his play *La putain respectueuse* (Paris: Gallimard, 1946) would focus on the collectivity as a mechanism for restoring the power of the dominant group.

55. The figure of "Mamadou" was of course central to the marketing of "Banania" products, which featured the face of a smiling African man apparently thrilled with his exposure to French universalism, and which Senghor spoke out against so vociferously: "Mais je déchirerai les rires *banania* sur tous les murs de France" ("I will tear down those Banania smiles from the walls of France"). See Léopold Sédar Senghor, "Poème liminaire," in *Œuvre poétique* (Paris: Seuil, 1990), 7. On this question, see Mireille Rosello, *Declining the Stereotype: Ethnicity and Representation in French Cultures* (Hanover, N.Y.: University Press of New England, 1998).

56. This type of belief has characterized the French electoral landscape for many years now, and came to prominence with the rise of extreme-right politics during the 1980s. In a review of Bernard Stasi's *Laïcité et République: Rapport de la commission de réflection sur l'application du principe de laïcité dans la République* (Paris: La Documentation Française, 2004), Emmanuel Terray has used the term "hysteria" to describe the official response to the perceived threat to secularism. See Emmanuel Terray, "Headscarf Hysteria," *New Left Review* 26 (March–April 2004): 118–127.

57. See Frantz Fanon, "L'homme de couleur et la Blanche," in *Peau noire, masques blancs* (Paris: Seuil, 1952), 51–66; Fanon knew Richard Wright and had read his work, in fact even mentioning *Native Son* in *Peau noire, masques blancs* in his discussion of the Negro's "sentiment d'infériorité" (inferiority complex), 112–113.

58. In a paper entitled "Paul Smaïl m'a tué ou histoire parisienne d'un faux-beur écrivain," delivered at Florida State University at the conference "Textual Ownership in Francophone African Writing" on October 22, 2004, Azouz Begag demonstrated the appeal and comforting nature to a French audience (confirmed by an extraordinary print run) of a text written about contemporary immigration in France by an impostor. Furthermore, as Begag demonstrated, the inauthenticity of the narrative was immediately detectable by Beur writers because of the vocabulary and terminology it employed.

59. Hans-Jürgen Lüsebrink, *Schrift, Buch und Lektüre in der französischsprachigen Literatur Afrikas: Zur Wahrnehmung und Funktion von Schriftlichkeit*

und Buchlektüre in einem kulturellen Epochenumbruch der Neuzeit (Tübingen, Niemeyer, 1990).

60. As discussed in Gbanou (87), the excerpt Diaw recites reminds Mouralis of Prosper Mérimée's *Tamango.*

61. Interesting parallels emerge here between the discourse surrounding the alleged rape of Ginette Tontisane and J. M. Coetzee's novel *Disgrace* (London: Viking, 1999). In the latter, the reader is taken on a troubling journey into post-Apartheid South Africa, framed under the aegis of complicated relations between men and women and, perhaps more importantly, between one Black African man and a young white woman upon whom violence is visited in what might constitute "retribution" for earlier generations of white dominance.

62. Feuser is quoting from Marius-François Guyard's book *La littérature comparée* (Paris: PUF, 1969).

63. Arnold Rampersad, introduction to *Native Son,* by Richard Wright (New York: Harper, 1993), xxv.

64. Writing in 1986, Feuser makes the point that Sembene, "whose English is virtually non-existent even today" (*"Native Son,"* 105), must have read Wright in translation. The Sembene scholar David Murphy confirmed this in an e-mail message to me on November 3, 2004: "I doubt if he had enough English to read American texts in the original back in the 1950s."

65. Ekue Akoua, *Le crime de la rue des notables* (Lomé, Togo: Editions NEA, 1989).

66. As Charles R. Larson contends, "the larger issue, which extends well beyond the domain of the vanity publishers, is that of a general lapse of ethics among both African publishers and, to a lesser extent, their European counterparts." *The Ordeal of the African Writer* (New York: Zed Books, 2001), 60.

67. For a brilliant analysis of the Sambo figure as an example of "the interrelationship of the global and the local and the current configurations of race, racialization, and racism" in France, see Leora Auslander and Thomas C. Holt, "Sambo in Paris: Race and Racism in the Iconography of the Everyday," in Peabody and Stovall, *The Color of Liberty,* 151.

68. Lamine Diakhaté, review of *Le docker noir* in *Présence Africaine,* no. 13 (1957): 153–154.

69. This question was addressed by Jean-Marc Moura at the conference "Textual Ownership in Francophone African Writing," held at Florida State University, October 22–23, 2004. See Jean-Marc Moura, "Textual Ownership in *L'étrange destin de Wangrin* (The Fortunes of Wangrin) by Amadou Hambaté Bâ," in Hargreaves, Hitchcott, and Thomas, "Textual Ownership in Francophone African Writing," 91–99.

70. See Françoise Lionnet and Shu-mei Shih, "Thinking Through the Mirror, Transnationally," in *Minor Transnationalism,* ed. Françoise Lionnet and Shu-mei Shih (Durham, N.C.: Duke University Press, 2005), 1–23.

4. RHETORICAL MEDIATIONS
OF SLAVERY

1. Jean-Loup Amselle, *Branchements: Anthropologie de l'universalité des cultures* (Paris: Flammarion, 2001), 7–8.

2. Jean Baudrillard, *Screened Out,* trans. Chris Turner (London: Verso, 2002), 155.

3. Saskia Sassen, *Globalization and Its Discontents: Essays on the New Mobility of People and Money* (New York: New Press, 1998), 81.

4. Ousmane Sembene, *Le docker noir* (Paris: Présence Africaine, 1973; first pub. 1956); and Bernard Dadié, *Un nègre à Paris* (Paris: Présence Africaine, 1959).

5. Henriette Akofa, with Olivier de Broca, *Une esclave moderne* (Paris: Michel Lafon, 2000).

6. Roger Botte, "Le spectre de l'esclavage," *Les temps modernes,* nos. 620–621 (August–November 2002): 145–164.

7. See also Fatou Keïta, *Rebelle* (Paris: Présence Africaine, 1998); this novel highlights tenuous links between the hegemonic parameters of Frenchness and the imperatives of a multicultural society.

8. F. Abiola Irele, *The African Imagination: Literature in Africa and the Black Diaspora* (Oxford: Oxford University Press, 2001), 46–47.

9. Homi K. Bhabha, *The Location of Culture* (London: Routledge, 1994), 15.

10. See for example Richard Watts, *Packaging Post/Coloniality: The Manufacture of Literary Identity in the Francophone World* (Lanham, Md.: Lexington Books, 2005).

11. Sekai Nzenza-Shand, "Take Me Back to the Village: African Women and the Dynamics of Health and Human Rights in Tanzania and Zimbabwe," in *Engendering Human Rights: Cultural and Socio-economic Realities in Africa,* ed. Obioma Nnaemeka and Joy Ngozi Ezeilo (New York: Palgrave Macmillan, 2005), 66.

12. See Christopher L. Miller, *Blank Darkness: Africanist Discourse in French* (Chicago: University of Chicago Press, 1985).

13. The "migrant impulse" and "demystification of France" will be discussed further in chapter 6.

14. This is a real organization that is active in France. Visit http://www.esclavagemoderne.org for further information. Other groups have been active in denouncing the exploitation of immigrant workers. See "'Nous sommes les indigènes de la République!' Appel pour les Assises de l'anti-colonialisme post-colonial," http://toutesegaux.free.fr/article.php3?id_article=90; and Sylvie O'Dy, *Esclaves en France* (Paris: Albin Michel, 2001). Sylvie O'Dy is a chief editor for the magazine *L'express* and the vice-president of the Comité contre l'esclavage moderne (CCEM). See Gilbert Charles, "Cosette du tiers-monde," http://livres.lexpress.fr/critique.asp?idC=2220&idR=12&idTC=3&idG=8, and the website of the International Organization for Migration (IOM) at http://www.iom.int/. For scholarly writings on the legacy of slavery in France and its historical links to the Hexagon, see Jean-Pierre N'Diaye, *Négriers modernes: Les travailleurs noirs en France* (Paris: Présence Africaine, 1970); and Roger Botte, "Traite et esclavage, du passé au présent," Vues d'Afrique, *Esprit,* no. 317 (August–September 2005): 188–199.

15. Janet MacGaffey and Rémy Bazenguissa-Ganga have extensively explored the correlation between the shifting demands and exigencies of French immigration law and the rise of trade practices by individuals outside of legalistic frameworks. See their *Congo-Paris: Transnational Traders on the Margins of the Law* (Bloomington: Indiana University Press, 2000).

16. See http://press.coe.int/cp/2005/240a(2005).htm.

17. See http://press.coe.int/cp/2005/415a(2005).htm. For the official position of the French National Assembly, see "Rapport d'information, deposé . . . par la mission d'information commune sur les diverses formes de l'esclavage moderne," December 12, 2001, http://www.assembleenationale.fr/rap-info/i3459-11.asp.

18. Ousmane Sembene, "La Noire de . . . " in *Voltaïque* (Paris: Présence Africain, 1962), published in English as "Black Girl," trans. Ellen Conroy Kennedy, in *Under African Skies: Modern African Stories,* ed. Charles R. Larson (New York: Noonday Press, 1997), 42–54.

19. Mireille Rosello, *Postcolonial Hospitality: The Immigrant as Guest* (Stanford, Calif.: Stanford University Press, 2001), 122.

20. Fatou Diome, *La préférence nationale* (Paris: Présence Africaine, 2001), 65.

5. AFRO-PARISIANISM AND AFRICAN FEMINISMS

1. Salman Rushdie, *East, West* (London: Jonathan Cape, 1994), 141.

2. Adrienne Rich, "Notes toward a Politics of Location," in *Blood, Bread, and Poetry: Selected Prose, 1979–1985* (New York: W. W. Norton, 1986), 210–231.

3. Dominic Thomas, *Nation-Building, Propaganda, and Literature in Francophone Africa* (Bloomington: Indiana University Press, 2002), 17.

4. Obioma Nnaemeka and Joy Ngozi Ezeilo, "Context(ure)s of Human Rights —Local Realities, Global Contexts," introduction to *Engendering Human Rights: Cultural and Socio-economic Realities in Africa,* ed. Obioma Nnaemeka and Joy Ngozi Ezeilo (New York: Palgrave Macmillan, 2005), 18.

5. Alec G. Hargreaves, "Testimony, Co-authorship and Dispossession among Women of Maghrebi Origin in France," in "Textual Ownership in Francophone African Writing," ed. Alec G. Hargreaves, Nicki Hitchcott, and Dominic Thomas, special issue of *Research in African Literatures* 37, no. 1 (Spring 2006): 42–54. The quotation is from the introduction to the edited volume. See Leila with Marie-Thérèse Cuny, *Mariée de force* (Paris: Oh! Editions, 2004); Jamila Aït-Abbas, *La Fatiha: Née en France, mariée de force en Algérie* (Paris: Michel Lafon, 2003); Samira Bellil and Josée Stoquart, *Dans l'enfer des tournantes* (Paris: Denoël, 2002); and Souad with Marie-Thérèse Cuny, *Brûlée vive* (Paris: Oh! Editions, 2003). These questions are currently very much the subject of debate within the European Union itself. See also Jody K. Biehl, "The Death of a Muslim Woman: 'The Whore Lived Like a German,'" *Der Spiegel,* March 2, 2005, http://service .spiegel.de/cache/international; and Ayaan Hirsi Ali, *Insoumise* (Paris: Editions Robert Laffont, 2005), for reference to the Netherlands.

6. Bill Ashcroft, *Post-colonial Transformation* (London: Routledge, 2001), 214.

7. Laurence Porgès, "Un thème sensible: L'excision en Afrique et dans les pays d'immigration africaine," *Afrique contemporaine,* no. 196 (October–December 2000): 49.

8. I am consciously embracing Nnaemeka's insistence on the plural "feminisms": "to speak of feminism in Africa is to speak of feminisms in the plural within Africa and between Africa and other continents in recognition of the multiplicity of perspectives" and "it will be more accurate to argue not in terms of a monolith (*African feminism*) but rather in the context of a pluralism (*African feminisms*) that captures the fluidity and dynamism of the different cultural imperatives, historical forces, and localized realities conditioning women's activism/ movements in Africa—from the indigenous variants to the state-sponsored configurations in the postcolonial era." Obioma Nnaemeka, "Mapping African Feminisms," in *Readings in Gender in Africa,* ed. Andrea Cornwall (Bloomington: Indiana University Press, 2005), 31, 32.

9. Fatou Keïta, *Rebelle* (Paris: Présence Africaine, 1998).

10. Obioma Nnaemeka, "The Challenges of Border-Crossing: African Women and Transnational Feminisms," in *Female Circumcision and the Politics of Knowledge: African Women in Imperialist Discourses*, ed. Obioma Nnaemeka (Westport, Conn.: Praeger, 2005), 4.

11. Roland Robertson, "Glocalization: Time-Space and Homogeneity-Heterogeneity," in *Global Modernities*, ed. Mike Featherstone, Scott Lash, and Roland Robertson (London: Sage, 1995), 25–44. On the notion of "interpenetration," see Bill Ashcroft, *Post-colonial Transformation* (London: Routledge, 2001), 214.

12. Jean-Loup Amselle, *Branchements: Anthropologie de l'universalité des cultures* (Paris: Flammarion, 2001), 47.

13. Obioma Nnaemeka, "If Female Circumcision Did Not Exist, Western Feminism Would Invent It," in *Eye to Eye: Women Practising Development across Cultures*, ed. Susan Perry and Celeste Schenck (London: Zed Books, 2001), 174, 172. The latter point is crucial, since, as Nnaemeka says, "it is unwise for Western women to think that they are fully capable of solving their own problems, whereas 'Third World' women need their help because they are totally incapable of doing so" (183).

14. Sekai Nzenza-Shand, "Take Me Back to the Village: African Women and the Dynamics of Health and Human Rights in Tanzania and Zimbabwe," in Nnaemeka and Ezeilo, *Engendering Human Rights,* 66. Naturally, this position is quite contrary to that of Corinne Packer, who has argued that "a principal reason why the human rights discourse has not yet made that much of an impact on the practice of FC [female circumcision] is because, in many cases, it has been the first discourse of its kind to be introduced to individuals unfamiliar with the notion of human rights." Corinne Packer, "Understanding the Sociocultural and Traditional Context of Female Circumcision and the Impact of the Human Rights Discourse," in Nnaemeka and Ezeilo, *Engendering Human Rights,* 242.

15. One should not forget contributions made by African writers outside of the domain of fiction. See for example Awa Thiam, *La parole aux négresses* (Paris: Denöel, 1978).

16. Eloïse A. Brière, "Confronting the Western Gaze," in Nnaemeka, *Female Circumcision and the Politics of Knowledge,* 166–167. Additionally, Brière addresses certain problematic aspects of Anne Laure Folly's documentary *Femmes aux yeux ouverts/Women with Open Eyes* (San Francisco: California Newsreel, 1994), and Pratibha Parmar and Alice Walker's *Warrior Marks* (New York: Women Make Movies, 1993). Alternatively, Ange-Marie Hancock accords more value to the manner in which Walker "straddles a unique position as a woman of African descent from a predominantly Western cultural orientation" and of the potentiality of Walker's contribution, so long as "egalitarian multicultural coalition building addresses differential power among women." Ange-Marie Hancock, "Overcoming Willful Blindness: Building Egalitarian Multicultural Women's Coalitions," in Nnaemeka, *Female Circumcision and the Politics of Knowledge,* 252.

17. Etienne Balibar, "Is There a 'Neo-racism'?" in *Race, Nation, Class: Ambiguous Identities*, ed. Etienne Balibar and Immanuel Wallerstein (London: Verso, 1991), 21. In turn, Catherine Raissiguier has convincingly demonstrated how Islam functions in the French context: "'Islam' is used here to represent a whole set of undesirable immigrants who will not/cannot be integrated into French society. These immigrants are from sub-Saharan Africa and the Maghreb. They, like their

religion (assumed to be Islam and equated with radical fundamentalism) and their culture (reduced to a monolithic backward and dangerous whole), are invading and polluting the national space"; and "The re-articulation of existing forms of racism, xenophobia, and nationalism in France with deeply rooted patriarchal (and hetero-normative) understandings of citizenship has created a context where some immigrant women and their daughters find themselves particularly vulnerable to processes of exclusion and marginalization." Catherine Raissiguier, "Women from the Maghreb and Sub-Saharan Africa in France: Fighting for Health and Basic Human Rights," in Nnaemeka and Ezeilo, *Engendering Human Rights,* 111, 124.

18. A varied lexicon in both English and French has been deployed to describe the practice; terms include "excision" (*excision*), "female circumcision" (*circoncision féminine*), and "female genital cutting" or "female genital mutilation" (FGM; *mutilations génitales féminines,* MGF). See Porgès, "Un thème sensible," 72. Excision has been the subject of numerous studies that have addressed the reasons for the practice or tradition, its health risks, and of course its implications for human rights. I have found the following books and essays helpful in different ways to thinking and teaching on and around the question of excision: Nnaemeka and Ezeilo, *Engendering Human Rights;* Nnaemeka, *Female Circumcision and the Politics of Knowledge;* Nahid Toubia, *Female Genital Mutilation: A Call for Global Action* (New York: Women Ink, 1995); Nawal El Saadawi, *The Hidden Face of Eve: Women in the Arab World,* trans. Sherif Hetata (London: Zed Books, 1980); Evelyne Accad, *The Excised* (Colorado Springs, Colo.: Three Continents Press, 1994); Françoise Couchard, *L'excision* (Paris: Presses Universitaires de France, 2003); Martine Lefeuvre-Déotte, *L'excision en procès: Un différend culturel?* (Paris: L'Harmattan, 1997); Michel Erlich, *La femme blessée: Essai sur les mutilations sexuelles féminines* (Paris: L'Harmattan, 1986); Molly Melching, "Abandoning Female Genital Cutting," in Perry and Schenck, *Eye to Eye,* 156–170; Alice Walker and Pratibha Parmar, *Warrior Marks: Female Genital Mutilation and the Sexual Blinding of Women* (New York: Harcourt Brace, 1993); Theresa M. Klingenberg, "The Cultural Practice of Female Genital Mutilation and the Implications for Social Work," *Social Work Perspectives* 7, no. 1 (Spring 1997): 7–12; and Melissa Parker, "Rethinking Female Circumcision," *Africa: Journal of the International African Institute/Revue de l'Institut africain international* 65, no. 4 (1995): 506–523. See also the websites of the World Health Organization, UNICEF, and Amnesty International; organizations such as the Commission pour l'abolition des mutilations sexuelles (CAMS), the Comité inter-africain sur les pratiques traditionelles ayant effet sur la santé des femmes et des enfants, and the Comité national sur les pratiques néfastes à la santé de la femme et de l'enfant (COSEPRAT, Senegal); and films by Boureima Nikiema (*Ma fille ne sera pas excisée,* Burkina Faso), Cheikh Oumar Sissoko (*Finzan,* Mali), Anne-Laure Folly, (*Femmes aux yeux ouverts,* France); Jean-Pierre Zirn (*L'Afrique accusée,* France); and Ousmane Sembene (*Molaade,* Senegal).

19. Françoise Lionnet, "Feminisms and Universalisms: 'Universal Rights' and the Legal Debate around the Practice of Female Excision in France," in *Feminist Postcolonial Theory: A Reader,* ed. Reina Lewis and Sara Mills (New York: Routledge, 2003), 370.

20. Françoise Lionnet, *Postcolonial Representations: Women, Literature, Identity* (Ithaca, N.Y.: Cornell University Press, 1995), 162.

21. See for example Linda Weil-Curiel, "Female Genital Mutilation in France: A Crime Punishable by Law," in Perry and Schenck, *Eye to Eye,* 190–197. Similar debates have recently been held in the Italian Somali community, and in Germany. On the latter, see Tobe Levin, "Female Genital Mutilation: Campaigns in Germany," in Nnaemeka and Ezeilo, *Engendering Human Rights,* 285–301. The juridical position on female circumcision has been carefully summarized by Corinne Packer: "It is certainly a delicate matter when Westerners condemn the practices and beliefs of non-Western communities. To be sure, careful attention to argument is needed to maintain legitimacy . . . Despite some views to the contrary, the human rights guaranteed within the universal instruments are guaranteed to all equally. Human rights and the human dignity and life they protect are universal values that transcend all cultural rights . . . Human rights reflect minimal ethical imperatives shared by all and codified into law. On this basis, 'outsiders' may have a say on how a community treats its individuals and advocate change. The recognition that FC is a violation of the rights of women and children lends legitimacy to the concerns of the international community." Packer, "Understanding the Sociocultural and Traditional Context," 231.

22. Chima Korieh, "'Other' Bodies: Western Feminism, Race, and Representation in Female Circumcision Discourse," in Nnaemeka, *Female Circumcision and the Politics of Knowledge,* 119.

23. Sondra Hale, "Colonial Discourse and Ethnographic Residuals: The 'Female Circumcision' Debate and the Politics of Knowledge," in Nnaemeka, *Female Circumcision and the Politics of Knowledge,* 209, 213.

24. Calixthe Beyala, *Lettre d'une Africaine à ses sœurs occidentales* (Paris: Spengler, 1995), and *Lettre d'une Afro-française à ses compatriotes* (Paris: Editions Mango, 2000). The most complete studies of the work of Calixthe Beyala are Nicki Hitchcott, *Women Writers in Francophone Africa* (Oxford: Berg, 2000), and "Calixthe Beyala: Performances of Migration," unpublished ms.; Rangira Béatrice Gallimore, *L'œuvre romanesque de Calixthe Beyala: Le renouveau de l'écriture en Afrique francophone sub-saharienne* (Paris: L'Harmattan, 1997); Odile Cazenave, *Femmes rebelles: Naissance d'un nouveau roman africain au féminin* (Paris: L'Harmattan, 1996); Jean-Marie Volet, *La parole aux africaines ou l'idée de pouvoir chez les romancières d'expression française de l'Afrique sub-saharienne* (Amsterdam: Rodopi, 1993); and Pierrette Herzberger-Fofana, *Littérature féminine francophone d'Afrique noire* (Paris: L'Harmattan, 1993).

25. Jacques Chevrier, "Calixthe Beyala: Quand la littérature féminine africaine devient féministe," *Notre librairie,* no. 146 (October–December 2001): 22, 24; Calixthe Beyala, *C'est le soleil qui m'a brûlée* (Paris: Stock, 1987). Similarly, in *Femme nue, femme noire* (Paris: Albin Michel, 2003), Beyala subverts the title of Senghor's famous colonial-era ode to the beauty of blackness and the African woman in order to address the emancipation of African women in France in the postcolonial era, precisely outside of the reductive characterization of women from the positions of domestic servants and objects of male desire. In this case, the diasporic experience allows for a reformulation of relations outside of local pressure—though these are not necessarily intrinsic to sociocultural relations in France, of which she remains highly critical. In an interview with Bennetta Jules-Rosette, Beyala mentioned that "an image of a certain type of sexuality stereotypes me as a black woman writer." "Interview: Calixthe Beyala," in *Black Paris: The African Writers' Landscape,* by Bennetta Jules-Rosette (Urbana: University of Illi-

nois Press, 1998, 204. Zadie Smith has also addressed the manner in which women writers have been objectified, and these questions inform her novel *On Beauty* (London: Penguin, 2005). And the novelist Sami Tchak has devoted a work of nonfiction to some of these questions, *La sexualité féminine en Afrique* (Paris: L'Harmattan, 1999).

26. Nicki Hitchcott, "Calixthe Beyala: Black Face(s) on French TV," *Modern and Contemporary France* 12, no. 4 (November 2004): 479.

27. Useful additional references provided by Hitchcott include Antonio Perotti, "Présence et représentation de l'immigration et des minorités ethniques à la télévision française," *Migrations société* 3, no. 18 (November 1991): 39–55; Marie-France Malonga, "Présence et représentation des 'minorités visibles' à la télévision française," unpublished ms., "Ethnic Minorities: Which Place and Which Image on French Television? Televisual Representation of People of Extra European Origin," http://www.lse.ac.uk/collections/EMTEL/Minorities/papers/franceminorepres.doc, and "Fictions TV: Des Noirs dans l'ombre," *Africultures* 27 (2000): 34–37; and J. M. McGonacle, "Ethnicity and Visibility in Contemporary French Television," *French Cultural Studies* 13, no. 3 (October 2002): 281–292.

28. Bennetta Jules-Rosette, "Parisianism: The African Writers' Reality," in *Black Paris,* 188.

29. See also Obioma Nnaemeka, "African Women, Colonial Discourses, and Imperialist Interventions: Female Circumcision as Impetus," in Nnaemeka, *Female Circumcision and the Politics of Knowledge,* 27–45.

30. Obioma Nnaemeka, "Nego-feminism: Theorizing, Practicing, and Pruning Africa's Way," *Signs: Journal of Women in Culture and Society* 29, no. 2 (Winter 2004): 377–378.

31. Niara Sudarkasa, "'The Status of Women' in Indigenous African Societies," in *Feminist Frontiers: Rethinking Sex, Gender, and Society,* ed. Laurel Richardson and Verta Taylor (New York: McGraw Hill, 1989), 157.

32. Chandra Talpade Mohanty, "Under Western Eyes: Feminist Scholarship and the Colonial Discourses," in Lewis and Mills, *Feminist Postcolonial Theory,* 60.

33. Nnaemeka has demonstrated how these struggles are recuperated by Western feminists, leading to "the decontextualization and banalization of African women's lives as they take centre stage in the narratives of feminist insurgence against female circumcision." Nnaemeka, "If Female Circumcision Did Not Exist," 175.

34. See Jean-Marie Volet, "Calixthe Beyala, or the Literary Success of a Cameroonian Living in Paris," *World Literature Today* 67, no. 2 (Spring 1993): 309–314; and Nicki Hitchcott, "Calixthe Beyala and the Post-colonial Woman," in *Post-colonial Cultures in France,* ed. Alec G. Hargreaves and Mark McKinney (London: Routledge, 1997), 211–225.

35. Laye Camara, *L'enfant noir* (Paris: Plon, 1954); Cheikh Hamidou Kane, *L'aventure ambiguë* (Paris: Julliard, 1961).

36. Simone de Beauvoir, *Le deuxième sexe* (Paris: Gallimard, 1949).

37. See also Françoise Lionnet, Obioma Nnaemeka, Susan H. Perry, and Celeste Schenck, eds., "Development Cultures: New Environments, New Realities, New Strategies," special issue of *Signs: Journal of Women in Culture and Society* 29, no. 2 (Winter 2004); Aminata Traoré, *Le viol de l'imaginaire* (Paris: Actes Sud/Fayard, 2002), and *L'Afrique dans un monde sans frontières* (Arles: Actes Sud, 1999); and Perry and Schenck, *Eye to Eye.*

38. On this topic, see for example Alec G. Hargreaves, *Immigration, "Race," and Ethnicity in Contemporary France* (London: Routledge, 1995): "The desire to exercise personal control in the fields of sexuality and matrimony is indicative of important attitudinal changes among young people of immigrant origin compared with their parents . . . In most Third World countries it has been customary for parents to arrange marriages for their children. Those who migrate often expect to retain this prerogative and to use it in such a way as to ensure that succeeding generations remain faithful to the cultural heritage of their ancestors" (110).

39. Ange-Marie Hancock, "Overcoming Willful Blindness: Building Egalitarian Multicultural Coalitions," in Nnaemeka, *Female Circumcision and the Politics of Knowledge,* 252.

40. Seyla Benhabib, *The Claims of Culture: Equality and Diversity in the Global Era* (Princeton, N.J.: Princeton University Press, 2002), 100.

41. Vicky Kirby, "Out of Africa: 'Our Bodies Ourselves,'" in Nnaemeka, *Female Circumcision and the Politics of Knowledge,* 83.

42. Françoise Lionnet, "Excision," in *Encyclopedia of African Religions and Philosophy,* ed. V. Y. Mudimbe (Amsterdam: Kluwer, forthcoming).

43. See references provided by Hancock to Molara Ogundipe-Leslie, *Recreating Ourselves: African Women and Critical Transformations* (Trenton, N.J.: Africa World Press, 1994); and Philomena E. Okeke, "Postmodern Feminism and Knowledge Production: The African Context," *Africa Today* 43, no. 3 (1999): 223–234.

44. Nnaemeka has argued along similar lines: "the subtext of the barbarism of African and Muslim cultures, and the relevance (even indispensability) of the West in purging the barbaric flaw, mark another era where colonialism and missionary zeal determined what 'civilization' was, and figured out how and when to force it on people who did not ask for it. Only imperialist arrogance can imagine what Africans want, determine what they need, and devise ways to deliver the goods." "If Female Circumcision Did Not Exist," 178. Of course, this is a classic example of how people's "identity as immigrants supersedes their 'Africanness'" (Lionnet, *Postcolonial Representations,* 164) on French soil.

6. FASHION MATTERS

1. Ousmane Sembene, "Black Girl," trans. Ellen Conroy Kennedy, in *Under African Skies: Modern African Stories,* ed. Charles R. Larson (New York: Noonday Press, 1997), 49; originally published as "La Noire de . . . ," in *Voltaïque* (Paris: Présence Africaine, 1962), 162.

2. Achille Mbembe, *On the Postcolony* (Berkeley and Los Angeles: University of California Press, 2001), 131–133.

3. Albert Memmi, *The Colonizer and the Colonized,* trans. Howard Greenfield (Boston: Beacon Press, 1991; first pub. 1957), 121.

4. This "quest" has often been playfully invoked, since many *sapeurs* were housed at the Maisons des étudiants congolais (Congolese Student House) in Paris; the acronym MEC is pronounced the same way in French as *Mecque* (Mecca), thereby associating the secular quest of *La sape* with the religious pilgrimage. Given *La sape*'s masculinist qualities, it is also interesting to note that *mec* is the French word for "guy."

5. Alain Mabanckou, *Bleu-Blanc-Rouge* (Paris: Présence Africaine, 1998); and Daniel Biyaoula, *L'impasse* (Paris: Présence Africaine, 1996), and *Agonies*

(Paris: Présence Africaine, 1998). See for example Jean Allman, ed., *Fashioning Africa: Power and the Politics of Dress* (Bloomington: Indiana University Press, 2004). Shifting styles associated with *alhajis* (men who have completed the pilgrimage to Mecca) and "Hausa style" or *agbada* (a term that designates upwardly mobile entrepreneurs or politicians in Nigeria) are discussed in Misty L. Bastian, "Female '*Alhajis*' and Entrepreneurial Fashions: Flexible Identities in Southeastern Nigerian Clothing Practice," in *Clothing and Difference: Embodied Identities in Colonial and Post-colonial Africa,* ed. Hildi Hendrickson (Durham, N.C.: Duke University Press, 1996), 97–132; and Andrew M. Ivaska has shown how, "as visual signs, fashions like the miniskirt in the late sixties in Tanzania were extraordinary indices of social conflict, registering debates over national culture and 'modern development,' the construction and crises of new femininities and masculinities, generational conflicts over resources, and contests over public space in a postcolonial capital." Andrew M. Ivaska, "'Anti-mini Militants Meet Modern Misses': Urban Style, Gender, and the Politics of 'National Culture' in 1960s Dar es Salaam, Tanzania," in *Material Strategies: Dress and Gender in Historical Perspective,* ed. Barbara Burman and Carole Turbin (Malden, Mass.: Blackwell, 2003), 234.

6. Janet MacGaffey and Rémy Bazenguissa-Ganga describe one woman as a *sapeur,* when their account indicates that she is in fact a transnational trader. See Janet MacGaffey and Rémy Bazenguissa-Ganga, *Congo-Paris: Transnational Traders on the Margins of the Law* (Bloomington: Indiana University Press, 2000), 151.

7. Barbara Burman and Carole Turbin, "Material Strategies Engendered," introduction to Burman and Turbin, *Material Strategies,* 6. As Philip Holden and Richard J. Ruppel have argued, "any discussion of masculinity cannot ignore the social position and the representation of women." Introduction to *Imperial Desire: Dissident Sexualities and Colonial Literature,* ed. Philip Holden and Richard J. Ruppel (Minneapolis: University of Minnesota Press, 2003), xiii. As we saw in the previous chapter, questions of gender and identity are central in *Black France,* and a clear understanding of the cultural and social circumstances that inform gender questions as they pertain to excision, feminism, and masculinist codes in *La sape* is explored in this chapter.

8. Jean-Loup Amselle, *Branchements: Anthropologie de l'universalité des cultures* (Paris: Flammarion, 2001), 7.

9. Whereas both soldiers and students were encouraged to come to France during the colonial period, French laws have become much stricter since the 1970s, beginning with the "zero immigration" policies of 1974. Many francophone sub-Saharan African youth want to leave Africa for complex economic, political, and social reasons, but find fewer and fewer host nations willing to provide them with entry visas. The *sans-papiers* affair of 1996 was but one example of harsh governmental responses to illegal and undocumented subjects, and as "Fortress Europe" becomes more real (with the so-called global war on terror fueling debates on immigration), incidents such as that which took place in October 2005 in Bou-Izakarn in Morocco, when thousands of African migrants awaiting passage to Spain were placed in the desert in holding camps, will surely multiply.

10. MacGaffey and Bazenguissa-Ganga, *Congo-Paris,* 3.

11. Justin-Daniel Gandoulou, *Au cœur de la sape: Mœurs et aventures de Congolais à Paris* (Paris: L'Harmattan, 1989), first published as *Entre Paris et Bacongo* (Paris: Editions Centre Pompidou, 1984).

12. Elie Goldschmidt, "Migrants congolais en route vers l'Europe," *Les temps modernes,* nos. 620–621 (August–November 2002): 208–239.

13. F. Abiola Irele, *The African Imagination: Literature in Africa and the Black Diaspora* (Oxford: Oxford University Press, 2001); Christopher L. Miller, *Nationalists and Nomads: Essays on Francophone African Literature and Culture* (Chicago: University of Chicago Press, 1998); and Manthia Diawara, *In Search of Africa* (Cambridge, Mass.: Harvard University Press, 1998).

14. Lydie Moudileno, "La fiction de la migration: Manipulation des corps et des récits dans *Bleu blanc rouge* d'Alain Mabanckou," *Présence africaine,* nos. 163–164 (2001): 182.

15. Tyler Stovall, *Paris Noir: African Americans in the City of Light* (New York: Houghton Mifflin, 1996); and Bennetta Jules-Rosette, *Black Paris: The African Writers' Landscape* (Urbana: University of Illinois Press, 1998).

16. Justin-Daniel Gandoulou, *Dandies à Bacongo: Le culte de l'élégance dans la société congolaise contemporaine* (Paris: L'Harmattan, 1989), 62.

17. Eric de Rosny, "L'Afrique des migrations: Les échappées de la jeunesse de Douala," *Etudes: Revue de culture contemporaine,* no. 3965 (May 2002): 623.

18. Didier Gondola, "Dream and Drama: The Search for Elegance among Congolese Youth," *African Studies Review* 42, no. 1 (April 1999): 40–41, also published as "La Sape des *milikistes:* Théâtre de l'artifice et représentation onirique," *Cahiers d'études africaines,* no. 153.39–1 (1999): 13–47. See also Charles Tshimanga, *Jeunesse, formation et société au Congo/Kinshasa, 1890–1960* (Paris: L'Harmattan, 2001).

19. Ackbar Abbas, "On Fascination: Walter Benjamin's Images," *New German Critique* 48 (Autumn 1989): 50. See Walter Benjamin, *Charles Baudelaire: A Lyric Poet in the Era of High Capitalism,* trans. Harry Zohn (London: New Left Books, 1973).

20. In this instance, Abbas is alluding to Benjamin. For further parallels, see Domna C. Stanton, *The Aristocrat as Art: A Study of the* Honnête Homme *and the* Dandy *in Seventeenth- and Nineteenth-Century French Literature* (New York: Columbia University Press, 1980).

21. Gayatri Spivak, "Mapping the Present," interview by Meyda Yegenoglu and Mahmut Mutman, *New Formations* 45 (Winter 2001–2002): 10. See also Ngũgĩ wa Thiong'o, *Decolonizing the Mind: The Politics of Language in African Literature* (London: James Currey, 1986).

22. Tahar Ben Jelloun, *Hospitalité française: Racisme et immigration maghrébine* (Paris: Seuil, 1984), 61.

23. Ferdinand Oyono, *Une vie de boy* (Paris: Julliard, 1956).

24. Jean Comaroff, *Body of Power, Spirit of Resistance* (Chicago: University of Chicago Press, 1985), 3.

25. Phyllis M. Martin, "Dressing Well," in *Leisure and Society in Colonial Brazzaville* (Cambridge: Cambridge University Press, 1995), 155.

26. For a supranational approach to these questions in the African context, see Hildi Hendrickson's introduction to *Clothing and Difference:* "our African case studies allow us to state that the body surface has been a powerful arena in which colonial relations have been enacted and contested" (15).

27. Pierre Bourdieu, *Masculine Domination* (Stanford, Calif.: Stanford University Press, 2001), 101.

28. On the question of stereotyping and the apparent mutation and survival of these constructs into contemporary politics, see Mireille Rosello, *Declining the*

Stereotype: Ethnicity and Representation in French Cultures (Hanover, N.H.: University Press of New England, 1998); and Pascal Blanchard and Nicolas Bancel, "De l'indigène à l'immigré: Le retour du colonial," *Hommes et migrations,* no. 1207 (May–June 1997): 100–113. See also Fanon's work on Creole and French expression as identity markers for students from the Antilles in the metropole in *Peau noire, masques blancs* (Paris: Seuil, 1995; first pub. 1952).

29. Jean de Brunhoff, *Le roi Babar* (Paris: Hachette, 1988; first pub. 1939), published in English as *The Story of Babar, the Little Elephant,* trans Merle S. Haas.

30. Ariel Dorfman, *The Empire's Old Clothes* (New York: Penguin, 1996; first pub. 1983), 18.

31. Homi K. Bhabha, *The Location of Culture* (London: Routledge, 1994), 86, 88–89.

32. Leslie W. Rabine, *The Global Circulation of African Fashion* (Oxford: Berg, 2002). Many of these concerns are shared by Margaret Maynard in her recent *Dress and Globalisation* (Manchester: Manchester University Press, 2004).

33. Paul Gilroy, *Between Camps: Race, Identity, and Nationalism at the End of the Colour Line* (London: Penguin, 2000), 251.

34. Rachel Lee, "Dissenting Literacy and Transnationalism," unpublished ms.

35. Sony Labou Tansi, *La vie et demie* (Paris: Seuil, 1979); Nkem Nwankwo, *My Mercedes Is Bigger than Yours* (London: André Deutsch Limited, 1975); and Ousmane Sembene, *Xala* (Paris: Présence Africaine, 1973).

36. Simon Njami, *African gigolo* (Paris: Seghers, 1989).

37. Allrefer.com, http://reference.allrefer.com/country-guide-study/zaire/zaire 214.html.

38. Radio France internationale, "Biographie: Papa Wemba," http://www. rfimusique.com/siteFr/biographie/biographie_8839.asp. See also Michela Wrong, "The Importance of Being Elegant," in *In the Footsteps of Mr. Kurz: Living on the Brink of Disaster in Mobutu's Congo* (New York: Harper Collins, 2001), 169–191.

39. See Chéri Samba, *Chéri Samba* (Paris: Hazan, 1997); and André Magnin and Robert Storr, eds., *J'aime Chéri Samba* (Arles: Actes Sud/Fondation Cartier pour l'art contemporain, 2004).

40. Jean Allman, "Fashioning Africa: Power and the Politics of Dress," introduction to Allman, *Fashioning Africa,* 1.

41. Judith Butler's work has of course been central in achieving a broader understanding of how gender itself is constructed. See her *Gender Trouble: Feminism and the Subversion of Identity* (London: Routledge, 1990), and *Bodies That Matter* (London: Routledge, 1993).

42. Ruth P. Rubinstein, *Dress Codes: Meanings and Messages in American Culture* (Boulder, Colo.: Westview Press, 2001), 124.

43. Joanne Entwistle, *The Fashioned Body: Fashion, Dress, and Modern Social Theory* (Cambridge: Polity Press, 2000), 127.

44. Maurizia Boscagli, *Eye on the Flesh: Fashions of Masculinity in the Early Twentieth Century* (Boulder, Colo.: Westview Press, 1996), 166–167.

45. Eve Kosofsky Sedgwick, *Between Men: English Literature and Male Homosocial Desire* (New York: Columbia University Press, 1985), 1, 2–4.

46. Ange-Marie Hancock, "Overcoming Willful Blindness: Building Egalitarian Multicultural Coalitions," in *Female Circumcision and the Politics of Knowledge: African Women in Imperialist Discourses,* ed. Obioma Nnaemeka (Westport, Conn.: Praeger Publishers, 2005), 254.

47. "Popular Music, Urban Society, and Changing Gender Relations in Kinshasa, Zaire (1950–1990)," in *Gendered Encounters: Challenging Cultural Boundaries and Social Hierarchies in Africa,* ed. Maria Grosz-Ngaté and Omari H. Kokole (New York: Routledge, 1997), 65–66. See also Didier Gondola's exhaustive study of Brazzaville and Kinshasa, *Villes miroirs: Migrations et identités urbaines à Kinshasa et Brazzaville, 1930–1970* (Paris: L'Harmattan, 1996), in particular "L'espace du migrant: Les modifications de l'après-guerre," 141–164, and "Musique populaire et société urbaine: Essai d'interprétation," 193–231.

48. As Gondola points out, "the word *Mario* is now commonly used in Lingala for 'gigolo'" (Gondola, "Popular Music," 82). In fact, as Gondola shows, "in most African cities gender relations evolved in favor of women due to economic transformations. The phenomenon of *nana Benz* [a title used to designate successful African businesswomen] originating in West Africa is now common in major African cities" (Gondola, "Popular Music," 81). See also Jules-Rosette, *Black Paris,* 163–168; and her interview with Simon Njami in *Black Paris,* 196–200. Nicki Hitchcott has shown how in Calixthe Beyala's novel *Le petit prince de Belleville* (Paris: Albin Michel, 1992) "Abdou's masculinity is threatened. He has to learn how not to be a 'man' just as Beyala's female protagonists have learnt how not to be 'women.' Gender roles are destabilized and then constantly renegotiated as these modern African women become post-colonial travellers." Nicki Hitchcott, *Women Writers in Francophone Africa* (Oxford: Berg, 2000), 145.

49. Carol Beckwith and Angela Fisher, *African Ceremonies,* vol. 1 (New York: Harry N. Abrams, 1999), 68. These links are perhaps also playfully implied in the title of a volume edited by Calvin Thomas, *Straight with a Twist: Queer Theory and the Subject of Heterosexuality* (Urbana: University of Illinois Press, 2000).

50. Tim Edwards, *Men in the Mirror: Men's Fashion, Masculinity, and Consumer Society* (London: Cassell, 1997), 108.

51. Catherine S. Ramírez, "Crimes of Fashion: The Pachua and Chicana Style Politics," *Meridians: Feminism, Race, Transnationalism* 2, no. 2 (2002): 3.

52. See for example James Laver, *Taste and Fashion: From the French Revolution until Today* (London: George G. Harrap, 1937).

53. Hendrickson, introduction to *Clothing and Difference,* 15.

54. Jean Baudrillard, *Simulacra and Simulation,* trans. Sheila Faria Glaser (Ann Arbor: University of Michigan Press, 1994), 19.

55. See David Ndachi Tagne, "Koffi Olomidé: Le dandysme comme mode de vie," *Mots pluriels,* no. 10 (May 1999), http://www.arts.uwa.edu.au/MotsPluriels/MP1099dnt.html.

56. Roland Barthes, *Système de la mode* (Paris: Seuil, 1967).

57. See Alonzo Westbrook, *Hip Hoptionary: The Dictionary of Hip Hop Terminology* (New York: Broadway Books, 2002). The fascination for the "glitter" of material goods comes up in several novels considered in *Black France:* in Ousmane Socé's *Mirages de Paris* (examined in chapter 2) we hear of local African traders eagerly acquiring poor-quality French products known as *pacotille,* and in Fatou Diome's *Le ventre de l'Atlantique* (examined in chapter 7) such products are among the gifts the "man from Barbès" brings with him on his various trips back to Senegal.

58. For more information on selected design houses, see Gandoulou, *Au cœur de la sape,* 143.

59. Examples of variations of this practice are available in Merzak Allouache's 1996 film *Salut Cousin!* in which the character Mok adapts Jean de La Fontaine's

fables to the rhythms of hip-hop performance. On this, see Mireille Rosello, *Post-colonial Hospitality: The Immigrant as Guest* (Stanford, Calif.: Stanford University Press, 2001), and also the film *8 Mile,* directed by Curtis Hanson and featuring Eminem, and Gang Starr's song "Battle" on its soundtrack.

60. See Jean-Jacques Sewanou-Dabla, "Alain Mabanckou, sous le signe du binaire," *Notre librairie,* no. 146 (October–December 2001): 46–48.

61. Alain Mabanckou, "A l'écoute d'Alain Mabanckou, lauréat du Grand prix littéraire de l'Afrique noire, 1999," interview by Pierrette Herzberger-Fofana, *Mots pluriels,* no. 12 (December 1999), http://www.arts.uwa.edu.au/MotsPluriels/MP1299mabanckou.html.

62. Françoise Lionnet, "Immigration, Poster Art, and Transgressive Citizenship: France, 1968–1988." *SubStance* 76–77 (1995): 103.

63. The two phrases translated here as "public housing" are, in the original French text, "Z.U.P.," standing for "zone à urbaniser en priorité," and "H.L.M.," standing for "habitation à loyer modéré." The former designates a zone that is scheduled for priority housing development, and the latter, rent-controlled government or public housing. Mr. Rosa seems to use these terms interchangeably to designate government housing.

64. See for example Rosello, *Declining the Stereotype.*

65. Edouard Glissant, *Caribbean Discourse: Selected Essays,* trans. J. Michael Dash (Charlottesville: University of Virginia Press, 1989), 14.

66. See Glissant's essay "Reversion and Diversion," in *Caribbean Discourse,* 14–26. For Glissant, "diversion" is "formed . . . from an interweaving of negative forces that go unchallenged. . . . Diversion is the ultimate resort of a population whose domination by an Other is concealed" (19–20), while "reversion" refers to an "obsession with a single origin" (16).

67. Mabanckou is now on the faculty at the University of California–Los Angeles.

68. Alain Mabanckou, *Verre cassé* (Paris: Seuil, 2005).

69. See Laye Camara, *L'enfant noir* (Paris: Plon, 1954); Bernard Dadié, *Un nègre à Paris* (Paris: Présence Africaine, 1959); Cheikh Hamidou Kane, *L'aventure ambiguë* (Paris: Julliard, 1961); and Aminata Sow Fall, *Le revenant* (Dakar: Nouvelles Editions Africaines, 1976) for additional examples.

70. Similar structural shifts between Africa and France have become a common feature in recent texts by African authors, most noticeably in the works of Calixthe Beyala, *Le petit prince de Belleville* (Paris: Albin Michel, 1992), and *Les honneurs perdus* (Paris: Albin Michel, 1996); and Biyaoula.

71. Gondola argues that the term *parisien* is "outmoded" ("Dream and Drama," 28).

72. The fictional element and the evidentiary mode are of course constantly blurred, since the *sapeurs* do actually exist. See for example the extensive interviews conducted by Gandoulou, "Histoires de vies," in his *Au cœur de la sape,* 53–89.

7. AFRICAN YOUTH IN
THE GLOBAL ECONOMY

1. Aimé Césaire, *Notebook of a Return to My Native Land,* trans. Mireille Rosello (Newcastle upon Tyne: Bloodaxe Books, 1995), 91.

2. Fatou Diome, *Le ventre de l'Atlantique* (Paris: Editions Anne Carrière, 2003).

3. Development politics and globalization have become central issues in contemporary African fiction. See for example Sony Labou Tansi, *Le commencement des douleurs* (Paris: Seuil, 1995); and Bessora, *Petroleum* (Paris: Denöel, 2004); and Xavier Garnier's article "Derrière les 'vitrines du progrès'" in a special issue of *Notre librairie* devoted to these questions, "Littérature et développement," no. 157 (January–March, 2005): 38–43.

4. Saskia Sassen, *Globalization and Its Discontents: Essays on the New Mobility of People and Money* (New York: New Press, 1998), xxxvi.

5. Achille Mbembe, "On Private Indirect Government," in *On the Postcolony* (Berkeley and Los Angeles: University of California Press, 2001), 67.

6. Arjun Appadurai, "Grassroots Globalization and the Research Imagination," in *Globalization,* ed. Arjun Appadurai (Durham, N.C.: Duke University Press, 2001), 5.

7. Fredric Jameson, "Notes on Globalization as a Philosophical Issue," in *The Cultures of Globalization,* ed. Fredric Jameson and Masao Miyoshi (Durham, N.C.: Duke University Press, 1998), 57.

8. Xavier Garnier, "L'exil lettré de Fatou Diome," *Notre librairie,* nos. 155–156 (July–December 2004): 30.

9. Philippe Hugon, "L'Afrique dans la mondialisation," Vues d'Afrique, *Esprit,* no. 317 (August–September 2005): 158–164.

10. Mireille Rosello, *Postcolonial Hospitality: The Immigrant as Guest* (Stanford, Calif.: Stanford University Press, 2001), 1.

11. Etienne Balibar, *We, the People of Europe: Reflections on Transnational Citizenship* (Princeton, N.J.: Princeton University Press, 2004), 111. See also Sassen, "The De Facto Transnationalizing of Immigration Policy," in *Globalization,* 5–30; and Janet MacGaffey and Rémy Bazenguissa-Ganga, *Congo-Paris: Transnational Traders on the Margins of the Law* (Bloomington: Indiana University Press, 2000).

12. Eric de Rosny, "L'Afrique des migrations: Les échappées de la jeunesse de Douala," *Etudes: Revue de culture contemporaine,* no. 3965 (May 2002): 623.

13. Fatou Diome, *La préférence nationale* (Paris: Présence Africaine, 2001).

14. See for example Christopher L. Miller on Senegalese women writers in *Theories of Africans: Francophone Literature and Anthropology in Africa* (Chicago: Chicago University Press, 1990).

15. Joseph E. Stiglitz, *Globalization and Its Discontents* (New York: W. W. Norton, 2002), 5.

16. Michel Samuel, *Le prolétariat africain en France* (Paris: Françoise Maspéro, 1978).

17. See also the testimonies provided in Jean-Yves Carfantan, ed., *Rêves d'en France: Des Africains parlent; Qui les écoutent?* (Paris: L'Harmattan, 1979).

18. One should note that the man from Barbès is called "Tonton," the familiar term employed in France for "Uncle." In the African context, this position of seniority in the family hierarchy and the title itself are often accompanied by significant respect—in this case, social capital is transferred onto the figure of the returning migrant in recognition of material "success."

19. Pierre Nora, "General Introduction: Between Memory and History," in *Realms of Memory: Rethinking the French Past,* trans. Arthur Goldhammer (New York: Columbia University Press, 1996), 2.

20. Maurice Agulhon, "Paris: A Traversal from East to West," in *Realms of Memory: The Construction of the French Past,* ed. Pierre Nora, English edition

ed. Lawrence D. Kritzman, trans. Arthur Goldhammer (New York: Columbia University Press, 1998), 525.

21. Henri Loyrette, "The Eiffel Tower," in Nora, *Realms of Memory: The Construction of the French Past,* 360.

22. See Alain Mabanckou's novel *Bleu-Blanc-Rouge* (Paris: Présence Africaine, 1998).

23. Justin-Daniel Gandoulou, *Dandies à Bacongo: Le culte de l'élégance dans la société congolaise contemporaine* (Paris: L'Harmattan, 1989), 62; and Didier Gondola, "Dream and Drama: The Search for Elegance among Congolese Youth," *African Studies Review* 42, no. 1 (April 1999): 40–41. See also Justin-Daniel Gandoulou, *Au cœur de la sape: Mœurs et aventures de Congolais à Paris* (Paris: L'Harmattan, 1989); and chapter 6 of this book.

24. Others struggle and experience considerable stress entertaining the lie, and in secret welcome the opportunity to be home, dreading the imminent return into exile: "One dies alone on the journey, but one often leaves on the adventure for others" (Diome, *Le ventre,* 278). In order to protect their image and keep the myth alive, migrants end up suffering a double exile: "Identitarian pride is the dopamine of the exiled" (188).

25. It might be worth noting that Dadié's "travel writings" of the 1950s and 1960s, describing New York, Paris, and Rome, were always already marked by a profound transnationality. See *La ville où nul ne meurt* (Paris: Présence Africaine, 1968), published in English as *The City Where No One Dies,* trans. Janis A. Mayes (Washington, D.C.: Three Continents Press, 1986), and *Patron de New York* (Paris: Présence Africaine, 1969), published in English as *One Way: Bernard Dadié Observes America,* trans. Jo Patterson (Urbana: University of Illinois Press, 1994).

26. Sassen has made tremendous contributions to the understanding of economic and social globalization in other books, such as *The Global City: New York, London, Tokyo* (Princeton, N.J.: Princeton University Press, 1991). However, it might be worth noting that Paris operates as a different kind of global city than the one Sassen has in mind when she argues that "inside global cities we see a new geography of centrality and marginality. The downtowns of global cities and metropolitan business centers receive massive investments in real estate and telecommunications while low-income city areas are starved for resources" (Sassen, *Globalization,* xxvi), since the French authorities have made a concerted effort to develop the *banlieues* at the peripheries of French cities. See, for example, Alec G. Hargreaves, "Socio-economic Structures," in *Immigration, "Race," and Ethnicity in Contemporary France* (London: Routledge, 1995), 38–84.

27. See for example the work of Pap Khouma, *Io, venditore di elefanti: Una vita per forza fra Dakar, Parigi e Milano* (Milan: Garzanti, 1990).

28. The work of Emmanuel Dongala also indicates this, showing young Congolese youth to have become avid consumers of Western films and Japanese comics. See his *Les petits garçons naissent aussi des étoiles* (Paris: Le Serpent à Plumes, 1997), published in English as *Little Boys Come from the Stars,* trans. Joël Réjouis and Val Vinokurov (New York: Farrar, Straus and Giroux, 2001).

29. Rebecca Saunders, "Uncanny Presence: The Foreigner at the Gate of Globalization," *Comparative Studies of South Asia, Africa, and the Middle East* 21, nos. 1–2 (2001): 88–98.

30. In fact, GDP has more recently also been employed in revisionary analyses of imperialism. See for example Nial Ferguson, *Empire: The Rise and Demise of*

the British World Order and the Lessons for Global Power (New York: Basic Books, 2004).

31. See for example World Bank, *Sénégal: Stabilisation, ajustement partiel et stagnation,* report no. 11506-SE, 1993; and Ibrahima Thioub, Momar-Coumba Diop, and C. Boone, "Economic Liberalization in Senegal: Shifting Politics of Indigenous Business Interests," *African Studies Review* 41, no. 2 (September 1998): 63–89. On trade agreements and arrangements under the General Agreement on Tariffs and Trade, see *Trade Policy Review: Senegal,* vols. 1–2 (Geneva: General Agreement on Tariffs and Trade, 1994).

32. S. M. Ravi Kanbur, "The Theory of Structural Adjustment and Trade Policy," in Jonathan H. Frimpong-Ansah, S. M. Ravi Kanbur, and Peter Svedberg, eds., *Trade and Development in Sub-Saharan Africa* (Manchester: Manchester University Press, 1991), 188.

33. Makhtar Diouf, *L'Afrique dans la mondialisation* (Paris: L'Harmattan, 2002). See also Thandika Mkandawire and Charles C. Soludo, *Our Continent, Our Future: African Perspectives on Structural Adjustment* (Dakar: CODESRIA, 1999); and François Boye, "Economic Mechanisms in Historical Perspective," in *Senegal: Essays in Statecraft,* ed. Momar-Coumba Diop (Dakar: CODESRIA, 1993), 28–84. Many of these problems were anticipated some time ago by Immanuel Wallerstein, "Africa in a Capitalist World," in *Africa and the Modern World* (Trenton, N.J.: Africa World Press, 1986), 47–76.

34. "A Success and Challenge: AGETIP in Senegal," http://lnweb18.worldbank. org/oed/oeddoclib.nsf/DocUNIDViewForJavaSearch/88629E1A3D3B14A585256 7F5005D8F6F?opendocument.

35. See International Labour Organization, 89th session, June 2001, Report V (1), "Promotion of Cooperatives," http://www.ilo.org/public/english/standards/ relm/ilc/ilc89/rep-v-1.htm (the quotation is from chapter 1, section 1.1). See also "Structural Adjustment Failed Senegal" ("After twenty years of structural adjustment, Senegal finds itself listed by the UN as a Least Developed Country"), an interview with Demba Dembele, linked from http://www.oneworld.ca/. For an assessment of the impact of structural adjustment programs on African women, see Sekai Nzenza-Shand, "Take Me Back to the Village: African Women and the Dynamics of Health and Human Rights in Tanzania and Zimbabwe," in *Engendering Human Rights: Cultural and Socio-economic Realities in Africa,* ed. Obioma Nnaemeka and Joy Ngozi Ezeilo (New York: Palgrave Macmillan, 2005), 61–79.

36. The futility of his attempts is echoed in other texts explored in chapter 4, such as Ousmane Sembene's short story "La Noire de . . . " and Henriette Akofa and Olivier de Broca's *Une esclave moderne,* texts whose central protagonists ignored warnings concerning the perils inherent to migration. See Ousmane Sembene, "La noire de . . . ," in *Voltaïque* (Paris: Présence Africaine, 1962); and Henriette Akofa, with Olivier de Broca, *Une esclave moderne* (Paris: Michel Lafon, 2000).

37. Ousmane Sembene, *Le docker noir* (Paris: Présence Africaine, 1956).

38. See J. R. Essomba's *Le paradis du nord* (Paris: Présence Africaine, 1996) for an additional example of this concept.

39. Manthia Diawara, "Toward a Regional Imaginary in Africa," in Jameson and Miyoshi, *The Cultures of Globalization,* 111. See also Oladeji O. Ojo, "The CFA Franc Devaluation and the Future of Monetary Cooperation in Africa," in

Africa and Europe: The Changing Economic Relationship, ed. Oladeji O. Ojo (London: Zed Books, 1996), 111–128.

40. Momar-Coumba Diop, "L'aboutissement d'une si longue quête," in *Le Sénégal contemporain* (Paris: Karthala, 2002), 25.

41. Mbembe, "On Private Indirect Government," 67.

42. See Evelyne Combeau-Mari, ed., *Sports et loisirs dans les colonies, XIXe–XXe siècles* (Paris: Editions SEDES, 2004); Phyllis Martin, "Colonialism, Youth, and Football in French Equatorial Africa," *International Journal of the History of Sport* 8, no. 1 (May 1991): 56–71; and Philippe Liotard, "Sport, mémoire coloniale et enjeux identitaires," in *La fracture coloniale: La société française au prisme de l'héritage colonial,* ed. Pascal Blanchard, Nicolas Bancel, and Sandrine Lemaire (Paris: La Découverte, 2005), 227–236.

43. This is a popular catchphrase that came into use in France to designate the multiethnic make-up of immigrant youth minorities. See Alec G. Hargreaves, "The Contribution of North and Sub-Saharan African Immigrant Minorities to the Redefinition of Contemporary French Culture," in *Francophone Postcolonial Studies: A Critical Introduction,* ed. Charles Forsdick and David Murphy (London: Arnold, 2003), 145–154.

44. Salman Rushdie, *East, West* (London: Jonathan Cape, 1994), 141.

45. Mongo Beti, *Main basse sur le Cameroun: Autopsie d'une décolonisation* (Paris: François Maspéro, 1972), and *La France contre l'Afrique: Retour au Cameroun* (Paris: La Découverte, 1993).

46. Etienne Balibar has provided an incisive analysis of "the system of identity verifications (generally occurring within the territory) allowing a triage of travelers admitted to and rejected from a given national territory. For the mass of humans today, these are the most decisive borders, but they are no longer 'lines': instead they are *detention zones* and *filtering systems* such as those located in the center or on the periphery of major international airports. It is well known that these transit zones are zones of 'nonright' in which guarantees of individual freedom are suspended for a variable length of time, and where foreigners again become noncitizens and pariahs." Balibar, *We, the People of Europe,* 111.

47. For further discussion of the tenuous relationship between the French national soccer team and immigrants, see Mireille Rosello, "Football Games and National Symbols: Reconfiguration of the French-Algerian Border through Philosophy and Popular Culture," in *France and the Maghreb: Performative Encounters* (Gainesville: University Press of Florida, 2005), 25–47.

48. Achille Mbembe, "At the Edge of the World: Boundaries, Territoriality, and Sovereignty in Africa," in Appadurai, *Globalization,* 50–51.

49. Obioma Nnaemeka, "Nego-feminism: Theorizing, Practicing, and Pruning Africa's Way," *Signs: Journal of Women in Culture and Society* 29, no. 2 (Winter 2004): 370, 375.

50. Diop, "L'aboutissement d'une si longue quête," 25. On *sopi* (political transition), see Linda J. Beck, "Le clientélisme au Sénégal: Un adieu sans regrets?" in Diop, *Le Sénégal contemporain,* 529–547.

51. Donal Cruise O'Brien, "Le sens de l'Etat au Sénégal," in Diop, *Le Sénégal contemporain,* 506. See also Momar-Coumba Diop, ed., *Sénégal: Trajectoires d'un état* (Dakar: CODESRIA, 1992).

52. Ousmane Sembene, "Sembene présente *Molaade* à Cannes: Une présence africaine plus importante est possible," interview by Walfadjiri, http://www.africatime.com/togo/nouv_pana.asp?no_nouvelle=119602&no_categorie=.

CONCLUSION

1. Black de France, http://www.blackdefrance.com.

2. Richard Senghor, "Le surgissement d'une 'question noire' en France," *Esprit*, no. 321 (January 2006), 5–19.

3. See Mireille Rosello, "Representing Illegal Immigrants in France: From *clandestins* to *l'affaire des sans-papiers de Saint-Bernard*," *Journal of European Studies* 38 (1998): 137–151; Madjiguène Cissé, *Parole de sans-papiers* (Paris: La Dispute/Snédit, 1999); Ababacar Diop, *Dans la peau d'un sans-papiers* (Paris: Seuil, 1997); Georges Courade, "Des papiers et des hommes: L'épreuve des politiques d'endiguement," *Politique Africaine* 67 (October 1997): 3–30; Bernard Stasi, *Laïcité et République: Rapport de la commission de réflection sur l'application du principe de laïcité dans la République* (Paris: La Documentation Française, 2004); and Emmanuel Terray, "Headscarf Hysteria!" *New Left Review* 26 (March–April 2004): 118–127.

4. Catherine Raissiguier, "Women from the Maghreb and Sub-Saharan Africa in France: Fighting for Health and Basic Human Rights," in *Engendering Human Rights: Cultural and Socio-economic Realities in Africa*, ed. Obioma Nnaemeka and Joy Ngozi Ezeilo (New York: Palgrave Macmillan, 2005), 111.

5. See Daniel Bourmaud, "La nouvelle politique africaine de la France à l'épreuve," *Esprit*, no. 317 (August–September 2005): 17–27; François Gèze, "L'héritage colonial au cœur de la politique étrangère française," in *La fracture coloniale: La société française au prisme de l'héritage colonial*, ed. Pascal Blanchard, Nicolas Bancel, and Sandrine Lemaire (Paris: La Découverte, 2005), 155–163; Tamar Golan, "A Certain Mystery: How Can France Do Everything That It Does in Africa—and Get Away with It?" *African Affairs* 80, no. 318 (January 1981): 3–11; Jean-Paul Gourévitch, *L'Afrique, le fric, la France: L'aide, la dette, l'immigration, l'avenir; Vérités et mesonges* (Paris: Le Pré aux Clercs, 1997); François-Xavier Verschave, *La françafrique, le plus long scandale de la République* (Paris: Stock, 1998); and "L'héritage colonial: Un trou de mémoire," *Hommes et migrations*, no. 1227 (November–December 2000).

6. Patrick Weil, *La République et sa diversité: Immigration, intégration, discriminations* (Paris: Seuil, 2005), 88. See also Michel Wieviorka, *La différence: Identités culturelles; Enjeux, débats et politiques* (Paris: Editions de l'Aube, 2005), 82–102; Catherine Withol de Wenden, Olivier Roy, Alexis Tadié, Marie Mendras, Khalid Hamdani, and Antoine Garapon, "La France des émeutes," *Esprit*, no. 320 (December 2005): 22–43; and Yazid Sabeg and Yacine Sabeg, *Discrimination positive: Pourquoi la France ne peut y échapper* (Paris: Calmann-Lévy, 2004). During the month of November 2005, Begag found himself at the center of a public controversy in France over Minister of the Interior Nicolas Sarkozy's handling of civil unrest in the Paris *banlieues*.

7. Gaston Kelman, *Je suis noir et je n'aime pas le manioc* (Paris: Max Milo Editions, 2003).

8. Mireille Rosello has pointed out that "Beyala goes as far as to use the taboo word 'quotas' and she even invents a daring acronym: 'des quotas à durée déterminée—QDD' [fixed-term quotas]." Mireille Rosello, "Tactical Universalism and New Multiculturalist Claims in Postcolonial France," in *Francophone Postcolonial Studies: A Critical Introduction*, ed. Charles Forsdick and David Murphy (London: Arnold, 2003), 143.

9. See a report published one year before the tragic fires, "La lutte des mal-logés," *Cité Black,* no. 35 (July–August 2004): 1, 20; and also coverage of the fires themselves in "Le drame des mal-logés noirs," *Cité Black,* no. 58 (September 12, 2005): 4, 24; "Manifestation de soutien aux victimes du Boulevard Vincent Auriol," *Cité Black,* no. 58 (September 12, 2005): 25.

10. Calixthe Beyala, *Lettre d'une Afro-française à ses compatriotes* (Paris: Editions Mango, 2000), 52.

11. Danielle Marx-Scouras, *La France de Zebda, 1981–2004: Faire de la musique un acte politique* (Paris: Les Editions Autrement, 2005).

12. See for example Carrie Tarr, "French Cinema and Post-colonial Minorities," in *Post-colonial Cultures in France,* ed. Alec G. Hargreaves and Mark McKinney (London: Routledge, 1997), 59–83; and Jean-Pierre Chrétien, "Regards africains au cinéma," *Esprit,* no. 317 (August–September 2005): 86–92.

13. See for example Koffi Kwahulé, *Bintou* (Carnières-Morlanwelz, Belgium: Editions Lansman, 1997); and Achille Ngoye, *Ballet noir à Château-Rouge* (Paris: Gallimard, 2001); for the most comprehensive study to date of African detective fiction, see Francis Higginson, "Blood and the Canon: The Advent of Francophone African Crime Fiction," unpublished ms.

14. Nicki Hitchcott, "Calixthe Beyala: Black Face(s) on French TV," *Modern and Contemporary France* 12, no. 4 (November 2004): 480.

15. Abdourahman A. Waberi, *Transit* (Paris: Gallimard, 2003) and *Aux Etats-Unis d'Afrique* (Paris: Lattès, 2006); Sami Tchak, *Place des fêtes* (Paris: Gallimard, 2001); Bilguissa Diallo, *Diasporama* (Paris: Editions Anibwe, 2005); and Sayouba Traoré, *Loin de mon village, c'est la brousse* (La Roque d'Anthéron, France: Editions Vents d'Ailleurs, 2005).

16. See Bernard Magnier's overview of francophone sub-Saharan African literature, "Le livre africain: Un livre comme les autres," *Esprit,* no. 317 (August–September 2005): 53–60.

17. The exhibit could be visited during 2004–2005 at the Museum Kunst Palast in Düsseldorf, the Hayward Gallery in London, the Centre Georges Pompidou in Paris, and finally at the Mori Art Museum in Tokyo.

18. Simon Njami, "Identity and History," trans. Gail de Courcy-Ireland, in *Africa Remix: Contemporary Art of a Continent,* ed. Simon Njami et al. (Ostfildern-Ruit, Germany: Hatje Cantz Verlag, 2005), 55. See also the French catalogue: Simon Njami et al., eds., *Africa Remix: L'art contemporain d'un continent* (Paris: Editions du Centre Pompidou, 2005).

19. See Marie Poinsot, ed., "Les chantiers de l'histoire," special issue, *Hommes et migrations,* no. 1255 (May–June 2005), for examples of similar historiographic projects in Britain, Germany, and the Netherlands; and Lionel Arnaud, ed., *Les minorités ethniques dans l'Union européenne: Politiques, mobilisations, identités* (Paris: La Découverte, 2005).

20. Boniface Mongo-Mboussa, "Grammaire de l'immigration," in *L'indocilité: Supplément au Désir d'Afrique* (Paris: Gallimard, 2005), 115.

21. Etienne Balibar, "De la préférence nationale à l'invention de la politique," in *Droit de cité* (Paris: Presses Universitaires de France, 2002), 130. See Suzanne Gearhart, who has argued that "civility lies in the ambivalence of identification and the ambiguity of repression to the extent that they are viewed or lived not as limitations to be overcome but rather as conditions of sociability and freedom. This means that civility cannot be identified with national culture—but equally important, it cannot be simply identified with minority or immigrant culture either."

Suzanne Gearheart, "Psychoanalysis, Transnationalism, and Minority Cultures," in *Minor Transnationalism,* ed. Françoise Lionnet and Shu-mei Shih (Durham, N.C.: Duke University Press, 2005), 40.

22. Achille Mbembe, "La République et l'impensé de la 'race,'" in Blanchard, Bancel, and Lemaire, *La fracture coloniale,* 140, 153.

23. Pascal Blanchard, Eric Deroo, and Gilles Manceron, *Le Paris noir* (Paris: Editions Hazan, 2001); Pascal Blanchard, Eric Deroo, Driis El-Yazami, Pierre Fournié, and Gilles Manceron, *Le Paris arabe: Deux siècles de présence des Orientaux et des Maghrébins, 1830–2003* (Paris: La Découverte, 2003); Pascal Blanchard and Eric Deroo, *Le Paris Asie: Du rêve d'Asie à Chinatown, 1854–2004* (Paris: La Découverte, 2004; and Blanchard, Bancel, and Lemaire, *La fracture coloniale.*

24. Salman Rushdie, "The New Empire within Britain," in *Imaginary Homelands: Essays and Criticism: 1981–1991* (London: Granta, 1991), 129–138.

25. See Aimé Césaire, *Nègre je suis, nègre je resterai: Entretiens avec Françoise Vergès* (Paris: Albin Michel, 2005), 15.

Bibliography

Abbas, Ackbar. "On Fascination: Walter Benjamin's Images." *New German Critique* 48 (Autumn 1989): 43–62.

Abdelkrim-Chikh, Rabia. "Les femmes exogames: Entre la loi de Dieu et les droits de l'homme." In *L'Islam en France: Islam, état et société,* ed. Bruno Etienne, 235–254. Paris: CNRS, 1991.

Accad, Evelyne. *The Excised.* Colorado Springs, Colo.: Three Continents Press, 1994.

Ageron, Charles Robert. "L'exposition coloniale de 1931: Mythe républicain ou mythe impérial." In *La République,* vol. 1 of *Les lieux de mémoire,* ed. Pierre Nora, 493–515. Paris: Gallimard, 1997.

Agulhon, Maurice. "Paris: A Traversal from East to West." In *Realms of Memory: The Construction of the French Past,* ed. Pierre Nora, English edition ed. Lawrence D. Kritzman, trans. Arthur Goldhammer, 523–552. New York: Columbia University Press, 1998.

Aissou, A. *Les Beurs, l'école et la France.* Paris: L'Harmattan, 1987.

Aït-Abbas, Jamila. *La Fatiha: Née en France, mariée de force en Algérie.* Paris: Michel Lafon, 2003.

Akhenaton. *Métèque et Mat.* Sound recording. EMI International.

Akofa, Henriette, with Olivier de Broca. *Une esclave moderne.* Paris: Michel Lafon, 2000.

Akoua, Ekue. *Le crime de la rue des notables.* Lomé, Togo: Nouvelles Editions Africaines, 1989.

Ali, Ayaan Hirsi. *Insoumise.* Paris: Editions Robert Laffont, 2005.

Allman, Jean, ed. *Fashioning Africa: Power and the Politics of Dress.* Bloomington: Indiana University Press, 2004.

Allouache, Merzak, dir. *Salut Cousin!* Artémis Productions and Flash Back Audiovisuel, 1996.

Amar, Marianne, and Pierre Milza. *L'immigration en France au XXème siècle.* Paris: Armand Colin, 1990.

Amselle, Jean-Loup. *Affirmative Exclusion: Cultural Pluralism and the Rule of Custom in France.* Trans. Jean Marie Todd. Ithaca, N.Y.: Cornell University Press, 2003.

———. *Branchements: Anthropologie de l'universalité des cultures.* Paris: Flammarion, 2001.

———. *Logiques métisses: Anthropologie de l'identité en Afrique et ailleurs.* Paris: Payot, 1990.

———. *Mestizo Logics: Anthropology of Identity in Africa and Elsewhere.* Trans. Claudia Royal. Stanford, Calif.: Stanford University Press, 1998.

———. *Vers un multiculturalisme français: L'empire de la coutume.* Paris: Flammarion, 2001.

Amselle, Jean-Loup, and Elikia M'Bokolo, eds. *Au cœur de l'ethnie: Ethnies, tribalisme et état en Afrique.* Paris: La Découverte, 1985.

Andriamirado, Sennen. "Le Pen, quel dangers pour les Africains?" *Jeune Afrique,* no. 1426 (May 4, 1998): 13–15.

Appadurai, Arjun. "Grassroots Globalization and the Research Imagination." In *Globalization,* ed. Arjun Appadurai, 1–21. Durham, N.C.: Duke University Press, 2001.

————, ed. *Globalization*. Durham, N.C.: Duke University Press, 2001.

Appiah, Kwame Anthony. *In My Father's House: Africa in the Philosophy of Culture*. New York: Oxford University Press, 1992.

Apter, Emily. "On Translation in a Global Market." In "Translation," special issue of *Public Culture* 13, no. 1 (Winter 2001): 1–12.

Arnaud, Lionel, ed. *Les minorités ethniques dans l'Union européenne: Politiques, mobilisations, identités*. Paris: La Découverte, 2005.

Ashcroft, Bill. *Post-colonial Transformation*. London: Routledge, 2001.

Ashcroft, Bill, Gareth Griffiths, and Helen Tiffin. *The Empire Writes Back: Theory and Practice in Post-colonial Literatures*. London: Routledge, 1989.

Augé, Marc. *Oblivion*. Trans. Marjolijn de Jager. Minneapolis: University of Minnesota Press, 2004.

August, Thomas G. *The Selling of the Empire: British and French Imperialist Propaganda, 1890–1940*. Westport, Conn.: Greenwood Press, 1985.

Auslander, Leora, and Thomas C. Holt. "Sambo in Paris: Race and Racism in the Iconography of the Everyday." In *The Color of Liberty: Histories of Race in France,* ed. Sue Peabody and Tyler Stovall, 147–184. Durham, N.C.: Duke University Press, 2003.

Baker, Léandre-Alain. *Ici s'arrête le voyage*. Paris: L'Harmattan, 1989.

Bakhtin, Mikhail. *Dialogism*. Trans. Caryl Emerson and Michael Holquist. Austin: University of Texas Press, 1981.

Baldwin, Kate A. *Beyond the Color Line and the Iron Curtain: Reading Encounters between Black and Red, 1922–1963*. Durham, N.C.: Duke University Press, 2002.

Balibar, Etienne. "De la préférence nationale à l'invention de la politique." In *Droit de cité,* 89–132. Paris: Presses Universitaires de France, 2002.

————. "Is There a 'Neo-racism'?" In *Race, Nation, Class: Ambiguous Identities,* ed. Etienne Balibar and Immanuel Wallerstein, 17–28. London: Verso, 1991.

————. "Racism and Crisis." In *Race, Nation, Class: Ambiguous Identities,* ed. Etienne Balibar and Immanuel Wallerstein, 217–227. London: Verso, 1991.

————. "Racism and Nationalism." In *Race, Nation, Class: Ambiguous Identities,* ed. Etienne Balibar and Immanuel Wallerstein, 37–67. London: Verso, 1991.

————. *We, the People of Europe: Reflections on Transnational Citizenship*. Princeton, N.J.: Princeton University Press, 2004.

Balibar, Etienne, Monique Chemillier-Gendreau, Jacqueline Costa-Lascoux, and Emmanuel Terray. *Sans-papiers: L'archaïsme fatal*. Paris: La Découverte et Syros, 1999.

Bamba, Drissa. *Moi, Drissa, immigré africain: L'identité africaine aujourd'hui*. Paris: L'Harmattan, 2002.

Bancel, Nicolas, Pascal Blanchard, Gilles Boëtsch, Eric Deroo, and Sandrine Lemaire, eds. *Zoos humains: De la Vénus hottentote aux reality shows*. Paris: La Découverte, 2002.

Bancel, Nicolas, Pascal Blanchard, and Françoise Vergès. *La République coloniale: Essai sur une utopie*. Paris: Albin Michel, 2003.

Barber, Benjamin R. *Jihad versus McWorld: How Globalism and Tribalism Are Reshaping the World*. New York: Crown, 1995.

Bardolph, Jacqueline. *Etudes postcoloniales et littérature*. Paris: Champion, 2001.

Barreau, J.-C. *De l'immigration en général et de la nation française en particulier*. Paris: Le Pré aux Clercs, 1992.

Barthes, Roland. *Le plaisir du texte*. Paris: Seuil, 1973.

———. *Système de la mode*. Paris: Seuil, 1967.

Bastian, Misty L. "Female '*Alhajis*' and Entrepreneurial Fashions: Flexible Identities in Southeastern Nigerian Clothing Practice." In *Clothing and Difference: Embodied Identities in Colonial and Post-colonial Africa*, ed. Hildi Hendrickson, 97–132. Durham, N.C.: Duke University Press, 1996.

Baucom, Ian. *Out of Place: Englishness, Empire, and the Locations of Identity*. Princeton, N.J.: Princeton University Press, 1999.

Baudrillard, Jean. *Screened Out*. Trans. Chris Turner. London: Verso, 2002.

———. *Simulacra and Simulation*. Trans. Sheila Faria Glaser. Ann Arbor: University of Michigan Press, 1994.

Bayart, Jean-François. *Le gouvernement du monde*. Paris: Fayart, 2004.

———. "The 'Social Capital' of the Felonious State." In *The Criminalization of the State in Africa*, ed. Jean-François Bayart, Stephen Ellis, and Béatrice Hibou, 32–48. Oxford: James Currey; Bloomington: Indiana University Press, 1999.

Beauvoir, Simone de. *Le deuxième sexe*. Paris: Gallimard, 1949.

Beck, Linda J. "Le clientélisme au Sénégal: Un adieu sans regrets?" In *Le Sénégal contemporain*, ed. Momar-Coumba Diop, 529–547. Paris: Karthala, 2002.

Beckwith, Carol, and Angela Fisher. *African Ceremonies*. Vol. 1. New York: Harry N. Abrams, 1999.

Begag, Azouz. *Béni ou le paradis privé*. Paris: Seuil, 1986.

———. *Le gone du Châaba*. Paris: Seuil, 1986.

Behdad, Ali. *Belated Travelers: Orientalism in the Age of Colonial Dissolution*. Durham, N.C.: Duke University Press, 1994.

———. *A Forgetful Nation: On Immigration and Cultural Identity in the United States*. Durham, N.C.: Duke University Press, 2005.

———. "Postcolonial Theory and the Predicament of 'Minor Literature.'" In *Minor Transnationalism*, ed. Françoise Lionnet and Shu-mei Shih, 223–236. Durham, N.C.: Duke University Press, 2005.

Belghoul, Farida. *Georgette!* Paris: IM'média, 1994. First published 1986.

Bellil, Samira, and Josée Stoquart, *Dans l'enfer des tournantes*. Paris: Denoël, 2002.

Ben Jelloun, Tahar. *Hospitalité française: Racisme et immigration maghrébine*. Paris: Seuil, 1984.

———. *Racism Explained to My Daughter*. Trans. Carol Volk. New York: New Press, 1999.

———. *Le racisme expliqué à ma fille*. Paris: Seuil, 1990.

Benhabib, Seyla. *The Claims of Culture: Equality and Diversity in the Global Era*. Princeton, N.J.: Princeton University Press, 2002.

Beniamino, Michel. *La francophonie littéraire: Essai pour une théorie*. Paris: L'Harmattan, 1999.

Benjamin, Walter. *Charles Baudelaire: A Lyric Poet in the Era of High Capitalism*. Trans. Harry Zohn. London: New Left Books, 1973.

Bénot, Yves. *Les parlementaires africains à Paris, 1914–1958*. Paris: Editions Chaka, 1989.

Béranger, Diane. "Les chiffres de l'immigration en France." *Regards sur l'actualité*, no. 299 (March 2004): 6–9.

Bergougniou, Jean-Michel, Rémi Clignet, and Philippe David. *"Villages noirs" et visiteurs africains et malgaches en France et en Europe, 1870–1940*. Paris: Karthala, 2001.

Bernabé, Jean, Patrick Chamoiseau, and Raphaël Confiant. *Eloge de la créolité.* Paris: Gallimard, 1989.

Bertoncello, Brigitte. *Colporteurs africains à Marseille: Un siècle d'aventures.* Paris: Autrement, 2004.

Bertoncello, Brigitte, and Sylvie Bredeloup, eds. "Marseille, carrefour d'Afrique." *Hommes et migrations,* no. 1224 (March–April 2000).

Bessora. *Petroleum.* Paris: Denöel, 2004.

Beti, Mongo. *La France contre l'Afrique: Retour au Cameroun.* Paris: La Découverte, 1993.

———. *Main basse sur le Cameroun: Autopsie d'une décolonisation.* Paris: François Maspéro, 1972.

———. *Mission terminée.* Paris: Buchet-Chastel, 1957.

———. *Le pauvre Christ de Bomba.* Paris: Robert Laffont, 1956.

———. *Le roi miraculé.* Paris: Buchet-Chastel, 1958.

———, as Eza Boto. *Ville cruelle.* Paris: Editions Africaines, 1954.

Beyala, Calixthe. *Assèze l'Africaine.* Paris: Albin Michel, 1994.

———. *C'est le soleil qui m'a brûlée.* Paris: Stock, 1987.

———. *Femme nue, femme noire.* Paris: Albin Michel, 2003.

———. *Les honneurs perdus.* Paris: Albin Michel, 1996.

———. *Maman a un amant.* Paris: Albin Michel, 1993.

———. *Lettre d'une Africaine a ses sœurs occidentales.* Paris: Spengler, 1995.

———. *Lettre d'une Afro-française à ses compatriotes.* Paris: Editions Mango, 2000.

———. *Le petit prince de Belleville.* Paris: Albin Michel, 1992.

Beye, Ben Diogaye, dir. *Les princes noirs de Saint-Germain-des-Prés.* 1975.

Bhabha, Homi K. *The Location of Culture.* London: Routledge, 1994.

Billon, Yves, dir. *Paris Black Night.* Zarafa Films, L'Harmattan. 1991.

Biyaoula, Daniel. *Agonies.* Paris: Présence Africaine, 1998.

———. *L'impasse.* Paris: Présence Africaine, 1996.

Bjornson, Richard. *The African Quest for Freedom and Identity: Cameroonian Writing and the National Experience.* Bloomington: Indiana University Press, 1991.

Blair, Dorothy S. *African Literature in French.* Cambridge: Cambridge University Press, 1976.

Blanchard, Pascal, and Nicolas Bancel. *De l'indigène à l'immigré.* Paris: Gallimard, 1998.

———. "De l'indigène à l'immigré: Le retour du colonial." *Hommes et migrations,* no. 1207 (May–June 1997): 100–113.

———. "Les origines républicaines de la fracture coloniale." In *La fracture coloniale: La société française au prisme de l'héritage colonial,* ed. Pascal Blanchard, Nicolas Bancel, and Sandrine Lemaire, 33–43. Paris: La Découverte, 2005.

Blanchard, Pascal, Nicolas Bancel, and Sandrine Lemaire, eds. *La fracture coloniale: La société française au prisme de l'héritage colonial.* Paris: La Découverte, 2005.

———. "La fracture coloniale: Une crise française." In *La fracture coloniale: La société française au prisme de l'héritage colonial,* ed. Pascal Blanchard, Nicolas Bancel, and Sandrine Lemaire, 9–30. Paris: La Découverte, 2005.

Blanchard, Pascal, and Gilles Boëtsch. *Marseille porte sud: Un siècle d'histoire coloniale et d'immigration.* Paris: La Découverte, 2005.

Blanchard, Pascal, and Eric Deroo. "Contrôler: Paris, capitale coloniale." In *Culture impériale: Les colonies au cœur de la République, 1931–1961,* ed. Pascal Blanchard and Sandrine Lemaire, 107–122. Paris: Editions Autrement, 2004.

———. *Le Paris Asie: Du rêve d'Asie à Chinatown, 1854–2004.* Paris: La Découverte, 2004.

Blanchard, Pascal, Eric Deroo, and Gilles Manceron, *Le Paris noir.* Paris: Editions Hazan, 2001.

Blanchard, Pascal, Eric Deroo, Driis El-Yazami, Pierre Fournié, and Gilles Manceron. *Le Paris arabe: Deux siècles de présence des Orientaux et des Maghrébins, 1830–2003.* Paris: La Découverte, 2003.

Blanchard, Pascal, and Sandrine Lemaire. "Les colonies au cœur de la République." In *Culture impériale: Les colonies au cœur de la République, 1931–1961,* ed. Pascal Blanchard and Sandrine Lemaire, 5–32. Paris: Les Editions Autrement, 2004.

———, eds. *Culture impériale: Les colonies au cœur de la République, 1931–1961.* Paris: Les Editions Autrement, 2004.

Blatt, David. "Immigrant Politics in a Republican Nation." In *Post-colonial Cultures in France,* ed. Alec G. Hargreaves and Mark McKinney, 40–51. London: Routledge, 1997.

Bokiba, André-Patient. *Ecriture et identité dans la littérature africaine.* Paris: L'Harmattan, 1998.

———. ed. *Le siècle Senghor.* Paris: L'Harmattan, 2001.

Boscagli, Maurizia. *Eye on the Flesh: Fashions of Masculinity in the Early Twentieth Century.* Boulder, Colo.: Westview Press, 1996.

Boto, Eza. See Beti, Mongo.

Botte, Roger. "Le spectre de l'esclavage." *Les temps modernes,* nos. 620–621 (August–November 2002): 145–164.

———. "Traite et esclavage, du passé au présent." Vues d'Afrique. *Esprit,* no. 317 (August–September 2005): 188–199.

Boukoum, Saïdou. *Chaîne.* Paris: Editions Denöel, 1974.

Bourdieu, Pierre. *La distinction: Critique sociale du jugement.* Paris: Editions de Minuit, 1979.

———. *Masculine Domination.* Stanford, Calif.: Stanford University Press, 2001.

Bourmaud, Daniel. "La nouvelle politique africaine de la France à l'épreuve." *Esprit,* no. 317 (August–September 2005): 17–27.

Boye, François. "Economic Mechanisms in Historical Perspective." In *Senegal: Essays in Statecraft,* ed. Momar-Coumba Diop, 28–84. Dakar: CODESRIA, 1993.

Brière, Eloise A. "Confronting the Western Gaze." In *Female Circumcision and the Politics of Knowledge: African Women in Imperialist Discourses,* ed. Obioma Nnaemeka, 165–180. Westport, Conn.: Praeger Publishers, 2005.

———. *Le roman camerounais et ses discours.* Ivry: Editions Nouvelles du Sud, 1993.

Brunhoff, Jean de. *Le roi Babar.* Paris: Hachette, 1988. First published 1939.

Brunschwig, Henri. *L'avènement de l'Afrique noire du XIXe siècle à nos jours.* Paris: Armand Colin, 1963.

———. *Mythes et réalités de l'impérialisme colonial français, 1871–1914.* Paris: Armand Colin, 1960.

———. *Noirs et Blancs dans l'Afrique noire française: Ou comment le colonisé devient colonisateur, 1870–1914.* Paris: Flammarion, 1983.

Burman, Barbara, and Carole Turbin. "Material Strategies Engendered." Introduction to *Material Strategies: Dress and Gender in Historical Perspective,* ed. Barbara Burman and Carole Turbin, 1–11. Malden, Mass.: Blackwell, 2003.

———, eds. *Material Strategies: Dress and Gender in Historical Perspective.* Malden, Mass.: Blackwell, 2003.

Butler, Judith. *Bodies That Matter.* London: Routledge, 1993.

———. *Gender Trouble: Feminism and the Subversion of Identity.* London: Routledge, 1990.

Cabaculu, Mwamba. "L'épistolarité dans l'œuvre de Bernard B. Dadié: Le cas de *Un nègre à Paris.*" In *Bernard Bilin Dadié: Conscience critique de son temps,* ed. Valy Sidibé and Bruno Gnaoulé-Oupoh, 185–190. Abidjan, Ivory Coast: Centre d'Edition et de Diffusion Africaines, 1999.

Campbell, James. *Exiled in Paris: Richard Wright, James Baldwin, Samuel Beckett, and Others on the Left Bank.* Berkeley and Los Angeles: University of California Press, 2003.

Camara, Laye. *The African Child.* Trans. James Kirkup and Ernest Jones. New York: Noonday Press, 1954.

———. *The Dark Child.* Trans. James Kirkup. London: Collins, 1955.

———. *Dramouss.* Paris: Plon, 1966.

———. *A Dream of Africa.* Trans. James Kirkup. Glasgow: William Collins Sons, 1968.

———. *L'enfant noir.* Paris, Plon, 1954.

Camus, Albert. *L'étranger.* Paris: Gallimard, 1942.

Cannon, Steve. "Paname City Rapping: B-Boys in the Banlieues and Beyond." In *Post-colonial Cultures in France,* ed. Alec G. Hargreaves and Mark McKinney, 150–166. London: Routledge, 1997.

Casanova, Pascale. *The World Republic of Letters.* Trans. M. B. DeBevoise. Cambridge, Mass.: Harvard University Press, 2004.

Cazenave, Odile. *Afrique sur Seine: A New Generation of African Writers in Paris.* Lanham, Md.: Lexington Books, 2005.

———. *Afrique sur Seine: Une nouvelle génération de romanciers africains à Paris.* Paris: L'Harmattan, 2003.

———. *Femmes rebelles: Naissance d'un nouveau roman africain au féminin.* Paris: L'Harmattan, 1996.

Césaire, Aimé. *Cahier d'un retour au pays natal.* Paris: Présence Africaine, 1939.

———. *Discours sur le colonialisme.* Paris: Présence Africaine, 1955.

———. *Nègre je suis, nègre je resterai: Entretiens avec Françoise Vergès.* Paris: Albin Michel, 2005.

Cévaër, Françoise. *Ces écrivains d'Afrique noire.* Ivry-sur-Seine: Nouvelles du Sud, 1998.

Chanda, Tirthandar. "Les écrivains noirs d'Angleterre: Naissance d'une tradition." *Notre librairie,* nos. 155–156 (July–December 2004): 88–95.

Charpy, Manuel, and Souley Hassane. *Lettres d'émigrés: Africains d'ici et d'ailleurs.* Paris: Editions Nicolas, 2004.

Chemla, Yves. "Dire l'ailleurs." *Notre librairie,* nos. 155–156 (July–December 2004): 48–53.

Chevrier, Jacques. "Afrique(s)-sur-Seine: Autour de la notion de 'migritude.'" *Notre librairie,* nos. 155–156 (July–December 2004): 96–100.

———. "Calixthe Beyala: Quand la littérature féminine africaine devient féministe." *Notre librairie,* no. 146 (October–December 2001): 22–24.

————. "Lecture d'un Nègre à Paris: Où il est prouvé qu'on peut être Parisien et raisonner comme un Agni." *L'Afrique littéraire et artistique* 85 (1989): 42–50.

————. "La littérature francophone et ses héros." *Esprit,* no. 317 (August–September 2005): 70–85.

————. *Littérature nègre.* Paris: Armand Colin, 1984.

Chonez, Claudine. "De *L'enfant noir* à la libération de l'homme." *Présence Africaine,* no. 3 (1948): 515–518.

Chow, Rey. *The Protestant Ethnic and the Spirit of Capitalism.* New York: Columbia University Press, 2002.

Chrétien, Jean-Pierre, "L'Afrique face aux défis du monde." *Esprit,* no. 317 (August–September 2005): 8–16.

————. "Regards africains au cinéma." *Esprit,* no. 317 (August–September 2005): 86–92.

Cissé, Madjiguène. *Parole de sans-papiers.* Paris: La Dispute/Snédit, 1999.

Cité black. "Le drame des mal-logés noirs." No. 58 (September 12, 2005): 4, 24.

————. "La lutte des mal-logés." No. 35 (July–August 2004): 1, 20.

————. "Manifestation de soutien aux victimes du Boulevard Vincent Auriol." No. 58 (September 12, 2005): 25.

Clifford, James. "Museums as Contact Zones." In *Routes: Travel and Translation in the Late Twentieth Century,* 188–219. Cambridge, Mass.: Harvard University Press, 1997.

————. *Routes: Travel and Translation in the Late Twentieth Century.* Cambridge, Mass.: Harvard University Press, 1997.

Coetzee, J. M. *Disgrace.* London: Viking, 1999.

Cohen, William B. *The French Encounter with Africans: White Response to Blacks, 1530–1880.* Bloomington: Indiana University Press, 1980.

Comaroff, Jean. *Body of Power, Spirit of Resistance.* Chicago: University of Chicago Press, 1985.

Combeau-Mari, Evelyne, ed. *Sports et loisirs dans les colonies, XIXe–XXe siècles.* Paris: Editions SEDES, 2004.

Conklin, Alice L. *A Mission to Civilize: The Republican Ideal of Empire in France and West Africa, 1895–1930.* Stanford, Calif.: Stanford University Press, 1997.

————. "Redefining 'Frenchness': Citizenship, Race Regeneration, and Imperial Motherhood in France and West Africa, 1914–40." In *Domesticating the Empire: Race, Gender, and Family Life in French and Dutch Colonialism,* ed. Julia Clancy-Smith and Frances Gourda, 65–83. Charlottesville: University Press of Virginia, 1998.

Cooper, Wayne F. *Claude McKay: Rebel Sojourner in the Harlem Renaissance; A Biography.* Baton Rouge: Louisiana State University Press, 1987.

Coquery-Vidrovitch, Catherine. *L'Afrique et les Africains au XIXe siècle.* Paris: Armand Collin, 1999.

————. "Colonisation, coopération, partenariat: Les différentes étapes (1950–2000)." In *Etudiants africains en France, 1951–2001,* ed. Michel Sot, 29–48. Paris: Karthala, 2002.

Coryell, Schofield. "Itinéraire d'un écrivain engagé: Richard Wright le subversif." *Le monde diplomatique,* August 2003.

Couao-Zotti, Florent, et al. *L'Europe, vues d'Afrique.* Bamako: Figuier; Paris: Cavalier Bleu, 2004.

Couchard, Françoise. *L'excision.* Paris: Presses Universitaires de France, 2003.

Dadié, Bernard. *An African in Paris.* Trans. Karen C. Hatch. Urbana: University of Illinois Press, 1994.

———. *The City Where No One Dies.* Trans. Janis A. Mayes. Washington, D.C.: Three Continents Press, 1986.

———. *Climbié.* Paris: Seghers, 1956.

———. *Climbié.* Trans. Karen C. Chapman. London: Heinemann, 1971.

———. Interview by Bennetta Jules-Rosette. In *Black Paris: The African Writers' Landscape,* by Bennetta Jules-Rosette, 140–146. Urbana: University of Illinois Press, 1998.

———. *Un nègre à Paris.* Paris: Présence Africaine, 1959.

———. *One Way: Bernard Dadié Observes America.* Trans. Jo Patterson. Urbana: University of Illinois Press, 1994.

———. *Patron de New York.* Paris: Présence Africaine, 1969.

———. *La ville où nul ne meurt.* Paris: Présence Africaine, 1968.

d'Almeida-Topor, Hélène. "Le nombre d'étudiants africains en France (1951–2000)." In *Etudiants africains en France, 1951–2001,* ed. Michel Sot, 109–115. Paris: Karthala, 2002.

Daly, Mary. *Gyn/Ecology: The Metaethics of Radical Feminism.* Boston: Beacon Press, 1978.

Delavignette, Robert. "Faidherbe." In *Les politiques d'expansion impérialiste,* Colonies et empires, 1. sér., Etudes coloniales 5, 75–92. Paris: Presses Universitaires de France, 1949.

Deltombe, Thomas, and Mathieu Rigouste. "L'ennemi intérieur: La construction médiatique de la figure de l''Arabe.'" In *La fracture coloniale: La société française au prisme de l'héritage colonial,* ed. Pascal Blanchard, Nicolas Bancel, and Sandrine Lemaire, 191–198. Paris: La Découverte, 2005.

Derive, Jean. "*Un nègre à Paris:* Contexte littéraire et idéologique." In *Bernard Dadié: Hommages et études,* 189–209. Ivry-sur-Seine: Nouvelles du Sud, 1992.

Dewitte, Philippe. "Un centre de l'histoire de l'immigration: Pourquoi et comment?" *Hommes et migrations,* no. 1247 (January–February 2004): 6–16.

———. *Deux siècles d'immigration en France.* Paris: La Documentation Française, 2003.

———, ed. "Diasporas caribéennes." *Hommes et migrations,* no. 1237 (May–June 2002).

———. *Les mouvements nègres en France, 1919–1939.* Paris: L'Harmattan, 1985.

———. "Vers la création d'un 'musée' de l'immigration?" *Hommes et migrations,* no. 1238 (July–August 2002).

———, ed. Special dossier. "Vers un lieu de mémoire de l'immigration." *Hommes et Migrations,* no. 1247 (January–February 2004): 1–66.

Diagne, Ahmadou Mapaté. *Les trois volontés de Malic.* Paris: Larose, 1920.

Diakhaté, Lamine. Review of *Le docker noir. Présence africaine,* no. 13 (1957): 153–154.

Diallo, Bakary. *Force-Bonté.* Paris: Rieder, 1926.

Diallo, Bilguissa. *Diasporama.* Paris: Editions Anibwe, 2005.

Diawara, Manthia. *In Search of Africa.* Cambridge, Mass.: Harvard University Press, 1998.

———. "Toward a Regional Imaginary in Africa." In *The Cultures of Globalization,* ed. Fredric Jameson and Masao Miyoshi, 103–124. Durham, N.C.: Duke University Press, 1998.

————. *We Won't Budge: An African Exile in the World.* New York: Basic Civitas Books, 2003.

Diome, Fatou. *La préférence nationale.* Paris: Présence Africaine, 2001.

————. *Le ventre de l'Atlantique.* Paris: Editions Anne Carrière, 2003.

Diop, Ababacar. *Dans la peau d'un sans-papiers.* Paris: Seuil, 1997.

Diop, Cheikh Anta. *L'Afrique noire précoloniale: Etude comparée des systèmes politiques et sociaux de l'Europe et de l'Afrique noire, de l'antiquité à la formation des états modernes.* Paris: Présence Africaine, 1960.

————. *Antériorité des civilisations nègres: Mythe ou vérité historique?* Paris: Présence Africaine, 1967.

————. *Civilisation ou barbarie.* Paris: Présence Africaine, 1981.

————. *Nations nègres et culture: De l'antiquité négro-égyptienne aux problèmes culturels de l'Afrique noire aujourd'hui.* Paris: Présence Africaine, 1954.

————. *L'unité culturelle de l'Afrique noire.* Paris: Présence Africaine, 1960.

Diop, Momar-Coumba. "L'aboutissement d'une si longue quête." In *Le Sénégal contemporain,* ed. Momar-Coumba Diop, 11–34. Paris: Karthala, 2002.

————, ed. *Le Sénégal contemporain.* Paris: Karthala, 2002.

————, ed. *Sénégal: Trajectoires d'un état.* Dakar: CODESRIA, 1992.

Diop, Papa Samba. "Le pays d'origine comme espace de creation littéraire." *Notre librairie,* nos. 155–156 (July–December 2004): 54–61.

Diouf, Makhtar. *L'Afrique dans la mondialisation.* Paris: L'Harmattan, 2002.

Diouf, Mamadou. "Africain, citoyen du monde du XXIe siècle." In *Etudiants africains en France, 1951–2001,* ed. Michel Sot, 169–173. Paris: Karthala, 2002.

————. "Postface." In *Les intellectuels africains en France,* by Abdoulaye Gueye, 241–246. Paris: L'Harmattan, 2001.

————. *Sénégal: Ethnies et nations.* Paris: L'Harmattan, 1994.

Dongala, Emmanuel. *Jazz et vin de palme.* Paris: Le Serpent à Plumes, 1982.

————. *Little Boys Come from the Stars.* Trans. Joël Réjouis and Val Vinokurov. New York: Farrar, Straus and Giroux, 2001.

————. *Les petits garçons naissent aussi des étoiles.* Paris: Le Serpent à Plumes, 1997.

Dorfman, Ariel. *The Empire's Old Clothes.* New York: Penguin, 1996. First published 1983.

Doukouré, Cheik, dir. *Paris selon Moussa.* 2003.

Dozon, Jean-Pierre. *Frères et sujets: La France et l'Afrique en perspective.* Paris: Flammarion, 2003.

Dufoix, Stéphane. *Les diasporas.* Paris: Presses Universitaires de France, 2003.

Durand, Jean-François, ed. *Regards sur les littératures coloniales: Afrique francophone; Découvertes.* Paris: L'Harmattan, 1999.

Echenberg, Myron. *Colonial Conscripts: The Tirailleurs Sénégalais in French West Africa, 1857–1960.* Portsmouth, N.H.: Heinemann, 1991.

Edwards, Brent Hayes. *The Practice of Diaspora: Literature, Translation, and the Rise of Black Internationalism.* Cambridge, Mass.: Harvard University Press, 2003.

Edwards, Tim. *Men in the Mirror: Men's Fashion, Masculinity, and Consumer Society.* London: Cassell, 1997.

Effa, Gaston-Paul. *Tout ce bleu.* Paris: Grasset, 1996.

————. *Voici le dernier jour du monde.* Monaco: Editions du Rocher, 2005.

8 Mile. Directed by Curtis Hanson. Universal Studios, 2002.

Ekué, Lauren. *Icône urbaine.* Paris: Editions Anibwe, 2005.

Entwistle, Joanne. *The Fashioned Body: Fashion, Dress, and Modern Social Theory.* Cambridge: Polity Press, 2000.

Equateur. "Sony Labou Tansi." *Equateur,* no. 1 (October–November 1986).

Erlich, Michel. *La femme blessée: Essai sur les mutilations sexuelles féminines.* Paris: L'Harmattan, 1986.

Essomba, J. R. *Le paradis du nord.* Paris: Présence Africaine, 1996.

Etienne, Bruno. *La France et l'Islam.* Paris: Hachette, 1989.

Etoké, Natalie. *Un amour sans papiers.* Paris: Editions Cultures Croisées, 1999.

Ezra, Elizabeth. *The Colonial Unconscious: Race and Culture in Interwar France.* Ithaca, N.Y.: Cornell University Press, 2000.

Fabre, Michel. *From Harlem to Paris: Black American Writers in France, 1840–1980.* Urbana: University of Illinois Press, 1991.

———. *La rive noire: Les écrivains noirs américains à Paris, 1830–1995.* Marseille: André Dimanche, 1999.

Fall, Mar. *Des Africains noirs en France: Des tirailleurs sénégalais aux Blacks.* Paris: L'Harmattan, 1986.

Fanon, Frantz. *Black Skin, White Masks.* Trans. Charles Lam Markmann. New York: Grove Press, 1967.

———. *Peau noire, masques blancs.* Paris: Seuil, 1995. First published 1952.

———. *Toward the African Revolution.* Trans. Haakon Chevalier. New York: Grove Press, 1967.

———. *The Wretched of the Earth.* Trans. Constance Farrington. New York: Grove Press, 1963.

Fanoudh-Siefer, Léon. *Le mythe du nègre et de l'Afrique noire dans la littérature française, de 1800 à la 2e guerre mondiale.* Paris: Klincksieck, 1968.

Farah, Nurrudin. *Yesterday, Tomorrow: Voices from the Somali Diaspora.* New York: Cassell, 2000.

Farine, Philippe, ed. "Colonisation, immigration: Le complexe impérial." Special issue of *Migrations société* 14, nos. 81–82 (May–August 1982).

Faure, Michaël. *Voyage au pays de la double peine.* Paris: L'Esprit Frappeur, 2000.

Favell, Adrian. *Philosophies of Integration: Immigration and the Idea of Citizenship in France and Britain.* Basingstoke: Palgrave, 1998.

Federal Bureau of Investigation. File on Richard Nathaniel Wright. http://foia.fbi.gov/foiaindex/rnwright.htm.

Ferguson, Nial. *Empire: The Rise and Demise of the British World Order and the Lessons for Global Power.* New York: Basic Books, 2004.

Ferro, Marc. *Histoire des colonisations, des conquêtes aux indépendances, XIIIème–XXème siècle.* Paris: Seuil, 1994.

Feuser, Wilfried F. "*Native Son* and Sembene Ousmane's *Le docker noir.*" *Komparatistische Hefte* 14 (1986): 103–116.

———. "Richard Wright's *Native Son* and Sembene Ousmane's *Le docker noir.*" In *Essays in Comparative African Literature,* ed. Wilfried F. Feuser and I. N. C. Aniebo, 252–267. Lagos, Nigeria: Centre for Black and African Arts and Civilization, 2001.

Folly, Anne Laure, dir. *Femmes aux yeux ouverts/Women with Open Eyes.* San Francisco: California Newsreel, 1994.

Fonkoua, Romuald. "Diasporas littéraires: Quels statuts? Ecrire après les dictatures." *Notre librairie,* nos. 155–156 (July–December 2004): 22–29.

Forsdick, Charles, and David Murphy, eds. *Francophone Postcolonial Studies: A Critical Introduction.* London: Arnold, 2003.

Frémeaux, Jacques. "L'union française: Le rêve d'une *France unie.*" In *Culture impériale: Les colonies au cœur de la République, 1931–1961,* ed. Pascal Blanchard and Sandrine Lemaire, 163–174. Paris: Les Editions Autrement, 2004.

Frohning Deleporte, Sarah. "Trois musées, une question, une République." In *La fracture coloniale: La société française au prisme de l'héritage colonial,* ed. Pascal Blanchard, Nicolas Bancel, and Sandrine Lemaire, 105–111. Paris: La Découverte, 2005.

Gafaiti, Hafid. "Nationalism, Colonialism, and Ethnic Discourse in the Construction of French Identity." In *French Civilization and Its Discontents: Nationalism, Colonialism, Race,* ed. Tyler Stovall and Georges Van Den Abbeele, 189–212. Lanham, Md.: Lexington Books, 2003.

Gallap, J. "Phénotypes et discriminations des Noirs en France: Question de méthode." *Migrants-formation,* no. 94 (September 1993), 39–54.

Gallimore, Rangira Béatrice. *L'œuvre romanesque de Calixthe Beyala: Le renouveau de l'écriture en Afrique francophone sub-saharienne.* Paris: L'Harmattan, 1997.

Gandoulou, Justin-Daniel. *Au cœur de la sape: Mœurs et aventures de Congolais à Paris.* Paris: L'Harmattan, 1989. First published as *Entre Paris et Bacongo* (Paris: Editions Centre Pompidou, 1984).

———. *Dandies à Bacongo: Le culte de l'élégance dans la société congolaise contemporaine.* Paris: L'Harmattan, 1989.

Gang Starr. "Battle." On the soundtrack album of *8 Mile,* directed by Curtis Hanson. Produced by DJ Premier for Gang Starr Productions. Interscope Records, 2002.

Gardinier, David E. "Historical Origins of Francophone Africa." In *Political Reform in Francophone Africa,* ed. John F. Clark and David E. Gardinier, 9–22. Boulder, Colo.: Westview Press, 1997.

Garnier, Xavier. "Derrière les 'vitrines du progrès.'" *Notre librairie,* no. 157 (January–March, 2005): 38–43.

———. "L'exil lettré de Fatou Diome." *Notre librairie,* nos. 155–156 (July–December 2004): 30–35.

Gaspard, F., and F. Khosrokhavar. *Le foulard et la République.* Paris: La Découverte, 1995.

Gates, Henry Louis. *The Signifying Monkey: A Theory of African-American Literary Criticism.* New York: Oxford University Press, 1988.

Gautier, Madeleine. "Un romancier de la race noire: Richard Wright." *Présence africaine,* no. 1 (November–December 1947): 163–165.

Gbanou, Sélom Komlan. "Textes, contextes et intertextes dans les romans *Le docker noir* de Sembene Ousmane et *Le crime de la rue des notables* de Ekue Akoua T." *Palabres: Revue culturelle africaine* 1, nos. 3–4 (1997): 81–93.

Gearhart, Suzanne. "Psychoanalysis, Transnationalism, and Minority Cultures." In *Minor Transnationalism,* ed. Françoise Lionnet and Shu-mei Shih, 27–40. Durham, N.C.: Duke University Press, 2005.

Genet, Jean. *The Blacks.* New York: Grove Press, 1960.

Gèze, François. "L'héritage colonial au cœur de la politique étrangère française." In *La fracture coloniale: La société française au prisme de l'héritage colonial,* ed. Pascal Blanchard, Nicolas Bancel, and Sandrine Lemaire, 155–163. Paris: La Découverte, 2005.

Gide, André. *Retour du Tchad.* Paris: Gallimard, 1928.

———. *Voyage au Congo.* Paris: Gallimard, 1927.

Gilou, Thomas, dir. *Black Mic Mac.* 1986.

Gilroy, Paul. *Between Camps: Race, Identity, and Nationalism at the End of the Colour Line.* London: Penguin, 2000.

———. *The Black Atlantic: Modernity and Double Consciousness.* Cambridge, Mass.: Harvard University Press, 1993.

———. *Postcolonial Melancholia.* New York: Columbia University Press, 2005.

———. *There Ain't No Black in the Union Jack: The Cultural Politics of Race and Nation.* Chicago: University of Chicago Press, 1987.

Girardet, Raoul. *L'idée coloniale en France de 1871 à 1962.* Paris: Editions de la Table Ronde, 1962.

Glissant, Edouard. *Caribbean Discourse: Selected Essays.* Trans. J. Michael Dash. Charlottesville: University of Virginia Press, 1989.

———. *Le discours antillais.* Paris: Seuil, 1981.

———. "Terre à terre." *Les temps modernes,* no. 36 (September 1948): 429–438.

Golan, Tamar. "A Certain Mystery: How Can France Do Everything That It Does in Africa—and Get Away with It?" *African Affairs* 80, no. 318 (January 1981): 3–11.

Goldschmidt, Elie. "Migrants congolais en route vers l'Europe." *Les temps modernes,* nos. 620–621 (August–November 2002): 208–239.

Gomes, Flora, dir. *Nha Fala.* 2003.

Gondola, Didier. "'But I Ain't African, I'm American!': Black American Exiles and the Construction of Racial Identities in Twentieth-Century France." In *Blackening Europe: The African American Presence,* ed. Heike Raphael-Hernandez, 201–215. New York: Routledge, 2004.

———. "Dream and Drama: The Search for Elegance among Congolese Youth." *African Studies Review* 42, no. 1 (April 1999): 23–48.

———. "Popular Music, Urban Society, and Changing Gender Relations in Kinshasa, Zaire (1950–1990)." In *Gendered Encounters: Challenging Cultural Boundaries and Social Hierarchies in Africa,* ed. Maria Grosz-Ngaté and Omari H. Kokole, 65–84. New York: Routledge, 1997.

———. "La sape des *milikistes:* Théâtre de l'artifice et représentation onirique." *Cahiers d'études africaines,* no. 153 (1999): 13–47.

Gourévitch, Jean-Paul. *L'Afrique, le fric, la France: L'aide, la dette, l'immigration, l'avenir; Vérités et mesonges.* Paris: Le Pré aux Clercs, 1997.

Goussault, Bénédicte. *Paroles de sans-papiers.* Paris: Les Editions de l'Atelier/Les Editions Ouvrières, 1999.

Granotier, B. *Les travailleurs immigrés en France.* Paris: Maspéro, 1971.

Green, Charles, ed. *Globalization and Survival in the Black Diaspora: The New Urban Challenge.* Albany: State University of New York Press, 1997.

Green, Nancy L. *Repenser les migrations.* Paris: Presses Universitaires de France, 2002.

Guénif-Souilamas, Nacira. "La réduction à son corps de l'indigène de la République." In *La fracture coloniale: La société française au prisme de l'héritage colonial,* ed. Pascal Blanchard, Nicolas Bancel, and Sandrine Lemaire, 199–208. Paris: La Découverte, 2005.

Gueye, Abdoulaye. "Les chercheurs africains en demande d'Occident." *Esprit,* no. 317 (August–September 2005): 219–227.

———. *Les intellectuels africains en France.* Paris: L'Harmattan, 2001.

Guillon, Michelle. "La mosaïque des migrations africaines." *Esprit,* no. 317 (August–September 2005): 165–176.

Guimont, Fabienne. *Les étudiants africains en France, 1950–1965.* Paris: L'Harmattan, 1997.

Guyard, Marius-François. *La littérature comparée.* Paris: PUF, 1969.

Hajjat, Abdellali. *Immigration postcoloniale et mémoire.* Paris: L'Harmattan, 2005.

Hale, Sondra. "Colonial Discourse and Ethnographic Residuals: The 'Female Circumcision' Debate and the Politics of Knowledge." In *Female Circumcision and the Politics of Knowledge: African Women in Imperialist Discourses,* ed. Obioma Nnaemeka, 209–218. Westport, Conn.: Praeger Publishers, 2005.

Halen, Pierre. "Pour en finir avec une phraséologie encombrante: La question de l'Autre et de l'exotisme dans l'approche critique des littératures coloniales et post-coloniales." In *Regards sur les littératures coloniales: Afrique francophone; Découvertes,* ed. Jean-François Durand, 41–62. Paris: L'Harmattan, 1999.

Hall, Catherine. *Civilising Subjects: Metropole and Colony in the English Imagination, 1830–1867.* Chicago: University of Chicago Press, 2002.

Hall, Stuart. "Race, Articulation, and Societies Structured in Dominance." In *Black British Cultural Studies: A Reader,* ed. Houston A. Baker, Manthia Diawara, and Ruth H. Lindeborg, 16–60. Chicago: University of Chicago Press, 1996. First published 1980.

Hancock, Ange-Marie. "Overcoming Willful Blindness: Building Egalitarian Multicultural Coalitions." In *Female Circumcision and the Politics of Knowledge: African Women in Imperialist Discourses,* ed. Obioma Nnaemeka, 245–274. Westport, Conn.: Praeger Publishers, 2005.

Hardt, Michael, and Antonio Negri. *Empire.* Cambridge, Mass.: Harvard University Press, 2001.

———. *Multitude.* New York: Penguin, 2004.

Hardy, Georges. *Une conquête morale: L'enseignement en A.O.F.* Paris: Armand Colin, 1917.

———. *L'enseignement au Sénégal de 1817 à 1857.* Paris: Larose, 1920.

Hargreaves, Alec G. "The Contribution of North and Sub-Saharan African Immigrant Minorities to the Redefinition of Contemporary French Culture." In *Francophone Postcolonial Studies: A Critical Introduction,* ed. Charles Forsdick and David Murphy, 145–154. London: Arnold, 2003.

———. *Immigration, "Race," and Ethnicity in Contemporary France.* London: Routledge, 1995.

———. "Multiculturalism." In *Political Ideologies in Contemporary France,* ed. Christopher Flood and Laurence Bell, 180–199. London: Cassell, 1997.

———. "Testimony, Co-authorship and Dispossession among Women of Maghrebi Origin in France." In "Textual Ownership in Francophone African Writing," ed. Alec G. Hargreaves, Nicki Hitchcott, and Dominic Thomas, special issue of *Research in African Literatures* 37, no. 1 (Spring 2006): 42–54.

———. *Voices from the North African Immigrant Community in France: Immigration and Identity in Beur Fiction.* London: Berg, 1991.

Hargreaves, Alec G., and Mark McKinney, eds. *Post-colonial Cultures in France.* London: Routledge, 1997.

Hazoumé, Paul. *Doguicimi.* Paris: Larose, 1938.

Hendrickson, Hildi, ed. *Clothing and Difference: Embodied Identities in Colonial and Post-colonial Africa.* Durham, N.C.: Duke University Press, 1996.

Herzberger-Fofana, Pierrette. *Littérature féminine francophone d'Afrique noire.* Paris: L'Harmattan, 1993.

Higginson, Francis. "*Le docker noir* or Race, Revolution, and the Novel." In "Blood and the Canon: The Advent of Francophone African Crime Fiction." Unpublished ms.

Hill, Edwin. "Imagining *Métissage:* The Politics and Practice of *Métissage* in the French Colonial Exposition and Ousmane Socé's *Mirages de Paris.*" *Social Identities* 8, no. 4 (2002): 619–645.

Hill-Lubin, Mildred A. "*Présence Africaine:* A Voice in the Wilderness, a Record of Black Kinship." In *The Surreptitious Speech:* Présence Africaine *and the Politics of Otherness, 1947–1987,* ed. V. Y. Mudimbe, 157–173. Chicago: University of Chicago Press, 1992.

Hitchcott, Nicki. "Calixthe Beyala and the Post-colonial Woman." In *Post-colonial Cultures in France,* ed. Alec G. Hargreaves and Mark McKinney, 211–225. London: Routledge, 1997.

———. "Calixthe Beyala: Black Face(s) on French TV." *Modern and Contemporary France* 12, no. 4 (November 2004): 473–482.

———. *Calixthe Beyala: Performances of Migration.* Unpublished ms.

———. "Calixthe Beyala: Prizes, Plagiarism, and 'Authenticity.'" In "Textual Ownership in Francophone African Writing," ed. Alec G. Hargreaves, Nicki Hitchcott, and Dominic Thomas, special issue of *Research in African Literatures* 37, no. 1 (Spring 2006): 100–109.

———. *Women Writers in Francophone Africa.* Oxford: Berg, 2000.

Hoffman, Léon-François. *Le nègre romantique: Personnage littéraire et obsession collective.* Paris: Payot, 1973.

Holden, Philip, and Richard J. Ruppel. Introduction to *Imperial Desire: Dissident Sexualities and Colonial Literature,* ed. Philip Holden and Richard J. Ruppel, ix–xxvi. Minneapolis: University of Minnesota Press, 2003.

Hommes et migrations. "L'héritage colonial: Un trou de mémoire." No. 1228 (November–December 2000).

———. "Imaginaire colonial: Figures de l'immigré." No. 1207 (May–June 1997).

———. "L'immigration dans l'histoire nationale." No. 1114 (September 1988).

———. "Vers un lieu de mémoire de l'immigration." No. 1247 (January–February 2004).

Honig, Bonnie. *Democracy and the Foreigner.* Princeton, N.J.: Princeton University Press, 2001.

Horne, John. "Immigrant Workers in France during World War I." *French Historical Studies* 14 (1985): 57–88.

Huannou, Adrien. *La question des littératures nationales en Afrique noire.* Abidjan, Ivory Coast: CEDA, 1989.

Huggan, Graham. *The Post-colonial Exotic: Marketing the Margins.* London: Routledge, 2001.

Hugon, Philippe. "L'Afrique dans la mondialisation." *Esprit,* no. 317 (August–September 2005): 158–164.

Huntington, Samuel. *The Clash of Civilizations.* New York: Simon and Schuster, 1996.

Ilboudo, Monique. *Le mal de peau.* Paris: Gallimard, 2001.

Intik. "Si chacun faisait de son mieux." Intik and Nabil Bouaiche. © Sony Music Entertainment (France), 1999.

Irele, F. Abiola. *The African Imagination: Literature in Africa and the Black Diaspora.* Oxford: Oxford University Press, 2001.

———. "In Praise of Alienation." In *The Surreptitious Speech:* Présence Africaine *and the Politics of Otherness, 1947–1987,* ed. V. Y. Mudimbe, 201–224. Chicago: University of Chicago Press, 1992.

———. "Négritude—Literature and Ideology." *Journal of Modern African Studies* 3, no. 4 (December 1965): 499–526.

————. "Négritude or Black Cultural Nationalism." *Journal of Modern African Studies* 3, no. 3 (October 1965): 321–348.

Irele, F. Abiola, ed. "Léopold Sédar Senghor." Special issue of *Research in African Literatures* 33, no. 4 (Winter 2002).

Ivaska, Andrew M. "'Anti-mini Militants Meet Modern Misses': Urban Style, Gender, and the Politics of 'National Culture' in 1960s Dar es Salaam, Tanzania." In *Material Strategies: Dress and Gender in Historical Perspective,* ed. Barbara Burman and Carole Turbin, 214–237. Malden, Mass.: Blackwell, 2003.

James, Caryn. "Stop! Thief! An Author's Mind Is Being Stolen!" *New York Times,* June 25, 2004.

Jameson, Fredric. "Notes on Globalization as a Philosophical Issue." In *The Cultures of Globalization,* ed. Fredric Jameson and Masao Miyoshi, 54–77. Durham, N.C.: Duke University Press, 1998.

Joseph, May. "New Hybrid Identities and Performance." In *Performing Hybridity,* ed. May Joseph and Jennifer Natalya Fink, 1–24. Minneapolis: University of Minnesota Press, 1999.

Joxe, Alain. *Empire of Disorder.* New York: Semiotext(e), 2002.

Jules-Rosette, Bennetta. "Antithetical Africa: The Conferences and Festivals of *Présence Africaine,* 1956–73." In *Black Paris: The African Writers' Landscape,* 48–78. Urbana: University of Illinois Press, 1998.

————. *Black Paris: The African Writers' Landscape.* Urbana: University of Illinois Press, 1998.

————. "Conjugating Cultural Realities: *Présence Africaine.*" In *The Surreptitious Speech: Présence Africaine and the Politics of Otherness, 1947–1987,* ed. V. Y. Mudimbe, 14–44. Chicago: University of Chicago Press, 1992.

Julien, Ch.-André. *Les techniciens de la colonisation (XIXe–XXe siècles).* Colonies et empires, 1. sér., Etudes coloniales 1. Paris: Presses Universitaires de France, 1947.

Julien, Eileen. *African Novels and the Question of Orality.* Bloomington: Indiana University Press, 1992.

Kanbur, S. M. Ravi. "The Theory of Structural Adjustment and Trade Policy." In *Trade and Development in Sub-Saharan Africa,* ed. Jonathan H. Frimpong-Ansah, S. M. Ravi Kanbur, and Peter Svedberg, 188–202. Manchester: Manchester University Press, 1991.

Kane, Cheikh Hamidou. *Ambiguous Adventure.* Trans. Katherine Woods. London: Heinemann, 1972.

————. *L'aventure ambiguë.* Paris: Julliard, 1961.

Kane, Mohamadou. *Roman africain et tradition.* Dakar: Les Nouvelles Editions Africaines, 1982.

Keïta, Fatou. *Rebelle.* Paris: Présence Africaine, 1998.

Kelman, Gaston. *Je suis noir et je n'aime pas le manioc.* Paris: Max Milo Editions, 2003.

Kemedjo, Cilas. "The Western Anticolonialist of the Postcolonial Age: The Reformist Syndrome and the Memory of Decolonization in (Post-) Imperial French Thought." In *Remembering Africa,* ed. Elisabeth Mudimbe, 32–55. Portsmouth, N.H.: Heinemann, 2002.

Kepel, Gilles. *Les banlieues de l'Islam.* Paris: Seuil, 1987.

Kessas, Ferrudja. *Beur's Story.* Paris: L'Harmattan, 1990.

Kesteloot, Lilyan. *Black Writers in French: A Literary History of Negritude.* Trans. Ellen Conroy Kennedy. Philadelphia, Penn.: Temple University Press, 1974.

———. "Situation actuelle des écrivains noirs." In *Les écrivains noirs de langue française: Naissance d'une littérature,* 273–315. Brussels: Institut de sociologie de l'Université libre de Bruxelles, 1963.

Khouma, Pap. *Io, venditore di elefanti: Una vita per forza fra Dakar, Parigi e Milano.* Milan: Garzanti, 1990.

King, Adele. *Rereading Camara Laye.* Lincoln: University of Nebraska Press, 2002.

Kirby, Vicki. "Out of Africa: 'Our Bodies Ourselves.'" In *Female Circumcision and the Politics of Knowledge: African Women in Imperialist Discourses,* ed. Obioma Nnaemeka, 81–96. Westport, Conn.: Praeger Publishers, 2005.

Klingenberg, Theresa M. "The Cultural Practice of Female Genital Mutilation and the Implications for Social Work." *Social Work Perspectives* 7, no. 1 (Spring 1997): 7–12.

Konaré, Kadiatou. *Le Paris des Africains.* Paris: Cauris Editions, 2002.

Kone, Mamadou, dir. *Un village africain à Paris.* 1980.

Korieh, Chima. "'Other' Bodies: Western Feminism, Race, and Representation in Female Circumcision Discourse." In *Female Circumcision and the Politics of Knowledge: African Women in Imperialist Discourses,* ed. Obioma Nnaemeka, 111–132. Westport, Conn.: Praeger Publishers, 2005.

Kotchy, Barthélémy. "Critique des institutions coloniales." In *La critique sociale dans l'œuvre théâtrale de Bernard Dadié,* 94–123. Paris: L'Harmattan, 1984.

Kristeva, Julia. "Bakhtine, le mot, le dialogue et le roman." *Critique,* no. 239 (April 1967): 438–465.

———. *Le texte du roman.* La Haye: Mouton, 1970.

Kritzman, Lawrence. "Identity Crises: France, Culture, and the Idea of the Nation." *SubStance* 76–77 (1995): 5–20.

Kwahulé, Koffi. *Bintou.* Carnières-Morlanwelz, Belgium: Editions Lansman, 1997.

Laronde, Michel. *Autour du roman beur: Immigration et identité.* Paris: L'Harmattan, 1993.

———. "Les littératures des immigrations en France: Question de nomenclature et directions de recherche." *Le Maghreb littéraire* 1, no. 2 (1997): 25–44.

Larson, Charles R. *The Ordeal of the African Writer.* New York: Zed Books, 2001.

Laver, James. *Taste and Fashion: From the French Revolution until Today.* London: George G. Harrap, 1937.

Lebel, Roland. *L'Afrique occidentale dans la littérature française.* Paris: Larose, 1925.

———. *Etudes de littérature coloniale en France.* Paris: Larose, 1931.

Lebon, André. *Immigration et présence étrangère en France.* Paris: Ministère des Affaires Sociales, de la Santé et de la Ville, Direction de la population et des migrations, 1993.

———. *Immigration et présence étrangère en France en 1999: Premiers enseignements du recencement.* Paris: La Documentation Française, 2001.

Lebovics, Herman. "The Dance of the Museums." In *Bringing the Empire Back Home: France in the Global Age,* 143–177. Durham, N.C.: Duke University Press, 2004.

Le Brusq, Arnauld. "De 'notre' mémoire à 'leur' histoire: Les métamorphoses du Palais des colonies." In *La fracture coloniale: La société française au prisme de l'héritage colonial,* ed. Pascal Blanchard, Nicolas Bancel, and Sandrine Lemaire, 255–262. Paris: La Découverte, 2005.

Lee, Rachel. "Dissenting Literacy and Transnationalism." Unpublished ms.

Lefeuvre-Déotte, Martine. *L'excision en procès: Un différend culturel?* Paris: L'Harmattan, 1997.

Leila, with Marie-Thérèse Cuny. *Mariée de force.* Paris: Oh! Editions, 2004.

Leiris, Michel. *L'Afrique fantôme.* Paris: Gallimard, 1934.

———. "Martinique, Guadeloupe, Haïti." *Les temps modernes,* no. 52 (February 1950): 1345–1368.

———. "Poèmes." *Les temps modernes,* no. 37 (October 1948): 607–625.

Lemaire, Sandrine. "Colonisation et immigration: Des 'points aveugles' de l'histoire à l'école?" In *La fracture coloniale: La société française au prisme de l'héritage colonial,* ed. Pascal Blanchard, Nicolas Bancel, and Sandrine Lemaire, 93–104. Paris: La Découverte, 2005.

———. "Promouvoir: Fabriquer du colonial." In *Culture impériale: Les colonies au cœur de la République, 1931–1961,* ed. Pascal Blanchard and Sandrine Lemaire, 45–60. Paris: Editions Autrement, 2004.

Levin, Tobe. "Female Genital Mutilation: Campaigns in Germany." In *Engendering Human Rights: Cultural and Socio-economic Realities in Africa,* ed. Obioma Nnaemeka and Joy Ngozi Ezeilo, 285–301. New York: Palgrave Macmillan, 2005.

Lionnet, Françoise. "Excision." In *Encyclopedia of African Religions and Philosophy,* general editor V. Y. Mudimbe. Amsterdam: Kluwer, forthcoming.

———. "Feminisms and Universalisms: 'Universal Rights' and the Legal Debate around the Practice of Female Excision in France." In *Feminist Postcolonial Theory: A Reader,* ed. Reina Lewis and Sara Mills, 368–380. New York: Routledge, 2003.

———. "Immigration, Poster Art, and Transgressive Citizenship: France, 1968–1988." *SubStance* 76–77 (1995): 93–108.

———. "*Logiques métisses:* Cultural Appropriation and Postcolonial Representations." In *Postcolonial Subjects: Francophone Women Writers,* ed. Mary Jean Green, Karen Gould, Micheline Rice-Maximin, Keith L. Walker, and Jack A. Yaeger, 321–343. Minneapolis: University of Minnesota, 1996.

———. "The Mirror and The Tomb: Africa, Museums, and Representation." *African Arts* 34, no. 3 (Fall 2001): 50–59.

———. *Postcolonial Representations: Women, Literature, Identity.* Ithaca, N.Y.: Cornell University Press, 1995.

———. "Transcolonialismes: Echoes et dissonances de Jane Austen à Marie-Thérèse Humbert et d'Emily Brontë à Maryse Condé." In *Ecrire en langue étrangère et de cultures dans le monde francophone,* ed. Robert Dion, Hans-Jürgen Lüsebrink, and János Riesz, 227–243. Quebec City: Editions Nota Bene, 2002.

———. "Transnationalism, Postcolonialism, or Transcolonialism? Reflections on Los Angeles, Geography, and the Uses of Theory." *Emergences: Journal for the Study of Media and Composite Cultures* 10, no. 1 (May 2000): 25–35.

Lionnet, Françoise, Obioma Nnaemeka, Susan H. Perry, and Celeste Schenck, eds. "Development Cultures: New Environments, New Realities, New Strategies." Special issue, *Signs: Journal of Women in Culture and Society* 29, no. 2 (Winter 2004).

Lionnet, Françoise, and Shu-mei Shih, eds. *Minor Transnationalism.* Durham, N.C.: Duke University Press, 2005.

———. "Thinking through the Mirror, Transnationally." In *Minor Transnationalism,* ed. Françoise Lionnet and Shu-mei Shih, 1–23. Durham, N.C.: Duke University Press, 2005.

Little, Roger. "Reflections on a Triangular Trade in Borrowing and Stealing: Textual Exploitation in a Selection of African, Caribbean, and European Writers in French." In "Textual Ownership in Francophone African Writing," ed. Alec G. Hargreaves, Nicki Hitchcott, and Dominic Thomas, special issue of *Research in African Literatures* 37, no. 1 (Spring 2006): 16–27.

———. "Seeds of Postcolonialism: Black Slavery and Cultural Difference to 1800." In *Francophone Postcolonial Studies: A Critical Introduction,* ed. Charles Forsdick and David Murphy, 17–26. London: Arnold, 2003.

Loba, Aké. *Kocumba, l'étudiant noir.* Paris: Flammarion, 1960.

Loingsigh, Aedín Ní. "Immigration, Tourism, and Postcolonial Reinventions of Travel." In *Francophone Postcolonial Studies: A Critical Introduction,* ed. Charles Forsdick and David Murphy, 156–165. London: Arnold, 2003.

Lopes, Henri. *Ma grand-mère bantoue et mes ancêtres les Gaulois.* Paris: Gallimard, 2003.

Loufti, Martine Astier. *Littérature et colonialisme: L'expansion coloniale vue dans la littérature romanesque française.* Paris: Mouton, 1971.

Lowe, Lisa. *Immigrant Acts: On Asian American Cultural Politics.* Durham, N.C.: Duke University Press, 1996.

Loyrette, Henri. "The Eiffel Tower." In *Realms of Memory: The Construction of the French Past,* ed. Pierre Nora, English edition ed. Lawrence D. Kritzman, trans. Arthur Goldhammer, 349–374. New York: Columbia University Press, 1998.

Lüsebrink, Hans-Jürgen. "Acculturation coloniale et pédagogie interculturelle: L'œuvre de Georges Hardy." In *Sénégal-forum: Littérature et histoire,* ed. Papa Samba Diop, 113–122. Frankfurt: IKO Verlag, 1995.

———. "Les expositions coloniales: Lieux d'exhibition et de débats identitaires." In *La conquête de l'espace public colonial: Prises de parole et formes de participation d'écrivains et d'intellectuels africains dans la presse à l'époque coloniale,* 175–202. Frankfurt: IKO Verlag für Interkulturelle Kommunikation, 2003.

———. "Métissage et société coloniale." In *La conquête de l'espace public colonial: Prises de parole et formes de participation d'écrivains et d'intellectuels africains dans la presse à l'époque coloniale,* 203–218. Frankfurt: IKO Verlag für Interkulturelle Kommunikation, 2003.

———. *Schrift, Buch und Lektüre in der französischsprachigen Literatur Afrikas: Zur Wahrnehmung und Funktion von Schriftlichkeit und Buchlektüre in einem kulturellen Epochenumbruch der Neuzeit.* Tübingen: Niemeyer, 1990.

Mabanckou, Alain. "A l'écoute d'Alain Mabanckou, lauréat du Grand prix littéraire de l'Afrique noire, 1999." Interview by Pierrette Herzberger-Fofana. *Mots pluriels,* no. 12 (December 1999). http://www.arts.uwa.edu.au/MotsPluriels/MP1299mabanckou.html.

———. *African Psycho.* Paris: Le Serpent à Plumes, 2003.

———. *Les arbres aussi versent des larmes.* Paris: L'Harmattan, 1997.

———. *Au jour le jour.* Paris: Maison Rhodanienne, 1993.

———. *Bleu-Blanc-Rouge.* Paris: Présence Africaine, 1998.

———. *Et Dieu seul sait comment je dors.* Paris: Présence Africaine, 2002.

———. *La légende de l'errance.* Paris: L'Harmattan, 1995.

———. *Quand le coq annoncera l'aube d'un autre jour.* Paris: L'Harmattan, 1999.

———. *L'usure des lendemains.* Paris: Nouvelles du Sud, 1995.

———. *Verre cassé.* Paris: Seuil, 2005.

MacGaffey, Janet, and Rémy Bazenguissa-Ganga. *Congo-Paris: Transnational Traders on the Margins of the Law*. Bloomington: Indiana University Press, 2000.

Magnier, Bernard. "'Beurs noirs' à Black Babel." *Notre librairie*, no. 103 (October–December 1990): 102–107.

———. "Le livre africain: Un livre comme les autres." *Esprit*, no. 317 (August–September 2005): 53–60.

Magnin, André, and Robert Storr, eds. *J'aime Chéri Samba*. Arles: Actes Sud/Fondation Cartier pour l'art contemporain, 2004.

Makouta-Mboukou, J.-P. *Le français en Afrique noire: Histoire et méthodes de l'enseignement du français en Afrique noire*. Paris: Bordas, 1973.

———. *Introduction à l'étude du roman négro-africain de langue française: Problèmes culturels et littéraires*. Abidjan, Ivory Coast: Les Nouvelles Editions Africaines, 1980.

Malonga, Marie-France. "Fictions TV: Des Noirs dans l'ombre." *Africultures* 27 (2000): 34–37.

———. "Présence et représentation des 'minorités visibles' à la télévision française." Unpublished ms. A summary was published as "Présence et représentation des 'minorités visibles' à la télévision française: Une étude du Conseil supérieur de l'audiovisuel," *La lettre du CSA* 129, pp. 12–14.

Manceron, Gilles. "De la débauche de propagande au 'trou de mémoire' colonial." In *Marianne et les colonies: Une introduction à l'histoire coloniale de la France*, 267–282. Paris: La Découverte, 2003.

Manchuelle, François. *Les diasporas des travailleurs soninké (1848–1960): Migrants volontaires*. Paris: Karthala, 2004.

Manning, Patrick. *Francophone sub-Saharan Africa, 1880–1985*. Cambridge: Cambridge University Press, 1998.

Martin, Phyllis M. "Colonialism, Youth, and Football in French Equatorial Africa." *International Journal of the History of Sport* 8, no. 1 (May 1991): 56–71.

———. "Dressing Well." In *Leisure and Society in Colonial Brazzaville*, 154–172. Cambridge: Cambridge University Press, 1995.

Marx-Scouras, Danielle. *La France de Zebda, 1981–2004: Faire de la musique un acte politique*. Paris: Les Editions Autrement, 2005.

Maynard, Margaret. *Dress and Globalisation*. Manchester: Manchester University Press, 2004.

M'Barga, Jean-Pierre. "Excision: fonctions et conséquences de sa répression en milieu migrant en France." In *L'immigration face aux lois de la République*, ed. E. Rude-Antoine, 165–175. Paris: Karthala, 1992.

Mbembe, Achille. "At the Edge of the World: Boundaries, Territoriality, and Sovereignty in Africa." Trans. Steven Rendall. In *Globalization*, ed. Arjun Appadurai, 22–51. Durham, N.C.: Duke University Press, 2001.

———. *Les jeunes et l'ordre politique en Afrique noire*. Paris: L'Harmattan, 1985.

———. *On the Postcolony*. Berkeley and Los Angeles: University of California Press, 2001.

———. "La République et l'impensé de la 'race.'" In *La fracture coloniale: La société française au prisme de l'héritage colonial*, ed. Pascal Blanchard, Nicolas Bancel, and Sandrine Lemaire, 139–153. Paris: La Découverte, 2005.

M'Bokolo, Elikia. "Comparisons and Contrasts in Equatorial Africa: Gabon, Congo, and the Central African Republic." In *History of Central Africa: The Contemporary Years since 1960*, ed. David Birmingham and Phyllis M. Martin, 67–95. New York: Longman, 1998.

McGonacle, J. M. "Ethnicity and Visibility in Contemporary French Television." *French Cultural Studies* 13, no. 3 (October 2002): 281–292.

McKay, Claude. *Banjo*. Trans. Ida Treat and Paul-Vaillant Couturier. Paris: Rieder, 1931.

———. *Banjo: A Story without a Plot*. New York: Harper and Brothers, 1929.

Melching, Molly. "Abandoning Female Genital Cutting." In *Eye to Eye: Women Practising Development across Cultures,* ed. Susan Perry and Celeste Schenck, 156–170. London: Zed Books, 2001.

Memmi, Albert. *The Colonizer and the Colonized*. Trans. Howard Greenfield. Boston: Beacon Press, 1991. First published 1957.

———. *Portrait du décolonisé arabo-musulman et de quelques autres*. Paris: Gallimard, 2004.

Mestiri, Ezzedine. *L'immigration*. Paris: La Découverte, 1990.

Miano, Léonora. *L'intérieur de la nuit*. Paris: Plon, 2005.

Michel, Marc. *Les Africains et la Grande Guerre: L'appel à l'Afrique, 1914–1918*. Paris: Karthala, 2003.

Midiohouan, Guy Ossito. *Ecrire en pays colonisé: Plaidoyer pour une nouvelle approche des rapports entre la littérature négro-africaine d'expression française et le pouvoir colonial*. Paris: L'Harmattan, 2002.

———. *L'idéologie dans la littérature négro-africaine d'expression française*. Paris: L'Harmattan, 1986.

Miller, Christopher L. *Blank Darkness: Africanist Discourse in French*. Chicago: University of Chicago Press, 1985.

———. *The French Atlantic Triangle: Literature and Culture of the Slave Trade*. Durham, N.C.: Duke University Press, forthcoming.

———. *Nationalists and Nomads: Essays on Francophone African Literature and Culture*. Chicago: Chicago University Press, 1998.

———. *Theories of Africans: Francophone Literature and Anthropology in Africa*. Chicago: University of Chicago Press, 1990.

Mkandawire, Thandika, and Charles C. Soludo. *Our Continent, Our Future: African Perspectives on Structural Adjustment*. Dakar: CODESRIA, 1999.

Mohanty, Chandra Talpade. "Under Western Eyes: Feminist Scholarship and the Colonial Discourses." In *Feminist Postcolonial Theory: A Reader,* ed. Reina Lewis and Sara Mills, 49–74. New York: Routledge, 2003.

Le monde. "Les chanteurs de NTM condamnés à la prison ferme pour outrage à la police." November 16, 1996.

Mongo-Mboussa, Boniface. "Grammaire de l'immigration." *L'indocilité: Supplément au Désir d'Afrique,* 101–115. Paris: Gallimard, 2005.

———. "Les méandres de la mémoire dans la littérature africaine." *Hommes et migrations,* no. 1228 (November–December 2000): 68–79.

Mortimer, Mildred. *Journeys through the French African Novel*. Portsmouth, N.H.: Heinemann, 1990.

Moudileno, Lydie. "La fiction de la migration: Manipulation des corps et des récits dans *Bleu blanc rouge* d'Alain Mabanckou." *Présence africaine,* nos. 163–164 (2001): 182–189.

———. "Littérature et postcolonie." *Africultures,* no. 26 (March 2000): 9–13.

Moura, Jean-Marc. "Des études postcoloniales dans l'espace littéraire francophone." In *Exotisme et lettres francophones,* 191–216. Paris: Presses Universitaires de France, 2003.

———. "Littérature coloniale et exotisme: Examen d'une opposition de la théorie littéraire coloniale." In *Regards sur les littératures coloniales: Afrique fran-*

cophone; Découverte, ed. Jean-François Durand, 21–39. Paris: L'Harmattan, 1999.

———. *Littératures francophones et théorie postcoloniale.* Paris: Presses Universitaires de France, 1999.

———. "Textual Ownership in *L'étrange destin de Wangrin* (The Fortunes of Wangrin) by Amadou Hambaté Bâ." In "Textual Ownership in Francophone African Writing," ed. Alec G. Hargreaves, Nicki Hitchcott, and Dominic Thomas, special issue of *Research in African Literatures* 37, no. 1 (Spring 2006): 91–99.

Mouralis, Bernard. "L'écriture, le réel et l'action: Le cas de Georges Hardy dans Egarste ou la vocation coloniale." In *Regards sur les littératures coloniales: Afrique francophone; Découvertes,* ed. Jean-François Durand, 63–84. Paris: L'Harmattan, 1999.

———. *Littérature et développement: Essai sur le statut, la fonction et la représentation de la littérature négro-africaine d'expression française.* Paris: Silex, 1984.

———. *République et colonies: Entre histoire et mémoire; La République française et l'Afrique.* Paris: Présence Africaine, 1999.

Mousset, Christian. "La musique africaine et la France." In *Etudiants africains en France, 1951–2001,* ed. Michel Sot, 163–167. Paris: Karthala, 2002.

Mudimbe, V. Y. *Entre les eaux.* Paris: Présence Africaine, 1973.

———. *The Idea of Africa.* Bloomington: Indiana University Press, 1994.

———. *The Invention of Africa: Gnosis, Philosophy, and the Order of Knowledge.* Bloomington: Indiana University Press, 1988.

Mudimbe, V. Y., ed. *The Surreptitious Speech:* Présence Africaine *and the Politics of Otherness, 1947–1987.* Chicago: University of Chicago Press, 1992.

Mudimbe-Boyi, Elisabeth. "Harlem Renaissance and Africa: An Ambiguous Adventure." In *The Surreptitious Speech:* Présence Africaine *and the Politics of Otherness, 1947–1987,* ed. V. Y. Mudimbe, 174–184. Chicago: University of Chicago Press, 1992.

———. "Travel Representation and Difference, or How Can One Be a Parisian?" *Research in African Literature* 23, no. 3 (Fall 1992): 25–39.

Murphy, David. "La danse et la parole: L'exil et l'identité chez les Noirs de Marseille dans *Banjo* de Claude McKay et *Le docker noir* d'Ousmane Sembene." *Canadian Review of Comparative Literature* 27, no. 3 (September 2000): 462–479.

N'Diaye, J.-P. *Enquête sur les étudiants noirs en France.* Paris: Editions Réalités Africaines, 1962.

———. *Négriers modernes: Les travailleurs noirs en France.* Paris: Présence Africaine, 1970.

N'Djehoya, Blaise. *Nègre de Potemkine.* Paris: Lieu Commun, 1988.

N'Dongo, Sally. *Exil, connais pas.* Paris: Editions du Cerf, 1976.

Newland, Courttia, and Kadija Sesay, eds. *IC3: The Penguin Book of New Black Writing in Britain.* London: Hamish Hamilton, 2000.

Ngoye, Achille. *Agence Black Bafoussa.* Paris: Gallimard, 1996.

———. *Ballet noir à Château-Rouge.* Paris: Gallimard, 2001.

Ngũgĩ wa Thiong'o. *Decolonizing the Mind: The Politics of Language in African Literature.* London: James Currey, 1986.

Nini, Soraya. *Ils disent que je suis une beurette . . .* Paris: Fixot, 1993.

Njami, Simon. *African gigolo.* Paris: Seghers, 1989.

———. "Identity and History," In *Africa Remix: Contemporary Art of a Conti-nent,* ed. Simon Njami et al., 55–56. Trans. Gail de Courcy-Ireland. Ost-fildern-Ruit, Germany: Hatje Cantz Verlag, 2005.

Njami, Simon, et al. *Africa Remix: L'art contemporain d'un continent.* Paris: Edi-tions du Centre Pompidou, 2005.

———. *Africa Remix: Contemporary Art of a Continent.* Ostfildern-Ruit, Ger-many: Hatje Cantz Verlag, 2005.

Nkashama, Ngandu Pius. *Vie et mœurs d'un primitif en Essone quatre-vingt-onze.* Paris: L'Harmattan, 1987.

Nnaemeka, Obioma. "African Women, Colonial Discourses, and Imperialist Inter-ventions: Female Circumcision as Impetus." In *Female Circumcision and the Politics of Knowledge: African Women in Imperialist Discourses,* ed. Obioma Nnaemeka, 27–45. Westport, Conn.: Praeger Publishers, 2005.

———. "The Challenges of Border-Crossing: African Women and Transnational Feminisms." In *Female Circumcision and the Politics of Knowledge: African Women in Imperialist Discourses,* ed. Obioma Nnaemeka, 3–18. Westport, Conn.: Praeger Publishers, 2005.

———. "Context(ure)s of Human Rights—Local Realities, Global Contexts." In-troduction to *Engendering Human Rights: Cultural and Socio-economic Re-alities in Africa,* ed. Obioma Nnaemeka and Joy Ngozi Ezeilo, 3–24. New York: Palgrave Macmillan, 2005.

———, ed. *Female Circumcision and the Politics of Knowledge: African Women in Imperialist Discourses.* Westport, Conn.: Praeger Publishers, 2005.

———. "If Female Circumcision Did Not Exist, Western Feminism Would Invent It." In *Eye to Eye: Women Practising Development across Cultures,* ed. Su-san Perry and Celeste Schenck, 171–189. London: Zed Books, 2001.

———. "Mapping African Feminisms." In *Readings in Gender in Africa,* ed. An-drea Cornwall, 31–41. Bloomington: Indiana University Press, 2005.

———. "Nego-feminism: Theorizing, Practicing, and Pruning Africa's Way." *Signs: Journal of Women in Culture and Society* 29, no. 2 (Winter 2004): 357–385.

Nnaemeka, Obioma, and Joy Ngozi Ezeilo, eds. *Engendering Human Rights: Cul-tural and Socio-economic Realities in Africa.* New York: Palgrave Macmil-lan, 2005.

Noiriel, Gérard. *Le creuset français: Histoire de l'immigration, XIXème–XXème siècles.* Paris: Seuil, 1988.

———. "Histoire, mémoire, engagement civique." *Hommes et migrations,* no. 1247 (January–February 2004): 17–26.

Nokan, Charles. *Le soleil noir point.* Paris: Présence Africaine, 1962.

Nora, Pierre. "General Introduction: Between Memory and History." In *Realms of Memory: Rethinking the French Past,* 1–2. Trans. Arthur Goldhammer. New York: Columbia University Press, 1996.

———, ed. *Les lieux de mémoire.* 7 vols. Paris: Gallimard, 1984–1992.

———, ed. *Realms of Memory: The Construction of the French Past.* English edi-tion ed. Lawrence D. Kritzman. Trans. Arthur Goldhammer. New York: Co-lumbia University Press, 1998.

Notre librairie. "Images du noir dans la littérature occidentale. 1. Du Moyen Age à la conquête coloniale." No. 91 (January–February 1988).

———. "Littérature et développement." No. 157 (January–March, 2005).

———. "Nouvelle génération." No. 146 (October–December 2001).

Nwankwo, Nkem. *My Mercedes Is Bigger than Yours.* London: André Deutsch Limited, 1975.

Nzabatsinda, André. "La figure de l'artiste dans le récit d'Ousmane Sembene." *Etudes françaises* 31, no. 1 (Summer 1995): 51–60.

Nzenza-Shand, Sekai. "Take Me Back to the Village: African Women and the Dynamics of Health and Human Rights in Tanzania and Zimbabwe." In *Engendering Human Rights: Cultural and Socio-economic Realities in Africa,* ed. Obioma Nnaemeka and Joy Ngozi Ezeilo, 61–79. New York: Palgrave Macmillan, 2005.

O'Brien, Donal Cruise. "Le sens de l'Etat au Sénégal." In *Le Sénégal contemporain,* ed. Momar-Coumba Diop, 501–506. Paris: Karthala, 2002.

Ogundipe-Leslie, Molara. *Recreating Ourselves: African Women and Critical Transformations.* Trenton, N.J.: Africa World Press, 1994.

Ojo, Oladeji O. "The CFA Franc Devaluation and the Future of Monetary Cooperation in Africa." In *Africa and Europe: The Changing Economic Relationship,* ed. Oladeji O. Ojo, 111–128. London: Zed Books, 1996.

Okeke, Philomena E. "Postmodern Feminism and Knowledge Production: The African Context." *Africa Today* 43, no. 3 (1999): 223–234.

Okin, Susan Moller. "Is Multiculturalism Bad for Women?" In *Is Multiculturalism Bad for Women?* ed. Joshua Cohen, Matthew Howard, and Martha C. Nussbaum, 9–24. Princeton, N.J.: Princeton University Press, 1999.

Okpewho, Isidore, Carole Boyce Davies, and Ali Mazrui, eds. *The African Diaspora: African Origins and New World Identities.* Bloomington: Indiana University Press, 1999.

Olakunle, George. "Alice Walker's Africa: Globalization and the Province of Fiction." *Comparative Literature* 53, no. 4 (Fall 2001): 354–372.

Onama, Charles. *La France et ses tirailleurs: Enquête sur les combattants de la République.* Paris: Duboiris, 2003.

Ouedraogo, Hamadou B., dir. *L'exil.* 1981.

Ouologuem, Yambo. *Bound to Violence.* Trans. Ralph Manheim. London: Heinemann, 1971.

———. *Le devoir de violence.* Paris: Seuil, 1968.

———. *Lettre à la France nègre.* Paris: Le Serpent à Plumes, 2003. First published 1969.

Oussou-Essui, Denis. *La souche calcinée.* Paris: L'Harmattan, 2004. First published 1973.

Oyono, Ferdinand. *Chemin d'Europe.* Paris: Julliard, 1960.

———. *Une vie de boy.* Paris: Juilliard, 1956.

Packer, Corinne. "Understanding the Sociocultural and Traditional Context of Female Circumcision and the Impact of the Human Rights Discourse." In *Engendering Human Rights: Cultural and Socio-economic Realities in Africa,* ed. Obioma Nnaemeka and Joy Ezeilo, 223–247. New York: Palgrave Macmillan, 2005.

Palermo, Lynn E. "Identity under Construction: Representing the Colonies at the Paris *Exposition Universelle* of 1889." In *The Color of Liberty: Histories of Race in France,* ed. Sue Peabody and Tyler Stovall, 285–301. Durham, N.C.: Duke University Press, 2003.

Pamuk, Orhan. *Snow.* New York: Alfred A. Knopf, 2004.

Parker, Melissa. "Rethinking Female Circumcision." *Africa: Journal of the International African Institute/Revue de l'Institut africain international* 65, no. 4 (1995): 506–523.

Parmar, Pratibha, prod. and dir., and Alice Walker, prod. *Warrior Marks.* New York: Women Make Movies, 1993.

Peabody, Susan, and Tyler Stovall, eds. *The Color of Liberty: Histories of Race in France.* Durham, N.C.: Duke University Press, 2003.

———. "Race, France, Histories." In *The Color of Liberty: Histories of Race in France,* ed. Susan Peabody and Tyler Stovall, 1–7. Durham, N.C.: Duke University Press, 2003.

Perotti, Antonio. "Présence et représentation de l'immigration et des minorités ethniques à la télévision française." *Migrations société* 3, no. 18 (November 1991): 39–55.

Perry, Susan, and Celeste Schenk, eds. *Eye to Eye: Women Practicising Development across Cultures.* London: Zed Books, 2001.

Petitjean, Gérard. "Polygamie: Les femmes d'à côté." *Le nouvel observateur,* no. 1389 (June 2–26, 1991): 52–53.

Poinsot, Marie, ed. "Les chantiers de l'histoire." Special issue, *Hommes et migrations,* no. 1255 (May–June 2005).

Poiret, C. "Le phénomène polygamique en France." *Migrants-formation,* no. 91 (December 1992): 24–42.

Porgès, Laurence. "Un thème sensible: L'excision en Afrique et dans les pays d'immigration africaine." *Afrique contemporaine,* no. 196 (October–December 2000): 49–74.

Prencipe, Lorenzo. "Médias et immigration: Un rapport difficile." *Migrations société* 14, nos. 81–82 (May–August 2002): 139–156.

"La prison pour NTM: L'insulte faite aux jeunes." *L'événement du Jeudi,* no. 629 (November 21–27, 1996).

Procter, James, ed. *Writing Black Britain: An Interdisciplinary Anthology.* Manchester: Manchester University Press, 2000.

Rabine, Leslie W. *The Global Circulation of African Fashion.* Oxford: Berg, 2002.

Raissiguier, Catherine. "Women from the Maghreb and Sub-Saharan Africa in France: Fighting for Health and Basic Human Rights." In *Engendering Human Rights: Cultural and Socio-economic Realities in Africa,* ed. Obioma Nnaemeka and Joy Ngozi Ezeilo, 111–128. New York: Palgrave Macmillan, 2005.

Ramírez, Catherine S. "Crimes of Fashion: The Pachua and Chicana Style Politics." *Meridians: Feminism, Race, Transnationalism* 2, no. 2 (2002): 1–35.

Rampersad, Arnold. Introduction to *Native Son,* by Richard Wright, xi–xxviii. New York: Harper, 1993.

Rich, Adrienne. "Notes toward a Politics of Location." In *Blood, Bread, and Poetry: Selected Prose, 1979–1985,* 210–231. New York: W. W. Norton, 1986.

Richard, Jean-Luc. *Partir ou rester? Les destinées des jeunes issus de l'immigration étrangère en France.* Paris: Presses Universitaires de France, 2004.

Ricœur, Paul. *La mémoire, l'histoire, l'oubli.* Paris: Seuil, 2000.

Riesz, János. "*Le dernier voyage du Négrier Sirius:* Le roman dans le roman." In *Sénégal-Forum: Littérature et histoire,* ed. Papa Samba Diop, 178–196. Frankfurt: IKO Verlag, 1995.

———. "La folie des tirailleurs sénégalais: Fait historique et thème littéraire de la littérature coloniale à la littérature africaine de langue française." In *Black Accents: Writing in French from Africa, Mauritius, and the Caribbean,* ed. J. P. Little and Roger Little, 139–156. London: Grant and Cutler, 1997.

———. "Regards critiques sur la société coloniale, à partir de deux romans de Robert Randau et de Robert Delavignette." In *Regards sur les littératures coloniales: Afrique francophone; Approfondissements,* ed. Jean-François Durand, 51–77. Paris: L'Harmattan, 1999.

———. "The *Tirailleur sénégalais* Who Did Not Want to Be a 'Grand Enfant': Bakary Diallo's *Force-Bonté* (1926) Reconsidered." *Research in African Literatures* 27, no. 4 (Winter 1996): 157–179.

Riesz, János, and Joachim Schultz, eds. *Tirailleurs sénégalais.* Frankfurt-am-Main: Peter Lang Verlag, 1989.

Roberts, Allen F., and Mary Nooter-Roberts, eds. *Passport to Paradise: The Senegalese Mourides.* Los Angeles: UCLA, Fowler Museum of Cultural History, 2003.

Robertson, Roland. "Glocalization: Time-Space and Homogeneity-Heterogeneity." In *Global Modernities,* ed. Mike Featherstone, Scott Lash, and Roland Robertson, 25–44. London: Sage, 1995.

Rosello, Mireille. "The 'Beur Nation': Toward a Theory of 'Departenance.'" Trans. Richard Bjornson. *Research in African Literatures* 24, no. 3 (Fall 1993): 13–24.

———. *Declining the Stereotype: Ethnicity and Representation in French Cultures.* Hanover, N.H.: University Press of New England, 1998.

———. "Football Games and National Symbols: Reconfiguration of the French-Algerian Border through Philosophy and Popular Culture." In *France and the Maghreb: Performative Encounters,* 25–47. Gainesville: University Press of Florida, 2005.

———. *Postcolonial Hospitality: The Immigrant as Guest.* Stanford, Calif.: Stanford University Press, 2001.

———. "Representing Illegal Immigrants in France: From *clandestins* to *l'affaire des sans-papiers de Saint-Bernard.*" *Journal of European Studies* 38 (1998): 137–151.

———. "Tactical Universalism and New Multiculturalist Claims in Postcolonial France." In *Francophone Postcolonial Studies: A Critical Introduction,* ed. Charles Forsdick and David Murphy, 135–143. London: Arnold, 2003.

Rosny, Eric de. "L'Afrique des migrations: Les échappées de la jeunesse de Douala." *Etudes: Revue de culture contemporaine,* no. 3965 (May 2002): 623–633.

Ross, Kristin. *Fast Cars, Clean Bodies: Decolonization and the Reordering of French Culture.* Cambridge, Mass.: MIT Press, 1995.

Rougerie, R. J. "Les enfants de l'oncle Tom par Richard Wright." *Présence africaine,* no. 3 (1948): 518–519.

Rowley, Hazel. *Richard Wright: The Life and Times.* New York: Henry Holt, 2003.

Rubinstein, Ruth P. *Dress Codes: Meanings and Messages in American Culture.* Boulder, Colo.: Westview Press, 2001.

Rushdie, Salman. *East, West.* London: Jonathan Cape, 1994.

———. "The New Empire within Britain." In *Imaginary Homelands: Essays and Criticism, 1981–1991,* 129–138. London: Granta, 1991.

Saadawi, Nawal El. *The Hidden Face of Eve: Women in the Arab World.* Trans. Sherif Hetata. London: Zed Books, 1980.

Sabeg, Yazid, and Yacine Sabeg. *Discrimination positive: Pourquoi la France ne peut y échapper.* Paris: Calmann-Lévy, 2004.

Safran, William. "Diasporas in Modern Societies: Myths of Homeland and Return." *Diaspora* 1 (1991): 83–99.

Said, Edward. *Orientalism.* New York: Pantheon, 1978.

Samba, Chéri. *Chéri Samba.* Paris: Hazan, 1997.

Samuel, Michel. *Le prolétariat africain en France.* Paris: Françoise Maspéro, 1978.

Sartre, Jean-Paul. "Orphée noir." *Les temps modernes,* no. 37 (October 1948): 577–606.

———. Preface to *The Wretched of the Earth,* by Frantz Fanon. London: Penguin, 1971.

———. "Présence noire." *Présence africaine,* no. 1 (November–December 1947): 28–29.

———. *La putain respectueuse.* Paris: Gallimard, 1946.

Sassen, Saskia. *The Global City: New York, London, Tokyo.* Princeton, N.J.: Princeton University Press, 1991.

———. *Globalization and Its Discontents: Essays on the New Mobility of People and Money.* New York: New Press, 1998.

———. "Spatialities and Temporalities of the Global: Elements for a Theorization," *Public Culture* 12, no. 1 (Winter 2000): 215–232.

Saunders, Rebecca. "Uncanny Presence: The Foreigner at the Gate of Globalization." *Comparative Studies of South Asia, Africa, and the Middle East* 21, nos. 1–2 (2001): 88–98.

Sedgwick, Eve Kosofsky. *Between Men: English Literature and Male Homosocial Desire.* New York: Columbia University Press, 1985.

Sembene, Ousmane. *Black Docker.* Trans. Ros Schwartz. London: Heinemann, 1987.

———. "Black Girl." Trans. Ellen Conroy Kennedy. In *Under African Skies: Modern African Stories,* ed. Charles R. Larson, 42–54. New York: Noonday Press, 1997.

———. *Le docker noir.* Paris: Présence Africaine, 1973. First published 1956.

———. "Interview with Ousmane Sembene at Filmi Doomireew, Dakar, 30 November 1995." Interview by David Murphy. In *Sembene: Imagining Alternatives in Film and Fiction,* by David Murphy, 227–228. Oxford: James Currey, 2000.

———. "Letters from France." In *Tribal Scars,* 54–77. London: Heinemann, 1974.

———. "La Noire de. . . ." In *Voltaïque,* 149–174. Paris: Présence Africaine, 1962.

———. "Sembène présente *Molaade* à Cannes: Une présence africaine plus importante est possible." Interview by Walfadjiri. http://www.africatime.com/togo/nouv_pana.asp?no_nouvelle=119602&no_categorie=.

———. *Xala.* Paris: Présence Africaine, 1973.

Senghor, Lamine. *La violation d'un pays.* Paris: Bureau d'Editions, de Diffusion et de Publicité, 1927.

Senghor, Léopold Sédar. *Ce que je crois: Négritude, francité et civilisation de l'universel.* Paris: Bernard Grasset, 1988.

———. *Liberté I: Négritude et humanisme.* Paris: Seuil, 1964.

———. *Liberté II: Nation et voie africaine du socialisme.* Paris: Seuil, 1971.

———. *Liberté III: Négritude et civilisation de l'universel.* Paris: Seuil, 1977.

———. *Liberté IV: Socialisme et planification.* Paris: Seuil, 1983.

———. *Œuvre poétique.* Paris: Seuil, 1990.

Senghor, Richard. "Le surgissement d'une 'question noire' en France." *Esprit,* no. 321 (January 2006), 5–19.

Sepinwall, Alyssa Goldstein. "Eliminating Race, Eliminating Difference: Blacks, Jews, and the Abbé Grégoire." In *The Color of Liberty: Histories of Race in France,* ed. Susan Peabody and Tyler Stovall, 28–41. Durham, N.C.: Duke University Press, 2003.

Sewanou-Dabla, Jean-Jacques. "Alain Mabanckou, sous le signe du binaire." *Notre librairie,* no. 146 (October–December 2001): 46–48.

Shack, William A. *Harlem in Montmartre: A Paris Jazz Story between the Great Wars.* Berkeley and Los Angeles: University of California Press, 2001.

Sharpley-Whiting, T. *Black Venus: Sexualized Savages, Primal Fears, and Primitive Narratives in French.* Durham, N.C.: Duke University Press, 1999.

Silverman, Maxim. *Deconstructing the Nation: Immigration, Racism, and Citizenship in Modern France.* London: Routledge, 1992.

Siméant, Johanna. *La cause des sans-papiers.* Paris: Presses de Sciences Po, 1998.

Simpson Fletcher, Yaël. "Catholics, Communists, and Colonial Subjects: Working-Class Militancy and Racial Difference in Postwar Marseilles." In *The Color of Liberty: Histories of Race in France,* ed. Sue Peabody and Tyler Stovall, 338–350. Durham, N.C.: Duke University Press, 2003.

Smith, Annette. *Gobineau et l'histoire naturelle.* Geneva: Droz, 1984.

Smith, Zadie. *On Beauty.* London: Penguin, 2005.

Socé, Ousmane. *Karim: Roman sénégalais.* Paris: Nouvelles Editions Latines, 1935.

———. *Mirages de Paris.* Paris: Nouvelles Editions Latines, 1937.

Sontag, Susan. *Regarding the Pain of Others.* New York: Penguin, 2003.

Sony Labou Tansi. *Le commencement des douleurs.* Paris: Seuil, 1995.

———. *La vie et demie.* Paris: Seuil, 1979.

Sot, Michel, ed. *Etudiants africains en France, 1951–2001.* Paris: Karthala, 2002.

Souad, with Marie-Thérèse Cuny. *Brûlée vive.* Paris: Oh! Editions, 2003.

Sow Fall, Aminata. *Le revenant.* Dakar: Nouvelles Editions Africaines, 1976.

Spivak, Gayatri. "Mapping the Present." Interview by Meyda Yegenoglu and Mahmut Mutman. *New Formations* 45 (Winter 2001–2002): 9–23.

Stanton, Domna C. *The Aristocrat as Art: A Study of the* Honnête Homme *and the* Dandy *in Seventeenth- and Nineteenth-Century French Literature.* New York: Columbia University Press, 1980.

Stasi, Bernard. *Laïcité et République: Rapport de la commission de réflection sur l'application du principe de laïcité dans la République.* Paris: La Documentation Française, 2004.

Stein, Mark. *Black British Literature: Novels of Transformation.* Columbus: Ohio State University Press, 2004.

Stiglitz, Joseph E. *Globalization and Its Discontents.* New York: W. W. Norton, 2002.

Stoler, Ann Laura. *Carnal Knowledge and Imperial Power: Race and the Intimate in Colonial Rule.* Berkeley and Los Angeles: University of California Press, 2002.

Stora, Benjamin. *La gangrène et l'oubli.* Paris: La Découverte, 1991.

Stovall, Tyler. "Colour-Blind France? Colonial Workers during the First World War." *Race and Class* 35, no. 2 (October–December 1993): 35–55.

———. "From Red Belt to Black Belt: Race, Class, and Urban Marginality in Twentieth-Century Paris." In *The Color of Liberty: Histories of Race in France,* ed. Susan Peabody and Tyler Stovall, 351–369. Durham, N.C.: Duke University Press, 2003.

———. "Love, Labor, and Race: Colonial Men and White Women in France during the Great War." In *French Civilization and Its Discontents: Nationalism, Colonialism, Race,* ed. Tyler Stovall and Georges Van Den Abbeele, 297–321. Lanham, Md.: Lexington Books, 2003.

———. *Paris Noir: African Americans in the City of Light.* New York: Houghton Mifflin, 1996.

Stovall, Tyler, and Georges Van Den Abbeele, eds. *French Civilization and Its Discontents: Nationalism, Colonialism, Race.* Lanham, Md.: Lexington Books, 2003.

Sudarkasa, Niara. "'The Status of Women' in Indigenous African Societies." In *Feminist Frontiers: Rethinking Sex, Gender, and Society,* ed. Laurel Richardson and Verta Taylor, 152–158. New York: McGraw Hill, 1989.

Suret-Canale, Jean. "Le système administratif." In *Afrique noire: L'ère coloniale, 1900–1945,* 93–121. Paris: Editions Sociales, 1964.

Taguieff, Pierre-André. *La couleur et le sang: Doctrines racistes à la française.* Paris: Fayard, 2002.

———. "The Doctrine of the National Front in France (1972–1989): A 'Revolutionary' Programme?" *New Political Science,* nos. 16–17 (Fall–Winter 1989): 29–70.

———. "Le Front national: Du désert à l'enracinement." In *Face au racisme,* vol. 2, *Analyses, hypothèses, perspectives,* 83–104. Paris: La Découverte, 1991.

———. *La République enlisée: Pluralisme, communautarisme et citoyenneté.* Paris: Editions des Syrtes, 2005.

Tallon, Brigitte, and Maurice Lemoine, eds. "Black: Africains, Antillais . . . Cultures noires en France." Special issue of *Autrement,* no. 49 (April 1983).

Tandonnet, Maxime. *Migrations: La nouvelle vague.* Paris: L'Harmattan, 2003.

Tarr, Carrie. "French Cinema and Post-colonial Minorities." In *Post-colonial Cultures in France,* ed. Alec G. Hargreaves and Mark McKinney, 59–83. London: Routledge, 1997.

Tchak, Sami. *Place des fêtes.* Paris: Gallimard, 2001.

———. *La sexualité féminine en Afrique.* Paris: L'Harmattan, 1999.

Tchicaya, Aleth-Felix. *Lumière de femme.* Paris: Hatier, 2003.

Terray, Emmanuel. "Headscarf Hysteria." *New Left Review* 26 (March–April 2004): 118–127.

Thiam, Awa. *La parole aux négresses.* Paris: Denöel, 1978.

Thioub, Ibrahima, Momar-Coumba Diop, and C. Boone. "Economic Liberalization in Senegal: Shifting Politics of Indigenous Business Interests." *African Studies Review* 41, no. 2 (September 1998): 63–89.

Thomas, Calvin. *Straight with a Twist: Queer Theory and the Subject of Heterosexuality.* Urbana: University of Illinois Press, 2000.

Thomas, Dominic. "Constructing National and Cultural Identities in Sub-Saharan Francophone Africa." In *Not on Any Map: Essays on Postcoloniality and Cultural Nationalism,* ed. Stuart Murray, 115–134. University of Exeter Press, 1997.

———. *Nation-Building, Propaganda, and Literature in Francophone Africa.* Bloomington: Indiana University Press, 2002.

Tillery, Tyrone. *Claude McKay: A Black Poet's Struggle for Identity.* Amherst: University of Massachusetts Press, 1992.

Timera, Mahamet. *Les Soninkés en France: D'une histoire à l'autre.* Paris: Karthala, 1996.

Todd, Emmanuel. *Le destin des immigrés: Assimilation et ségrégation dans les démocraties occidentales.* Paris: Seuil, 1994.

Todorov, Tvetan. *Les abus de la mémoire.* Paris: Arléa, 1995.

———. *The Conquest of America: The Question of the Other.* Trans. Richard Howard. New York: Harper and Row, 1984.

———. *Nous et les autres.* Paris: Seuil, 1989.

Toubia, Nahid. *Female Genital Mutilation: A Call for Global Action.* New York: Women Ink, 1995.

Toubon, Jacques. *Mission de préfiguration du Centre de ressources et de mémoire de l'immigration.* Paris: La Documentation Française, 2004.

Trade Policy Review: Senegal. Vols. 1–2. Geneva: General Agreement on Tariffs and Trade, 1994.

Traoré, Aminata. *L'Afrique dans un monde sans frontières.* Arles: Actes Sud, 1999.

———. *Lettre au président des Français à propos de la Côte d'Ivoire et de l'Afrique en général.* Paris: Fayard, 2005.

———. *Le viol de l'imaginaire.* Paris: Actes Sud/Fayard, 2002.

Traoré, Sayouba. "Un Burkinabé dans la brousse." Interview by Eloïse Brezault. *Notre librairie,* no. 158 (April–June 2005): 48–50.

———. *Loin de mon village, c'est la brousse.* La Roque d'Anthéron, France: Editions Vents d'Ailleurs, 2005.

Tribalat, Michèle, ed. *Cent ans d'immigration: Etrangers d'hier, Français d'aujourd'hui.* Paris: Presses Universitaires de France, 1991.

———. *De l'immigration à l'assimilation: Enquête sur les populations d'origine étrangère en France.* Paris: La Découverte, 1996.

Tshimanga, Charles. *Jeunesse, formation et société au Congo/Kinshasa, 1890–1960.* Paris: L'Harmattan, 2001.

Verschave, François-Xavier. *La françafrique: Le plus long scandale de la République.* Paris: Stock, 1998.

———. *Noir silence: Qui arrêtera la françafrique?* Paris: Editions des Arènes, 2000.

Verschave, François-Xavier, and Philippe Hauser. *Au mépris des peuples: Le néocolonialisme franco-africain.* Paris: La Fabrique Editions, 2004.

Vieyra, Paulin S., dir. *Afrique sur Seine.* 1957.

Volet, Jean-Marie. "Calixthe Beyala, or the Literary Success of a Cameroonian Living in Paris." *World Literature Today* 67, no. 2 (Spring 1993): 309–314.

———. *La parole aux africaines ou l'idée de pouvoir chez les romancières d'expression française de l'Afrique sub-Saharienne.* Amsterdam: Rodopi, 1993.

Waberi, Abdourahman A. *Aux Etats-Unis d'Afrique.* Paris: Lattès, 2006.

———. "Les enfants de la postcolonie: Esquisse d'une nouvelle génération d'écrivains francophones d'Afrique noire." *Notre librairie,* no. 135 (September–December 1998): 8–15.

———. "Paris on my Mind." In *Rift, Routes, Rails,* 81–86. Paris: Gallimard, 2001.

———. *Transit.* Paris: Gallimard, 2003.

Wacquant, Loïc. "Banlieues françaises et ghetto noir américain: De l'amalgame à la comparaison." *French Politics and Society* 10, no. 4 (Autumn 1992): 81–103.

Walker, Alice, and Pratibha Parmar. *Warrior Marks: Female Genital Mutilation and the Sexual Blinding of Women.* New York: Harcourt Brace, 1993.

Wallerstein, Immanuel. "Africa in a Capitalist World." In *Africa and the Modern World,* 47–76. Trenton, N.J.: Africa World Press, 1986.

Warne, Chris. "The Impact of World Music in France." In *Post-colonial Cultures in France,* ed. Alec G. Hargreaves and Mark McKinney, 133–149. London: Routledge, 1997.

Watts, Richard. *Packaging Post/Coloniality: The Manufacture of Literary Identity in the Francophone World.* Lanham, Md.: Lexington Books, 2005.

Weil, Patrick. *La France et ses étrangers: L'aventure d'une politique de l'immigration, 1938–1991.* Paris: Calmann-Lévy, 1991.

———. *Qu'est-ce qu'un Français? Histoire de la nationalité française depuis la Révolution.* Paris: Grasset, 2002.

———. *La République et sa diversité: Immigration, intégration, discriminations.* Paris: Seuil, 2005.

Weil-Curiel, Linda. "Female Genital Mutilation in France: A Crime Punishable by Law." In *Eye to Eye: Women Practising Development across Cultures,* ed. Susan Perry and Celeste Schenck, 190–197. London: Zed Books, 2001.

West, Sandra L. "Paris." In *Encyclopedia of the Harlem Renaissance,* ed. Aberjhani and Sandra L. West, 253–256. New York: Checkmark Books, 2003.

Westbrook, Alonzo. *Hip Hoptionary: The Dictionary of Hip Hop Terminology.* New York: Broadway Books, 2002.

White, Edmund. *The Flâneur: A Stroll through the Paradoxes of Paris.* London: Bloomsbury, 2001.

Wieviorka, Michel. "La crise du modèle français d'intégration." *Regards sur l'actualité,* no. 161 (May 1990): 3–15.

———. "Culture, société et démocratie." In *Une société fragmentée? Le multiculturalisme en débat,* ed. Michel Wieviorka, 11–60. Paris: La Découverte and Syros, 1996.

———. "Un débat nécéssaire." In *Une société fragmentée? Le multiculturalisme en débat,* ed. Michel Wieviorka, 5–8. Paris: La Découverte and Syros, 1996.

———. *La différence: Identités culturelles; Enjeux, débats et politiques.* Paris: Editions de l'Aube, 2005.

———. *L'espace du racisme.* Paris: Seuil, 1991.

———. *Le racisme, une introduction.* Paris: La Découverte et Syros, 1998.

Withol de Wenden, Catherine. *Citoyenneté, nationalité et immigration.* Paris: Arcantère, 1987.

———. *Les immigrés et la politique.* Paris: Presses de la Fondation Nationale des Sciences Politiques, 1988.

Withol de Wenden, Catherine, Olivier Roy, Alexis Tadié, Marie Mendras, Khalid Hamdani, and Antoine Garapon. "La France des émeutes." *Esprit,* no. 320 (December 2005): 22–43.

Wolitz, Seth I. "L'art du plagiat, ou une brève défense de Ouologuem." *Research in African Literatures* 4, no. 1 (Spring 1973): 130–134.

World Bank. *Sénégal: Stabilisation, ajustement partiel et stagnation.* Report no. 11506-SE, 1993.

Wright, Richard. "Claire étoile du matin." Trans. Boris Vian. *Présence africaine,* no. 1 (November–December 1947): 120–135.

———. *Un enfant du pays.* Trans. Hélène Bokanowsky and Marcel Duhamel. Paris: Albin Michel, 1947.

———. "Le feu dans la nuée." Parts 1 and 2. Trans. Marcel Duhamel. *Les temps modernes,* no. 1 (October 1, 1945), 22–47; no. 2 (November 1, 1945), 291–319.

———. "J'ai essayé d'être communiste." Trans. René Guyonnet. *Les temps modernes,* no. 45 (July 1949): 1–45.

———. "Littérature noire américaine." Trans. René Guyonnet. *Les temps modernes,* no. 35 (August 1948): 193–221.

———. *Native Son.* New York: Harper Collins, 1993. First published 1940.

———. *The Outsider.* New York: Harper and Brothers, 1953.

———. "Tradition and Industrialization: The Plight of the Tragic Elite in Africa." Special issue of *Présence africaine,* nos. 8–10 (June–November 1956): 347–360.

————. *Le transfuge.* Paris: Gallimard, 1953.

Wrong, Michela. "The Importance of Being Elegant." In *In the Footsteps of Mr. Kurz: Living on the Brink of Disaster in Mobutu's Congo,* 169–191. New York: Harper Collins, 2001.

Zerguine, Valérie. "Fier d'être noir." *De l'air: Reportages d'un monde à l'autre* 11 (June–July 2002): 7–15.

Zobel, Joseph. *La rue Cases-Nègres.* Paris: Présence Africaine, 1974.

Index

DOMINIC THOMAS is Chair of the Department of French and Francophone Studies and Professor of Comparative Literature at the University of California, Los Angeles. He is author of *Nation-Building, Propaganda, and Literature in Francophone Africa* (Indiana University Press, 2002).

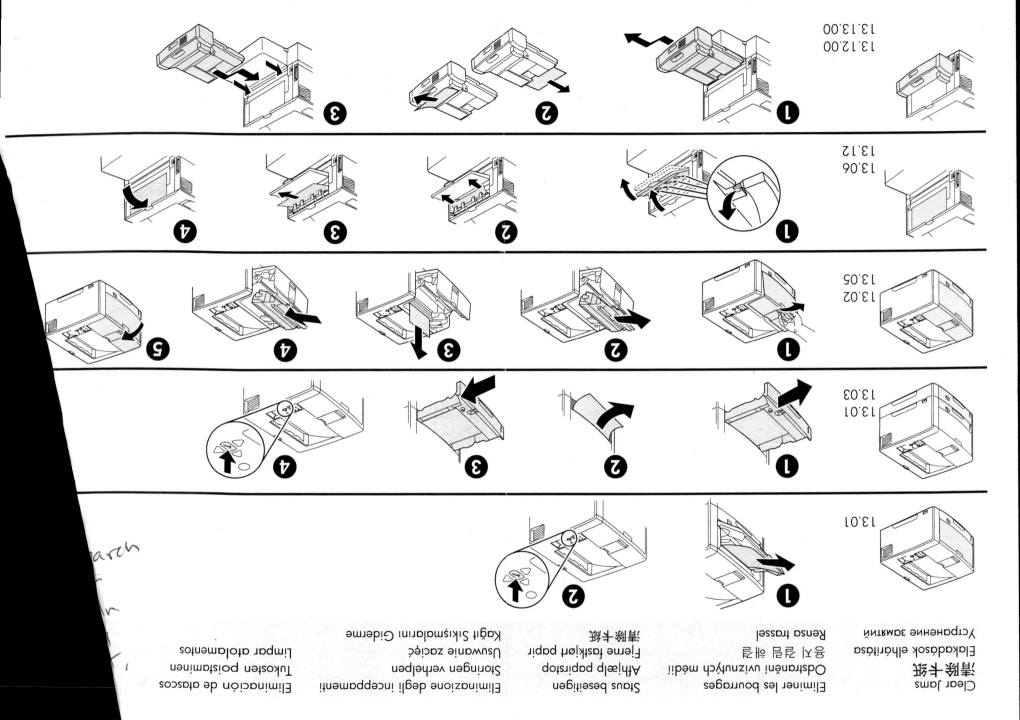

HP LaserJet 5200 printers

Clear Jams
清除卡紙
Eliminer les bourrages
용지 걸림 해결
Rensa trassel
Устранение замятий
Elakadások elhárítása

Odstranění uvíznutých médií
清除卡纸
Fjerne fastkjørt papir
Staus beseitigen

Afhjælp papirstop
Storingen verhelpen
Eliminazione degli inceppamenti
Usuwanie zacięć

Kağıt Sıkışmalarını Giderme
Tukosten poistaminen
Limpar atolamentos
Eliminación de atascos

Main actor

- Ministry of Housing
  - int'l donors: WB, AFD, UN-Habitat, Cities Alliance, etc
- Al Omrane
  - "private developers"
    - Addoha
- rural + municipal communes
- neighborhood reps
- "community organizations"
- maybe Agency of Social Development

(some issues) ↓

- MoH needs numbers

+

- Private developers don't actually want to become involved, despite subsidies
  - when they do, they often cheat

+

neighborhoods reps have electoral incentive for slums to remain

- ma
- Islamic
- collective (guiche)
- private

Sa
Fin
Unc
Lan
Ins

Project Options

- resettlement on land plots
- resettlement to apartments
- restructuring

Finance:

- state subsidizes housing, but households must finance majority
  - usually informally ☆
    - informal loans
    -
- sometimes, new evictions

Real Estate Development:

- major housing bubble
- tons of new construction
- luxury housing on the oceanfront + megaprojects
- funded by the Gulf

How to connect to slum resettlement program? ←

☆transnational dimensions

☆Martin Murray - new cities + segregation

☆Goldman - speculative urbanization (Bangalore)

- world city tied to new development

UNA waterfront city improvement districts